Beginner's Guide to DarkBASIC Game Programming

Jonathan S. Harbour with Joshua R. Smith

THOMSON

COURSE TECHNOLOGY

Professional ■ Technical ■ Reference

Publisher: Stacy L. Hiquet

Marketing Manager: Heather Hurley

Acquisitions Editor: Mitzi Foster Koontz

Project Editor/Copy Editor: Cathleen Snyder

Technical Reviewer: André LaMothe

Interior Layout: Marian Hartsough Associates

Cover Designer: Mike Tanamachi

Indexer: Kelly Talbot

Proofreader: Kim V. Benbow

Microsoft, Windows, DirectX, DirectDraw, DirectMusic, DirectPlay, DirectSound, Visual Basic, Visual C++, Windows NT, Xbox, and/or other Microsoft products referenced herein are either registered trademarks or trademarks of Microsoft Corporation in the U.S. and/or other countries. All other trademarks are the property of their respective owners.

Important: Premier Press cannot provide software support. Please contact the appropriate software manufacturer's technical support line or Web site for assistance.

Premier Press and the author have attempted throughout this book to distinguish proprietary trademarks from descriptive terms by following the capitalization style used by the manufacturer.

Information contained in this book has been obtained by Premier Press from sources believed to be reliable. However, because of the possibility of human or mechanical error by our sources, Premier Press, or others, the Publisher does not guarantee the accuracy, adequacy, or completeness of any information and is not responsible for any errors or omissions or the results obtained from use of such information. Readers should be particularly aware of the fact that the Internet is an ever-changing entity. Some facts may have changed since this book went to press.

ISBN: 1-59200-009-6

Library of Congress Catalog Card Number: 2002116163

Printed in Canada

03 04 05 06 07 WC 10 9 8 7 6 5 4 3 2

Thomson Course Technology PTR,
a division of Thomson Course Technology
25 Thomson Place
Boston, MA 02210
http://www.courseptr.com

Beginner's Guide to DarkBASIC Game Programming

D0713317

This book is dedicated to the next generation—
Jeremiah, April, Jason, Kayleigh, and Stephen—
and to my parents,
Ed and Vicki Harbour

—Jonathan

For my loving wife,
Hope Smith

—Joshua

Acknowledgments

I would like to thank everyone who helped make this book a reality. Thanks to my close family and friends for their encouragement. Jennifer, I love you, but you owe me five dollars. Jeremiah and Kayleigh, someday when you are old enough to read this, I want you to know that you are my inspiration.

Thank you to the staff at Premier Press and Course Technology who helped to see this book through to completion. My deepest gratitude and appreciation go out to Cathleen Snyder, Emi Smith, Mitzi Koontz, André LaMothe, Marian Hartsough, Kim Benbow, and Kelly Talbot.

Many thanks to the team at Dark Basic Software Ltd for developing a great product. For eager support, suggestions, and free software: Lee Bamber, Christopher Bamber, Malcolm Bamber, Rick Vanner, Mike Johnson, Simon Benge, Richard Davey, Guy Savoie, Andy Bolt, and Darren Ithell. And to all the DarkBASIC fans around the world, keep up the good work!

—Jonathan

I would like to thank everyone who has made writing this book possible. I'd first and foremost like to thank God for giving me the skills and resolve to complete this book. Thanks to my family and friends for all their support. Thank you to my wife, Hope, for all the hours she put up with missing me for the sake of this book, and for the valuable input she provided.

I'd like to thank Jonathan for the opportunity to co-author with him. This has been a fun experience and I would gladly do it again. I'm thankful for our friendship.

—Joshua

About the Authors

JONATHAN S. HARBOUR (right) has been fascinated with computers since his first experience with a Commodore PET in 1979. He has been writing code for 15 years, having started with Microsoft BASIC and Turbo Pascal on a Tandy 1000. Jonathan graduated from DeVry Institute of Technology in 1997, with a Bachelor's degree in Computer Information Systems. He has since worked for cellular, aerospace, pharmaceutical, education, medical research, and healthcare companies. In his sparc time, Jonathan enjoys spending time with his family, reading, playing video games, and restoring his 1968 Mustang.

JOSHUA R. SMITH is a full-time professional game developer at Semi-Logic Entertainments in Palo Cedro, California. He has worked on several commercial games, such as *Real War* and *Hot Wheels: Stunt Track Driver 2.* Joshua is an expert programmer, enjoys writing code in C, Shockwave, and Lingo, and is a long-time fan of the BASIC language. He is currently living in Redding, California with his wife, Hope. In his spare time, Joshua enjoys playing video games, reading science fiction, and spending time with his family and friends.

Contents at a Glance

Contents

CHAPTER 2
INTRODUCTION TO COMPUTER
PROGRAMMING 51

CHAPTER 3
BASIC COMMANDS,
VARIABLES, AND DATA TYPES 81

Chapter 4
Characters, Strings,
and Text Output 107

Chapter 5
Looping Commands 135

Chapter 6
Making Programs Think: Branching
Statements and Subroutines 161

Chapter 7
More Power to the Numbers:
Data Sequences and Arrays 181

CHAPTER 8
NUMBER CRUNCHING:
MATHEMATICAL AND RELATIONAL
OPERATORS AND COMMANDS 201

CHAPTER 11
THE ART OF USING ANIMATED
SPRITES FOR 2D GAMES 311

CHAPTER 12
PROGRAMMING THE KEYBOARD,
MOUSE, AND JOYSTICK ▪ ▪ ▪ ▪ ▪ ▪ ▪ ▪ ▪ ▪ ▪ 343

CHAPTER 13
ADDING SOUND EFFECTS
TO YOUR GAME 405

CHAPTER 14
PLAYING SOME TUNES:
CD AUDIO, MIDI, AND MP3 MUSIC . . . 439

Chapter 15
Loading and Saving
Information Using Files • • • • • • • • 457

Chapter 16
Playing Intro Movies
and Cut-Scenes 507

Part III
Advanced Topics: 3D Graphics and Multiplayer Programming 529

CHAPTER 17
FUNDAMENTALS OF 3D
GRAPHICS PROGRAMMING 531

Chapter 18
Multiplayer Programming:
The Crazy CARnage Game 587

Foreword

My first memory of a computer game was a set of paddles linked to a black and white TV. The object of the game was to bat the ball past your opponent to score points. I was a child at the time, but I played those paddles to pieces. My first memory of a computer was the VIC20—the property of my uncle, who would let me play it from time to time. You can guess what my Christmas present was. Due to the price my parents had to pay, it was my only present, and it was the biggest present I would ever get. It was my future in a box.

My childhood was spent playing computer games. Every so often I would write one. They were all terrible, but because they were mine I was proud of every single one of them. Through childhood, school, university, and the workplace I learned many programming languages, though none had the same enjoyment factor as good old BASIC. At university, my games were good enough to sell, and I made a little money. When it was time to enter the workplace, it was not the grades that got me the job—it was those terrible games I had created in my spare time. It was in the workplace that the idea for DarkBASIC was born.

I was working with Lego Media International when coding began for DarkBASIC. At the time, I was assisting in the creation of a programming language interface that would control the behaviour and responses of robots built out of Lego. Prior to my time at Lego, I worked on game creation tools that used a drag-and-drop methodology to create 2D games and applications. In my spare time, I had also cobbled together a 3D game called POBS, which taught me all the inner workings of a 3D game and how to code it on the PC. By the time my contract was complete for Lego, I resigned my position as software engineer and formed Dark Basic Software Ltd. That Christmas, DarkBASIC was launched from a little-known Web site in a corner of the Internet.

DarkBASIC was something I wanted as much for myself as for anyone else. I had done no serious marketing, no advertising, and I was still learning the ropes. I was not at all sure anyone else would give it a second glance. I didn't have much money, so I used every form of free advertising I could find—Web site links, search engine submissions, magazine demos, and anything else that would spread the word. I designed and maintained the Web site, a shareware company processed the orders, and the CDs were duplicated individually and labeled by hand. It was very much a cottage industry.

In the years that followed, Dark Basic Software Ltd got bigger. I took on a commercial director, then an artist, then another project. That project took on seven more artists, two musicians, and several consultants. All the while, the DarkBASIC language got bigger. Translations, new commands, and new media all formed part of a growing collection of software. As technology evolved, so did we. Starting from scratch, we hired another programmer and artist to contribute to our next big project. To stay ahead of technology, we needed a new modern language that could be expanded for years to come. In the summer of 2002, DarkBASIC Professional was born.

I have come a long way since those early days with the bat and ball game I played so much. If those early computers had not come with BASIC, would I be writing this now? Perhaps. If I had not written those early (but terrible) games, would I later have been paid large sums of money to play on my computer? Probably not. Let's suppose a few years from now a programmer working for a game company is asked to write the foreword to a book. Maybe this programmer will mention the early days, and how a little-known language called DarkBASIC inspired him to do great things. Might that programmer be you? If that happens, then I will be happy.

Best Regards,
Lee Bamber
Dark Basic Software Ltd

LETTER FROM THE SERIES EDITOR

In the beginning there was *only* assembly language game programming. Sure, BASIC was available on all 8-bit machines in the '70s and '80s, but it was more for learning and for the hobbyist, rather than for professional development. Time passed, computers got faster, compilers got better, and slowly a few brave souls tried using C to create games with lots of assembly language speed-up routines for time-critical code. In the mid '90s, games were developed completely in C/C++ with very little assembly language (maybe a rasterizer or two).

While all this was going on, Microsoft, Borland, and others continued to develop BASIC-type languages such as Visual Basic, Delphi, and so forth. However, none caught on more than Microsoft's Visual Basic. In fact, Visual Basic is Microsoft's flagship language product—*not* Visual C++, as many would think. So what does this have to do with DarkBASIC and game programming? Well, the point I am making is that we finally have sufficient technology, both hardware and software, to make a language based on BASIC a completely viable platform for creating 3D games. You can almost think of the language as a scripting platform to control the incredibly powerful hardware in today's machines.

Beginner's Guide to DarkBASIC Game Programming is what this is all about. Whether you are a complete newbie to computer programming or an experienced C/C++ programmer, you will be amazed at the simplicity and power of DarkBASIC. This language leverages BASIC-like syntax along with extremely high-level functionality supporting 2D/3D graphics, networking, input/output, and more. With 20 lines of code, you can literally write a 3D application—it's that amazing! Moreover, with DarkBASIC Professional you can easily write complete 3D game applications that rival the speed of pure C/C++, but that can be written in a fraction of the time!

The goal of *Beginner's Guide to DarkBASIC Game Programming* is to teach you three things—BASIC programming with the DarkBASIC platform, general game programming techniques, and 2D/3D graphics. Amazingly, this book pulls it all off, and a lot more. The authors, Jonathan and Joshua, teamed to bring you an amazing amount of code and text that one author simply couldn't have accomplished on his own. Their mastery of the platform, in addition to their experience as seasoned game programmers, allows them to really focus on showing you what you need to know to create games using the DarkBASIC platform.

So if you're looking to learn how to program in BASIC, you don't feel like writing Fahrenheit to Celsius conversion programs, and you think games might be more interesting, then you came to the right place. Or, if you do want to learn to make games, but you are put off by the thought of learning C/C++ or Java, then this is also the book for you. Finally, if you are a C/C++ game developer and you want a good reference for DarkBASIC as a tool to create smaller game applications or demos, this book will satisfy that need too!

In closing, I am very excited about this book and what it represents. For once, the amazing power of 3D graphics and game programming has been placed in the hands of beginners with the DarkBASIC platform. This book is the key to exploring your creative ideas without 100,000 lines to make a cube spin!

Sincerely,

André LaMothe
Series Editor for the Premier Game Development Series

Introduction

Congratulations, you have just found the one and only book you will need to learn the basics of game programming! This is a totally self-contained book that includes all the software you need to write cutting-edge DirectX-enabled games using tools developed by Dark Basic Software Ltd. Have you ever wanted to write your own *Half-Life* or *Quake III* mod? Why bother learning a complicated mod programming language when you can do the same thing with DarkBASIC (the Professional version, that is)? DarkBASIC is a computer programming language and a complete integrated development environment that is totally focused and optimized for game development.

Does that sound complicated? Nothing could be further from the truth! DarkBASIC is the easiest compiled computer language in the world, hands down. You will be shocked by how much you can do right from the start, before you have learned any of the advanced tricks and techniques that the experts use. In case you were wondering, DarkBASIC is being used to create professional games that are sold today. You, too, will learn to use DarkBASIC to write your own games, and you will be able to get started right away. This book is not a manual on theory, but rather on practical tips for the aspiring game programmer. Will *you* write the next blockbuster game with DarkBASIC?

A Little Background . . .

My name is Jonathan Harbour, and I am a professional programmer, not just a writer. I work on real-world programs that impact others every day—in other words, I don't just write games. My work environment is one in which phrases like "application development," "software specifications," "analysis and design," and "database schema" are used on a daily basis. My motto goes something like this: "Stop talking about it and just make it work." I have a very practical attitude toward computer programming because I like to do things that work well.

Joshua Smith, my co-author, is currently a programmer at Semi-Logic Entertainments in Northern California (http://www.slegames.com). He has worked on such games as *Real War, Real War: Rogue States, Michelle Kwan Figure Skating, Guard Force,* and *Full-On Rally* for Planet Hot Wheels. Suffice it to say, Joshua knows the inner workings of real retail games, what makes them tick, and how to write code that works. You will gain some of Joshua's insight into the video game industry throughout this book. We divided this book right down the middle, worked on various chapters individually, and then combined them into a seamless whole.

Joshua and I have been buddies for about 20 years now. We are part of the "Nintendo generation" because we both grew up playing video games in the 1980s and 1990s. But playing was only part of the story. We both have a lifetime fascination with games and have spent much of our time over the years learning to write games, and then mastering the tricks of the trade. In the early days, we spent many a weekend playing games while trying to write our own. We used to take turns at *Super Mario World* or *Contra III* on the SNES, while the other would type away on the PC. At the time, video game consoles like the SNES and Genesis were far more powerful than even a high-end PC. Back then, if you wanted to play a great game, you either went to an arcade or bought a console. The PC's sound and graphics capabilities were a joke. How things have changed today!

Given our backgrounds, why do you suppose we love DarkBASIC so much? Because DarkBASIC is awesome! You can do anything with it. You know, this might sound ridiculous, but you could write your own Web browser with DarkBASIC! (In fact, DarkBASIC would be a great tool for developing a virtual reality Web browser, a gateway into cyberspace, due to the incredible built-in 3D and TCP/IP commands.) The only problem with DarkBASIC is that it sort of takes away the magic behind game development because it is so incredibly easy to use. What I wouldn't have given ten years ago for a product like DarkBASIC! It runs on the latest versions of Windows, supports DirectX (8.1 or later), and features more than a thousand commands that are all geared toward game development. Ten years ago, I bought my first Sound Blaster audio card. How's that for progress, after only a decade? The most compelling thing about DarkBASIC is that you can write solid, fast-running code after a very short learning curve. Once you get started and get a feel for what DarkBASIC can do, you will be hooked!

Consider yourself lucky, my friend. Whereas it once was a black art just to get a sprite up on a PC screen, you can now load and draw a sprite in DarkBASIC with perhaps two lines of code. Two lines of code! I'm not talking about some hidden cache of game library code *in addition to* those two lines. I mean two lines of code, period! A compiled executable program out of two lines of code—DirectX full-screen display with a sprite on the screen! Consider yourself lucky to have such an amazing tool as you start on the path of discovery in the art of writing games. Since the black art behind the technology is no longer a problem with DarkBASIC, aspiring game programmers can focus on the fun stuff—writing a game. Just think, in the early days of the video game industry, you had to write special code for every single video card and sound card, *individually!*

Of course, DirectX has solved the problem of hardware standards, but DirectX itself is now incredibly complicated (sort of like coming full circle, don't you think?). DarkBASIC solves the problem of trying to write DirectX programs. Instead of pulling your hair out just to get a pixel on the screen, with DarkBASIC you can load a complete 3D model of a car or an airplane and render it on the screen fully textured. You will be able to do this within a few minutes of installing DarkBASIC, instead of after days and weeks of determined coding.

Is This Book for You?

The goal of this book is to introduce beginners to the basics of writing games using a very simple language. I chose DarkBASIC because it meets these qualifications. You will be surprised by how easy it is to write a game in DarkBASIC. At the same time, you will be amazed by how many powerful features the language includes. DarkBASIC is suitable for more than just games, too. You will probably find, as I have, that DarkBASIC is great for all kinds of programs, such as graphics demos, business presentations, or even file viewers. It is a great resource for graphic art students who want to quickly and easily demonstrate their 3D models, scenes, and movies that they created with 3D Studio Max (which DarkBASIC supports natively). You can even use DarkBASIC to write your own MP3 player, because DarkBASIC Professional makes it easy to load and play MP3 music files!

This book was most certainly not written for experienced programmers. If you have a knack for new software and you are able to install DarkBASIC and within minutes write a simple program without breaking a sweat, then you are too advanced for this book. However, if you have experience writing code but would like to know more about DarkBASIC Professional (the latest version from Dark Basic Software Ltd, which was released in late 2002), then I think you will find this book useful because it covers both versions. (In fact, the book is possibly a little slanted toward DarkBASIC Professional.)

This book really starts at the beginning, and I mean *really*. I don't expect you to need another book or an online tutorial to get up to speed with DarkBASIC. On the contrary, I assume you know nothing about *programming* period—let alone game programming. There are chapters in this book on basic statements, math, conditional statements, basic language syntax, and looping—everything you need to get started, even if you have never written a program. In fact, I would prefer that you know nothing about programming because it is easier that way—you haven't learned any bad habits yet! Although many books make the claim, most fail miserably to cater to the complete beginner. The title of this book clearly describes the intended audience.

It is difficult to write a book without jumping right into the advanced material and showing off what a product can do. It is easier to write an advanced book because you are able to get right to the point and you don't have to bother with any introductory material. That is probably the biggest hurdle for a computer book author—understanding the beginner. I hope that this book has succeeded in that regard, and that anyone who has not written code will find it useful.

System Requirements

Most of the source code in this book will run on a low-end computer, with the exception of some of the high-end 3D commands. DarkBASIC supports advanced features found on the latest video cards, such as pixel shaders and vertex shaders. Obviously, you will need a video card that supports such features if you want to use them.

There is absolutely no way around the fact that you must have DirectX (8.1 or later) installed before you run DarkBASIC. More than likely you already have DirectX installed, but just in case you do not, it has been conveniently included on the CD-ROM. The programs in this book are pretty forgiving of computer hardware and will run on most systems without any trouble. If your computer is too slow, you will notice right away that the programs are running too slowly, although they do run! However, here are the minimum system requirements for DarkBASIC Professional:

- Windows 98, Me, 2000, XP
- Pentium II 300 MHz
- 128 MB of memory
- 1.0 GB of free hard drive space
- 32-MB 3D-accelerated video card with transform and lighting (T&L)

Book Summary

This book is divided into four parts, as described in the following paragraphs.

Part I: The Basics of Computer Programming. Part I will teach you how to get started programming DarkBASIC, with an introduction to the integrated development environment and the programming language. The first chapter is an overview of DarkBASIC and DarkBASIC Professional, showing some of the example programs that are installed with DarkBASIC. Chapters 2 through 8 provide a strong tutorial on basic computer programming concepts. If you have never written a program before, these early chapters will teach you how.

Part II: Game Fundamentals: Graphics, Sound, Input Devices, and File Access. Part II includes the most important subjects for game programming with DarkBASIC. This Part begins with a chapter on basic graphics commands and moves on to chapters on bitmaps, sprites, input devices (keyboard, mouse, and joystick), sound effects, music, file access, and playing movies (of the AVI variety). This is truly the bulk of the material in the book; it is where you will likely learn the most about DarkBASIC.

Part III: Advanced Topics: 3D Graphics and Multiplayer Programming. Part III covers advanced game programming topics that extend your knowledge of DarkBASIC into the subjects of 3D graphics and multiplayer programming. This Part includes a complete game called Crazy CARnage, a two-player networked vehicle combat game.

Part IV: Appendixes. Part IV includes the appendixes. This Part provides reference material that will be helpful as you are working through the book, including answers to the chapter quizzes, recommended books and Web sites, an ASCII chart, and a description of what is on the CD-ROM.

PART I

THE
BASICS OF
COMPUTER
PROGRAMMING

Welcome to Part I of *Beginner's Guide to DarkBASIC Game Programming*. Part I includes eight chapters that introduce you to computer programming with DarkBASIC. Starting with an overview of the basic capabilities of DarkBASIC and a tour of the integrated development environment, Part I then delves into the basics of writing computer programs, with coverage of basic syntax, variables, data types, looping, branching, arrays, and basic relational operators. By the time you are finished with this Part, you will have a solid understanding of the DarkBASIC language and you will know how to write simple computer programs. You will also have gained an understanding of how the DarkBASIC compiler works to create an executable program.

CHAPTER 1

WELCOME TO DARKBASIC

DarkBASIC is a fantastic programming tool for creating games of all types. Anyone who has at least minimal experience with a computer can use DarkBASIC to create quality presentations, demonstrations, simulations, and even games. This chapter provides an overview of DarkBASIC, with a tour of the development environment and a demonstration of some sample programs that come with DarkBASIC. It also explores the DarkMATTER add-on and update for DarkBASIC and contains an introduction to DarkBASIC Professional, the new and improved version of DarkBASIC that features a completely rewritten graphics engine based on DirectX 8.1. There are so many things to talk about that I want to jump in and explain all of them right away, but this chapter should give you a solid introduction that will prepare you for the chapters to come. At the end of this chapter is a tutorial on installing DarkBASIC.

This chapter covers the following topics:

- Introduction to DarkBASIC
- Features of the DarkBASIC Language
- The DarkBASIC Development Environment
- DarkEDIT: The "Official" External Editor
- DarkMATTER and the DarkBASIC Update
- Introduction to DarkBASIC Professional
- Installing DarkBASIC

Introduction to DarkBASIC

DarkBASIC is a language that makes programming fun and intuitive, and allows you to write intense graphics programs quickly and easily, without any formal knowledge or training. It is the perfect choice for prototyping software and creating presentations, product demonstrations, and yes—games! DarkBASIC completely hides the details and takes care of all the difficult work behind the scenes, allowing you to focus on what the program needs to do rather than how to do it.

It is a professional-grade compiler with an integrated development environment that lets you write, load, and save the source code that makes up programs, and then compile it into standalone executable programs that run in Windows and use DirectX.

This book focuses on teaching you how to be a programmer, first and foremost. I make no assumptions about whether you know how a command works. The subjects in this book are organized so that basic topics are covered first, with each chapter covering a more challenging aspect of programming with the DarkBASIC language. If you have never written a computer program before, you will have no trouble working your way through this chapter and those that follow.

Let me show you a few examples of what you can do with DarkBASIC. By the time you have finished this book, you will be able to write games and demos just like these. Figure 1.1 shows a first-person shooter (FPS) demo called *FPSEngine*, which is on the CD-ROM if you want to load and run the program.

Figure 1.2 shows a complete game called *Mr. Putts Mini Golf*, written by Roger Yarrow. The game is included on the CD-ROM; you can visit Roger's Web site at http://www.krunchopia.com.

Figure 1.1
DarkBASIC is a multi-purpose programming language for any type of game, such as this first-person shooter demo.

Figure 1.2
Mr. Putts Mini Golf
*is just one of the
hundreds of games
written with
DarkBASIC.*

*Image courtesy of
Roger Yarrow*

What Is DarkBASIC?

DarkBASIC is essentially a scripting language sitting on top of a powerful 3D game
engine. You might think of the language as a "wrapper" for the game engine. The
low-level functions in DarkBASIC interface with DirectX 8.1 below the scripting language. You use this language to tell the game engine what to do, and the result is a
running game.

Because DarkBASIC was designed for writing games, it contains none of the complexity of languages such as Microsoft Visual C++ (the language most commonly
used for commercial games). DarkBASIC is a scripted game engine somewhat at
the level of commercial game engines. Think of DarkBASIC as one step above
DirectX, which is the case with the *Quake III Arena, Unreal Warfare,* and *Half-Life*
engines, and so on. DarkBASIC is not optimized like these other engines for a specific purpose (such as first-person shooters); rather, it provides a general-purpose
game engine for multiple genres. As you will find later in this chapter, DarkBASIC
Professional takes DarkBASIC to a whole new level (see Figure 1.3).

Indeed, you can write any game that you can imagine using DarkBASIC. But just as
DarkBASIC is not as fast as the *Quake III Arena* engine, you would be hard pressed
to write a 2D platform scroller or a planetarium simulation as a *Quake III* mod!

Figure 1.3
*The DarkBASIC
Professional logo
image*

There are comparisons that go both ways. For example, take a look at Figure 1.4, which shows a solar system simulation written by Roger Yarrow. As you see, you can use DarkBASIC for just about anything imaginable, and it is a terrific tool for simulations, scientific visualizations, and even business presentations.

DarkBASIC features a programming language with simple commands to invoke the awesome gaming power of DirectX 8.1, which includes extensions for advanced transform and lighting effects and the new pixel and vertex shader technologies (which involve loading tiny programs into the video card for manipulating each pixel on the screen individually). You don't need to know anything about DirectX to write a complete, professional DirectX game with DarkBASIC! The programming

Figure 1.4
*This solar system
demo simulates the
motion of planets
around the sun.*

*Image courtesy of
Roger Yarrow*

language resembles Microsoft QuickBasic, a descendant of the original BASIC (*Beginner's All-Purpose Symbolic Instruction Code*) language. DarkBASIC is a structured language with simple English-like commands. By combining the power of DirectX with the easy-to-use BASIC language, you can write a complete 3D game with only a few lines of source code! Compared to the several thousand lines of code you need to get even a rudimentary DirectX program up and running with C++, the power of DarkBASIC is obvious.

Who Created DarkBASIC?

DarkBASIC was created by Dark Basic Software Ltd and distributed by FastTrak Software Publishing Ltd. The main Web site for DarkBASIC is at http://www.darkbasic.com, where you can purchase DarkBASIC, keep up to date on the latest news, view screenshots of featured demos and games, and chat on the message boards (see Figure 1.5).

Dark Basic Software also maintains a separate Web site for DarkBASIC Professional, as shown in Figure 1.6. You can visit the Web site at http://www.darkbasicpro.com for the latest information about programming and product updates.

Figure 1.5 *You will find the main Web site for DarkBASIC at http://www.darkbasic.com.*

Figure 1.6

The Web site for DarkBASIC Professional is located at http://www.darkbasicpro.com.

Rapid Game Development

What makes DarkBASIC so popular is that it provides users with the ability to quickly and easily write graphically intense programs that utilize the latest 3D graphics cards. It only takes a few simple commands to load a 3D model with full texturing and lighting enabled, and to move that model around on the screen.

To help you get a feel for what DarkBASIC is all about, let me show you some additional examples that demonstrate its capabilities. Although there's a lot of source code involved, these programs demonstrate that anyone can write a game with little effort using DarkBASIC. At the same time, a DarkBASIC program listing is significantly shorter than similar source code written in most languages.

- **Iced Demo**. Figure 1.7 shows a DarkBASIC program called *Iced Demo*, a simple first-person shooter game written by Lee Bamber, one of the lead programmers who created DarkBASIC. (He's more than just an expert, he's *the man*!)

- **Jet Ski Demo**. *Jet Ski Demo* is another nice example of the capabilities of Dark-BASIC (see Figure 1.8). This program, also written by Lee Bamber, reminds me of *WaveRace* on the Nintendo 64, featuring some awesome wave effects.

Figure 1.7 Iced Demo *is a simple first-person shooter created with DarkBASIC.*

Figure 1.8 Jet Ski Demo *simulates riding on waves with realistic water movement.*

- **Room Demo**. *Room Demo*, also included with DarkBASIC and written by Lee Bamber, demonstrates special water effects, 3D character animation, ball-bouncing physics, rain effects, translucent water, and triggers that open and close doors (see Figure 1.9).

- **DarkSWARM Demo**. *DarkSWARM* demonstrates 2D graphics. It is also included with DarkBASIC and was written by Lee Bamber. *DarkSWARM* resembles a classic vertically oriented arcade game, but it is actually a full 3D game (see Figure 1.10). The player's ship, aliens, projectiles, and even the

Figure 1.9 Room Demo *demonstrates 3D character animation and special effects.*

score are rendered in 3D, while the camera angle represents the game in a 2D setting. This is a great way to enhance a game that would otherwise be limited to 2D.

- **Tank Demo**. *Tank Demo* is an extraordinary demonstration of the capabilities of DarkBASIC! This program, also provided with DarkBASIC and written by Lee Bamber, includes multi-level terrain over which you can drive in a tank, as shown in Figure 1.11. The tank moves realistically over the terrain, angling

Figure 1.10 *DarkSWARM resembles a classic 2D arcade game.*

Figure 1.11 Tank Demo *shows off the awesome capabilities of DarkBASIC in a war game setting.*

up, down, left, and right depending on the angle of the ground. *Tank Demo* also employs recoil physics, smoke, fog on the horizon, moving clouds, fire, transparent surfaces, and realistic terrain damage when a projectile explodes on the ground. By changing the camera angle to an overhead view, this game could be turned into a real-time strategy (RTS) game. It could also be a fantastic tank battle game for multiple players by adding multiplayer connectivity, destructible buildings, base camps, and power-ups!

What about Windows and DirectX?

Now you've seen some examples of the capabilities built into DarkBASIC. What makes it all possible? Most games today are developed in C or C++ using development tools such as Microsoft Visual C++ or Metrowerks CodeWarrior, and they are extraordinarily complex, requiring extensive game libraries and "engines" that power the graphics system, usually implemented in 3D. Suppose you want to write your own game in C++ using DirectX—the leading game development library for Windows PCs today. The amount of work involved in writing a simple game using C++ is phenomenal. Not only must you interface with Windows, but you must also learn how to program the DirectX SDK, all before you are even able to start on your game. In contrast, DarkBASIC handles those details in the background and lets you start working on your goal right away, without any extra work.

> **NOTE**
>
> Microsoft's DirectX game development library is comprised of components that abstract the computer system, providing a common set of interfaces regardless of the underlying hardware (such as the video card and sound card). Hardware manufacturers, such as Nvidia (makers of the GeForce4 Graphics Processing Unit) and Creative Labs (makers of the Sound Blaster Audigy sound card) include DirectX drivers with their products so that all games developed in current or earlier versions of DirectX will run without incident.
>
> DarkBASIC supports DirectX 7.0, which is comprised of seven main components—DirectDraw, DirectSound (for sound effects), DirectSound3D (for positional 3D sound), DirectMusic (for music playback), DirectInput (for mouse, joystick, and keyboard support), DirectPlay (for multiplayer networking), and Direct3D (for 3D graphics). DarkBASIC Professional supports and uses the advanced features of DirectX 8.1.

Suppose you have a great idea for a game that you want to develop. First you need to write your own DirectX library suited for the type of game you are planning. This library should include the 2D or 3D graphics engine that powers your game, as well as support for sound effects, background music, user input devices (including force-feedback joysticks, if applicable), and multiplayer networking (if your game will support more than one player). It is a rare game today that is released with no built-in multiplayer capabilities. (One exception that comes to mind is Sid Meier's *Civilization III*—a deep and engaging turn-based strategy game that is perhaps not practical in a multiplayer setting, but is extraordinarily fun and challenging nonetheless. But even this game has an add-on product that provides network play capability!)

By the time you have finished creating the core library and engine code needed to power your game, you probably will have given up on the game entirely and moved on to a new subject or game type—assuming you had the capabilities to develop a cutting-edge game engine in the first place. An alternative is to use a game engine such as *Quake III* and then write a modification (mod) for that engine. However, even that involves a great amount of C++ code and creation of your own 3D models.

What you need is a way to *quickly, easily,* and *spontaneously* crank out the prototype version of your game idea before you lose interest and before the complexities of game programming overwhelm you and stifle the creative enthusiasm that you felt upon coming up with the new game idea. That's where DarkBASIC comes in. Not only is DarkBASIC a fantastic prototyping language that lets you get a minimal demonstration of your game up and running very quickly, it is also full-featured and loaded with awesome tools that will let you follow through and take the game to completion. Although you *can* (and will) write awesome games with DarkBASIC, you could also use it to quickly prototype a game that you plan to eventually write in a more difficult language.

System Requirements

Okay now, what does it take to actually run DarkBASIC? I'll assume that you have a computer already because that's sort of a given, right? If you don't have a computer, I'll at least assume that you are using one at school, work, or a friend's house. You will need a Windows PC with DirectX 7.0a installed to run DarkBASIC or any program compiled with it. Here are the minimum recommended specifications for any PC running DarkBASIC:

- Windows 95, 98, 2000, Me, or XP
- 300 MHz Pentium II
- 64 MB of memory
- 500 MB of free hard drive space
- 4x CD-ROM drive
- 3D video card with 8 MB of video memory
- DirectX-compatible sound card

From my own personal experience, you will want a much more powerful system than the minimum specs listed above; otherwise, your games will not be able to run very fast. When it comes to writing games and graphics programs, you want a more powerful computer than the norm. I recommend at least a 2 GHz processor, 512 MB of RAM, and a GeForce4 or later video card. Most PCs today exceed even these specs; I am being conservative with the numbers.

DarkBASIC Professional supports the advanced features of DirectX 8.0+, so you will want a high-end video card to write programs that use those features. For example, I have a GeForce4 Ti4200 card with 64 MB of DDR video memory, and it is fully capable of handling the new features in DarkBASIC Pro.

> **TIP**
>
> If you are not familiar with terms such as T&L, pixel shading, and vertex shading, you might want to pick up one of the excellent books by Premier Press that deals with Direct3D. You can find detailed information about these books at http://www.premierpressbooks.com and in Appendix B, "Recommended Books and Web Sites."

Features of the DarkBASIC Language

DarkBASIC includes a rich development environment and language, runs in full-screen mode, and is fully compatible with Windows. It runs in full-screen mode because it is more than just a programming tool—it is a complete game development environment. The Windows user interface takes away from the mystique—or rather, immersion—that DarkBASIC provides.

Now, this is an important point. When you are running DarkBASIC and working on a game, the rest of your computer is irrelevant; you are fully engaged in what you are doing, with no distractions. This is a very important aspect that I believe makes DarkBASIC a great tool for beginners. Too often, the Windows user interface is a distraction! Although DarkBASIC helps you to focus on the game, you can still freely switch between DarkBASIC and other programs because it's Windows friendly.

DarkBASIC features automatic double buffering, which results in super-smooth animation at the highest possible frame rate using hardware 3D acceleration (if your video card supports it). Other general features

> **NOTE**
>
> Despite the immersion of DarkBASIC, which is great for beginners, experienced programmers often prefer a windowed interface, such as that provided by DarkEDIT. DarkBASIC Professional features a windowed IDE (*Integrated Development Environment*).

include commands to play back audio-video interleave (AVI) movie files, create 3D sound effects, and use TrueType fonts. Probably one of the most interesting features of DarkBASIC is the compiler, and how it creates standalone executable files that can be run on any PC. (I'll explain this capability in the following section.) Possibly the best feature of DarkBASIC is how it compiles programs.

No Run-Time Required

What happens when you have created a killer new game and you want to share it with your friends or send it to game companies to see whether they might publish it? Probably the most impressive and amazing feature of DarkBASIC is that it can create standalone executable files that require absolutely no run-time library! What is a run-time library, you might ask? It is a collection of functions that are built into a programming language and must be packaged with a program for it to run. Some languages (such as Visual Basic) store the run-time in one or more dynamic link library (DLL) files that must be installed before the program will run. DarkBASIC programs, on the other hand, store the DarkBASIC run-time library *inside* the executable, requiring no dependencies.

But DarkBASIC doesn't stop there! DarkBASIC executables can be compiled as standalone programs and distributed with all of the graphics and sounds needed by the game. Alternatively, these files can all be packaged together inside the executable file. Yes, you can compile an entire game—executable file, 3D model files, texture bitmap files, sound files, and music files—into the executable. DarkBASIC handles the situation automatically! You don't need to modify anything to load files from a disk or from inside the executable because it is done behind the scenes. This is a great feature, especially when you don't want others to steal your game files and use them in their own games without your permission.

> **NOTE**
>
> Compiled DarkBASIC programs are standalone executables that do not require any run-time library because they are self-contained. The only requirement is that DirectX 7.0 is installed.

BASIC Graphics

DarkBASIC includes all the commands you need to create 2D and 3D games, but it doesn't stop there! It also includes a plethora of 3D models, textures, bitmaps, sound effects, and music that you can use freely and distribute in your own games.

DarkBASIC includes all of the following 2D graphics features.

- Support for the bitmap graphics format
- Super-fast software and hardware blitting
- Mirror, stretch, blur, and fade bitmaps
- Huge animated sprites
- Transparency
- Fast collision detection

It also includes all of the following 3D graphics features.

- XOF and 3DS model files
- Landscape transformation
- Built-in 3D objects
- 3D object collision detection
- Full model manipulation and animation
- Ambient and directional lighting
- Texture filtering
- Alpha blending
- Translucent textures and fog

BASIC Commands

DarkBASIC includes a rich assortment of commands used to write programs. What is a command? It is what other languages (such as C++) call an *intrinsic function*—something built into the language. Fortunately, DarkBASIC has no concept of project files, include files, library files, and so on. Although you can break up large programs into multiple source code files (which is particularly useful when you want to share your custom code between programs), there is far less confusion when compiling and running programs developed with DarkBASIC because the interface is so incredibly simple to use!

In a nutshell, DarkBASIC uses a structured version of the classic BASIC language. By structured, I mean that it resembles QuickBasic more than old-school BASIC because it allows you to create your own subroutines and functions that return values. Old-school BASIC had a GoSub command that referred to line numbers—not to worry, DarkBASIC doesn't use line numbers. Although DarkBASIC borrowed features of QuickBasic to make it easy to write programs, it utterly leaves QuickBasic in the dust beyond the core language.

The DarkBASIC Development Environment

With all this talk about hardware features, capabilities of DarkBASIC, and so on, you are probably eager to get started writing real DarkBASIC programs. Don't worry, my friend, the next chapter jumps right in and includes a sample program—your first DarkBASIC program, in fact. For now, you should take a brief tour of the DarkBASIC development environment so you feel comfortable with it.

The Integrated Game Development Environment

Most modern programming languages include a complete integrated development environment. DarkBASIC takes that concept a step further with respect to games, featuring what I like to call an integrated *game* development environment, due to the awesome built-in game features. Let's get started with that tour, okay?

First you need to run DarkBASIC. Assuming you have installed it already, you will be able to run it from the Windows Start menu. Click Start, Programs, Dark Basic Software, Dark Basic. The DarkBASIC development environment will appear, as shown in Figure 1.12. Note that there are six menus across the top of the screen: File, Edit, View, Help, Run, and Media.

File Menu

Figure 1.13 shows the File menu, which includes several common system functions for loading and saving projects and building executables.

The commands on the File menu include

- **New Project**. The New Project menu item brings up the New Project Folder dialog box (see Figure 1.14). The Project field contains the name of the folder that DarkBASIC creates to hold the project files. Since DarkBASIC looks in the current folder for files that a game needs, you should store all of the graphics, sound, and other files inside the project folder.

Main menu   Pages   Command Line Interface

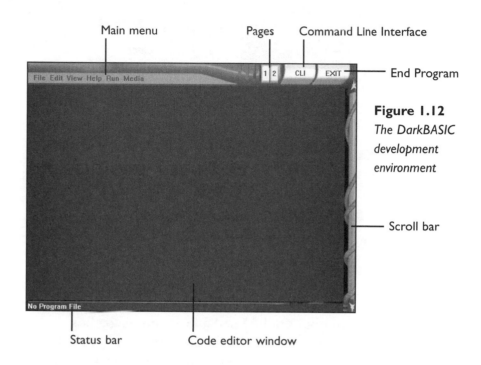

End Program

Figure 1.12
*The DarkBASIC
development
environment*

Scroll bar

Status bar   Code editor window

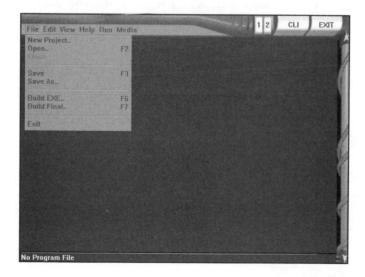

Figure 1.13 *The
File menu is used to
load and save pro-
jects in DarkBASIC.*

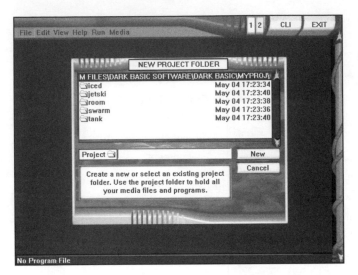

Figure 1.14 *The New Project Folder dialog box contains the name of the folder that holds the project files.*

- **Open**. The Open menu item brings up the Load a Program dialog box (shown in Figure 1.15), which allows you to load a DarkBASIC program by browsing through the folders on your computer. When you select a DarkBASIC program file (with a .dba extension), you can examine the Title, Author, and Date fields.
- **Close**. The Close menu item closes the current project file and clears the code editor window so you can start typing in a new program.

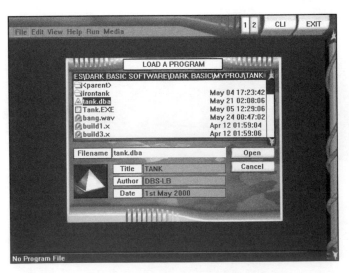

Figure 1.15 *The Load a Program dialog box lets you browse for a DarkBASIC project.*

- **Save**. The Save menu item saves the current project. Note that this applies only to the page that is in view. (There are two pages available in the code editor, as noted by the 1 and 2 buttons next to the CLI button at the top-right corner of the DarkBASIC screen; refer to Figure 1.16.)
- **Save As**. The Save As menu item brings up the Save a Program dialog box, as shown in Figure 1.17. You can type the program's title, author, and date in the appropriate fields. Then select the destination folder where you would like to save the .dba file.

Page buttons

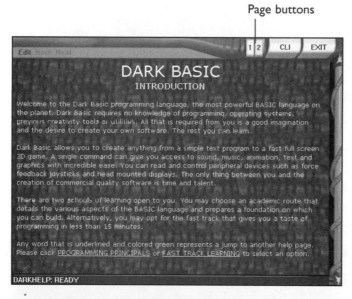

Figure 1.16 *The page-swapping buttons let you switch between one of the two source code windows available in the DarkBASIC editor.*

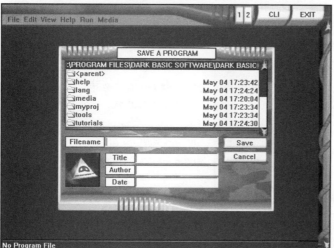

Figure 1.17 *The Save a Program dialog box lets you save the program currently in memory.*

- **Build EXE**. The Build EXE menu item brings up the Build Executable dialog box, shown in Figure 1.18. You can use this dialog box to create a standalone executable after you have finished writing a program. Note that this does not link all of the data files into the executable; that is accomplished using the Build Final menu item.
- **Build Final**. The Build Final menu item brings up the Build Final dialog box, as shown in Figure 1.19. Type in the name of the executable file, and DarkBASIC will build a standalone program with all of the graphics, sounds, and data files built into the executable and ready for distribution.

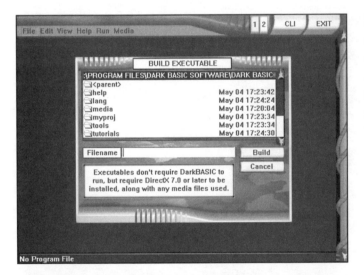

Figure 1.18 *The Build Executable dialog box lets you create an executable file that can be run outside of DarkBASIC.*

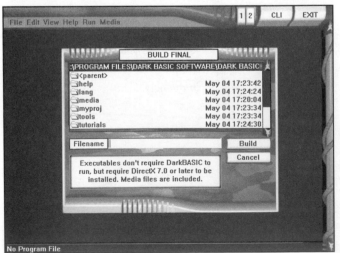

Figure 1.19 *The Build Final dialog box lets you create a standalone executable program with all of the graphics and sound files built in and with no run-time library required!*

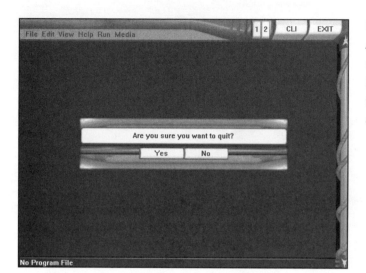

Figure 1.20
After you choose to exit the program, DarkBASIC confirms the action before closing.

- **Exit**. The Exit menu item is used to end the program. Before DarkBASIC closes, it asks you to confirm that you want to exit (see Figure 1.20). If you have a program currently in the editor, DarkBASIC will offer you an opportunity to save the file before quitting. You can also tell DarkBASIC to close by clicking the EXIT button at the top-right corner of the screen.

Edit Menu

The Edit menu, shown in Figure 1.21, contains the following commands. You might find these commands familiar, since they are standard in most Windows programs.

- **Undo**. The Undo menu item undoes the last edit action you performed in the code editor window. You can also invoke the Undo command by pressing Ctrl+Z.
- **Cut**. The Cut menu item removes the text from the code editor window and places it on the Windows Clipboard. You can also invoke the Cut command by pressing Ctrl+X.
- **Copy**. The Copy menu item copies the currently selected text to the Windows Clipboard. You can invoke the Copy command by pressing Ctrl+C.
- **Paste**. The Paste menu item pastes text from the Windows Clipboard into the code editor window. You can invoke the Paste command by pressing Ctrl+V.
- **Delete**. The Delete menu item deletes the selected text in the code editor window.

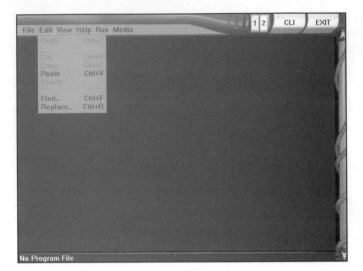

Figure 1.21 *The Edit menu includes copy/cut/paste and text search features.*

- **Find**. The Find menu item brings up the Search Text dialog box, shown in Figure 1.22.
- **Replace**. The Replace menu item brings up the Replace Text dialog box, shown in Figure 1.23, which allows you to replace one word or phrase with another throughout the source code in the code editor.

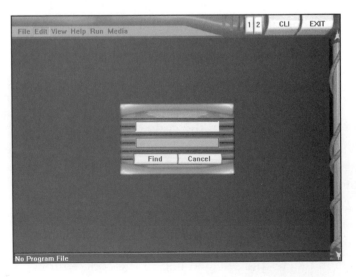

Figure 1.22 *The Search Text dialog box allows you to enter the text for the search process.*

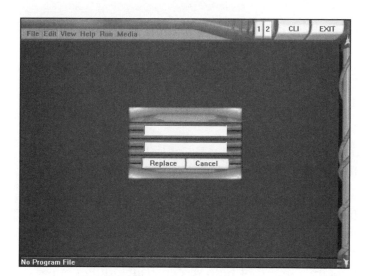

Figure 1.23 *The Replace Text dialog box allows you to replace one word or phrase with another.*

View Menu

The View menu, shown in Figure 1.24, includes the following commands.

- **Top.** The Top menu item moves the cursor to the top of the source code listing.
- **Bottom.** The Bottom menu item moves the cursor to the bottom of the source code listing.

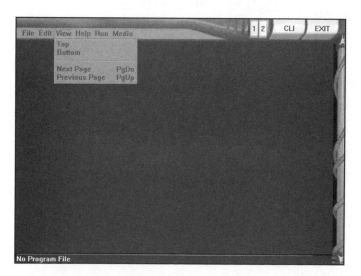

Figure 1.24
The View menu allows you to quickly jump through the source code.

- **Next Page**. The Next Page menu item moves the code listing down one page. You can also use the Page Down key to accomplish this.
- **Previous Page**. The Previous Page menu item moves the code listing up one page. You can also use the Page Up key to accomplish this.

Help Menu

The Help menu, shown in Figure 1.25, includes a long list of help commands that will bring up various screens in the DarkBASIC environment.

- **Context**. The Context menu item brings up a help screen related to a word currently highlighted in the code editor. For example, type the `PRINT` command in the code editor and then select Help, Context (or press F1) to get help for that command (see Figure 1.26).
- **Menu**. The Menu item brings up a menu of help screens (including complete tutorials) available within DarkBASIC that you can use while learning the language (see Figure 1.27). By clicking one of the help items, you will bring up additional help screens.
- **Recent**. The Recent menu item brings up the last help screen that you viewed.

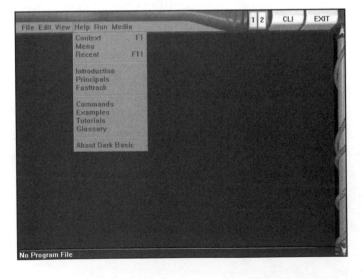

Figure 1.25 *The Help menu includes numerous help features.*

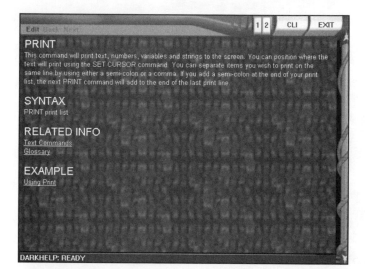

Figure 1.26
Context-sensitive help retrieves information about the currently highlighted text in the code editor.

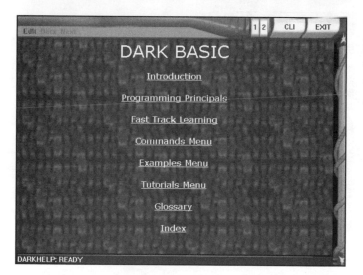

Figure 1.27
The Menu help screen displays a list of common help items.

- **Introduction**. The Introduction menu item brings up the Introduction help screen, which provides an overview of DarkBASIC with Web-style links to additional help screens (see Figure 1.28).

- **Principals**. The Principals menu item brings up the Programming Principals screen (shown in Figure 1.29), which provides an overview of the basic data types and commands built into DarkBASIC.

Figure 1.28

The Introduction help screen explains some of the features of DarkBASIC.

Figure 1.29

The Programming Principals help screen displays a list of commands built into DarkBASIC.

- **Fasttrack.** The Fasttrack menu item brings up the Fast Track Learning help screen (shown in Figure 1.30), which contains a series of tutorials geared to help you quickly get started writing programs with DarkBASIC.

- **Commands.** The Commands menu item brings up the Main Commands Menu help screen (shown in Figure 1.31), probably the most useful part of the DarkBASIC help system. This screen includes links to the main programming commands, grouped by function.

Figure 1.30 *The Fast Track Learning help screen includes numerous tutorials built into DarkBASIC that will help you start writing programs immediately.*

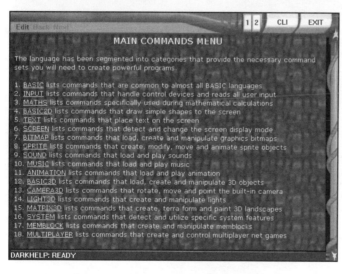

Figure 1.31 *The Main Commands Menu help screen displays a list of hyperlinked commands available in DarkBASIC.*

- **Examples**. The Examples menu item brings up the Main Examples Menu help screen (as shown in Figure 1.32), which is a huge list of samples that you can examine or run to see how various commands in DarkBASIC work.
- **Tutorials**. The Tutorials menu item brings up the Main Tutorials Menu help screen (shown in Figure 1.33), which explains how to solve specific types of programming problems with DarkBASIC.

Figure 1.32 *The Main Examples Menu help screen displays a list of example programs you can run.*

Figure 1.33 *The Main Tutorials Menu help screen includes some tutorials on programming with DarkBASIC.*

- **Glossary**. The Glossary menu item brings up the Glossary help screen (shown in Figure 1.34), a comprehensive list of terms and definitions for concepts related to game and graphics programming.

- **About Dark Basic**. The About Dark Basic menu item brings up the Dark Basic Credits screen, showing the members of the team who created and contributed to DarkBASIC (see Figure 1.35).

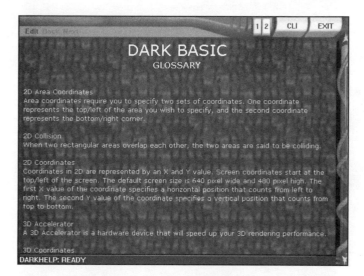

Figure 1.34 *The Glossary help screen displays a list of related terms and definitions.*

Figure 1.35 *The Dark Basic Credits screen displays the names of the individuals responsible for developing DarkBASIC.*

Run Menu

The Run menu, shown in Figure 1.36, includes two commands.

- **Compile**. The Compile menu item compiles the program internally using the scripting engine, and is basically used to verify that there are no errors in the source code. This command does not create an executable file.

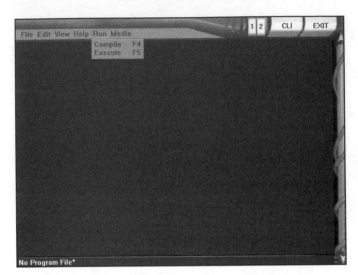

Figure 1.36 *The Run menu includes options to compile and execute your programs.*

- **Execute**. The Execute menu item causes the program to start running with the built-in double buffering and the Command Line Interface (CLI) available. When the program is running, hit the Esc key to bring up the CLI. You can then type in commands directly, and DarkBASIC will run them from the CLI. (I'll cover this in more detail in Chapter 2, "Introduction to Computer Programming.")

Media Menu

The Media menu, shown in Figure 1.37, includes commands to browse and edit media files, such as 3D models, bitmaps, waves, MIDIs, and AVIs. There are three commands in the Media menu.

- **Understanding Media**. The Understanding Media menu item brings up a help screen with the same name, as shown in Figure 1.38.
- **Specify an Editor**. The Specify an Editor menu item assigns external programs to the editor entries in the Media menu.
- **Media Browser**. The Media Browser menu item runs an external program called Media Browser, which comes with DarkBASIC (see Figure 1.39).

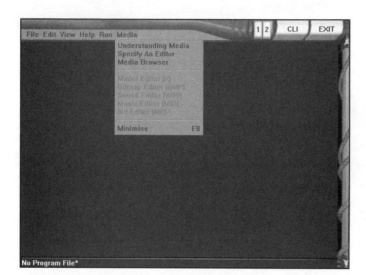

Figure 1.37 *The Media menu contains commands for browsing and editing media files.*

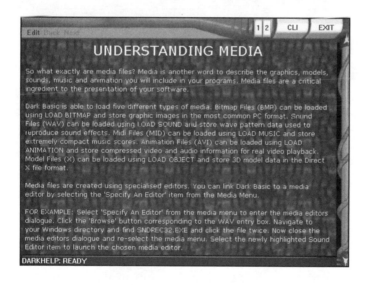

Figure 1.38 *The Understanding Media help screen*

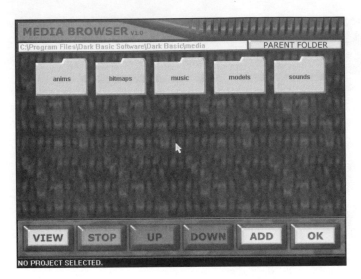

Figure 1.39 *The Media Browser program included with DarkBASIC*

DarkEDIT: The "Official" External Editor

You might be saying to yourself, "What a neat integrated environment, but it lacks a few of the Windows features I need, such as the mouse wheel. Can I develop DarkBASIC programs outside of the DarkBASIC environment?" The answer to that question is yes! There is a program called DarkEDIT that allows you to develop DarkBASIC programs outside of the environment. For those of you who are more familiar with Visual C++, Delphi, and Visual Basic, where the IDE runs in a window, DarkEDIT is the tool for you.

DarkEDIT tracks labels, functions, and other essentials, just like the DarkBASIC environment. It has the same keyboard layout as DarkBASIC but is more of a Windows-style program. If you are not looking for total immersion in the BASIC environment but you would still like to write DarkBASIC games, DarkEDIT is the right tool (see Figure 1.40).

As a matter of fact, DarkEDIT was adapted, revised, rewritten, and generally recycled for use in DarkBASIC Professional! The new editor in DarkBASIC Pro is more feature-rich than DarkEDIT, but the same DarkEDIT author worked on the editor for DarkBASIC Pro—Guy Savoie of Real Game Tools.

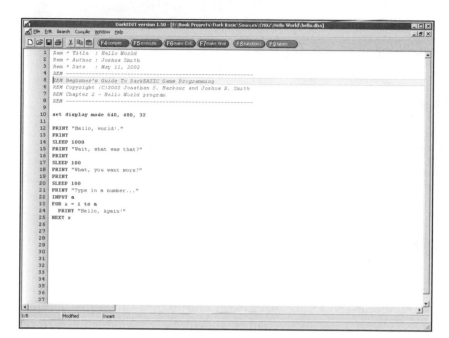

Figure 1.40
DarkEDIT is a text editor that runs outside of DarkBASIC and includes many features that are common in other source code editors.

DarkMATTER and the DarkBASIC Update

DarkMATTER is an add-on product for DarkBASIC that includes hundreds of high-quality, professional 3D models, textures, and sound effects that you can use royalty-free in your own programs. In addition, DarkMATTER includes the DarkBASIC Enhancement Pack, which updates the DarkBASIC language with new commands and features such as those used for creating multiplayer games.

DarkMATTER Features

I highly recommend that you purchase DarkMATTER if you intend to do any serious work with DarkBASIC, because it is invaluable. Some of the sample programs in this book use DarkMATTER 3D models and textures (courtesy of Dark Basic Software). Figure 1.41 shows the logo for DarkMATTER.

Figure 1.41
*The DarkMATTER
add-on logo*

DarkBASIC Update

DarkMATTER not only gives you a ton of 3D models, it also includes a complete updated version of DarkBASIC (version 1.13), which provides numerous new enhancements. One such enhancement is multiplayer commands that allow you to support multiple players in your DarkBASIC games!

Introduction to DarkBASIC Professional

DarkBASIC Professional is a totally new program with a new language, compiler, editor, and debugger. This version has been written from scratch using DirectX 8.1 and supports the latest features of DirectX. For this reason, DarkBASIC Professional operates differently than standard DarkBASIC. Figure 1.42 shows the new IDE for DarkBASIC Professional.

As Figure 1.42 shows, DarkBASIC Professional has a new feature called the DarkBASIC Pro Assistant. This is a new integrated help system that provides a quick reference for commands. There is another display mode in DarkBASIC Pro that looks more like a traditional programming language, with a project window showing project files, resources, and so on. Figure 1.43 shows the project view mode in DarkBASIC Pro.

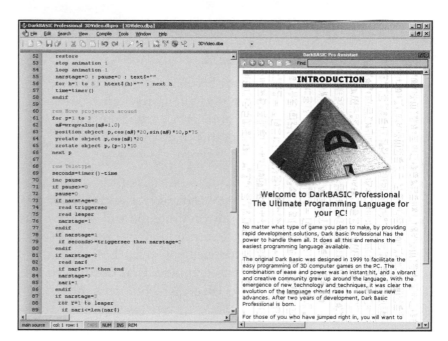

Figure 1.42
DarkBASIC Professional features a completely new IDE.

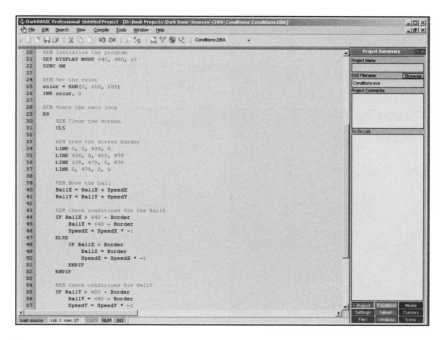

Figure 1.43
The project window in DarkBASIC Professional displays information about the current program.

New Features in DarkBASIC Professional

DarkBASIC Pro is a completely new product; it is not based on the source code from DarkBASIC. It features a completely rewritten graphics core engine based on DirectX 8.1. In contrast, DarkBASIC 1.0 was based on DirectX 7.0. Take a look at Figure 1.44 to see *FaceDemo*, one of the sample programs that comes with DarkBASIC Pro.

Although it's premature (in the extreme!) at this point to talk about the details, I will at least give you a glimpse of what to expect in later chapters. DarkBASIC Pro is packed with a lot of functionality that is based entirely on the good will and charitable nature of the authors. For instance, DarkBASIC Pro can load and render *Half-Life* maps, *Quake III Arena* maps, and generic binary space partition (BSP) maps, as well as 3D characters stored in .MD2 and .MD3 files. Of course, DarkBASIC Pro also supports 3D Studio MAX (.3DS) files, as well as Direct3D .X files, as the *LTypeDemo* program shows in Figure 1.45.

Figure 1.44
DarkBASIC Pro features a new graphics engine based on DirectX 8.1, demonstrated by the FaceDemo program.

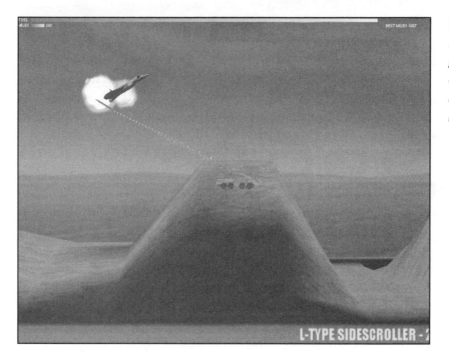

Figure 1.45
2D scrolling shooter games are even more exciting when they are rendered in 3D using DarkBASIC Pro!

Which Version Should You Focus On?

DarkBASIC programs will still run in the DarkBASIC Professional environment, but they require a few small changes, which I will point out when necessary. If you are an experienced DarkBASIC programmer who has invested time in standard DarkBASIC, you will learn all of the tricks and techniques that you might have missed before in the following chapters. At the same time, you will gain the knowledge and experience you need to delve into DarkBASIC Professional. In effect, this book gives you the option to choose which version you would like to use. If you already own DarkBASIC, you can install the DarkBASIC Professional Premier Trial Edition located on the CD-ROM to take advantage of the new features in DarkBASIC Pro. During the trial period, you can decide whether the new version is compelling enough to warrant an upgrade. Rest assured, by the time you have read this book you will definitely want to buy the full version, because it is awesome!

The last thing I want you to be concerned with is which version of DarkBASIC you need while reading this book. The book supports both versions. Although DarkBASIC Professional is a powerful new programming language that is mostly compatible with standard DarkBASIC projects, I'm going to focus primarily on standard DarkBASIC. The code and topics of discussion in this book are geared primarily for standard DarkBASIC, but in most cases I have included a DarkBASIC Professional version of the sample programs on the CD-ROM.

Installing DarkBASIC

In this section I will walk you through an installation of both DarkBASIC and DarkBASIC Professional, since you are likely to install the demo or retail versions of both to explore the features and benefits of each product.

Installing Standard DarkBASIC

The standard version of DarkBASIC is included on the CD-ROM for this book. Whether you are installing the retail version, the demo version from the DarkBASIC Web site, or the Premier Trial Edition from the CD-ROM, the following instructions should be applicable. When you insert the retail CD-ROM, you will see the menu shown in Figure 1.46.

Click the Install Dark Basic option to run the setup program. The Welcome screen will appear, as shown in Figure 1.47. If you have not yet installed DirectX, you will

Figure 1.46 *The CD-ROM menu for DarkBASIC*

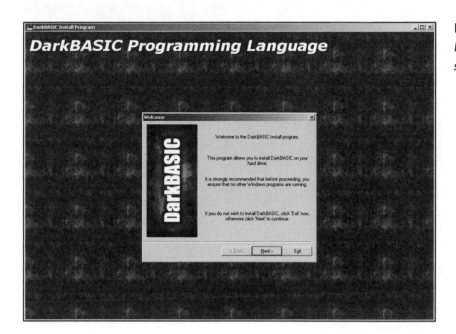

want to do so prior to installing DarkBASIC because DarkBASIC requires DirectX in order to work. Click the Next button to continue.

Next comes the end-user license agreement (also called the EULA) screen (shown in Figure 1.48). Click the Next button to continue.

The Choose the Version to Install screen (shown in Figure 1.49) contains two options—Full Installation and Minimum Installation. Leave the default of Full Installation selected, and then click the Next button to continue.

The next screen that appears is the Directory screen that allows you to choose the location to install DarkBASIC files (see Figure 1.50). Most of the time you will simply leave the default directory of C:\Program Files\Dark Basic Software\Dark Basic, but you can type in or browse for an alternative location if you want. Click the Next button to continue.

Depending on whether you have installed DarkBASIC before, you may or may not see a message box that asks you whether you want to create the new directory (see Figure 1.51). Click Yes to continue.

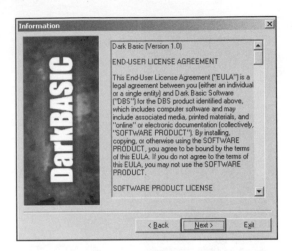

Figure 1.48 *The end-user license agreement screen*

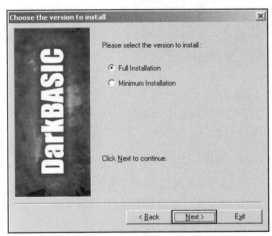

Figure 1.49 *The Choose the Version to Install screen*

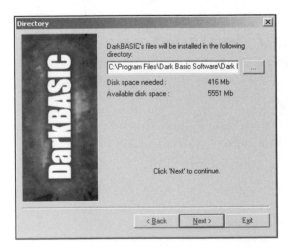

Figure 1.50 *The Directory screen*

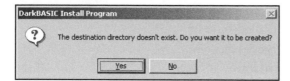

Figure 1.51 *The directory creation message box*

Finally, you will see the Confirmation screen (shown in Figure 1.52). Click the Start button to begin the actual install process of copying files to your hard drive.

As files are being copied to your hard drive, the Installing screen displays the progress of the install (see Figure 1.53).

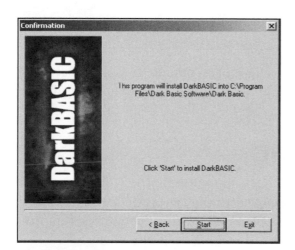

Figure 1.52 *The Confirmation screen*

Figure 1.53 *The Installing screen, which tracks the installation progress*

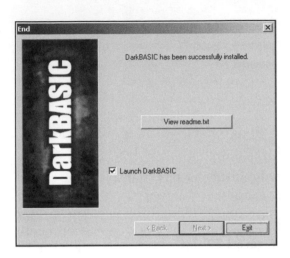

Figure 1.54 *The End screen, which signifies that the installation has been completed*

When the files have been copied and settings have been applied to your PC, the End screen will be displayed, as shown in Figure 1.54. You can now click Exit to exit the installer.

Installing DarkBASIC Professional

The installer for DarkBASIC Professional is similar to the DarkBASIC installer and just as easy to use. When you insert the retail CD-ROM or start the demo setup program, the menu shown in Figure 1.55 appears. If you have not already installed DirectX, you should install it now. If you have Windows 2000 or XP, select the first option (NT), but if you are running Windows 98 or Me, select the second option (98/ME). After you have installed DirectX, return to the DarkBASIC Professional installer.

Now proceed with the installation by clicking the Install Dark Basic Professional CD-ROM menu item. If you are installing the trial version from this book's CD-ROM, you might need to install DirectX from the main CD-ROM menu for the book, rather than from the DarkBASIC Professional install menu.

The InstallShield Wizard screen (shown in Figure 1.56) will appear when the installer starts. Click the Next button to continue.

Figure 1.55 *The CD-ROM menu interface for DarkBASIC Professional*

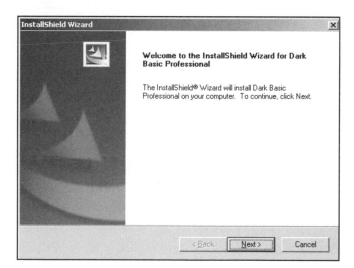

Figure 1.56 *The InstallShield Wizard welcome screen*

The end-user license agreement will be displayed, as shown in Figure 1.57. Click Yes to continue.

Figure 1.58 shows the Setup Type screen. In most cases you will want to select Full Installation, but you might want to select Minimum Installation if your hard drive is short on space. Click the Next button to continue.

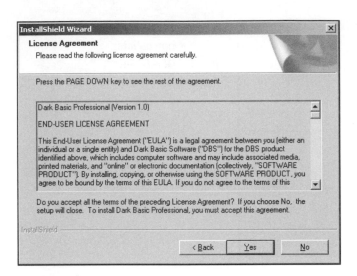

Figure 1.57
The EULA screen

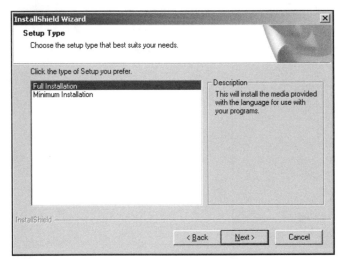

Figure 1.58 *The Setup Type screen, which allows you to set your installation options*

Now select the destination folder where the DarkBASIC Professional files will be copied, using the Choose Destination Location screen (see Figure 1.59). You can type in a new folder name or use the Browse button. Click Next to continue.

The installer will copy the files to your hard drive. As files are being copied, the Setup Status dialog box will show the progress of the install (see Figure 1.60).

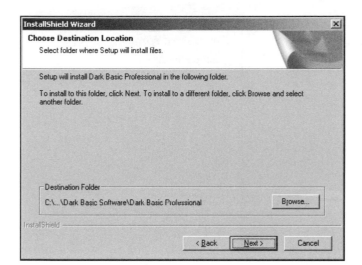

Figure 1.59 *The Choose Destination Location screen*

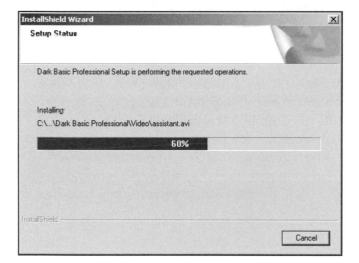

Figure 1.60 *The Setup Status screen, which displays the installation progress*

After the files have been copied and settings have been configured on your PC for running DarkBASIC Professional, the InstallShield Wizard Complete screen will appear (see Figure 1.61). Click the Finish button to exit. Your PC is now ready to run DarkBASIC Professional.

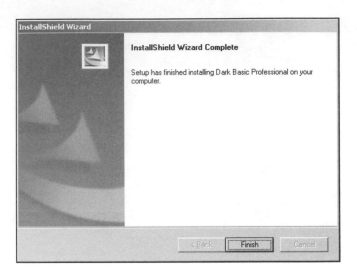

Figure 1.61 *The InstallShield Wizard Complete screen*

Summary

Well, there goes the first chapter. Are you feeling enthused about the capabilities of DarkBASIC yet? As you learned in this chapter, DarkBASIC is a complete, self-contained game creation tool capable of compiling standalone DirectX games. DarkBASIC handles all of the difficult work for you behind the scenes, allowing you to focus on quickly developing the program rather than spending most of your time learning how to program for Windows and DirectX. DarkBASIC-compiled programs are standalone executable files that have no dependency on a run-time file because the DarkBASIC run-time is built into the .exe file.

Chapter Quiz

Each chapter in this book will end with a quiz to help reinforce what you learned in the chapter. Each chapter quiz includes ten multiple-choice, true-false, or yes-no questions. You will find the answers for all of the chapter quizzes in Appendix A, "Answers to the Chapter Quizzes."

1. What company developed DarkBASIC?

   A. Real Game Tools

   B. Dark Basic Software Ltd

C. Light Productions

D. Sentient Creations

2. DarkBASIC takes advantage of what Windows-based technology?

    A. OpenGL

    B. ActiveX

    C. DirectX

    D. SQL

3. Which of the following commands is not listed on the File menu?

    A. Open

    B. Close

    C. Save

    D. Build EXE

4. DarkEDIT is an alternative for the DarkBASIC editor.

    A. True

    B. False

5. DarkBASIC was based on which of the following programming languages?

    A. BASIC

    B. C++

    C. Delphi

    D. Assembler

6. Which of the following is *not* a menu in DarkBASIC?

    A. File

    B. Help

    C. View

    D. Shop

7. What is the main Web site for DarkBASIC?

    A. http://www.darkbasic.com

    B. http://www.totaldb.com

    C. http://www.darkforces.com

    D. http://www.realgametools.com

8. BASIC stands for:

    A. Binary Attribute System in Concert

    B. Believing a Stupid Integer Call

    C. Beginner's All-Purpose Symbolic Instruction Code

    D. Buying All Spaghetti in California

9. What is the name of the DarkBASIC add-on product?

    A. DarkSTORM

    B. DarkFLIGHT

    C. DarkNESS

    D. DarkMATTER

10. Is there a run-time file required for DarkBASIC?

    A. Yes

    B. No

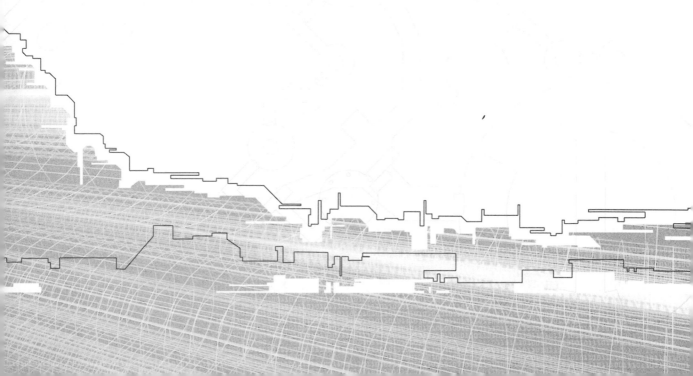

CHAPTER 2

INTRODUCTION TO COMPUTER PROGRAMMING

This chapter is an introductory course in computer programming, with no prior programming experience required. The first thing aspiring programmers often discover is that programming looks really complicated. The truth is, computer programs are made up of hundreds of different commands arranged in a specific order to accomplish a task. The program doesn't always have to be a game. In the context of DarkBASIC, most of the programs you will write using this book will be game-related. However, there is a lot of information to cover before you'll be ready to tackle your first complete game! This chapter explains not only how to get started writing source code in DarkBASIC, but how programs work.

This chapter covers the following topics:

- Short Course on Programming
- Video Game Basics
- Writing Your First DarkBASIC Program
- The Command Line Interface

Short Course on Programming

What's the best way to learn to write computer programs? You have probably wondered in amazement while playing the latest game, "How in the world did they *do that?*" I hope that by the time you've finished reading this book, you'll have a solid grasp on the answer! What I can tell you at this point is that it's a gradual process. First you learn the basics, and then you practice while learning more techniques. With some diligence you will learn how the pros work their magic. Eventually, you will gain the experience you need to become an expert programmer, but you must invest a lot of time in studying and practicing your programming skills, learning new languages and tricks along the way. As with most things in life, it just boils down to a lot of work—not necessarily hard work, but consistent effort. For that reason, it helps if you really enjoy programming in general—you must *love* to play and write games to get really good at it. If you are not fascinated by something, how will you muster the will to keep at it?

What Is a Computer Program?

First of all, you might be asking this simple question: What exactly is a computer program? I have already hinted at the answer, but in a nutshell, a computer program is something that accepts input (such as an entry from the keyboard), performs some computations (also called processing), and then sends the result to the output (usually the screen). Figure 2.1 illustrates this point.

There are many different ways to write a computer program, and I'm not just talking about the programming language. You can use any language to write a computer program, although some languages arc more suited for certain types of problems than others. When computer programs start to get really big, they tend to become unmanageable unless the programmer is well organized. For this reason, computer scientists came up with a fancy term called *methodology*. This word refers to the steps you can take to describe how a program is written, based on the way a programming language works. For instance, suppose you are writing a massively-multiplayer game that will be able to handle thousands of players online at the same time, interacting in a huge game world. The methodology for this game would describe how the computers are connected online in order for the game to work. One methodology might attempt to break up the game world into many smaller worlds linked together, while another methodology might describe a single huge game world.

Object-Oriented Programs

You might have heard of object-oriented programming (OOP) because it is used to write large and complex programs. Object-oriented programs are easy to handle when they get large because they are made up of many smaller related programs.

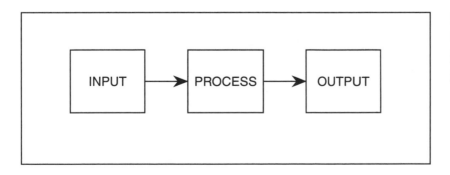

Figure 2.1 *The basis for computer programming is input, process, and output.*

Therefore, any time you need to solve a particular kind of problem in your program, you just plug in one of the smaller programs. As you might imagine, OOP excels at handling very large programs involving millions of lines of code, but it's more difficult to learn than other types of languages.

Structured Programs

Structured programming languages are easier to learn than OOP languages, which is one of the reasons why this book uses DarkBASIC, a powerful structured programming language. Structured programs are also called *procedural programs* because they are made up of multiple procedures, each of which is capable of solving a small problem. If this sounds similar to object-oriented programs, it's because OOP evolved from structured programming.

Structured programs tend to run faster than OOP programs. Although they are more difficult to manage when they get large, structured programs generally are easier to learn and use. Unlike OOP programs, structured programs don't require that you design an object before you start writing the actual program. Figure 2.2 shows an illustration of structured programming.

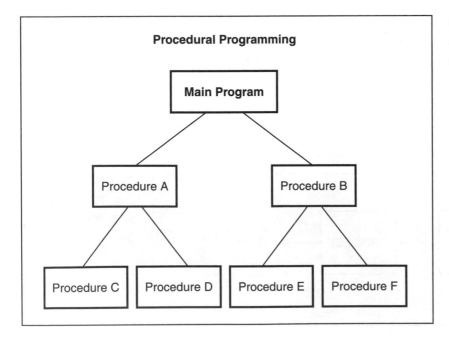

Figure 2.2 *A visual representation of a structured program*

DarkBASIC Is a Structured Language

DarkBASIC programs are completely self-contained executables that don't require any special run-time library because the library is built into the compiled program. (If you don't understand what I'm talking about, don't worry. I'll go over this information again in the next few chapters.) Figure 2.3 shows what the internal structure of a DarkBASIC program might look like in theory.

DarkBASIC allows you to compile your program to a standard Windows executable, which means that it runs like any other game you've played on your Windows PC, complete with support for DirectX. In fact, the greatest feature of DarkBASIC is that it lets you write DirectX games without even knowing any of the DirectX function calls. It's completely built in! Figure 2.4 shows the relationship between DarkBASIC, Windows, and DirectX.

Depending on your experience level, this might make sense or it might be something that you will pick up in time. A compiler is a program (like DarkBASIC) that converts your source code into an executable file. Like so many subjects involved in writing computer programs, this is one that I must defer until later in order to keep the subject matter more understandable and less rife with theory.

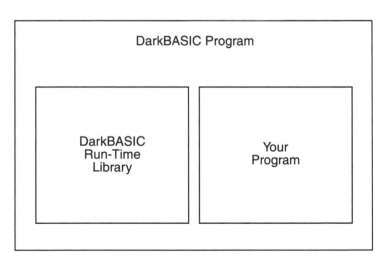

Figure 2.3 *DarkBASIC executables include both your compiled code and the run-time library.*

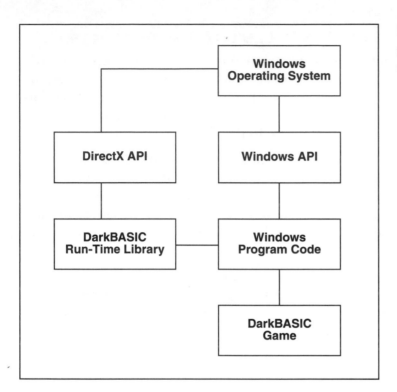

Figure 2.4 *DarkBASIC programs are closely tied to Windows and DirectX.*

Definition of a Computer Program

In a more technical sense, a computer program is a series of instructions that tells the computer what to do, usually in the context of solving a problem. A Web browser or word processing program is just a computer program made up of instructions—just like a fast-action first-person shooter game such as *Doom III* or *Unreal Tournament 2003*. It's all about the instructions—or, as we say in gaming circles, the code.

What is code? You might have heard the word used before, but without a clear frame of reference it can be somewhat confusing. *Code* refers to the source code instructions that make up a program. The instructions themselves are each designed to perform simple operations such as math, logic, or memory movement. These very low-level instructions tell the computer what to do. Of course, it's very difficult for humans to read and write these instructions in the computer's native format, which is referred to as *machine language*. This format is completely binary—that is, it consists of streams of 0s and 1s. These values are referred to as *bits*. A single bit can hold one piece of digital information. Figure 2.5 shows a game project made up of several parts.

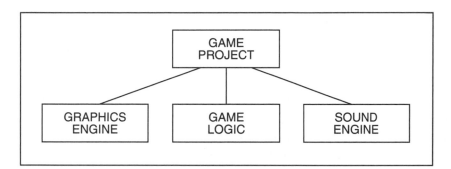

Figure 2.5
Computer programs are made up of separate parts, each of which accomplishes a task.

Video Game Bits

You might have heard the word *bit* used in the context of video games. Console makers, such as Sega, Nintendo, Sony, and Microsoft, love to talk about video games in terms of the bit strength of their consoles. For example, the Dreamcast was marketed as the very first 128-bit home video game machine. Where did the term "128-bit" come from? Generally, the number of bits that a video game system can handle is related to the computational power of the GPU (*Graphics Processing Unit*), which is different from the CPU (*Central Processing Unit*). This is really an interesting subject. Table 2.1 shows you the specifications of the major video game machines on the market today.

These figures seem to be much lower than those found on even a budget PC. Why do you suppose that a wide variety of console games seem to look and play so much better than PC games? Part of the reason is that console games are written very specifically for the hardware of the video game machine, while PC games have to support a wide variety of hardware configurations. Usually a high-end PC will totally

Table 2.1 Video Game Console Comparison Chart

Console	Processor	Graphics	Memory
Microsoft Xbox	733 MHz	256-bit, 233 MHz	64 MB
Nintendo GameCube	485 MHz	128-bit, 162 MHz	40 MB
Sony PlayStation 2	295 MHz	128-bit, 150 MHz	40 MB

blow away a console machine, but consoles generally attract a younger audience due to the lower price.

Since I'm on the subject of video games, what does it take to write a game? DarkBASIC excels at helping you write games, thanks to all of the wonderful built-in commands that were tailored just for this purpose. I'll cover this again in later chapters, but a game is basically a program that runs in a loop, which means that it keeps doing something over and over again until you tell it to end. It's this looping feature that keeps the game running smoothly. On the contrary, a turn-based game doesn't use a game loop like this unless the game uses animation that needs to be updated on a regular basis. When it comes to larger games that include animated graphics, artificial intelligence, sound effects, music, multiplayer support, and user input, the game loop can be quite complicated indeed! On top of it all, the game needs to run as fast as possible—even with 3D graphics in most cases! Check out Figure 2.6 for an illustration of the game loop.

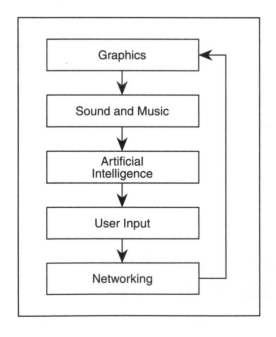

Figure 2.6
The game loop keeps the game running smoothly.

Solving Problems

Since computer programs are supposed to be written to solve a problem, what kinds of problems might need to be solved? The possibilities are innumerable. For example, there are computers and programs on airline jets that help the pilots take off, navigate, and land. Computer programs operate streetlights. There are even programs running in modern cars that help to achieve better gas mileage. We are surrounded by problems, in fact! The process for solving a problem with a computer is similar to the processes humans use to solve real-life problems. Every decision you make involves one or more pieces of input that you must weigh in order to make a decision. The result of your decision is the output of your "program."

Figure 2.7 shows a simple illustration of a decision the way a computer sees it. You see, computers treat every decision as a single entity. Even when there are many details that must be considered before making a decision, the computer must think about every decision separately. Humans, on the other hand, have the ability to quickly draw conclusions, sometimes without looking at every factor involved.

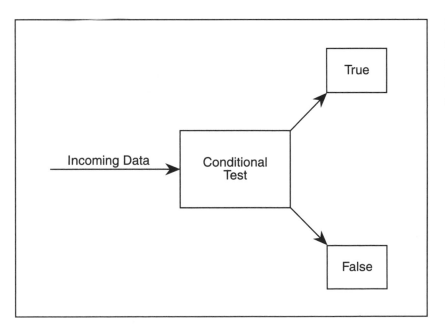

Figure 2.7
Computer problem-solving involves making decisions using simple logic tests.

Decisions, Decisions

Suppose you are purchasing a new video game console at the store. You want to buy a console with a large selection of games that appeal to you, but you also want it to last a long time before it becomes obsolete. Therefore, the game selection alone probably isn't good a single source of input for your decision. You intuitively weigh factors such as price, manufacturer, online multiplayer capabilities, and previous purchase decisions that went well or poorly before choosing a console.

Computer programs work the same way. A program is more limited than your mind, though, because programs have only a limited intelligence for adapting to new situations, while you are capable of adapting to any unforeseen condition. Computers excel at doing things precisely and quickly, but humans have intuition—we are able to see patterns and shapes that aren't apparent at the lowest detail, which is the narrow level that computers "see." Therefore, computers don't get the big picture like humans do.

To help with intuition, our minds like to categorize things as closely as possible, so we are able to recognize patterns quickly. As an infant, one of the first patterns that your mind memorizes is the face of your mother or father (usually both). Some of your mind's first problems involve seeing other faces and trying to decide whether they are Mom or Dad. This is a pattern-recognition problem that required a great deal of training and reinforcement—looking at familiar faces over and over again caused those patterns to be remembered and used for comparison. So, when you think about it, our minds are already programmed when we are born; they just need input. That is very similar to how a computer program works. First you write the program, putting as much or as little problem-solving ability into it as you choose, and then you send it out into the world. Of course, another thing humans have over computers is the built-in ability to learn.

Logic versus Intuition

Have you ever discovered something new and immediately found it difficult to compare that new thing to anything else you have seen in your life? Part of the enjoyment of discovering new things is the mystique of trying to categorize them. We leap upon solutions so quickly that it is fun to find something indescribable— at least at first. This is precisely why children have such a need to play, and why their lives are filled with such mystery, intrigue, and suspense. Children never know when something new will present itself to them. Adults are often not as fascinated by daily life, after having "seen it all." If you think about that observation for a minute and note how it applies to your life, doesn't it start to make sense? The wonder of childhood is very closely tied to our built-in ability to categorize things in the world. When a baby sees a new person's face, the baby might frown, look puzzled, or even cry, unhappy with the new situation. Often the baby is very quickly able to perform the "parent/not parent" test by comparing new faces with the most important faces in his or her mind. The infant's mind is an extraordinarily complex neural network. (A neural network is a pattern-recognition machine. Everything in the human mind is stored as a pattern, and our ability to organize and store patterns efficiently determines our intelligence.)

Do you suppose your brain really stores every letter of the alphabet and then searches that list of 26 letters from start to finish when you read the words in this book? Again, I ask that you take a moment to think about this, because it is more relevant to computer programming than you might imagine. No, you are reading these words and your mind is recognizing entire *words* as patterns, not just letters. Your mind will often misread words that have similar spellings (such as "grind" and "blind") because a neural network seeks out solutions as quickly as possible, not always with perfect accuracy. That is intuition in a nutshell.

One reason why programmers are so fascinated with writing code is because it puts your mind through a constant workout as you try to reprogram your mind to stop making assumptions about things. You must put a conscious halt to some patterns and try to think like the computer thinks (in the manner in which it processes data). The ability to quickly surmise the solution to a problem and write a program to solve it is what makes a good programmer, and it does take practice. As you write more and more code and solve one problem after another, you will start to get the hang of it.

Methodology of the Mind

I will elaborate on this more in the next section, but I wanted to give you more insight on writing computer programs. Over the years, I have learned that real programmers never get tired of writing code. No matter how boring the subject, a great programmer will have an inherent fascination with the "intuition bypass" that I described in the previous section. As you learn new techniques as a programmer, you will find that many solutions simply involve challenging your assumptions about what the computer will do in a given situation. As you have lived your daily life, your mind has started to develop more advanced ways to store patterns. This is what you might call the "methodology of the mind," developed with experience. Not only is the human mind able to store and organize patterns efficiently, it is also able to completely reprogram the method by which it does these things—something that computer scientists might never be able to build into a computer.

I have mentioned categories already. A category is a sort of bin in which your mind places like patterns; there can be a hierarchy of these storage bins of the mind. For instance, you might lump shells, seaweed, and sand together in a category called "the beach." Since seaweed comes from the ocean, your mind doesn't need to add water to the category—it is just an assumption that water goes along with these other beach-related items.

Now what if you have never seen a beach in your life, or even a picture of the ocean? It is hard to imagine, like trying to imagine what it would be like to have been blind from birth. Without ever having used your eyes, how would you imagine the many colors in the world? You might imagine shades of color that resemble different scents or textures or temperatures, but you'd never have any idea what different colors really look like.

As a programmer, you must learn to think outside of your assumptions to solve the most difficult problems in the best way. Not only will you become a better programmer, but you will be able to apply this skill to other areas of your life. After writing code for many years, I find that I am able to see things differently than others. Often, this is what causes non-programmers to think of programmers as a little strange. While most people will look at a sports car and admire the paint and body style, a typical programmer will be interested in such things as the engine displacement, fuel economy, and gear ratio.

Three Steps to Solving Logical Problems

There are three basic steps to solving a problem—input, calculations, and output. Consider a sample problem in which you are deciding which product to purchase at a store.

Input

Figure 2.8 shows three inputs for a decision that must be made. This represents the actual logic of a program (which could be the human brain or a computer, as the case may be). This problem involves selecting a product. The square labeled "Decision: Select a Product" could be a program or a thought process that uses the incoming information.

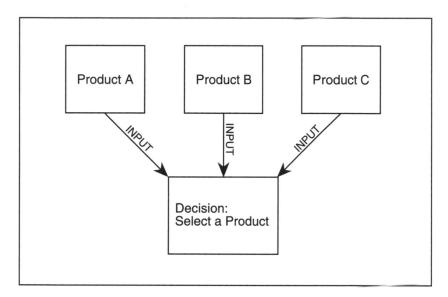

Figure 2.8
A problem that needs to be solved

Take a look at the sample problem to find the input, which is nothing more than the available data or facts. In the sample problem, three products represent the input: Product A, Product B, and Product C. Each of these inputs might be stored in the program using a *variable*— a piece of data that the program can use.

> **A *variable* is a location in the computer's memory that stores information that can be changed at any time.**

Calculation

The next step to solving a problem is to do something with the input. This step is called the calculation or *processing* step; it usually involves some type of algorithm designed to solve a specific problem. Figure 2.9 shows how you might select a product using specific criteria (also known as logic). This is really where all the action takes place, because the processing of the program occurs here. The program might run through many complex algorithms or just a simple equation.

> **An *algorithm* is a step-by-step process for solving a problem.**

Figure 2.9 shows a chain of test conditions involved in processing a decision. The decision is made only if all three conditions are true. Of course, in real life there might be any number of conditions, from just one to a hundred or even more.

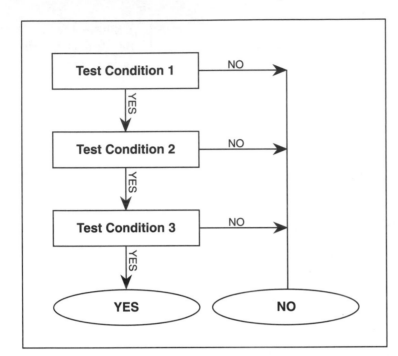

Figure 2.9 *Several conditions must be met before this decision returns true.*

Naturally, computers are more efficient than humans when a decision involves a very large number of conditions.

Output

The output of a decision (or an entire program) is usually the most obvious part, where you clearly see something on the screen or printer or perhaps receive the answer to a decision. The output from one process is often also the input for another process. There are many different methods to map out a program. Thinking in the simple terms of input, process, and output will help you understand how programs work.

Video Game Basics

Well, I have covered many different aspects of computer programming without getting too technical. As you might have guessed from the title, this book is not just about writing computer programs; it is about writing games.

A computer game or video game is a program, written with a programming language such as C++ or DarkBASIC, which allows a player to interact within an imaginary world. The goal of a video game is to compete with other players in a cooperative or adversarial competition or to play solo, usually with an emphasis on setting a new high score (which other players will attempt to beat later).

Why Do We Play Video Games?

Video games are fun because they are very good at simulating another world and then drawing the player into that world. They are excellent for developing keen hand-eye coordination and problem-solving skills through the achievement of goals with specific rewards. Often the completion of the game is reward enough, but many games do not have a specific ending point. Rather, some games are suited for pitting two or more friends against each other, either at the same time or in turns.

Competition helps to develop the skills you need to work with others and strive to better yourself, and video games are great at fostering competition. In addition, they are wonderful works of art that reflect the often arcane imaginings of the game designer. As such, game designers are like painters with virtual canvasses, capable of transporting someone to another world. Once a game has achieved a minimum acceptable standard on the visual and audible levels, players expect it to entertain through a gripping story or fantastic goal.

The Game Engine

Every game, from a simplistic card game like *Solitaire* to a complicated 3D first-person shooter like *Doom III*, has what is called a game engine. The *game engine* is the core set of commands that are executed repeatedly in a main game loop, which involves displaying images on the screen, playing sound effects, handling user input, and so on. Tall order, huh? Well, a game engine can be broken down into a few basic parts.

Game Graphics

In the old days, all games used two-dimensional images called sprites. It is a given that most games developed

> A *sprite* is a small image that may or may not be animated, with properties that define how it moves around on the screen. The source image for a sprite usually has a background color that is defined as the *transparent* color and is not displayed when the sprite is drawn on the screen. Engineers at Atari originally coined the word "sprite."

today will run entirely in 3D and feature three-dimensional objects throughout the game world rather than simply sprites. Not all games display 3D objects, but most games use a 3D world. DarkBASIC makes 3D programming easy by providing all the commands you need to load and draw 3D characters and worlds, as you'll see in later chapters!

Sound Effects and Music

Sound is quite often more important than the graphics in a game. It is clear that humans interact primarily through speech and sound. It should therefore be no surprise that sound is a vital part of any new game. In fact, now that games use 3D sound, it's no longer a great thing to simply have sound and music in a game. 3D sound provides the often eerie effect of being fully immersed in an environment filled with sounds from every direction.

Getting Input

User input is always needed, no matter what type of game you are writing. After all, a game without user input is nothing more than a technology demo! DarkBASIC is capable of handling any number of input devices that you can plug into your PC, including the newer USB (*Universal Serial Bus*) force-feedback joysticks. DarkBASIC handles the devices through a series of simple but robust commands, as you'll discover in Chapter 12, "Programming the Keyboard, Mouse, and Joystick."

Artificial Intelligence

Computer-controlled players are necessary for most types of games, and are absolutely essential for single-player games. Some multiplayer games, such as first-person shooters, do not have computer-controlled players and thus do not need AI (*Artificial Intelligence*) code. However, the vast majority of games—especially strategy games—do, so it is important to learn the tricks and techniques for simulating intelligence and challenging the player with competitive computer players.

Writing Your First DarkBASIC Program

Now that I've covered some basics of programming and an overview of video games, I'd like to give you some experience playing around with DarkBASIC. You should now have a basic grasp of what makes a computer program tick—even if you don't have a clue exactly how to put it to use yet. In other words, you have some theory but nothing useful yet! In this chapter and those that follow, you will apply the input-process-output model to game programming. I'll start with some basic concepts that will be useful in every DarkBASIC programming project, regardless of the subject.

Running DarkBASIC for the First Time

First, fire up DarkBASIC. If you haven't installed it yet, go ahead and do that now; I'll wait.

Ready to continue? Great! The first time you run DarkBASIC, you will see a screen that looks like Figure 2.10. If you followed along in the last chapter as I gave you a tour of DarkBASIC, you might have already seen this screen when DarkBASIC started. This check is only performed the first time you run DarkBASIC.

DarkBASIC performs this check to ensure that it will run on your PC. First, your video card must support 3D at a resolution of 640×480. The other three features (alpha blending, texture filtering, and fogging) are advanced features that DarkBASIC can use, but which are not required for it to run. To continue, just press any key.

The Introduction screen appears next, as shown in Figure 2.11. You saw this screen in the last chapter.

Figure 2.10 *DarkBASIC detects the capabilities of your 3D card the first time it runs.*

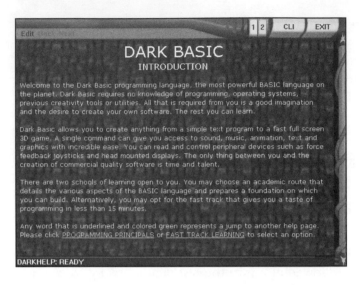

Figure 2.11 *The Introduction screen is loaded when you first run DarkBASIC, providing you with immediate help on how to get started.*

The "Hello World" Program

A program is made up of source code, which is the instruction manual that tells the computer what to do. When programming in DarkBASIC, you will type in *source code*, which is any text that instructs the computer what to do. Figure 2.12 shows an example of source code in the DarkBASIC editor.

Figure 2.12 *Sample source code in the DarkBASIC environment*

Entering the "Hello World" Source Code

One of the hardest parts of writing a computer game is typing in the source code. You have to keep everything in mind, from what commands you want to use to what variables you want to create. Most programming languages are case sensitive, which means that you not only have to spell everything correctly, but also verify the capitalization of each letter. Fortunately DarkBASIC is not case sensitive, so you can use whatever capitalization you prefer. If it is easier for you to type in the source code using all lowercase letters, DarkBASIC won't mind. For example, the print command will work equally well as print, PRINT, or pRiNt.

Go ahead—type in the program yourself and see how it runs. Type the following lines of source code into the DarkBASIC editor exactly as shown in Figure 2.12.

Before you do anything else, however, you need to fire up DarkBASIC (or DarkBASIC Professional, depending on which version you are using). In most cases, DarkBASIC is located in the Windows Start menu under Program Files, Dark Basic Software. If you can't find DarkBASIC in the Start menu, you might want to

Installing DarkBASIC

DarkBASIC is easy to install, but the installer differs depending on the version. Whether you are using DarkBASIC or DarkBASIC Professional, the installation process requires very little input and only takes a minute or two to complete. The CD-ROM that comes with this book includes the demo versions of both DarkBASIC and DarkBASIC Professional. The demo version of DarkBASIC is located in a folder called \DBV1 Install. Likewise, the demo version of DarkBASIC Professional is located in a folder called \DBPro Install. These demo versions will allow you to try DarkBASIC and read through the book before you purchase the retail version. In either case, Dark Basic Software Ltd has provided the latest version of each compiler at the time of this writing. For more information, browse to the official DarkBASIC Web sites at http://www.darkbasic.com and http://www.darkbasicpro.com.

make sure it was installed properly. The easiest way to tell is to run the install program and reinstall DarkBASIC from the CD-ROM.

```
REM --------------------------------
REM Beginner's Guide To Game Programming With DarkBASIC
REM Copyright (C)2002 Jonathan S. Harbour and Joshua R. Smith
REM Chapter 2 - Hello World program
REM --------------------------------

REM Display first message
CLS
PRINT
PRINT "Hello, world!."
PRINT

REM Pause for one second...
SLEEP 1000

REM Display second message
PRINT "Wait, what was that?"
PRINT

REM Pause for 1/10 second...
SLEEP 100

REM Display third message
PRINT "What, you want more?"
PRINT

REM Pause for 1/10 second...
SLEEP 100

REM Ask user to type in a number
PRINT "Type in a number..."
INPUT a

REM Display the message several times
FOR x = 1 to a
  PRINT "Hello, Again!"
NEXT x
```

This program includes several things that I have not introduced you to yet, but a little exposure to what is to come will just give you a sneak peek at coming chapters. You should be able to type this program into the DarkBASIC or DarkBASIC Professional code editor window and run the program by pressing F5. If you receive an error message, it is most likely due to a typing error. Simply check each line of the program and compare it with the printed program listing. Note that the comment lines at the top of the program are optional—you can leave out REM lines without hurting the program.

Quick Keyboard Shortcuts

Sometimes the mouse just isn't convenient enough. Your fingers are just finishing up a long stream of code, and the little effort it takes to move the mouse up to the Run menu is just too much. Yes, I'm speaking from experience here. DarkBASIC has that situation covered as well.

When you clicked on the Run menu, did you notice that each option has a function key listed next to it? The Compile option has F4, and the Run option has F5. This tells you that if you hit the F4 key while in DarkBASIC, the program will compile. If you hit the F5 key, the program will run.

Saving the Program

Always be sure to save a program you've typed in before running it. Programming is a scientific endeavor replete with mistakes, which will occasionally cause a compiler to crash—although DarkBASIC is particularly user friendly and has never crashed in my experience. Another reason to be sure you save your work is that you never know when the power will go out after a long programming session. I could tell you many different stories of people who did not save and lost a lot of work. (I won't mention my name in any of those stories.)

To save the program, choose File, Save, as shown in Figure 2.13. If this is the first time you have saved the project, the Save a Program dialog box will appear, allowing you to select the file to save. This dialog box also allows you to type in the name of the program, the author, and the date (see Figure 2.14).

Now comes an important step—naming the project. This can be easy if you follow a few guidelines. First, know what you are writing, and second, describe it in your project name. Once you have come up with a project name you like, just type it in the Filename field. DarkBASIC will take care of the rest, including creating the files and directories for you.

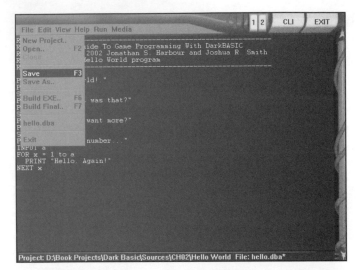

Figure 2.13
Saving the "Hello World" program using the File menu

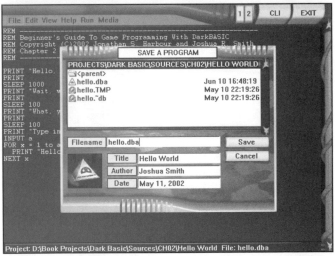

Figure 2.14 *The Save a Program dialog box lets you save a new program.*

Compiling the Program

You will need to check your source code for errors before running it. DarkBASIC will not run the program if you have entered illegal commands. You can attempt to run it, but it will not work if there is anything wrong. There is an easy way to compile and run your program—simply press the F5 key at any time and DarkBASIC will run it (that is, if there are no errors).

DarkBASIC is a fun programming environment to use, as you have probably noticed. It just seems like everything was designed for writing games, and it's very immersive. DarkBASIC isn't overloaded with an unbelievable amount of features that completely overwhelm anyone but an expert (like Visual C++).

Now that you've saved the program, compile it to make sure it doesn't contain any typos. To compile the program, select Run, Compile (see Figure 2.15).

Small programs such as this "Hello World" program compile in less than a second on most PCs, but larger programs can take a long time to compile. Figure 2.16 shows the compilation progress bar.

> **When you *compile* your source code, DarkBASIC turns it into something that can be run on the computer.**

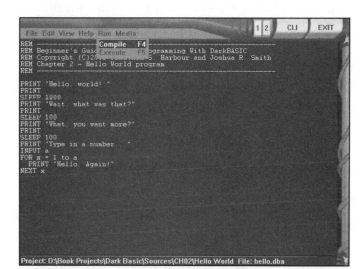

Figure 2.15 *You will find the Compile and Execute commands in the Run menu.*

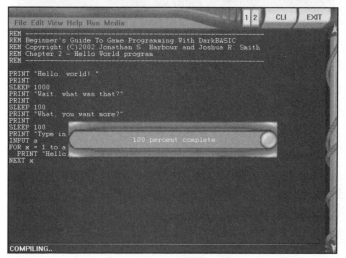

Figure 2.16 *The compilation progress bar shows the progress while a program is being compiled.*

Running the Program

Of course, you don't *have* to compile the program. You can just press F5, and DarkBASIC will automatically compile the program before running it. Figure 2.17 shows the output from the "Hello World" program.

Program Comments

Some of the most important source code in a program consists of lines that are never executed, called *comments*. Adding comments to source code is helpful in two ways. First, it tells you what you were thinking when you wrote that particular section of code. Second, it helps you remove code that you do not want run but that you want to save for later. They're also useful for including blank lines in the source code to separate sections of code and make it easier to read. DarkBASIC ignores blank lines, just like comment lines.

Making comments in DarkBASIC is very easy. There are three different commands (and a character) related to comments.

- REM
- REMSTART
- REMEND
- ` (single opening quote)

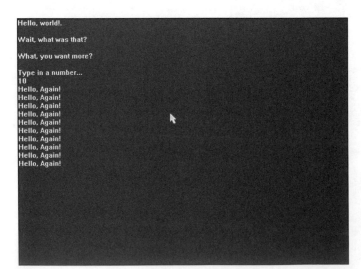

Figure 2.17

Output from the "Hello World" program

The single opening quote character, which looks like a reverse apostrophe, is the key normally associated with the ~ (tilde), and is found to the immediate left of the 1 key and above Tab on most keyboards. It is the most convenient way to add comments to your source code. After a few examples of using the other comment commands in upcoming chapters, I will use the quote character more often. Just wait; you'll see!

The REM Command

The REM command tells DarkBASIC that the line is a comment. The REM command must come first in the line, followed by the comment.

```
REM This is a comment that doesn't do anything.
REM Comment lines are ignored by DarkBASIC.
```

The REM command is short for *remark*, and it allows you to include comments that are ignored by DarkBASIC in a program.

The REMSTART...REMEND Commands

Often the REM command is just not enough to handle many lines in a lengthy comment. For example, you might want to add a header to your source code to give information about the program. You can include as many lines as you want in this header by defining those lines as comments. Adding REM to each line is easy to do, but there is a more elegant solution—the REMSTART and REMEND commands.

REMSTART indicates that a comment starts at that line. Anything following a REMSTART is considered a comment and is ignored by DarkBASIC until it reaches a REMEND command. Here is an example of the REMSTART and REMEND commands:

```
REMSTART
Program: Test.bas
Author: Joshua Smith
Date: April 3, 2002
Description: Demonstrates the use of comments.
REMEND
```

Starting and Stopping the Program

Now let's talk about program flow. DarkBASIC executes the source code from the top to the bottom, executing each line of the program one at a time. That means the first command in the source code file is the first command that DarkBASIC executes. Since DarkBASIC executes code in this manner, you can use an END command to end the program from any point. Otherwise, the program will simply end after the last line of the program executes.

The END Command

The END command ends the execution of your program wherever you put it. It can be placed in multiple locations. The following program shows how to use the END command.

```
REMSTART
Program:   FunWithComments.bas
Author:    Joshua Smith
Date:      April 3, 2002
Description: Demonstrates the use of comments.
REMEND

REM End the program!
END
```

This program might not do much, but it will end (little joke there). The END command is key in controlling the flow of your program, as you will discover in later chapters.

Why do you need an END command? Why not just place the last line of source code at the end of the file? If you want to stop your program from running, you need to use the END command. Nothing after the END command will run.

The Command Line Interface

The command line interface (CLI), which is built into DarkBASIC, allows you to debug a program while you are running it. The console is like a real-time DarkBASIC file that runs every command after you type it. You can print variables or ask for input. Anything that can be typed in source code can be typed in the CLI (see Figure 2.18).

> To *debug* a program is to remove all of the bugs from it. Sometimes it takes just as long to debug a program as it does to write it!

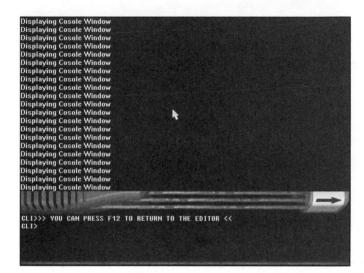

Figure 2.18 *The command line interface*

To gain access to the command line interface window while a program is running in the DarkBASIC IDE (*Integrated Development Environment*), just press the Esc key. The command line interface will pop up, interrupting your program. At that point you can enter whatever commands you want. To return to your program, just hit the Esc key again. I know this was a brief introduction to the CLI; it will be covered again in more detail in a later chapter. Note that DarkBASIC Professional operates differently and does not bring up the CLI. Instead, when you hit Esc, by default the program ends and control returns to the editor. DarkBASIC Professional has integrated the CLI into the debugging features of the new editor.

Summary

This chapter covered a lot of basics in a short amount of time, including how to create a new project, how to type in source code, and how to run your first DarkBASIC program. Congratulations, that's a great start! If you feel the need, go ahead and reread the chapter to strengthen your understanding of the material and become more familiar with the DarkBASIC editor and programming environment before moving on to the next chapter. But first, give the chapter quiz a try and see how well you do.

Chapter Quiz

The chapter quiz will help you to retain the information that was covered in this chapter, as well as give you an idea about how well you're doing at understanding the subjects. You can find the answers for this quiz in Appendix A, "Answers to the Chapter Quizzes."

1. Programming is the art of solving what?

   A. Crossword puzzles

   B. Problems

   C. Word searches

   D. Pizza toppings

2. Which is not part of the method for solving problems?

   A. Input

   B. Output

   C. Processing

   D. Pass on

3. Which command is used to make a comment?

   A. COMMENT

   B. REM

   C. COMMEND

   D. COMIT

4. What command is used to start a series of comments?

   A. COMMENTSTART

   B. REMSTART

   C. REMEND

   D. COMMENTEND

5. The END command will restart the program.

   A. True

   B. False

6. What is a good tool for debugging your program?

   A. Console
   B. REM statement
   C. END statement
   D. Mouse cursor

7. Why is it important to comment?

   A. It lets you know what you were thinking when you wrote the code.
   B. It's not important.
   C. To fill space.
   D. B and C

8. What is an algorithm?

   A. A musical term
   B. A step-by-step process used to solve a problem
   C. A graphics card
   D. A brand of cereal

9. What command do you use to end a program?

   A. STOP
   B. END
   C. HALT
   D. BYEBYE

10. What does REMEND do?

   A. Ends a series of comments
   B. Nothing
   C. Starts a series of comments
   D. Prints to the screen

CHAPTER 3

BASIC COMMANDS, VARIABLES, AND DATA TYPES

There are many commands in DarkBASIC; some are very easy to understand, but many are more complicated. To understand those commands, you will need to first cover some fundamental groundwork. Programming is more than just knowing all the commands. You need to understand how to use variables and learn the basic data types. When you have mastered the information in this chapter, you will be on the right track for writing full-blown programs in DarkBASIC.

This chapter explains everything you need to know about variables—what they are, how they are defined, and how they are used. Data types are next. There are three data types to cover—integer, decimal, and string. After I lay the groundwork, I will cover a few basic commands. At the end of this chapter, you will be on your way to writing entire programs, and I will show you several examples along the way.

This chapter covers the following topics:

- Understanding Variables
- Understanding Data Types
- Working with Basic Commands

Understanding Variables

I briefly mentioned variables in the last chapter (enough to tantalize you?), but this chapter is dedicated to the subject. One might go so far as to claim that variables are the foundation of computer programs. They provide a means to store data in a program. A variable is stored in memory and accessed through its name, like this:

```
HugeNumber = 3828549
ShoeSize = 12
Person$ = "Carrie-Anne Moss"
```

As you can see, variables can store numbers or words (also called *strings*).

What Is a Variable?

In the old days when programmers used machine and assembly language, they would create variables by simply grabbing a chunk of memory and then storing a number in the newly acquired spot. This was called *memory allocation*, which is a valid term in software today. Reserving a space in the computer's memory was a manual process that required the programmer to keep track of exactly where that space was located by creating a pointer—from which variables were derived.

To make the task easier, programmers developed assembly language, made up of words and symbols that are very closely related to machine instructions but are much easier to write. Assembly permitted the use of mnemonic words to replace the specific addresses in the memory where the information was stored. Rather than keep track of a pointer's address, which in turn pointed to another address in the memory where actual data was located, a mnemonic was used as the pointer. Mnemonics are easier to remember than physical addresses in memory, so this made writing programs much easier. Here is an example:

> *Assembly language* **is a very low-level programming language that uses mnemonic (symbols that are easy to remember) instructions to represent the machine language instruction set of the computer itself—actually, the microprocessor in the physical sense. These mnemonic instructions allow the programmer to perform mathematical, logical, memory, and input/output instructions using English words rather than pure binary, so** Add **might be used rather than** 00101010**. As you can imagine, it is very difficult to write programs at this level even with the mnemonics, so assembly is normally only used to write time-critical high-performance code, such as device drivers, graphics algorithms, and other system programs.**

```
MOV AX, 03h
INT 33h
```

Those two commands together tell the computer to get the mouse position. As you might imagine, assembly is difficult to master, and beginners always have an interrupt reference book handy. The first line moves the number 3 into the AX register. Registers are sort of like the piston chambers of a processor. Put something in the chamber and fire off an interrupt, and something will happen (only in this case, it is a number instead of a spurt of gasoline and air).

The second line is an interrupt call—the spark plug of assembly language. There are many interrupts in assembly that do all kinds of weird things, such as polling the mouse. Another popular old MS-DOS interrupt is INT 21h, which was very common in the old days when games were developed for MS-DOS (before Windows or DirectX came along).

The AX in the first line is the assembly equivalent of a variable, although that is a bit of a stretch because AX is actually a physical part of the processor. If you were to take a processor and look at it through a microscope, you would theoretically be able to locate that AX register amidst a tight cluster of registers in the core of the chip.

Over time, assembly language and all the difficult-to-remember mnemonic words such as `MOV` and `INT` were replaced by more advanced languages that were closer to human language. DarkBASIC is what you might call an ultra high-level language because it has so many built-in features. In contrast, assembly language is extremely low-level because it is closer to machine language in form. Fortunately for us, DarkBASIC keeps track of all the variables in a program, including the type of data stored in variables.

Variable Notation

So how do you define a variable? You simply give it a name. There are rules for defining a variable name. You cannot start a variable with a number or punctuation mark, and you cannot have a space in the name. Other than that, the sky is the limit. For example, if you want to store the number of shots fired from a gun, you would define the variable like this:

```
ShotsFired = 5
```

You might also want to store how many shots are in the gun. To do so, just define another variable the keeps track of that value.

```
ShotsInGun = 6
```

Performing Basic Math Operations with Variables

You can also perform math functions on variables, including the four basic mathematical functions—addition, subtraction, multiplication, and division. Addition problems use the plus sign (+), subtraction problems use the minus sign (–), multiplication problems use the asterisk (*), and division problems use the forward slash (/). Here is a short sample program called MathExample1, which demonstrates how to use the basic math operators. You can open this program from the CD-ROM or type it into DarkBASIC yourself. Figure 3.1 shows the output of MathExample1.

```
REMSTART
---------------------------------
Beginner's Guide To DarkBASIC Game Programming
Copyright (C)2002 Jonathan S. Harbour and Joshua R. Smith
Chapter 3 - MathExample1 program
---------------------------------
```

```
REMEND

REM the variable "Answer" will be equal to 4
Answer = 2 + 2
PRINT Answer

REM the variable "Answer" will be equal to 3
Answer = 5 - 2
PRINT Answer

REM the variable "Answer" will be equal to 4
Answer = 2 * 2
PRINT Answer

REM the variable "Answer" will be equal to
Answer = 4 / 2
PRINT Answer

REM wait for a key press
WAIT KEY
END
```

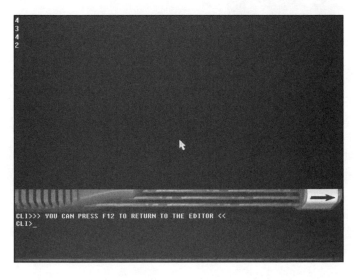

Figure 3.1 *The MathExample1 program demonstrates basic math operations.*

Using More Than One Variable in a Formula

Now, here's a trick: Instead of using plain numbers (which are called *literals* in computer-speak) in a variable, you can use other variables. For example, to calculate the speed at which an object is traveling (such as your car), you need a variable for distance and one for time. The speed is just distance divided by time. The following program, called MathExample2, shows how to solve this simple problem with DarkBASIC. Figure 3.2 shows the output of MathExample2.

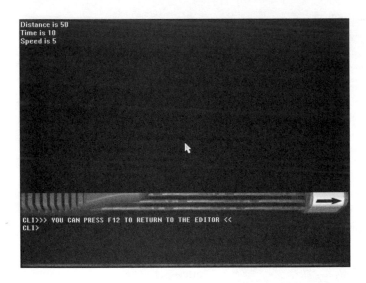

Figure 3.2 *The MathExample2 program demonstrates how to use variables in a calculation.*

```
REMSTART
-----------------------------------
Beginner's Guide To DarkBASIC Game Programming
Copyright (C)2002 Jonathan S. Harbour and Joshua R. Smith
Chapter 3 - MathExample2 program
-----------------------------------
REMEND

REM create some variables
Distance = 50
Time = 10
Speed = Distance / Time
```

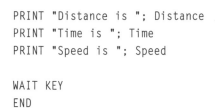

```
PRINT "Distance is "; Distance
PRINT "Time is "; Time
PRINT "Speed is "; Speed

WAIT KEY
END
```

Order of Operations

In DarkBASIC, mathematical operations have an order to them. Division and multiplication are performed first, followed by addition and subtraction. You can bypass that order if necessary by enclosing your problem in parentheses. Parentheses tell DarkBASIC to evaluate a certain part of the problem first. For example, in the equation $2 * 3 + 5$, the answer is determined by first multiplying 2 by 3 and then adding 5, which equals 11. Imagine if you were to first add 5 to 3 and then multiply by 2. The answer would be 16, which is incorrect. By using parentheses, though, you can force DarkBASIC to put priority on part of the calculation. $2 * (3 + 5) = 16$. The following program, called MathExample3, demonstrates the use of parentheses. Figure 3.3 shows the output of MathExample3.

```
REMSTART
-----------------------------------
Beginner's Guide To DarkBASIC Game Programming
Copyright (C)2002 Jonathan S. Harbour and Joshua R. Smith
Chapter 3 - MathExample3 Program
-----------------------------------
REMEND

REM this will evaluate to 3
Answer = 2 + 2 / 2
PRINT "2 + 2 / 2 ="; Answer

REM this will evaluate to 2
Answer = (2 + 2) / 2
PRINT "(2 + 2) / 2 ="; Answer

WAIT KEY
END
```

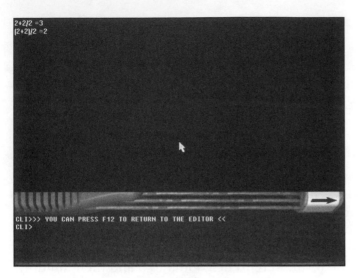

Figure 3.3 *The MathExample3 program demonstrates how to use parentheses to affect the order of operations in a math formula.*

This is known as order of operations. The only way to bypass this order is by using parentheses. Let me throw a few more problems at you; see if you can figure them out. Use Table 3.1 if you need a guide to the order of operations.

1. 4 + 3 / 3

2. (4 + 4) / 2

3. 4 + 4 * 2

4. 4 * (4 + 4)

The answers to these problems are

1. 5

2. 4

3. 12

4. 32

It's pretty complicated to keep the order of things in mind, especially when you are trying to write a program to solve a math problem for an algebra or calculus class! Table 3.1 lists the basic mathematical operations and the order in which they are evaluated.

Table 3.1 Order of Operations

Operator	Precedence	Description
( )	First	Parentheses to set precedence
*, /	Second	Multiplication and division
+, –	Third	Addition and subtraction

Variable Scope

Sometimes when you examine a problem, you need to determine its scope . . . that is, you need to determine how far the problem extends. Variables are similar in that they have a scope. There are two different types of scopes that variables obey—global and local.

Global Variables

Global variables are accessible anywhere in the program. It is like having a Palm Pilot in your pocket on the bus. Although you don't have access to your home computer, you still have access to all your information via the Palm Pilot. Information in a global variable is accessible anywhere in the program. Global variables are declared at the top of your source code with the DIM command.

```
DIM GlobalVariable(1)
```

Local Variables

Local variables are a different story. They are only visible (or available) in the current subroutine in which they reside. (I will describe subroutines in more detail in Chapter 6, "Making Programs Think: Branching Statements and Subroutines.") Figure 3.4 illustrates the difference between local and global variables. In this figure, the main program has global variables, while a subroutine has local variables (in other words, variables that have scope only within the subroutine). The subroutine can use the global variables, but the main program *cannot* use the variables inside the subroutine.

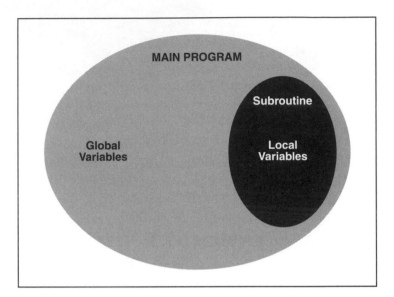

Figure 3.4 *The difference between local and global variables*

Your home computer is a good analogy to explain global and local variable scope. That's right; just think of your computer in light of this discussion. You have all kinds of information on it, such as your e-mail, photos, school or work assignments, and letters to friends. You can only access the files on your computer when you are at home and the computer is turned on. Or, suppose you are sharing files on your computer over the Internet, using something like an FTP (*File Transfer Protocol*) server or Web server. The FTP or Web files might be open to the public, but all of the other files on your computer that are not shared will not be visible. That relationship is similar to the local/global scope relationship.

Creating Global Variables Using the DIM Command

A variable generally stores one value at a time. Sometimes one value is just not enough. For example, you might want to keep track of ten different answers instead of one. You can extend the scope of a variable to encapsulate ten values by using the DIM command. DIM tells DarkBASIC to create an array.

> An *array* is an area of memory reserved for a sequential list of values of the same data type (such as integers or strings).

You can then use the multiple values assigned to your variable. You can reference each value by either a number or another

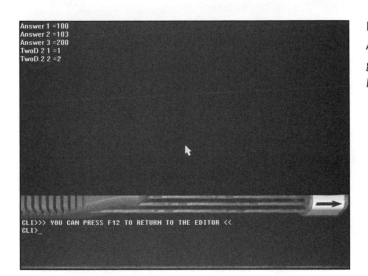

Figure 3.5 *The ArrayExample program demonstrates how to use arrays.*

variable. Here's another sample program, called ArrayExample, which shows you how to use two arrays in a program (see Figure 3.5). You will find this program on the CD in the Sources\Chapter03\ArrayExample folder.

```
REMSTART
-----------------------------------
Beginner's Guide To DarkBASIC Game Programming
Copyright (C)2002 Jonathan S. Harbour and Joshua R. Smith
Chapter 3 - ArrayExample Program
-----------------------------------
REMEND

DIM Answer(3)
Answer(1) = 100
Answer(2) = 103
NextOne = 3
Answer(NextOne) = 200
PRINT "Answer 1 ="; Answer(1)
PRINT "Answer 2 ="; Answer(2)
PRINT "Answer 3 ="; Answer(3)

DIM TwoD(2,2)
TwoD(2,1) = 1
```

```
TwoD(2,2) = 2
PRINT "TwoD 2 1 ="; TwoD(2,1)
PRINT "TwoD 2 2 ="; TwoD(2,2)

WAIT KEY
END
```

Arrays can have more than one dimension. Kind of like the *Twilight Zone*: "You've
entered a new dimension of sight and sound. . . ." The best way to visualize an array
is to imagine a row of squares. While the row is an entity itself, you can identify
each square in the row individually as well. To get to a particular square in a row,
you reference that square by its position. Arrays in DarkBASIC can be stored five
dimensions deep, which is far more than you will ever need. (If you ever do need
more than five dimensions, you might need to redesign the logic for your program.) Figure 3.6 illustrates a two-dimensional array with ten columns and seven
rows of boxes (which results in 70 elements in this array).

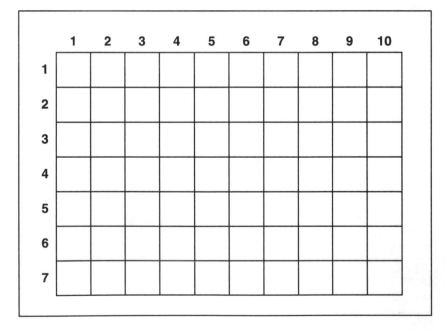

Figure 3.6 *A two-dimensional array can be illustrated with columns and rows of boxes, like the cells in a spread-sheet program.*

Understanding Data Types

Up to this point, I have been talking about variables and arrays, and how you can store values in them. I've shown you some illustrations to help you to understand the concepts. Now I would like to get into more detail by explaining the different types of information that you can store in a variable. In computer-speak, this is called the *data type*. I will explain each data type shortly; in the meantime, Table 3.2 introduces the data types and the notations required to create them.

Table 3.2 Variable Types

Data Type	Notation	Example
Integer	None	NumberOfCars
Real	#	Radius#
String	$	Name$

What Is a Data Type?

There are three types of data that make up the data types in DarkBASIC. While other programming languages (such as Visual Basic, C++, or Delphi) have many different data types, DarkBASIC keeps the list down to three items. As I have explained, DarkBASIC was designed specifically for writing games and graphics demos, and such programs don't often need the plethora of advanced data types available in other languages that were designed to solve programming problems (not specifically games, which is where DarkBASIC shines). There are some differences in this regard between DarkBASIC and DarkBASIC Professional, in that the latter supports many more data types than the former. I will reserve the discussion of the more advanced data types in DarkBASIC Pro for a later chapter. For now, an introduction to the basics is essential.

Basic Data Types

There are three basic data types—integer, decimal, and string. Each type is used in a special way to let DarkBASIC know what type of data a certain variable needs to store. For example, decimal variables (which keep track of floating-point or real numbers) must be referenced specifically with the pound sign (#) following the variable name. For example, Num# = 0.5 declares a variable called Num, gives it a decimal data type, and then sets the value to 0.5. In a sense, you might think of a variable's data type as a type of storage bin, such as the bins in the fruit and vegetable aisle at your local grocery store. There are separate bins for carrots, lettuce, potatoes, onions, peaches, apples, bananas, and so on. You would not want the fruits and vegetables to be piled together into a single large bin because that would make it difficult to sort it out and find what you want. The same theory applies to the way DarkBASIC keeps track of variables by identifying the type of value stored in each data type.

Integers

An integer can hold whole numbers. That is to say, an integer is a number that is not a fraction. 5.5 is not an integer because it has a fraction part, but 5 is. The following variables are integers.

```
A = 1
clicks = 5
counter = 0
scoredifference = -5
```

Integers can be positive or negative. To make a variable negative, just add a minus (–) sign in front of the value. Following is a sample program called IntegerExample, which demonstrates how to use integers (see Figure 3.7).

```
REMSTART
---------------------------------
Beginner's Guide To DarkBASIC Game Programming
Copyright (C)2002 Jonathan S. Harbour and Joshua R. Smith
Chapter 3 - IntegerExample Program
---------------------------------
REMEND

REM example of integers
Value1 = 48
Value2 = -2003
PRINT "Value 1 ="; Value1
PRINT "Value 2 ="; Value2
WAIT KEY
```

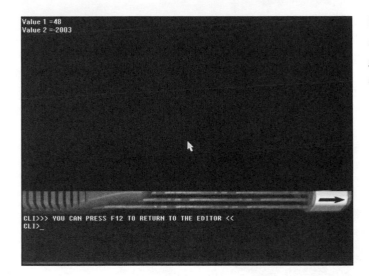

Figure 3.7 *The IntegerExample program demonstrates how to use integers.*

Decimals

A decimal can store a fraction; it is also called a *real number*. To define a variable as a decimal, add a # sign after the variable name. DarkBASIC will then know to use that variable as a decimal and as an integer. The following variables are real numbers.

```
PI# = 3.14159
xpos# = 5.332
ypos# = -1.334
zpos# = 2.234
```

Real numbers can be positive or negative; just like with integers, you simply add a minus (−) sign in front of the value to make it negative. The DecimalExample program, shown in Figure 3.8, demonstrates how to use floating-point variables in DarkBASIC. You will find this program on the CD in the Sources\Chapter03\DecimalExample folder.

```
REMSTART
---------------------------------
Beginner's Guide To DarkBASIC Game Programming
Copyright (C)2002 Jonathan S. Harbour and Joshua R. Smith
Chapter 3 - DecimalExample Program
---------------------------------
```

```
REMEND

REM example of integers
Value3# = 44.34
Value4# = -13.44
PRINT "Value 3 =";
PRINT Value3#
PRINT "Value 4 =";
PRINT Value4#
WAIT KEY
```

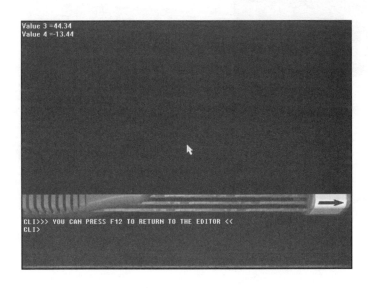

Figure 3.8 *The DecimalExample program demonstrates how to use decimals.*

Character Strings

A string is literally a string of characters that is not interpreted as a number. This means you can store any characters you wish in a string—including numbers, letters, symbols, and punctuation. Any numbers stored as part of a string are treated just like letters and punctuation marks and are just symbols as far as DarkBASIC is concerned. To define a variable as a string, add a $ sign after the variable name. All string values must be enclosed in quotes (""), which tell DarkBASIC where your string starts and ends. The following variables are strings.

```
MyName$ = "Dirk Gentry"
MySpaceShip$ = "UNSS Tadpole"
FirstFiveLetters$ = "ABCDE"
LastFiveLetters$ = "VWXYZ"
```

A string can also be blank, or what's called the *empty string*. To create an empty or blank string, you initialize the string by setting it equal to "". (Note that there is nothing between the quotes.) Figure 3.9 shows the StringExample program, which demonstrates how to use strings in DarkBASIC.

```
REMSTART
-----------------------------------
Beginner's Guide To DarkBASIC Game Programming
Copyright (C)2002 Jonathan S. Harbour and Joshua R. Smith
Chapter 3 - StringExample Program
-----------------------------------
REMEND

REM example of strings
String1$ = "Hello, this is a string generated in DarkBASIC"
String2$ = ""

PRINT String1$
PRINT String2$
WAIT KEY
```

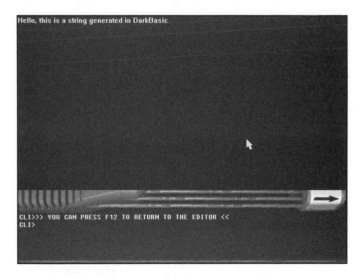

Figure 3.9 *The StringExample program demonstrates how to use strings.*

Converting Data Types

Sometimes you will need to convert a variable from one type to another. DarkBASIC provides the commands to do this. The STR$ command will convert any variable type (usually integer or decimal) to a string. This is useful when you need to display a variable on the screen because there are some display commands that work only with strings.

```
MyAge = 25
MyAgeString$ = "This is my age "+str$(MyAge)
```

The VAL command is the opposite of the STR$ command; it converts a string into a number for use in a calculation or formula. There are many times when you will need to convert from one data type to another. The VAL command can be very handy because it ignores any spaces or tabs in a string when converting to a number (which is useful, for example, when you are reading values from a text file).

```
MyAge$ = "25"
MyAge = VAL(MyAge$)
```

Working with Basic Commands

Now is where the real fun begins. You are going to cover some basic DarkBASIC commands that will haunt you . . . er, be with you, for the rest of the book.

The PRINT Command

PRINT is one of the most important commands in the DarkBASIC language. In Chapter 4, "Characters, Strings, and Text Output," you will learn some more variations of the PRINT command, but for now I want to give you the basics. The PRINT command takes a string as an argument. It looks like this:

```
PRINT "text to display"
```

Notice that any text you want to output with the PRINT command is surrounded by quotes. That is so DarkBASIC knows what text you are asking it to print. If you want to add two different strings of text, you would do something like this:

```
PRINT "Item1", "Item2"
```

> **An *argument* is a variable or literal value that is passed to a subroutine or DarkBASIC command.**

Note that a comma separates each individual parameter. The comma actually adds a tab to the output. If you want to append one variable or text value to the end of the last one without the tab jump, you can use a semicolon (;) instead. Appending text is very useful in DarkBASIC when you want to display values on the screen, such as the high score in a game. The PrintExample program (shown in Figure 3.10) demonstrates how to use the PRINT command to display text followed by a variable.

```
REMSTART
----------------------------------
Beginner's Guide To DarkBASIC Game Programming
Copyright (C)2002 Jonathan S. Harbour and Joshua R. Smith
Chapter 3 - PrintExample Program
----------------------------------
REMEND

Answer = 2 + 2
REM "The answer is 4" should be printed on the screen.
PRINT "The answer is ", Answer
WAIT KEY
```

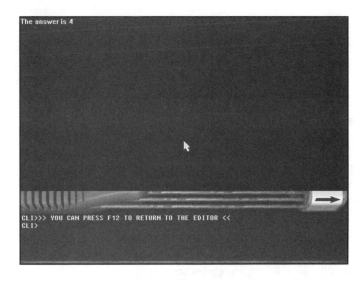

Figure 3.10 *The PrintExample program demonstrates how to use the* PRINT *command.*

> **NOTE**
>
> I realize that some program listings are very short, but the sample programs in this chapter and the next few chapters are included on the **CD-ROM** for easy retrieval and execution. It's all part of the learning experience! Later chapters will assume that you are more familiar with the code, and I will not use code to explain every topic.

The GET DATE$ Command

Sometimes you will need the current date in a program. You might need this to store the last time a program was run or to print it on the screen. DarkBASIC has a GET DATE$() command to retrieve the current computer date. Notice it has a $ at the end, which means that GET DATE$() returns a string. If you wanted to print the date, you would type the following code.

```
PRINT "The date is ", GET DATE$()
```

Did you notice that this command has a space between GET and DATE? DarkBASIC has some commands with spaces, which is somewhat difficult to comprehend at first, but once you have used them for a while, you will find these commands easy to remember.

The GET TIME$ Command

Another useful command is GET TIME$. You can use this command to keep track of how many hours you have been sitting at your computer programming in DarkBASIC. Notice that it's a string as well. All commands that give you information will return one of the three data types discussed earlier in this chapter.

```
PRINT "The time is ", GET TIME$()
```

The EXECUTE FILE Command

The EXECUTE FILE command is slightly more complicated. It might not seem like much, but it is quite useful when you are writing a menu program. The EXECUTE

FILE command runs any executable program (whether it is on a CD-ROM, the hard drive, or another accessible device or location) on your computer. I have written a program called sample.exe to use as an example.

The EXECUTE FILE command has three arguments. The first is the file name of a program to run (in this case, sample.exe). The ExecuteFileExample1 program (shown in Figure 3.11) demonstrates how to use the command.

Figure 3.11 *The ExecuteFileExample1 program demonstrates the* EXECUTE FILE *command.*

This program, along with the sample.exe file, can be found on the CD-ROM in the Sources\DarkBASIC\CH03 folder. If you are using DarkBASIC Pro, the folder name is Sources\DBPro\CH03.

```
REMSTART
----------------------------------
Beginner's Guide To Game Programming With DarkBASIC
Copyright (C)2002 Jonathan S. Harbour and Joshua R. Smith
Chapter 3 - ExecuteFileExample1 Program
----------------------------------
REMEND

REM this will execute sample.exe
EXECUTE FILE "sample.exe", "", ""
```

The second argument that EXECUTE FILE accepts is a command-line parameter. This is the line that sends the arguments to the program you are trying to run. If you wanted to pass your name to the sample.exe program as a command-line parameter, you would add "*your name*" to the second parameter, as the ExecuteFileExample2 program demonstrates (see Figure 3.12).

Figure 3.12 *The ExecuteFileExample2 program demonstrates how to pass a command-line parameter to a program that is being run.*

You will find this program, along with the sample.exe file, on the CD in the Sources\Chapter03\ExecuteFileExample2 folder.

```
REMSTART
------------------------------------
Beginner's Guide To Game Programming With DarkBASIC
Copyright (C)2002 Jonathan S. Harbour and Joshua R. Smith
Chapter 3 - ExecuteFileExample2 Program
------------------------------------
REMEND

REM this will execute sample.exe if it exists,
REM and add my name as an argument.
EXECUTE FILE "sample.exe", "Joshua", ""
```

The last argument used in EXECUTE FILE is the directory in which your program is located. This way DarkBASIC knows where to go to get the program for its data files. If nothing is specified here, the program will assume the current directory by default. If the program is not in the directory you specified, DarkBASIC will return an error. Figure 3.13 shows the output of the ExecuteFileExample3 program when the executable file can't be found.

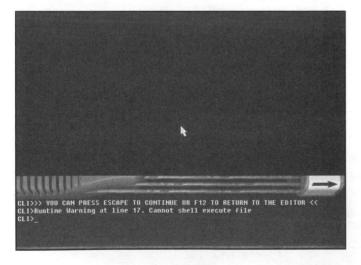

```
CLI>>> YOU CAN PRESS ESCAPE TO CONTINUE OR F12 TO RETURN TO THE EDITOR <<
CLI>Runtime Warning at line 17. Cannot shell execute file
CLI>_
```

Figure 3.13 *The output of ExecuteFileExample3 shows that an error occurred.*

```
REMSTART
------------------------------------
Beginner's Guide To Game Programming With DarkBASIC
Copyright (C)2002 Jonathan S. Harbour and Joshua R. Smith
Chapter 3 - ExecuteFileExample3 Program
------------------------------------
```

```
REMEND

REM this will execute sample.exe if exists and
REM send the argument, Joshua and Force the
REM Working Directory to C:\
EXECUTE FILE "sample.exe", "Joshua", "c:\"
```

Notice how DarkBASIC generated an error. You can fix this if you just copy sample.exe to C:\. If you do, the result of the ExecuteFileExample3 program should look like Figure 3.14.

Figure 3.14 *The ExecuteFileExample3 program, successfully run*

Chapter Project

All right, now for a fun chapter project. When I was in school, I did some fun exercises in my typing class. I would draw pictures with the typewriter. I thought I would let you enjoy the same experience, only with DarkBASIC! Notice that I start the program with comments. If you would prefer to load the project instead of typing it all in, it is located on the CD in the folder called Sources\DarkBASIC\CH03\Artist.

This program draws a picture of a smiley face, and it just happens to resemble a famous fellow involved in the DarkBASIC language (hint, hint!). It also contains variables to store your name and age so it can print them at the bottom of the picture. Once you have typed the program in, try modifying it to include your name and age. Creativity is key when writing games, even simple ones! Figure 3.15 shows the output of the Artist program.

```
----------------------------------
Beginner's Guide To DarkBASIC Game Programming
Copyright (C)2002 Jonathan S. Harbour and Joshua R. Smith
Chapter 3 - Artist Program
----------------------------------
REMEND

REM Place your name here
MyName$ = "Joshua Smith"
REM Place your age here
```

```
MyAge = 25

SET TEXT FONT "Courier New"
SET TEXT SIZE 18

PRINT "   ||||||||   "
PRINT "  /         \  "
PRINT "  |  O   O  |  "
PRINT "  |    [    |  "
PRINT "  |  ____  |  "
PRINT "   \ \__/ /  "
PRINT "    \    /    "
PRINT "     ^^^^^    "
PRINT
PRINT "I am a DarkBASIC programmer."
PRINT "And my programs are great."
PRINT "NAME ", MyName$
PRINT "AGE   ", MyAge
PRINT "DATE ", GET DATE$()
PRINT "TIME ", GET TIME$()
WAIT KEY
END
```

Figure 3.15 *This is what the Artist program looks like when it is run.*

Summary

This chapter covered many of the fundamentals of programming. Data types, variables, variable scope (local and global), math formulas, and variable notation—these are all basic subjects, but they are the key elements that are important to master if you want to be a successful programmer. As you progress through the next few chapters, you will gain a broader understanding of the nuts and bolts of DarkBASIC programming that were introduced in this chapter.

Chapter Quiz

The chapter quiz will help you retain the information that was covered in this chapter, and will give you an idea about how well you understand the subjects. Refer to Appendix A, "Answers to the Chapter Quizzes," to see how well you answered these questions.

1. What is an argument in DarkBASIC?

    A. A fight you get in with the computer
    B. A virtual boxing match
    C. The information a command needs to be processed correctly
    D. The current time

2. What is an array in DarkBASIC?

    A. A science fiction concept
    B. An area of memory reserved for program data
    C. A `PRINT` statement
    D. None of the above

3. What command defines a global variable?

    A. `REMSTART`
    B. `PRINT`
    C. `DIM`
    D. `EXECUTE FILE`

4. Which is evaluated first in the order of operations?

    A. Things enclosed in parentheses
    B. Addition
    C. Multiplication
    D. Division

5. What does the `PRINT` command do?

   A. Displays text on the screen
   B. Prints text to the printer
   C. Adds money to your virtual bank account
   D. Ends a program

6. In `EXECUTE FILE "jumpers.exe", ""` is a valid command.

   A. True
   B. False, there is no `EXECUTE FILE` command
   C. False, there are not enough arguments
   D. False, there are too many arguments

7. In DarkBASIC what does 2+2*2+6*(3+2) evaluate to?

   A. 17
   B. 46
   C. 36
   D. 14

8. Which is not a valid variable type?

   A. String
   B. Integer
   C. Real
   D. Caret

9. Which command converts a string into an integer?

   A. `STR$()`
   B. `VAL()`
   C. `STRINGTOINTEGER()`
   D. None of the above

10. Which command prints the current date on the computer?

    A. `PRINT GET TIME$()`
    B. `PRINT GET DATE$()`
    C. `PRINT WHATSTHEDATE()`
    D. `PRINT "Today"`

CHAPTER 4

CHARACTERS, STRINGS, AND TEXT OUTPUT

We are now heading into the fascinating subject of strings, which store characters, words, sentences, and any other types of information that you need to track. You can use strings to hold all other data types, which is useful when you need to make sure a user typed in the correct type of information (for example, a dollar amount). In this chapter, you will learn how to create, manipulate, and display strings.

This chapter shows you how to do all kinds of things with strings, from converting them to numbers to printing them to the screen using graphical fonts to reading substrings within a string. By then end of this chapter, you will be able to create a really cool game (in fact, it's a game I used to play when I was young). Now on to strings. . . .

This chapter covers the following topics:

- Introduction to Strings and Text Output
- Programming Strings
- Displaying Text on the Screen
- The Gab Lib Game

Introduction to Strings and Text Output

Strings, strings, strings. What does that make you think about? I think of one of Bach's concertos being performed in an orchestral hall. The cello is to the left of the piano, in tune with trombones and flutes. To the right, you have the violin section, adding to the harmony of the piece. "String" is one of those unfortunate overworked and overused words in the English language, and it has been used to mean many different things. (It is the bane of the foreigner learning English as a second language!)

What is so special about strings? They are the lines of text that bind together programs. Stringed instruments allow the flow of the melody and the harmony of a song; strings in DarkBASIC do essentially the same thing. They allow you to convey thoughts that you want to portray in your game. Computer scientists decided to use the word "string" to represent a series of characters in the computer's memory that display textual information. In the old days, everything was printed out by a printer, but today most output is sent to the high-resolution monitor sitting next to your computer. Regardless of the output device, a string is used to store and display text.

Strings are the most popular data type that programmers use. Why? String variables are versatile and capable of storing numbers, letters, and punctuation in any combination. One string can store your name, while another string can store how many oranges you have.

Programming Strings

Strings are easy to program or define in DarkBASIC. To give you a little perspective, I'll explain how strings work in most languages. They are more or less collections of characters. A character, of course, is a number, letter, or punctuation mark. In C you can define a string by creating a character array, whereas in C++ you just define a string class. In DarkBASIC it is much, much easier.

Declaring Strings

So how is a string declared? Simply by enclosing what you want to say in quotes (""). For example, "This sentence is declared as a string." Notice how the string was enclosed in quotes? The quotes tell DarkBASIC that what comes between them is a string.

Assigning Strings to Variables

To assign a string to a variable, you just add an = sign followed by the string. If you wanted to create a string called sentence$, containing "This sentence is declared as a string," you would type in the following code.

```
sentence$ = "This sentence is declared as a string"
```

Copying and Adding Strings

Sometimes declaring a string is just not enough. You might need to copy a string, which is quite simple in DarkBASIC. The following code will copy the string from the preceding example into a new variable called newsentence$.

```
sentence$ = "This sentence is declared as a string."
newsentence$ = sentence$
PRINT newsentence$
```

Sometimes you will need to add two strings, which will allow you to make more sense of the data you have within your strings. There are two strings in the following code—firstname$ and lastname$. Suppose you want to get the wholename$. You just add the strings together, like this:

```
firstname$ = "Joshua"
lastname$ = "Smith"
wholename$ = firstname$ + lastname$
PRINT wholename$
```

When you are running this program, you'll notice that wholename$ prints out, but there is no space between my first and last name. That does not help you when you are putting my whole name together. You need to add a space between the first and last name. The following code will show you how to do that.

```
firstname$ = "Joshua"
lastname$ = "Smith"
wholename$ = firstname$ + " " + lastname$
PRINT wholename$
```

String Conversion Commands

Now it's time to do some legwork with strings. You know how to define them, but what's the good of defining them if you don't have something to use them? DarkBASIC contains several commands that will convert strings into useful data.

The ASC Command

The ASC command converts a character (one letter) into its corresponding numeric ASCII value. The command returns the ASCII value of the *first* character in the string you input. The syntax to return a string as an integer is ASC(*String*).

What is an ASCII value? Good question! ASCII stands for *American Standard Code for Information Interchange*. Computers don't know what characters and words are, but they do understand numbers. Therefore, a standards committee assigned a specific numeric value to every single character on the keyboard, along with many special control characters, a long, long time ago. Appendix C, "ASCII Chart," contains a complete ASCII table, and I recommend that you flip back there now to see what it looks like. There are 256 ASCII values, which means there are 256 characters in the ASCII chart. For example, the uppercase A is equal to ASCII value 65. If you need to know an ASCII value for any reason, the ASC command will give it to you. The following code demonstrates a short program that will return an ASCII value.

```
REM This will return the value of 65
AsciiValue = ASC("A")
REM This will print the number 65
PRINT AsciiValue
```

The VAL Command

The VAL command, mentioned in Chapter 3, converts a string to an integer. It only converts strings that contain actual numbers, such as "123". Thus VAL is useful if you have a number stored in a string and you need to convert it to an actual integer for calculations. The syntax to return a string as an integer is VAL(*String$*).

The following code demonstrates the use of the VAL command.

```
REM This will return a value of 35
Number = VAL("35")
REM This will print the number 35
PRINT Number
```

What happens if you enter a word instead of a number? Good question, I'm glad you asked. I just so happened to check that out and guess what? VAL returned a 0 for the answer.

```
REM This will return a value of 0
Number = VAL("My String Here")
REM This will print the number 0
PRINT Number
```

The CHR$ Command

The CHR$ command converts a decimal number that represents an ASCII character into a single character string. Remember the ASC command? The CHR$ command performs the opposite operation—that is, it converts numbers to characters, rather than characters to numbers. The syntax for this command is CHR$(*number*), where *number* is the decimal integer of the ASCII value you want to convert to a string. This command returns the desired ASCII character as a string.

```
REM this will return the value of "A"
MyString$ = CHR$(65)
REM this will print "A"
PRINT MyString$
```

String Manipulation Commands

Now you have a long list of commands to use with strings, but what can you actually do with them? Strings are pretty complicated, yet simple at the same time. However, to understand the next series of commands, you will need a better understanding of strings.

As I said before, a string is a collection of characters. You can envision a string as an array of characters. See Figure 4.1 for an example of a string broken into an array of characters.

Now that you understand what a string is made of, the next series of commands will make strings a lot more interesting. They are string manipulation commands, which means you can use them to get information from strings.

The LEN Command

The LEN command returns the number of characters in a string, which is quite useful when used with other string manipulation commands. The LEN command syntax is LEN(*String*), where *String* is the string for which you want to compute the length.

Many string manipulation commands require you to know how large or small a string is before you manipulate it. If you do not know the length of a string, you could end up going outside the scope of the string and generating an error. For

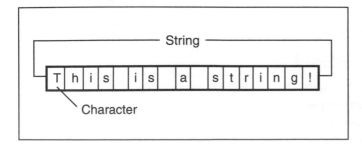

Figure 4.1 *This illustration shows how a string is represented in computer memory.*

instance, suppose you want to display a message on the right side of the screen, but you don't know how long the string will be. Suppose you are displaying the mouse position, like this:

```
MOUSE X/Y = (539,290)
```

Because the mouse could be up at (0,0) on the screen, the length of the message will change depending on the mouse position. The LEN command is useful for computing the length of a message right before it is displayed on the screen.

```
REM this will return the value of 17
Number = LEN("This is a string!")
REM this will print a 17
PRINT Number
```

The MID$ Command

The MID$ command lets you retrieve any character from the middle of a string (and also from the start or end of the string). All you need to know for this command is the position of the letter in your string. The MID$ command syntax is MID$(*String, Number*), which returns a string of the character found at the position in the string indicated by number.

```
REM this will set MyString$ to "This is my string!"
MyString$ = "This is my string!"
REM this will print a "T"
PRINT MID$(MyString$, 1)
REM this will print a "s"
PRINT MID$(MyString$, 12)
```

The RIGHT$ Command

The RIGHT$ command returns the rightmost set of characters in a string, which means that you can find out the last five characters of the "Hello World" string. (This would be "World," of course.) The RIGHT$ command syntax is RIGHT$(*String, Number*), which returns a string containing the rightmost letters up to the number specified.

```
MyString$ = "This is my string!"
REM this will print "string!"
PRINT RIGHT$(MyString$,7)
REM this will print a "ing!"
PRINT RIGHT$(MyString$,4)
```

The LEFT$ Command

The LEFT$ command is the exact opposite of the RIGHT$ command. That is, it returns the leftmost set of characters in a string. In the "Hello World" string, the first five characters are "Hello." The LEFT$ command syntax is LEFT$(*String*, *Number*), which returns a string containing the leftmost letters up to the number specified.

```
MyString$ = "This is my string!"
REM this will print a "This"
PRINT LEFT$(MyString$,4)
REM this will print a "This is my"
PRINT LEFT$(MyString$,10)
```

The STR$ Command

The STR$ command converts any integer into a string. This is a good command for converting numbers read from a file into strings. The STR$ command syntax is STR$(*integer value*), where *integer value* is returned as a string instead of an integer.

```
REM this will print a "4"
PRINT STR$(4)
REM this will print a "45"
PRINT STR$(45)
```

Displaying Text on the Screen

Now you've learned several commands for manipulating strings. The only thing that's lacking is some way to display the strings in a more precise manner than using PRINT. DarkBASIC provides a few commands to display text on the screen. However, before I jump into the text-printing commands, I'd like to talk for a minute about the computer screen.

First you need to understand what makes up the objects on a computer screen. The display is made up of thousands of small picture elements (also called pixels). A *pixel* is simply the smallest point on a display screen, comprised of red, green, and blue elements. Each of these elements can be lit independently and to a fine degree of luminosity, providing a mighty range of colors. In later chapters I'll show

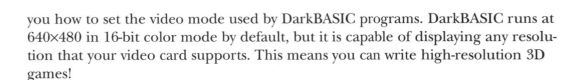

you how to set the video mode used by DarkBASIC programs. DarkBASIC runs at 640×480 in 16-bit color mode by default, but it is capable of displaying any resolution that your video card supports. This means you can write high-resolution 3D games!

The pixels on the screen are arranged in rows and columns. If your screen is set to 1024×768, there are 1024 pixels from left to right across the screen, and 768 rows of those 1024 pixels. As you can imagine, that adds up to a *ton* of pixels! To better understand this concept, take a look at Figure 4.2. Like a sheet of graph paper, the screen is represented by columns and rows described as X and Y, respectively.

The next few commands will help you position strings on the screen. Some commands will simply print text in a pseudo-graphics mode, while others will let you draw text anywhere on the screen.

The PRINT Command

We have already gone over the PRINT command, but it is good to review it. The PRINT command just prints whatever string or series of strings you want on the screen. It starts at the top and works its way down to the bottom. The PRINT command syntax is PRINT "*string to print*", where *string to print* is displayed on the screen. Remember that if you want to print anything other than a variable after a

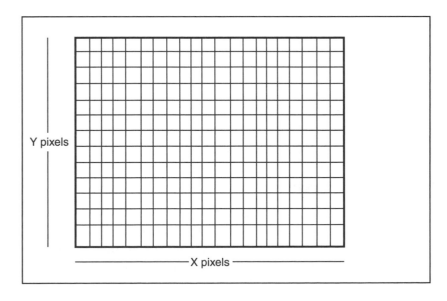

Figure 4.2 *The display screen is made up of many rows and columns of picture elements (pixels).*

Y pixels

X pixels

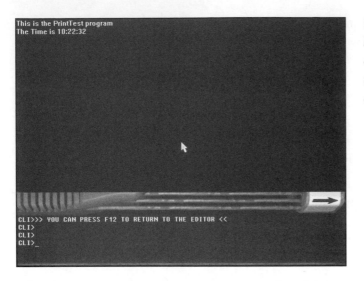

Figure 4.3 *The PrintTest program demonstrates some uses for the* PRINT *command.*

PRINT command, you must enclose it in quotes. Figure 4.3 shows the output from a program called PrintTest that demonstrates how to use the PRINT command. You will find this program on the CD in the Sources\Chapter04\PrintTest folder.

```
REM ---------------------------------
REM Beginner's Guide To DarkBASIC Game Programming
REM Copyright (C)2002 Jonathan S. Harbour and Joshua R. Smith
REM Chapter 4 - PrintTest Program
REM ---------------------------------

PRINT "This is the PrintTest program"

REM this will print a "The time is " followed by the current time.
TheTime$ = "The Time is " + GET TIME$()
PRINT TheTime$
WAIT KEY
```

The TEXT Command

The TEXT command is just like the PRINT command but with a twist. The TEXT command takes two additional arguments at the beginning of the command—the X and Y position at which you want to print the text. This allows you to place text anywhere you want on the screen. The syntax for the TEXT command is TEXT *X*, *Y*, *String*.

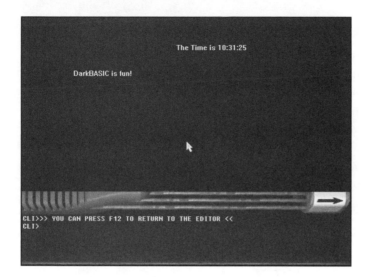

Figure 4.4 *The TextTest program demonstrates how to use the* TEXT *command.*

Figure 4.4 shows the output from the TextTest program, which follows. You will find this program on the CD in the Sources\Chapter04\TextTest folder.

```
REM this will print a "My Text is here" a little bit off set from the
REM upper left of the screen
TEXT 100,100, "DarkBASIC is fun!"

REM this will print a "The time is " followed by the current time
REM in the top center of the screen.
TheTime$ = "The Time is " + GET TIME$()
TEXT 300, 50, TheTime$
WAIT KEY
```

The CENTER TEXT Command

The CENTER TEXT command is just like the TEXT command but again with a twist. This command centers whatever you want to print around the X and Y positions that you enter. If you want to print someone's name on the top of the screen but you do not want to figure out the spacing, this command is for you. The syntax for the CENTER TEXT command is CENTER TEXT *X, Y, String*, where the *X* and *Y* values must be integers.

```
REM This will print "DarkBASIC is awesome!" centered on the screen.
Message$ = "DarkBASIC is awesome!"
CENTER TEXT 320, 240, Message$
```

The SET CURSOR Command

The SET CURSOR command is one of my favorites. There is a similar command in GWBASIC called locate. This command places the cursor anywhere you want on the screen. The TEXT command is simply this command plus a PRINT command. The syntax of the SET CURSOR command is SET CURSOR X, Y, where the X and Y values must be integers. Figure 4.5 shows the output from the CursorTest program, which follows. You will find this program on the CD in the Sources\Chapter04\CursorTest folder.

```
REM ---------------------------------
REM Beginner's Guide To DarkBASIC Game Programming
REM Copyright (C)2002 Jonathan S. Harbour and Joshua R. Smith
REM Chapter 4 - CursorTest Program
REM ---------------------------------

REM This will print a message at the top left
SET CURSOR 10, 100
PRINT "Who ya gonna call?"

REM This will print a message at the top right
SET CURSOR 500, 100
PRINT "DarkBASIC!"
WAIT KEY
```

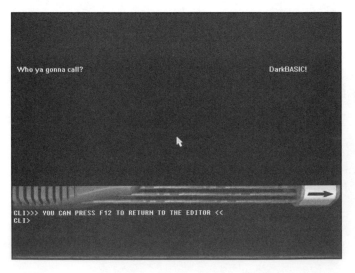

Figure 4.5 *The CursorTest program demonstrates how to use the* SET CURSOR *command.*

Font Commands

Now I have covered the basics of displaying text on the screen, but that text sure is ugly. In a word processing application, you have a choice of many different fonts, sizes, and styles. Well, DarkBASIC offers that to you as well. It provides a variety of commands to change the appearance, size, and other aspects of any text printed. I will not cover all of the commands in this chapter, but rest assured I will cover them in a future chapter.

Something to note about the text font commands: They only work with the TEXT or CENTER TEXT command. They will not work with the PRINT command, so if you want to change the appearance of your font, make sure you use the TEXT command.

Changing the Text Output Font and Size

The default font used to output text in DarkBASIC is the "system" font, which is monospaced and good for general-purpose messages. However, DarkBASIC gives you access to all the fonts installed on your PC, including TrueType fonts such as Times New Roman and Arial. You use the SET TEXT FONT command to change the font. The syntax of the command is SET TEXT FONT "*Font Name*".

SET TEXT SIZE is a complementary command to change the font size that is almost always used with SET TEXT FONT. The command sets the point size of the font, with common values of 10, 12, 14, 16, and 18, to name a few. Just like in a word processor, this command defines how large the text will appear on the screen. The average font size is usually 12 points. The syntax for the SET TEXT SIZE command is SET TEXT SIZE *Value*.

Figure 4.6 shows a comparison of different point sizes as output by the FontTest program that follows. You will find this program on the CD in the Sources\Chapter04\FontTest folder.

```
REM ---------------------------------
REM Beginner's Guide To DarkBASIC Game Programming
REM Copyright (C)2002 Jonathan S. Harbour and Joshua R. Smith
REM Chapter 4 - FontTest Program
REM ---------------------------------

REM Set font to Arial 18
SET TEXT FONT "Arial"
SET TEXT SIZE 18
```

```
TEXT 100,100, "This font is Arial 18"

REM Set font to Times New Roman 24
SET TEXT FONT "Times New Roman"
SET TEXT SIZE 24
TEXT 100,200, "This font is Times New Roman 24"
WAIT KEY
```

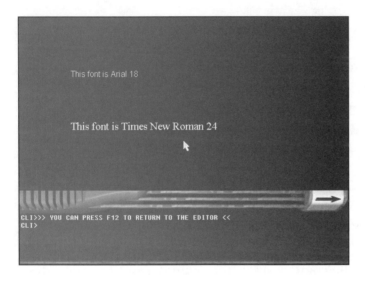

Figure 4.6 *The FontTest program demonstrates how to change the font type and size.*

Returning the Current Font Name

There might come a situation in which you need to know the name of the current font used for text output. To return the font name as a string, you use the TEXT FONT$ command, which has the format Font Name = TEXT FONT$(). Here is a sample snippet of code that shows how you might use the TEXT FONT$ command.

```
FontName$ = TEXT FONT$()
PRINT "The current font in use is "; FontName$
```

Font Size Commands

In DarkBASIC, size *does* matter. If the print is too small, no one will be able to read it; if it is too large, it won't fit on the screen. Therefore, you need to define the size of your fonts.

The TEXT SIZE Command

The TEXT SIZE command is like the TEXT FONT$ command. However, instead of returning the name of the font in use, it returns the size of the font as an integer. The syntax of the TEXT SIZE command is Font Size = TEXT SIZE(). The following sample snippet of code shows you how you might use the TEXT SIZE command.

```
FontSize = TEXT SIZE()
PRINT "The current font size is "; FontSize
```

The TEXT WIDTH Command

The TEXT WIDTH command can be very helpful at times. It gives you the width of a string in pixels, as it would appear on the screen. Remember, a string is made up of characters. The LEN command tells you how many characters are in a string, but font types and sizes vary widely when printed on the screen. That's where the TEXT WIDTH command is useful. For example, suppose you want to right-justify a string at the right edge of the screen. Without knowing the exact width of the string, you wouldn't be able to position it precisely without trial and error. The syntax for the TEXT WIDTH command is Width Value = TEXT WIDTH(*String*).

Here is a short program that will center a text message on the screen.

```
MyText$ = "DarkBASIC is a great programming language."
CurrentWidth = TEXT WIDTH(MyText$)
TEXT 320 - CurrentWidth / 2, 235, MyText$
```

The TEXT HEIGHT Command

The TEXT HEIGHT command returns the height of the string you want to print in pixels. This gives you the Y size of the text, whereas the TEXT WIDTH command gave you the X size of the text. The syntax for the TEXT HEIGHT command is Height Value = TEXT HEIGHT(*String*).

The BounceText Program

To demonstrate the font width and height commands, I've written a short program called BounceText, which is shown in Figure 4.7. The BounceText program is somewhat advanced at this time, using many commands that I have not yet discussed. However, I want to give you a glimpse of things to come and help to challenge your

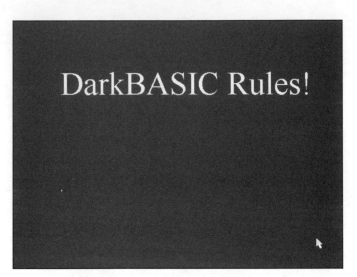

Figure 4.7 *The BounceText program demonstrates how to use the font width and height commands.*

creativity by delving into the unknown from time to time. You might find this program intriguing enough that you will want to experiment with it on your own by changing values, such as the speed at which the text moves across the screen. You will find this program on the CD in the Sources\Chapter04\BounceText folder.

```
REM ---------------------------------
REM Beginner's Guide To DarkBASIC Game Programming
REM Copyright (C)2002 Jonathan S. Harbour and Joshua R. Smith
REM Chapter 4 - Bounce Text Program
REM ---------------------------------

REM Initialize the program
MyText$ = "DarkBASIC Rules!"
SET TEXT FONT "Times New Roman"
SET TEXT SIZE 72
INK RGB(255,255,255), RGB(10,10,10)
Width = TEXT WIDTH(MyText$)
Height = TEXT HEIGHT(MyText$)
CurrentX = 320 - Width / 2
CurrentY = 240 - Height / 2
SpeedX = 2
SpeedY = -2
```

```
REM Manually control the screen
SYNC ON
DO
    REM Clear the screen
    CLS

    REM Update X position
    CurrentX = CurrentX + SpeedX
    IF CurrentX + Width > 635 THEN SpeedX = -4
    IF CurrentX < 5 THEN SpeedX = 4

    REM Update Y position
    CurrentY = CurrentY + SpeedY
    IF CurrentY + Height > 475 THEN SpeedY = -4
    IF CurrentY < 5 THEN SpeedY = 4

    REM Display the text message
    TEXT CurrentX, CurrentY, MyText$

    REM Update the screen
    SYNC
LOOP
END
```

Text Style Commands

Now we come to the fashionable part of the text commands—the text style commands. These commands allow you to alter the appearance of the text once again. You can change the text to bold, italic, or both.

Setting the Font to Normal

The SET TEXT TO NORMAL command sets the font style to normal, which removes any bold or italic font styles for the next text output command. Here is a snippet of code that demonstrates how to use this command:

```
SET TEXT FONT "Arial"
SET TEXT TO NORMAL
SET TEXT SIZE 16
TEXT 100,100, "This text is normal"
```

Setting the Font to Italic

The SET TEXT TO ITALIC command sets all the text that follows it to italics. That means your text will not be bold, but it will be in italics. Here is a snippet of code that demonstrates how to use this command:

```
SET TEXT FONT "Arial"
SET TEXT TO ITALIC
SET TEXT SIZE 16
TEXT 100,100, "This text is italic"
```

The SET TEXT TO BOLD Command

The SET TEXT TO BOLD command sets all the text that follows it to bold. That means your text will not be in italics, but it will be in bold. Here is a snippet of code that demonstrates how to use this command:

```
SET TEXT FONT "Arial"
SET TEXT TO BOLD
SET TEXT SIZE 16
TEXT 100,100, "This text is bold"
```

The SET TEXT TO BOLDITALIC Command

The SET TEXT TO BOLDITALIC command sets all the text that follows it to bold italics. That means your text will be in both bold and italics. Here is a snippet of code that demonstrates how to use this command:

```
SET TEXT FONT "Arial"
SET TEXT TO BOLDITALIC
SET TEXT SIZE 16
TEXT 100,100, "This text is bold and italic"
```

Determining the Current Text Style

The TEXT STYLE command returns an integer indicating the current font style in use (normal, italic, bold, or bold italic). The command returns a number from 0 to 3, corresponding to the current text style. Table 4.1 describes the four values returned by this command.

Table 4.1 Text Style Values

Return Value	Style
0	Normal
1	Bold
2	Italic
3	Bold and italic

I have written a short program that demonstrates how to use the TEXT STYLE command. The program is called TextStyles, and it is shown in Figure 4.8. You will find this program on the CD in the Sources\Chapter04\TextStyles folder.

```
REM --------------------------------
REM Beginner's Guide To Game Programming With DarkBASIC
REM Copyright (C)2002 Jonathan S. Harbour and Joshua R. Smith
REM Chapter 4 - TextStyles Program
REM --------------------------------

REM Create an array
DIM Styles$(4)
Styles$(0) = "NORMAL"
Styles$(1) = "BOLD"
Styles$(2) = "ITALIC"
Styles$(3) = "BOLD ITALIC"

REM Set the font name
SET TEXT FONT "Times New Roman"
SET TEXT SIZE 36

REM Print out the text style strings
SET TEXT TO NORMAL
TEXT 0, 0, "This text is " + Styles$( TEXT STYLE() )
```

```
SET TEXT TO BOLD
TEXT 0, 40, "This text is " + Styles$( TEXT STYLE() )
SET TEXT TO ITALIC
TEXT 0, 80, "This text is " + Styles$( TEXT STYLE() )
SET TEXT TO BOLDITALIC
TEXT 0, 120, "This text is " + Styles$( TEXT STYLE() )
WAIT KEY
END
```

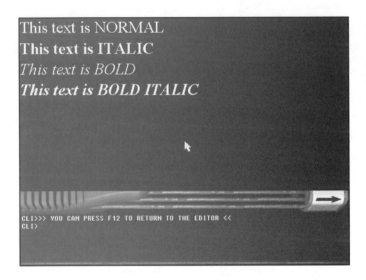

Figure 4.8 *The TextStyles program demonstrates how to use the* TEXT STYLE *command.*

Text Transparency

One last thing I need to cover for text appearance is text transparency. That is, what does the background of the text look like? Not the letters per se, but behind the letters. Each letter printed in DarkBASIC is really a square. Anything that is not part of a letter is black or whatever color you specify it to be. However, if you want to put text over a picture, you definitely do not want its background to be black. DarkBASIC has some commands to control transparency.

> *Transparency* **defines how much you can see through something. A piece of glass is transparent.** *Opacity* **refers to something that is completely non-transparent and opaque.**

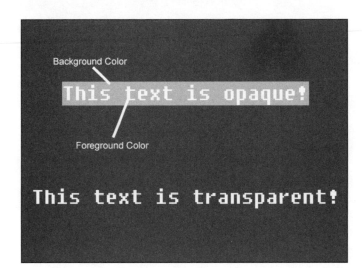

Figure 4.9
Transparency versus opacity

The SET TEXT OPAQUE Command

The SET TEXT OPAQUE command sets the text background to the current color specified in the INK command (which is covered in Chapter 9, "Basic Graphics Commands"). If text is printed over any pictures, it will look like a solid rectangle with words in the middle.

```
REM Set the background color to red
CLS RGB(255,0,0)
REM Set the font color to white on black
INK RGB(255,255,255), RGB(0,0,0)
REM Display the opaque text
SET TEXT OPAQUE
TEXT 100,100, "This Text is Opaque"
```

The SET TEXT TRANSPARENT Command

The SET TEXT TRANSPARENT command is the exact opposite of the SET TEXT OPAQUE command. That is, it sets the text background to clear so whatever is behind it can be seen.

```
REM Set the background color to red
CLS RGB(255,0,0)
REM Set the font color to white on black
INK RGB(255,255,255), RGB(0,0,0)
```

```
REM Display the transparent text
SET TEXT TRANSPARENT
TEXT 100,100, "This Text is Transparent"
```

The TEXT BACKGROUND TYPE Command

The TEXT BACKGROUND TYPE command returns the background type of the current font—either opaque or transparent. Like the TEXT STYLE command, TEXT BACKGROUND TYPE returns an integer. If the background is opaque, a 0 is returned; for transparent, a 1 is returned. The syntax for the command is Background Value = TEXT BACKGROUND TYPE().

The Gab Lib Game

I have talked a lot about strings and text in this chapter, so what better example than a Mad Lib game that uses a lot of strings? In case you have never heard of a Mad Lib, the concept is rather funny. You ask the user to type in various nouns, verbs, adjectives, and so on, and then you fill in the words of a story using the user's input.

Running the Gab Lib Game

Take a look at Figure 4.10, which shows the Gab Lib program asking the user for input.

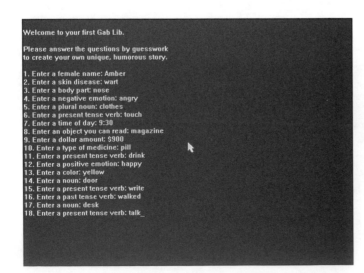

Figure 4.10 *The first part of the Gab Lib game asks the user to type in parts of speech that are then used to create a story.*

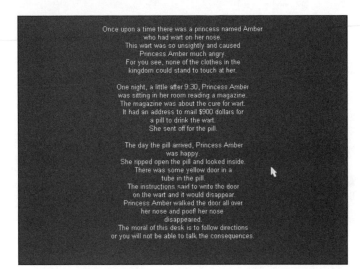

Figure 4.11 *The second part of the Gab Lib game uses the user input to print the story.*

Figure 4.11 shows the final output of the Gab Lib game, after it has assembled the user input into a story.

The Source Code for Gab Lib

It takes a while to type in the source code that make up the Gab Lib game, but the end result is worth it! However, if you're in a hurry you can just load the program from the CD-ROM under Sources\Chapter04\GabLib. The compiled program is also in that folder; if you want to run it directly from Windows Explorer, you can double-click GabLib.exe.

The best way to learn is by practicing, so I recommend typing in the source code for the Gab Lib game. You will learn much faster because the mental connections are strengthened through hand-eye coordination, which is what it takes to see a command before typing it into DarkBASIC. Regardless of the method of input, you run the game by pressing F5 or selecting Execute from the Run menu.

```
REM --------------------------------
REM Beginner's Guide To DarkBASIC Game Programming
REM Copyright (C)2002 Jonathan S. Harbour and Joshua R. Smith
REM Chapter 4 - MadLib Program
REM --------------------------------

SET TEXT FONT "Arial"
CLS
```

```
PRINT
PRINT "Welcome to your first Gab Lib."
PRINT
PRINT "Please guess the answer to the questions"
PRINT "to create your own unique, humorous story."
PRINT

REM Ask questions
INPUT "1. Enter a female name: ", NAME$
INPUT "2. Enter a skin problem: ", PROBLEM$
INPUT "3. Enter a body part: ", BODYPART1$
INPUT "4. Enter a negative emotion: ", EMOTION$
INPUT "5. Enter a plural noun: ", NOUN1$
INPUT "6. Enter a present tense verb: ", VERB1$
INPUT "7. Enter a time of day: ", TIME$
INPUT "8. Enter an object you can read: ", NOUN2$
INPUT "9. Enter a dollar amount: ", NUMBER$
INPUT "10. Enter a type of medicine: ", NOUN3$
INPUT "11. Enter a present tense verb: ", VERB2$
INPUT "12. Enter a positive emotion: ", EMOTION2$
INPUT "13. Enter a color: ", COLOR$
INPUT "14. Enter a noun: ", NOUN4$
INPUT "15. Enter a present tense verb: ", VERB3$
INPUT "16. Enter a past tense verb: ", VERBP$
INPUT "17. Enter a noun: ", NOUN5$
INPUT "18. Enter a present tense verb: ", VERB4$

REM Prepare to display story
SET TEXT SIZE 16
CLS

REM Calculate line height
offset = 480 / 30

REM First paragraph
a$ = "Once upon a time there was a princess named " + NAME$
CENTER TEXT 320, offset, a$
a$ = "who had a " + PROBLEM$ + " on her " + BODYPART1$ + "."
CENTER TEXT 320, offset * 2, a$
a$ = "This " + PROBLEM$ + " was so unsightly and caused"
```

```
CENTER TEXT 320, offset * 3, a$
a$ = "Princess " + NAME$ + " much " + EMOTION$ + "."
CENTER TEXT 320, offset * 4, a$
a$ = "For you see, none of the " + NOUN1$ + " in the"
CENTER TEXT 320, offset * 5, a$
a$ = "kingdom could stand to " + VERB1$ + " at her."
CENTER TEXT 320, offset * 6, a$

REM Second paragraph
a$ = "One night, a little after " + TIME$ + ", Princess " + NAME$
CENTER TEXT 320, offset * 8, a$
a$ = "was sitting in her room reading a " + NOUN2$ + "."
CENTER TEXT 320, offset * 9, a$
a$ = "The "+NOUN2$+" was about the cure for " + PROBLEM$ + "s."
CENTER TEXT 320, offset * 10, a$
a$ = "It had an address to mail " + NUMBER$ + " dollars for"
CENTER TEXT 320, offset * 11, a$
a$ = "a " + NOUN3$ + " to " + VERB2$ + " the " + PROBLEM$ + "."
CENTER TEXT 320, offset * 12, a$
a$ = "She sent off for the " + NOUN3$ + "."
CENTER TEXT 320, offset * 13, a$

REM Third paragraph
a$ = "The day the " + NOUN3$ + " arrived, Princess " + NAME$
CENTER TEXT 320, offset * 15, a$
a$ = "was " + EMOTION2$ + "."
CENTER TEXT 320, offset * 16, a$
a$ = "She ripped open the " + NOUN3$ + " and looked inside."
CENTER TEXT 320, offset * 17, a$
a$ = "There was some " + COLOR$ + " " + NOUN4$ + " in a"
CENTER TEXT 320, offset * 18, a$
a$ = "tube in the " + NOUN3$ + "."
CENTER TEXT 320, offset * 19, a$
a$ = "The instructions said to " + VERB3$ + " the " + NOUN4$
CENTER TEXT 320, offset * 20, a$
a$ = " on the " + PROBLEM$ + " and it would disappear."
CENTER TEXT 320, offset * 21, a$

REM Fourth paragraph
a$ = "Princess " + NAME$ + " " + VERBP$ + " the " + NOUN4$ + " all over"
```

```
CENTER TEXT 320, offset * 22, a$
a$ = "her " + BODYPART1$ + " and poof! her " + BODYPART1$ + " "
CENTER TEXT 320, offset * 23, a$
a$ = "disappeared."
CENTER TEXT 320, offset * 24, a$
a$ = "The moral of this " + NOUN5$ + " is to follow directions"
CENTER TEXT 320, offset * 25, a$
a$ = "or you will not be able to " + VERB4$ + " the consequences."
CENTER TEXT 320, offset * 26, a$

REM Wait for user to press a key
WAIT KEY
END
```

Summary

This chapter was dedicated to the study of strings, the most useful and versatile data type available in DarkBASIC. There are numerous text formatting, manipulation, and display commands built into DarkBASIC for manipulating strings. After you learned about string handling, you discovered how to display strings on the screen with user-definable fonts, which are necessary because DarkBASIC programs run in graphical full-screen mode. Finally, you put your newfound knowledge of strings to use in the Gab Lib game.

Chapter Quiz

The chapter quiz will help reinforce the material you have learned in this chapter and will provide feedback on your progress. For the answers to the quiz, refer to Appendix A, "Answers to the Chapter Quizzes."

1. Which symbol do you use to add two strings?

    A. =

    B. +

    C. ^

    D. /

2. Which command will convert a string to an integer?

   A. STR$
   B. VAL
   C. STRINGTONUM
   D. NUMBER$

3. Which command centers text in a given location?

   A. CENTER TEXT
   B. TEXT CENTER
   C. CENTER PRINT
   D. TEXT

4. What does the SET TEXT TRANSPARENT command do?

   A. Sets the background of the text to transparent
   B. Makes the text invisible
   C. Displays the word "Transparent" on the screen
   D. None of the above

5. What is the result of the following command: LEN("This is a string")?

   A. 42
   B. 19
   C. 16
   D. 02

6. What would the following source code print on the screen?

```
MyString$ = "This is my string!"
PRINT RIGHT$(MyString$,7)
```

   A. This is
   B. is my
   C. my string
   D. string!

7. What would the following source code print on the screen?

```
MyString$ = "This is my string!"
PRINT LEFT$(MyString$,6)
```

A. This is

B. is my

C. my string

D. string!

8. Which symbol attached to a variable denotes it as a string?

A. $

B. *

C. %

D. #

9. Which value would TEXT STYLE return if you were in bold mode?

A. 0

B. 1

C. 2

D. 3

10. Which command returns the font of the text being displayed?

A. FONT OF TEXT

B. FONT$

C. TEXT FONT$

D. SET FONT$

CHAPTER 5

LOOPING COMMANDS

Computers excel at processing huge amounts of data very quickly. Indeed, the most common task for a programmer is to write a program that automates a manual process, tasking a computer to perform the work that previously required a great deal of human effort to complete. The manual process almost always includes a human typing in data or performing some other task, such as filing paperwork. To automate a process, programmers usually employ loops that run through large lists of transactions or other processes and perform one or more tasks depending on the type of data in the list.

For example, most banks process thousands or even millions of financial transactions a day. This is only possible because computers quickly iterate through the transactions and process them very quickly, one at a time. In the days before computers revolutionized the banking industry—something that happened to most industries, in fact—vast hordes of tellers, accountants, statisticians, and auditors were required to process and balance the dreaded end-of-day pile of deposits, withdrawals, loans, and other financial tasks. Thanks to computers and their awesome looping capabilities, humans are free to perform tasks that are better suited to their nature, such as helping customers and making business decisions.

This chapter covers the following topics:

- Understanding the Importance of Looping
- Working with Looping Commands

Understanding the Importance of Looping

This chapter provides an overview of the looping commands built into DarkBASIC. There are four looping commands available, and it's important to understand the strengths and weaknesses of each. The four looping commands are

- FOR...NEXT
- DO...LOOP
- REPEAT...UNTIL
- WHILE...ENDWHILE

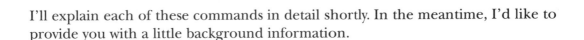

I'll explain each of these commands in detail shortly. In the meantime, I'd like to provide you with a little background information.

What Is a Loop?

A loop can be defined as anything that repeats something over and over. It has a starting point and an ending point. See Figure 5.1 for an example of a loop. It contains a circle with a big black dot. The big black dot indicates the beginning and ending points of the loop.

Although the computer doesn't actually use a circle to perform a loop, this is a suitable illustration of the concept. You have a starting point, which is the first instruction in the loop. The program then executes one instruction after another inside the loop until it reaches the last instruction. It then jumps back to the first instruction and begins the process again. So you see, it's not exactly like a circle, but I suppose that concept is where the term "loop" originally came from.

It's All About Iteration

It's all about iteration, the ability to get repetitive things done. A loop in DarkBASIC will help you complete some repetitive task. A single iteration is complete when you have reached the ending point, where DarkBASIC will decide

> *Iteration* is the process of repeating one or more commands until a series has been processed (or completely run).

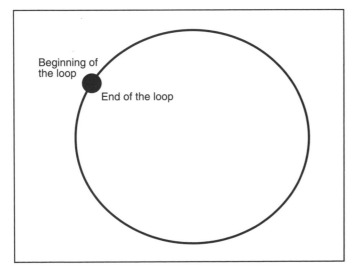

Beginning of the loop

End of the loop

Figure 5.1

A simple representation of a loop

whether you need to return to the starting point or continue with the program based on the conditions you have set.

My best example of a repetitive task is mowing the lawn. I know . . . what a bore, right? In fact, I'm writing this chapter right now instead of doing it. Mowing the lawn is indeed a repetitive task—not only in the number of times it needs to be done during the summer, but also the actual process of going around the yard, row after row. Mowing involves pushing—or if you are lucky, riding—the lawnmower back and forth across the yard, as straight as possible. Eventually, you complete a row and must turn around for the next row. This could be thought of as a loop, since you're performing the same task over and over until the yard is done.

Number Looping

At this point you might be wondering, "How will looping help me write a game with DarkBASIC?" I'm glad you asked! You might use looping in DarkBASIC to find the solution to a problem. Suppose you write a program that asks the user to type in 10 numbers, which the program will then add. Here's a short example—a program called Adder1 (see Figure 5.2). You will find this program on the CD in the Sources\Chapter05\Adder1 folder.

```
REM --------------------------------
REM Beginner's Guide To DarkBASIC  Game Programming
REM Copyright (C)2002 Jonathan S. Harbour and Joshua R. Smith
REM Chapter 5 - Adder1 Program
REM --------------------------------

REM This program will take a series of numbers and add them together
REM This program is written without the use of LOOPS
print "Enter #1: ";
INPUT a
Total = a
print "Enter #2: ";
INPUT a
Total = Total + a
print "Enter #3: ";
INPUT a
Total = Total + a
print "Enter #4: ";
INPUT a
Total = Total + a
```

```
print "Enter #5: ";
INPUT a
Total = Total + a
print "Enter #6: ";
INPUT a
Total = Total + a
print "Enter #7: ";
INPUT a
Total = Total + a
print "Enter #8: ";
INPUT a
Total = Total + a
print "Enter #9: ";
INPUT a
Total = Total + a
print "Enter #10: ";
INPUT a
Total = Total + a
print "Total is "+str$(Total)
WAIT KEY
```

Let me guess . . . after the third or fourth line of code things started to look familiar, and it only got worse with each passing line. It's called repetition! Any time you
find yourself typing in the same thing two or more times, it's a good hint that a
loop will be helpful.

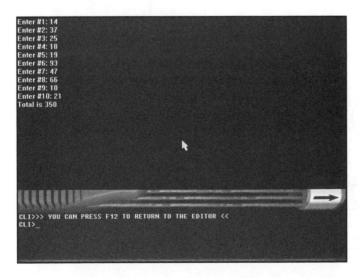

Figure 5.2 *The
Adder1 program
demonstrates multi-
ple additions without
loops.*

The Adder1 program has approximately 30 lines of code. Using a loop, that same program can probably be written with fewer than seven lines of code. But the real advantage is that those short seven lines of code can be employed to handle 50, 100, 1,000, or any number of iterations! It makes no difference at all to DarkBASIC because it is simple a repetitive loop, and programming languages excel at doing things like that.

When I was in high school, I used loops all the time in computer class. My teacher once asked us to write a program to accept a list of test grades and then return the average score. The assignment was easy using a loop! In the next section, I'll introduce you to the first looping command, FOR...NEXT, and then I'll show you how to convert that unwieldy Adder1 program into a more elegant solution.

Looping through an Array

There are other practical applications for loops that might be overlooked at times. You can use loops to read numbers in arrays. By looping through an array, you can perform complex tasks based on the data in the array (such as calculating the sum or an average). Figure 5.3 illustrates an array being passed though a loop.

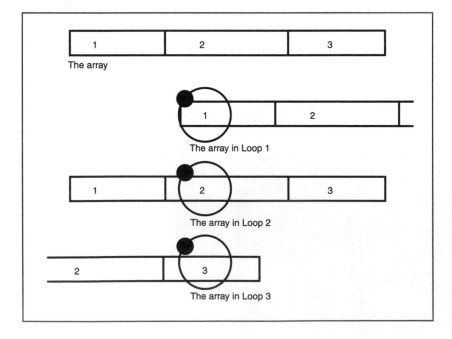

Figure 5.3 *An array within a loop*

Working with Looping Commands

DarkBASIC has many different commands for looping, each of which has its own unique way of defining the starting and ending points of the loop. As I mentioned briefly at the beginning of the chapter, there are four looping commands in DarkBASIC: FOR...NEXT, DO...LOOP, REPEAT...UNTIL, and WHILE...ENDWHILE. The difference between these commands is the condition each one uses to determine when the loop is finished.

What is a condition? It is a programming statement that resolves to either a true or false answer. A condition determines each iteration through a loop; if the condition is true, then the loop ends and the program continues. Chapter 8, "Number Crunching: Mathematical and Relational Operators and Commands," covers the myriad conditions supported in DarkBASIC, so I'll stick to very simple conditions now and save the more advanced subjects for later. For a quick reference, Table 5.1 shows the relational operators used to test a condition.

Table 5.1 Conditional Symbols

Symbol	Description
=	Equal
<>	Not equal
<	Less than
>	Greater than
<=	Less than or equal
>=	Greater than or equal

The FOR...NEXT Command

The first looping command up to bat is FOR...NEXT. It's deceptively simple, but it provides easily understandable results. With the FOR...NEXT command, you can define how many times you want the loop to run. A loop that runs forever—in which case the condition is always false—is called an infinite loop. Fortunately, the FOR...NEXT command is the most limited of the four looping commands because it runs a fixed number of times. The starting point of the loop is the FOR command; the ending point is the NEXT command. See Figure 5.4 for an example.

The command format for the FOR...NEXT loop is

```
FOR variable = starting number TO ending number
NEXT variable
```

The FOR command initiates the first loop by making the variable equal to the starting number. When DarkBASIC reaches the NEXT command, it returns to the FOR command and adds 1 to the variable. When the variable reaches the ending number, the NEXT command does not return to the FOR command. Instead, it continues through the source code.

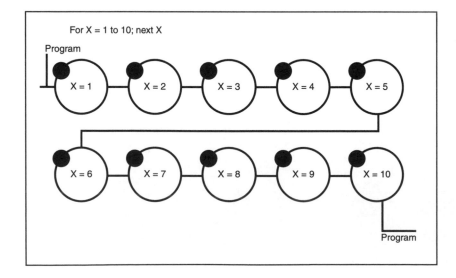

Figure 5.4

A FOR...NEXT *loop*

Using the FOR...NEXT Command

So let's use the FOR...NEXT loop in a practical sense. Why not shorten the Adder1 program to seven lines, like I said could be done? The Adder2 program (shown in Figure 5.5) follows. You will find this program on the CD in the Sources\Chapter05\Adder2 folder.

```
REM ---------------------------------
REM Beginner's Guide To Game Programming With DarkBASIC
REM Copyright (C)2002 Jonathan S. Harbour and Joshua R. Smith
REM Chapter 5 - Looping Commands
REM ---------------------------------

REM This program will take a series of numbers and add them together
REM This program is written with the use of a FOR...NEXT loop

Total = 0
FOR x = 1 to 10
print "Enter #"+str$(X)+": ";
INPUT a
Total = Total + a
NEXT x
print "Total is "+str$(Total)
WAIT KEY
```

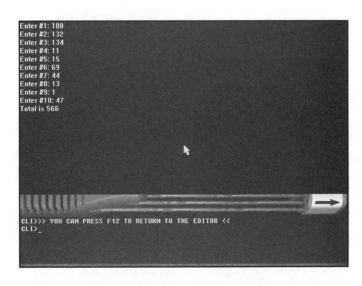

Figure 5.5 *The Adder2 program demonstrates multiple additions with a* FOR...NEXT *loop.*

It is pretty simple and yet so very powerful. With a single change of a number, you can make the program add 100 numbers or even 1,000 numbers! Try playing with the starting and ending values to see what kind of crazy combinations you can create.

Specialty Case: The STEP Parameter

Sometimes you need to count by something other than 1. For example, suppose you want to print every other number between 15 and 33. There is a special command for this, called STEP. It is placed at the end of a FOR command, and you can specify the increment by which you want to count. For example, if you want to loop between 15 and 33 by increments of 2, the FOR command would be FOR X = 15 to 33 STEP 2. See Figure 5.6 for a better representation of the STEP command.

The STEP command is also useful because it allows you to loop backward. Figure 5.7 demonstrates how you can use the STEP command to do so. A simple program that uses the STEP command backward follows.

The Countdown program (shown in Figure 5.8) demonstrates looping with a negative number. You will find this program on the CD in the Sources\Chapter05\Countdown folder.

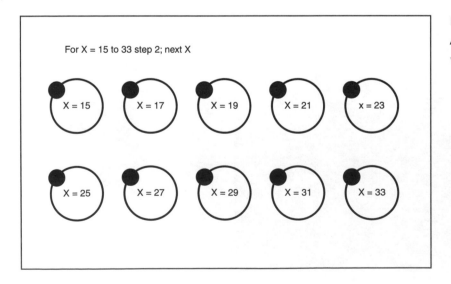

For X = 15 to 33 step 2; next X

X = 15   X = 17   X = 19   X = 21   x = 23

X = 25   X = 27   X = 29   X = 31   X = 33

Figure 5.6

A FOR...NEXT loop with a STEP of 2

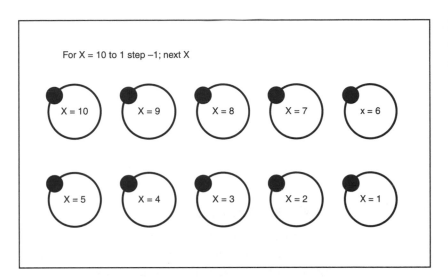

Figure 5.7
Count backward with a STEP *of -1.*

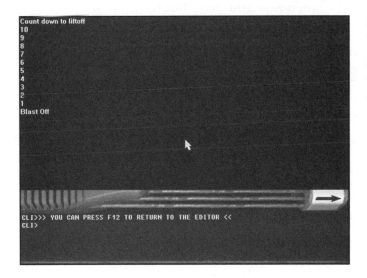

Figure 5.8
The Countdown program demonstrates one use of the STEP *command.*

```
REMSTART
----------------------------------
Beginner's Guide To Game Programming With DarkBASIC
Copyright (C)2002 Jonathan S. Harbour and Joshua R. Smith
Chapter 5 - Looping Commands
----------------------------------
REMEND
```

```
REM This program counts down from 10 to 1
REM This program is written with the use of a FOR...NEXT loop

PRINT "Count down to liftoff"
FOR X=10 to 1 step -1
 PRINT X
 SLEEP 500
 NEXT x
PRINT "Blast Off"
```

The DO...LOOP Command

Like FOR...NEXT, DO...LOOP is another looping command. The big difference between the two is that DO...LOOP is known as an infinite loop, which means that as long as you do not interrupt it, the loop will continue forever. Okay, forever is quite a long time and hardware can fail between now and then, but for all practical purposes DO...LOOP will run forever. See Figure 5.9 for an example of a DO...LOOP.

The format for the DO...LOOP command is the same as the FOR...NEXT command, except that you do not have to follow the DO or the LOOP with anything.

```
DO
 Source Code
 Source Code
 Source Code
LOOP
```

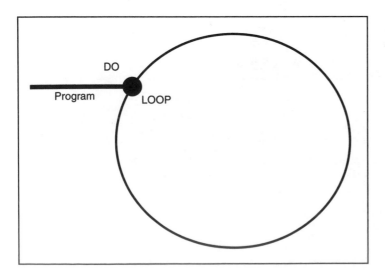

Figure 5.9
A DO...LOOP

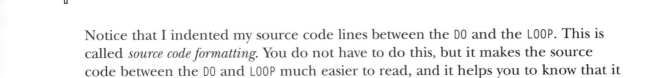

Notice that I indented my source code lines between the DO and the LOOP. This is called *source code formatting*. You do not have to do this, but it makes the source code between the DO and LOOP much easier to read, and it helps you to know that it is a separate section of source code.

Using the DO...LOOP Command

The following program shows you a practical use for the DO...LOOP command (see Figure 5.10). Warning: To exit this program, you will need to hit the F12 key (DBV1) or the Esc key (DBPro). Now on with the program. You will find this program on the CD in the Sources\Chapter05\BouncerWithDo1 folder.

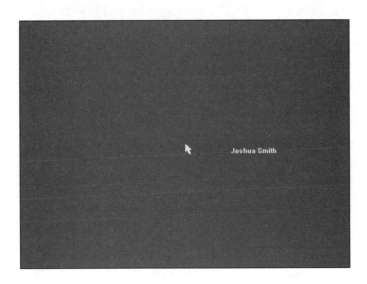

Figure 5.10
The BouncerWithDo1 program demonstrates infinite looping using DO...LOOP.

```
REMSTART
-----------------------------------
Beginner's Guide To DarkBASIC Game Programming
Copyright (C)2002 Jonathan S. Harbour and Joshua R. Smith
Chapter 5 - Looping Commands
-----------------------------------
REMEND

REM This program bounces your name around the screen
REM This program is written with the use of a DO...LOOP loop

PRINT "Please Type in your Name:"
INPUT NAME$
```

```
DO
 CLS
 TEXT RND(500),RND(350),NAME$
 SLEEP 500
LOOP
```

Don't worry about some of the commands you don't recognize; they will be addressed in later chapters. It's a pretty cool program to bounce whatever you typed around the screen.

Breaking Out with EXIT

DO...LOOP is useful if you have all the time in the world to sit in a loop. However, some of us have better things to do. The makers of DarkBASIC knew that, so they provided the EXIT command, which will break out of any DO...LOOP. No more sitting around, waiting for the end of the world as you know it. Figure 5.11 shows the great benefits of using the EXIT command.

The following program is just like the previous one you typed in, but with one slight difference—it breaks out after 10 prints for you. Do not worry about the IF command; I will cover it in Chapter 6, "Making Programs Think: Branching Statements and Subroutines." Figure 5.12 shows the output of the BouncerWithDo2 program, which follows. You will find this program on the CD in the Sources\Chapter05\BouncerWithDo2 folder.

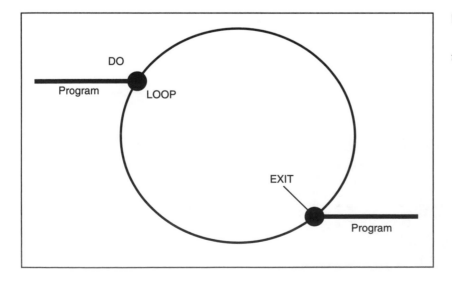

Figure 5.11
A DO...LOOP *with the* EXIT *command*

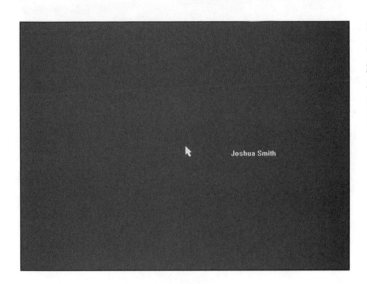

Figure 5.12 *The BouncerWithDo2 program demonstrates breaking a* DO...LOOP *using the* EXIT *command.*

```
REMSTART
-----------------------------------
Beginner's Guide To Game Programming With DarkBASIC
Copyright (C)2002 Jonathan S. Harbour and Joshua R. Smith
Chapter 5 - Looping Commands
-----------------------------------
REMEND

REM This program bounces your name around the screen
REM This program is written with the use of a DO...LOOP loop
REM This program will stop after the 10 time of bouncing

PRINT "Please Type in your Name:"
INPUT NAME$

count = 1
DO
 CLS
 TEXT RND(500),RND(350),NAME$
 SLEEP 500
 count = count + 1
 if count > 10 then EXIT
LOOP
```

The REPEAT...UNTIL Command

The DO...LOOP command is a great loop for just hanging around. The EXIT command ensures that you do not hang around forever, but what about the times when you want to loop for a while and stop when a condition is met? Welcome to the REPEAT...UNTIL command, your next stop in the wonderful world of loops.

The REPEAT...UNTIL command will do just that—repeat until a condition is met. See Figure 5.13 for an example of REPEAT...UNTIL.

The command format of REPEAT...UNTIL is

```
REPEAT
     Source Code
     Source Code
     Source Code
UNTIL condition
```

An important thing to note about the REPEAT...UNTIL command is that the source code inside it will run at least once. That is, all the code between the REPEAT and the UNTIL will run once. If the condition is met, the loop will not repeat.

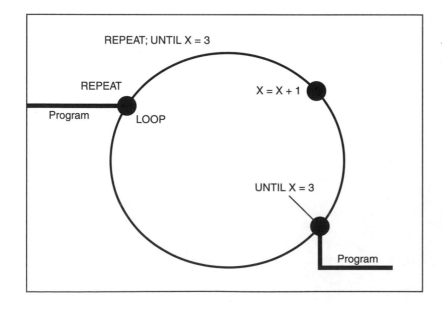

Figure 5.13
A REPEAT...UNTIL
loop

Using the REPEAT...UNTIL Command

Now you are going to rewrite the program you wrote in the DO...LOOP section. This time, the code will repeat until you hit the spacebar. Again, don't worry about the INKEY$ command; that will be covered in a later chapter as well. Figure 5.14 shows the output of the BouncerWithRepeat1 program.

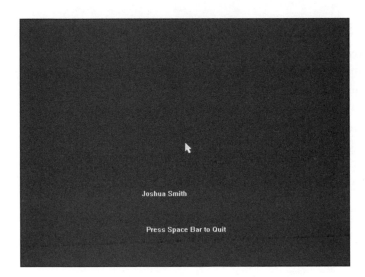

Figure 5.14 *The BouncerWithRepeat1 program demonstrates finite looping using the* REPEAT...UNTIL *loop.*

```
REMSTART
----------------------------------
Beginner's Guide To Game Programming With DarkBASIC
Copyright (C)2002 Jonathan S. Harbour and Joshua R. Smith
Chapter 5 - Looping Commands
----------------------------------
REMEND

REM This program bounces your name around the screen
REM This program is written with the use of a REPEAT...UNTIL loop
REM This program will stop after the spacebar has been hit

PRINT "Please Type in your Name:"
INPUT NAME$
```

```
REPEAT
 CLS
 TEXT RND(500),RND(350),NAME$
 CENTER TEXT 320,400,"Press Spacebar to Quit"
 SLEEP 500
UNTIL INKEY$()=" "
```

Breaking Out with EXIT

Remember the EXIT command from the DO...LOOP? Well, it's back. You can use the
EXIT command in the REPEAT...UNTIL command as well. Instead of having one condition to leave the loop, you can create multiple conditions to leave the loop. The
following program uses the REPEAT...UNTIL command with an EXIT command.
The program bounces your name around the screen and stops when the spacebar
is hit or after 10 loops. Figure 5.15 shows the output of the BouncerWithRepeat2
program. You will find this program on the CD in the
Sources\Chapter05\BouncerWithRepeat2 folder.

```
REMSTART
----------------------------------
Beginner's Guide To Game Programming With DarkBASIC
Copyright (C)2002 Jonathan S. Harbour and Joshua R. Smith
Chapter 5 - Looping Commands
----------------------------------
REMEND

PRINT "Please Type in your Name:"
INPUT NAME$

count = 1
REPEAT
 CLS
 TEXT RND(500),RND(350),NAME$
 CENTER TEXT 320,400,"Press Spacebar to Quit"
 SLEEP 500
 count = count + 1
 if count > 10 then EXIT
UNTIL INKEY$()=" "
```

Figure 5.15 *The BouncerWithRepeat2 program demonstrates finite looping with the* REPEAT...UNTIL *loop using the* EXIT *command.*

The WHILE...ENDWHILE Command

The last of the loop commands is the WHILE...ENDWHILE command. Its purpose is different than the REPEAT...UNTIL command, but it can act almost the same. Just like the REPEAT...UNTIL command, WHILE...ENDWHILE runs the code between the lines. However, unlike REPEAT...UNTIL, WHILE...ENDWHILE will not run the code between the lines if the condition is met before the loop is started. Figure 5.16 shows an illustration of a WHILE...ENDWHILE loop.

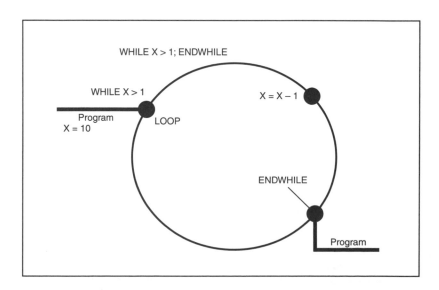

Figure 5.16 *A* WHILE...ENDWHILE *loop*

The command format of the WHILE...ENDWHILE command is

```
WHILE condition
     Source Code
     Source Code
     Source Code
ENDWHILE
```

Using the
WHILE...ENDWHILE Command

Okay, now it's time to rework the name-bouncing program. The main difference between this program and the previous REPEAT...UNTIL program is that it checks for the spacebar before it runs the code. Figure 5.17 shows the output of the BouncerWithWhile1 program. You will find this program on the CD in the Sources\Chapter05\BouncerWithWhile1 folder.

```
REMSTART
-----------------------------------
Beginner's Guide To Game Programming With DarkBASIC
Copyright (C)2002 Jonathan S. Harbour and Joshua R. Smith
Chapter 5 - Looping Commands
-----------------------------------
REMEND

REM This program bounces your name around the screen
REM This program is written with the use of a WHILE...ENDWHILE loop
REM This program will stop after the spacebar has been hit

PRINT "Please Type in your Name:"
INPUT NAME$

WHILE inkey$() <> " "
 CLS
 TEXT RND(500),RND(350),NAME$
 CENTER TEXT 320,400,"Press Spacebar to Quit"
 SLEEP 500
ENDWHILE
```

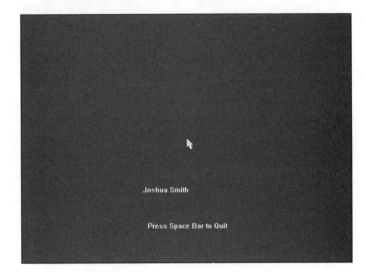

Figure 5.17 *The BouncerWithWhile1 program demonstrates finite looping using the* WHILE...ENDWHILE *loop.*

Breaking Out with EXIT

There are times when you need to break out of a loop. You can use the EXIT command to stop a loop and jump to the line that follows it. This is very useful for the programmer who has every command under his belt. Figure 5.18 shows the output of the BouncerWithWhile2 program.

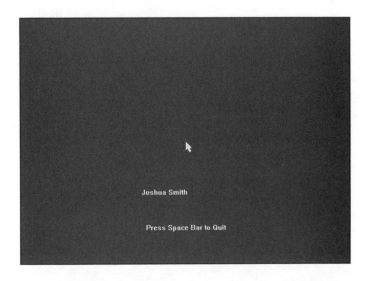

Figure 5.18 *The BouncerWithWhile2 program demonstrates finite looping with the* WHILE...ENDWHILE *loop using the* EXIT *command.*

You will find this program on the CD in the Sources\Chapter05\ BouncerWithWhile2 folder.

```
REMSTART
-----------------------------------
Beginner's Guide To Game Programming With DarkBASIC
Copyright (C)2002 Jonathan S. Harbour and Joshua R. Smith
Chapter 5 - Looping Commands
-----------------------------------
REMEND

PRINT "Please Type in your Name:"
INPUT NAME$

count = 1
WHILE inkey$() <> " "
 CLS
 TEXT RND(500),RND(350),NAME$
 CENTER TEXT 320,400,"Press Spacebar to Quit"
 SLEEP 500
 count = count + 1
 if count > 10 then EXIT
ENDWHILE
```

Combining Loops

There is one last topic that I need cover on the subject of loops before you move on to the chapter project—nesting loops. The loops I have shown you so far are single loops, meaning that only one loop is running at a time. DarkBASIC supports nested loops, meaning that more than one loop is running at a time. Nested loops are some of the best programming tricks to use. You can do things such as scroll through two variables in one sitting. Through the journey of game programming, you will find nested loops to be one of your greatest allies. Figure 5.19 shows what a nested loop looks like.

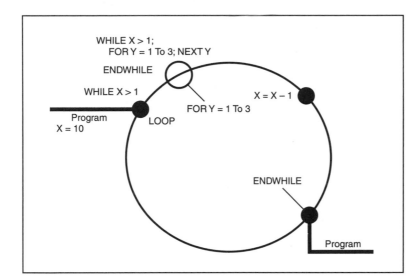

Figure 5.19 *A nested loop*

Sample Project

Okay, now it's time to put into practice what you have learned in this chapter. I have used two different kinds of loops in the chapter project, and I have a challenge for you. Try changing the loops to a different kind of loop, such as changing the REPEAT...UNTIL loop to a WHILE...ENDWHILE loop.

The chapter project is a simple math program to sharpen your skills. Just enter the two numbers and the program will add them for you. What you get after you have entered all the numbers is just as interesting. You will find this program on the CD in the Sources\Chapter05\MathFun folder.

```
REMSTART
----------------------------------
Beginner's Guide To Game Programming With DarkBASIC
Copyright (C)2002 Jonathan S. Harbour and Joshua R. Smith
Chapter 5 - Looping Commands
----------------------------------
REMEND

DIM Numbers1(50)
DIM Numbers2(50)
CLS
```

```
Total = 0
REPEAT
    PRINT "Enter a number between 1-50: "
    INPUT Total
UNTIL TOTAL<=50 and TOTAL >0

FOR X = 1 to Total
    PRINT "Enter First Number To Add: "
    INPUT a
    Numbers1(x) = a
    PRINT "Enter Second Number To Add:"
    INPUT a
    Numbers2(x) = a
    Answer = Numbers1(x)+Numbers2(x)
    PRINT Numbers1(x);
    PRINT "+";
    PRINT Numbers2(x);
    PRINT "=";
    PRINT Answer
    SLEEP 500
    CLS
NEXT X

PRINT "Now for the interesting stuff:"
SUM = 0
FOR x= 1 TO Total
    SUM = SUM + Numbers1(x) + Numbers2(x)
NEXT X

PRINT "The sum of all the numbers you entered is ";
PRINT SUM
PRINT "The Average of all the numbers you entered is ";
PRINT (SUM/Total)
WAIT KEY
```

Summary

This chapter was dedicated to the study of looping commands, which are essential for processing large sequences of numbers, strings, or any other information in DarkBASIC. There are several looping commands, such as WHILE...ENDWHILE,

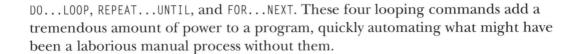

DO...LOOP, REPEAT...UNTIL, and FOR...NEXT. These four looping commands add a tremendous amount of power to a program, quickly automating what might have been a laborious manual process without them.

Chapter Quiz

The chapter quiz will help to reinforce the material you have learned in this chapter, and will provide you with feedback on how well you have learned the subjects that were covered. For the answers to the quiz, refer to Appendix A, "Answers to the Chapter Quizzes."

1. How many times will the following loop iterate?

    ```
    FOR X = 1 to 10
    NEXT X
    ```

    A. 1
    B. 5
    C. 10
    D. Forever

2. Which command will exit out of a loop?

    A. END
    B. EXIT
    C. STOP
    D. FINISH

3. Which word describes what happens in a FOR...NEXT loop?

    A. Processing
    B. 5
    C. 10
    D. Forever

4. Which of the following conditional statements means greater than?

    A. =
    B. >
    C. <
    D. <>

5. How would you make a FOR...NEXT loop count by 3s?

    A. STEP 3

    B. MOVEIT 3

    C. STEP -5

    D. STEP 5

6. Which command completes a REPEAT loop?

    A. ENDWHILE

    B. NEXT

    C. LOOP

    D. UNTIL

7. According to this chapter, what is a loop?

    A. A type of sport

    B. Anything that repeats itself

    C. An invalid variable

    D. None of the above

8. What is another term for a combined loop (one loop inside another)?

    A. Sub loop

    B. Nested loop

    C. Multiple loop

    D. Loop-de-loop

9. Which command completes a DO loop?

    A. ENDWHILE

    B. NEXT

    C. LOOP

    D. UNTIL

10. Which command completes a WHILE loop?

    A. ENDWHILE

    B. NEXT

    C. LOOP

    D. UNTIL

CHAPTER 6

MAKING PROGRAMS THINK: BRANCHING STATEMENTS AND SUBROUTINES

As programs become longer and more complicated, a common problem occurs. Regardless of programming language or computer system, there is a point at which logic commands reach a roadblock and the program cannot grow any larger without being broken into smaller parts. When the main procedure needs to do something specific, such as check the position of the mouse pointer on the screen, it is better to jump to another part of the program that specifically handles mouse input than to write the mouse code directly in the main procedure's source code. That way other parts of the program can use the mouse, and you don't have to rewrite the mouse commands every time.

This chapter will teach you how to break up a program into smaller parts, called *subroutines,* and how to use branching statements to call upon those subroutines when needed. *Branching* gives a program the logic it needs to perform more than one task based on certain conditions. There are times when you can write small portions of code directly inside a branching statement, but there are other times when that code is too lengthy and requires its own space. I'll show you how to create subroutines that perform specific processes in a game, and you will put this new information to use in later chapters. Basically, this is one of the most important chapters in the book!

This chapter covers the following topics:

- Introduction to Program Logic
- Conditional Logic Statements
- Understanding and Using Subroutines

Introduction to Program Logic

First I would like to talk about program logic, because you should understand it before you get into subroutines. DarkBASIC calls all subroutines *functions,* but I'll get to that in the second half of the chapter.

What is logic and how does it relate to programming? When I hear the word logic, I think of several descriptions—analysis, deductive reasoning, processing—the rival of intuition.

Computers are great at performing logical commands, but how does logic work in DarkBASIC? Most programming languages have a standard set of branching statements that you can use to create the logic in a program. The two branching statements in DarkBASIC are IF...THEN and IF...ELSE...ENDIF. These statements can be more formally described as *conditional statements*. Most programmers will know right away what you are talking about if you mention an IF statement, strange as that may sound at first.

What Is a Branching Statement?

Branching statements provide the program with a means to apply rules and tests to variables and then take action based on the results. They are built into programming languages so programmers can process the input and provide the output for a program. Without branching statements, the program would only be able to forward the input directly to the output without any processing. Although this might be something that you want the program to do (perhaps to display a text file on the screen or print a document), it is far more likely that you will need to *do something* with data that has been entered into the program. Branching statements allow you to create complex program logic. You might not be able to create something as complicated as a pattern-recognition neural network like the human brain (as described back in Chapter 2), but even the human brain works by simple rules. It is just that billions of those small rules are being followed synchronously.

Conditions are factors that limit something within a specific boundary. For example, a football field is a rectangle bordered by white lines that delineate the area in which legal plays can be made. The rules of the game dictate how the game is played, and these rules form a set of conditions that must be met in order to play the game correctly. Who enforces the rules of the game? The referees (and in some cases, the fans!).

The Key to Program Logic

Program logic and logical decisions are at the core of how computers work, providing a means to process data. At the highest level, programs should be designed to accomplish the following three tasks.

1. Receive some input data

2. Process the data

3. Output the result

The goal of any programmer should be to write programs that revolve around these three basic operations. Input, process, and output help to break down a problem into manageable pieces, and you should be able to clearly see how these three concepts apply to every program. When a program doesn't receive input, process data, or output something, it really isn't a useful program.

Obviously, these operations have a wide range of applications. Input could be from the keyboard, mouse, or joystick, but it could also be from a database, text file, serial or infrared port, network connection, or even a scanner or digital camera. Processing might involve translating, combining, or transforming the data to suit a specific purpose. In the case of a digital camera, processing might involve adjusting the brightness and cropping the photo. Output is the result of the processing, which might involve displaying something on the screen, in a printed report, or possibly to an output file or database. As you can see, input-process-output can be interpreted to mean many things. The important thing is that every program accomplishes at least this basic level of functionality.

Making the Program More Useful

In a computer program, you define a set of conditional statements (or branching commands) that enforce the rules of the program. There are usually many different areas of the program that perform these commands, depending on its state. For instance, a game might check the status of a joystick button. The condition in this case is a rule that if the button is pressed, something will happen (for example, the spaceship will fire a weapon or a player will shoot a gun). A more complicated example is reading the keyboard. There are approximately 100 keys on a typical AT-101 keyboard. Checking the scan codes (the special codes for each key) involves some logic, as does checking the mouse for input. The point is, without the ability to process input and provide a result, computer programs are not very useful. Imagine a car game in which you just watch the computer drive the cars around the screen. Sound like fun? Obviously, a game needs to interact with the user, and that is my point.

Conditional Logic Statements

There are two specific branching statements in DarkBASIC: IF...THEN and IF...ELSE...ENDIF. In this section, I'll describe both statements and show you how to use them.

The IF...THEN Statement

The most common branching statement used in programming languages is the
IF...THEN statement. Following is the general syntax of the statement as it is used in
DarkBASIC.

```
IF <condition is true> THEN <do something>
```

Do you see how the entire statement occurs on a single line? This is a *simple* statement. There is also a *compound* version of the IF...THEN statement, which is called
IF...ELSE...ENDIF.

The IF...ELSE...ENDIF Statement

What happens when you need to test more than one condition at a time? You
could use multiple IF...THEN statements, but there are times when it is easier just to
include an ELSE block within the statement. Following is the general format of the
IF...ELSE...ENDIF statement.

```
IF <condition is true>
    <do something>
ELSE
    <do something else>
ENDIF
```

There is one important distinction between the simple and compound statements.
The compound IF does not have a trailing THEN when an ENDIF is also used.
DarkBASIC identifies the THEN keyword to indicate that the whole statement occurs
on a single line, while an IF without a THEN indicates a compound statement.

The use of the ELSE keyword is equivalent to the following two individual branching
statements. Note the use of ENDIF to end each statement.

```
IF <condition is true>
    <perform primary commands>
ENDIF

IF <condition is false>
    <perform alternative commands>
ENDIF
```

As I mentioned, these two branching statements are equivalent to the
IF...ELSE...ENDIF statement. The ELSE saves a lot of time! Figure 6.1 shows an

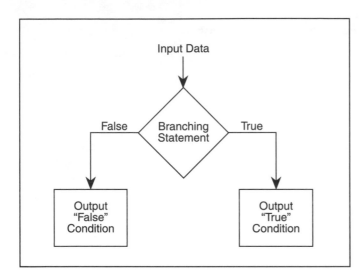

Figure 6.1
Illustration of a branching statement, showing the true or false result

illustration of the `IF...ELSE...ENDIF` statement, demonstrating how input is tested for a true or false condition and the program execution is directed down a specific path.

Using Branching Statements

Okay, I don't want to lose you! If you are new to branching statements or to programming in general, this discussion might not have sunk in yet. How about a realistic example? Here is how you might code the branching statement to determine which mouse button has been clicked.

```
IF MouseButton = 1
    PRINT "Left click"
ELSE
    PRINT "Right click"
ENDIF
```

You could have just as easily written this code using two `IF...THEN` statements instead of a single `IF...ELSE...ENDIF`, and the result would have been the same.

```
IF MouseButton = 1
    PRINT "Left click"
ENDIF

IF MouseButton = 2
```

```
    PRINT "Right click"
ENDIF
```

The better solution, of course, is to use the ELSE section instead of the second IF statement, which is relevant when there are one or two possible values to be tested. When there are more than two values that you need to check, you can use compound IF statements, as follows.

```
IF MouseButton = 1
    PRINT "Left click"
ELSE
    IF MouseButton = 2
        PRINT "Right click"
    ENDIF
ENDIF
```

> **TIP**
>
> Chapter 8, "Number Crunching: Mathematical and Relational Operators and Statements," covers the common relational operators, such as greater than (>), less than (<), and equal to (=), along with mathematical operators such as multiply (*) and divide (/). You can combine this information with what you learn in this chapter and the one that follows to have some very useful techniques available for writing programs.

Testing Program Logic: The Conditions Program

To demonstrate branching statements and program logic in DarkBASIC, I have written a program called Conditions that moves a ball around the screen. Any time the ball nears the edge of the screen, which is drawn with a border, the program will reverse the direction of the ball. The logic in this program determines when the ball is nearing the edge, and then deflects the ball so it doesn't go off the edge of the screen.

Running the Program

The Conditions program is located on the CD-ROM under Sources\DarkBASIC\ CH06\Conditions (for standard DarkBASIC) and under Sources\DBPro\CH06\ Conditions (for DarkBASIC Pro). You can run the program directly off the CD if you want, although you will need to copy the files to your hard drive to make any changes to the source code. Remember that you will need to turn off the read-only attribute for any files copied from a CD-ROM. (You can do this by right-clicking on a file in Windows Explorer and selecting Properties from the drop-down menu.) Figure 6.2 shows the Conditions program right after it has started.

Figure 6.2 *The Conditions program tests program logic with a bouncing ball.*

Figure 6.3 shows the ball right at the left edge of the screen, from where it will bounce back. The border around the edge shows the point on the screen from where the ball is bounced.

Figure 6.3 *The ball is bounced off the left wall in this shot of the Conditions program.*

Conditions Source Code

Following is the source code for the Conditions program. The important sections of code related to the program's logic are set in bold text. This program uses an advanced feature called SYNC that dramatically speeds up the program and eliminates flicker. To see the difference that the SYNC command makes, comment out the SYNC ON command in the initialization section. I'll explain the SYNC command and the other graphics commands used in this program in more detail in Chapter 9, "Basic Graphics Commands."

Now for the code listing. You can create a new project in DarkBASIC and type in the following code, or you can load this project off the CD-ROM (as described earlier). If you type in the program, remember to save the source code to a file called Conditions.dba after you're done. This is one of the most complex programs in the book so far! Trust me, it is worth the effort to type it in because you will learn a lot about logic statements and get a sneak peek at some graphics commands.

```
REMSTART
----------------------------------
Beginner's Guide To DarkBASIC Game Programming
Copyright (C)2002 Jonathan S. Harbour and Joshua R. Smith
Chapter 6 - Conditions Program
----------------------------------
REMEND

REM Create some variables
BallX = 320
BallY = 240
BallSize = 20
SpeedX = 4
Speedy = -5
Border = 25

REM Initialize the program
SYNC ON

REM Set the color
color = RGB(0, 200, 255)
INK color, 0

REM Start the main loop
```

```
DO
    REM Clear the screen
    CLS

    REM Draw the screen border
    LINE 0, 0, 639, 0
    LINE 639, 0, 639, 479
    LINE 639, 479, 0, 479
    LINE 0, 479, 0, 0

    REM Move the ball
    BallX = BallX + SpeedX
    BallY = BallY + SpeedY

    REM Check conditions for the BallX
    IF BallX > 640 - Border
        BallX = 640 - Border
        SpeedX = SpeedX * -1
    ELSE
        IF BallX < Border
            BallX = Border
            SpeedX = SpeedX * -1
        ENDIF
    ENDIF

    REM Check conditions for BallY
    IF BallY > 480 - Border
        BallY = 480 - Border
        SpeedY = SpeedY * -1
    ELSE
        IF BallY < Border
            BallY = Border
            SpeedY = SpeedY * -1
        ENDIF
    ENDIF

    REM Draw the ball
    CIRCLE BallX, BallY, BallSize

    REM Redraw the screen
    SYNC
LOOP
```

Understanding and Using Subroutines

Subroutines are important for breaking up a large program into smaller, more manageable pieces, leading to better code reuse and legibility. They are also important for creating program logic. Quite often, the conditional statements in a branching statement point to a subroutine to keep the branching statement short. If each case in a branching statement included a page of source code, it would be easy to lose track of the cases! Therefore, subroutines are essential parts of a programming language. Figure 6.4 illustrates the relationships between the main program and all of its functions, which are broken down into more detail at each level.

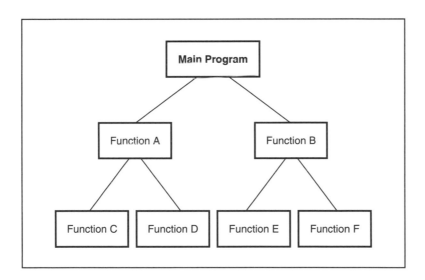

Figure 6.4

Structured programs have a hierarchy of functions from high levels to lower levels of detail.

What Is a Function?

First, let me clear up something regarding subroutines. A subroutine is a separate sequence of source code within a program that performs a recurring or distinct task. By recurring, I mean something that is repeated over and over. By distinct, I mean something that might be used only once, but for which it makes more sense to put the code in its own subroutine.

The next thing I want to make clear is that you must use the FUNCTION statement to create custom subroutines. For the sake of clarity, I will refer to subroutines and functions interchangeably; they are the same thing. I will use the uppercase

FUNCTION when referring to source code and the lowercase function when talking about functions in the general sense.

Following is the basic syntax of a function in DarkBASIC.

```
FUNCTION FunctionName([Parameters])
ENDFUNCTION [ReturnValue]
```

Let me explain how this works. You declare a function with a FUNCTION...ENDFUNCTION block of code. You give it a name and include any parameters that you want to be able to pass to the function, and then you provide an optional return value. Since there really is no easy way to explain this, let me show you a few examples. This first example is a function that displays a message on the screen.

```
FUNCTION PrintHello()
    PRINT "Hello!"
ENDFUNCTION
```

You can simply call this function by name anywhere in the program. The function prints out "Hello!" on the screen any time it is called. That is great as a first example, but it isn't very useful. A far more useful function would be one that lets you print out any message you want. Although the PRINT command does this already, it is helpful to demonstrate how parameters work. Here is an example of a function that includes a parameter.

```
FUNCTION PrintHello(Name$)
    PRINT "Hello, "; Name$; "!"
ENDFUNCTION
```

The parameter, Name$, includes a dollar sign at the end because that is how you pass a text message to a function in DarkBASIC. Number parameters don't need the dollar sign, only text messages (which are called *strings*) do. In fact, it is a good idea to refer to text variables in that manner, for instance by calling the parameter "Name string"—just how it sounds.

Using Functions

I want you to remember something very important about dealing with string variables. Any time you declare a string parameter, you must use the dollar sign along with the variable name everywhere in the function. If you were to write the previous line without the dollar sign, like the following line of code (note the variable name in bold), the output of the program would be very strange.

```
PRINT "Hello, "; Name; "!"
```

No matter what text message you send to the `PrintHello` function, it would always print 0 instead of the text you intended. Why is that, do you suppose?

Let me show you a complete program that uses the `PrintHello` function so you can see for yourself what happens when you leave off the dollar sign. Type the following code into a new project in DarkBASIC.

```
REMSTART
-----------------------------------
Beginner's Guide To DarkBASIC Game Programming
Copyright (C)2002 Jonathan S. Harbour and Joshua R. Smith
Chapter 6 - PrintHello Program
-----------------------------------
REMEND

CLS
PRINT
PrintHello("DarkBASIC")
END

FUNCTION PrintHello(Name$)
    PRINT "Hello, "; Name$; "!"
ENDFUNCTION
```

After typing in the program (or loading it off the CD-ROM from the Sources\CH06\PrintHello folder), save it and then run it. The display will look like Figure 6.5.

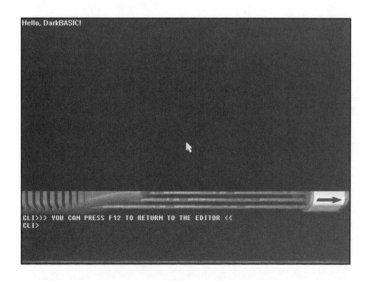

Figure 6.5 *The PrintHello program demonstrates how to pass parameters to a function.*

Now change the program as I explained by removing the dollar sign from the `Name$` variable inside the `PrintHello` function. The result is a 0 instead of the string "DarkBASIC."

As Austin Powers would say, "Positively smashing, baby!" Okay, maybe it's not that big of a deal, but I just want to make it clear that a lot of programming problems in DarkBASIC are a result of an error involving parameters. DarkBASIC is a very lenient programming language, allowing you to declare variables anywhere! That's why `Name` printed out 0 instead of the intended string—because DarkBASIC created a new variable called `Name` on the fly with a default value of 0.

Divide and Conquer

How about another example to give you a little more practice using parameters? I've written a program called RandomText that uses a custom function called `PrintAt`. This function prints a string on the screen at a specific location using parameters. Figure 6.6 shows the output of the program.

Here's the code listing for the RandomText program. There's one new command in this program that I haven't explained yet—`RANDOMIZE TIMER()`. The `RANDOMIZE` command initializes the random-number seed in DarkBASIC, which causes your program to generate random numbers each time it is run. Without `RANDOMIZE`, the program will generate the same numbers each time, even when you re-run the

Figure 6.6 *The RandomText program demonstrates how to use multiple parameters.*

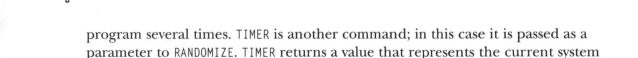

program several times. TIMER is another command; in this case it is passed as a parameter to RANDOMIZE. TIMER returns a value that represents the current system timer in milliseconds.

```
REMSTART
----------------------------------
Beginner's Guide To DarkBASIC Game Programming
Copyright (C)2002 Jonathan S. Harbour and Joshua R. Smith
Chapter 6 - RandomText Program
----------------------------------
REMEND

REM Initialize the program
CLS
PRINT
RANDOMIZE TIMER()

DO
    REM Select a random color
    color = RGB(RND(256), RND(256), RND(256))
    INK color, 0

    REM Print the message
    PrintAt(RND(640), RND(480), "I Love DarkBASIC!!")
LOOP
FUNCTION PrintAt(X, Y, Message$)

    SET CURSOR X, Y
    PRINT Message$
ENDFUNCTION
```

Returning Values

You can use functions not only to break up lengthy programs with many lines of code and to make code reusable, but also to perform calculations or logic and return a value. This is an important aspect of any programming language. Without the ability to return values from functions, a program would have to use variables for everything, including calculations, and the source code would quickly become unmanageable.

Remember the syntax of a function, which allowed you to return a value? Here's the definition again for reference.

```
FUNCTION FunctionName([Parameters])
ENDFUNCTION [ReturnValue]
```

The return value is added after the ENDFUNCTION keyword when you want the function to return some value. This value can be a string or a number (integer or decimal), derived from a calculation, variable, or by any other means. Following is an example of a function that returns a value.

```
FUNCTION RandomColor()
   Color = RGB(RND(256), RND(256), RND(256))
ENDFUNCTION Color
```

Pay close attention to the use of parentheses after the function name: RandomColor(). When you want to use this function in your own program, you must include the parentheses at the end, or else DarkBASIC will give you an error message. Some commands do not need the parentheses. Can you think of why this might be the case? The answer is related to the return value. Some commands return a value, and some do not. You can spot such commands in the source code because they include parentheses at the end. In general, a command that returns a value is called a function. Some languages even use the words "procedure" and "function" so it is easier to tell them apart. DarkBASIC is more flexible, allowing you to decide whether or not one of your custom functions will return a value. Sometimes it is helpful to think of it this way: Commands *do* something, while functions *return* something.

Testing Parameters and Return Values: The ReturnValue Program

To demonstrate how to return values from functions, I've written a program called ReturnValue (see Figure 6.7), located on the CD-ROM in the folder for this chapter. Type in the following code and run the program to see how it works. This program features three functions, two of which were designed to return a value and make the main program easier to read.

For example, the custom SetColor function that I wrote is easier to use than the built-in INK command.

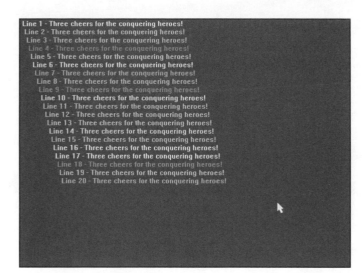

Figure 6.7 *The ReturnValue program demonstrates how to return values from functions.*

```
REMSTART
-----------------------------------
Beginner's Guide To DarkBASIC Game Programming
Copyright (C)2002 Jonathan S. Harbour and Joshua R. Smith
Chapter 6 - ReturnValue Program
-----------------------------------
REMEND

REM Initialize the program
CLS
PRINT

REM Print a message N times
FOR N = 1 TO 20
    REM Select a random color
    color = RandomColor()
    SetColor(color)

    REM Display message
    PRINT Spaces(N); "Line "; N; " - ";
    PRINT "Three cheers for the conquering heroes!"
NEXT N
```

```
WAIT KEY

REM End the program
END

REM The Spaces function returns a specified number of blanks
FUNCTION Spaces(Length)
    Temp$ = ""
    FOR A = 1 TO Length
        Temp$ = Temp$ + " "
    NEXT A
ENDFUNCTION Temp$

REM The RandomColor function returns a random color
FUNCTION RandomColor()
    Color = RGB(RND(256), RND(256), RND(256))
ENDFUNCTION Color

REM The SetColor function sets the foreground color
FUNCTION SetColor(Forecolor)
    INK Forecolor, 0
ENDFUNCTION
```

Writing Your Own Functions

You can create any custom function for your programs, with your own parameters and return values. As such, you can rewrite much of the DarkBASIC language to fit in with your own ideas of how programs should be written, or you can just combine DarkBASIC commands to perform higher-level processes. For instance, instead of just tracking the mouse, you might write your own function that moves a walking character on the screen based on where the mouse is clicked. Or you might move a spaceship around the screen using the mouse with a custom MoveShip function that you have created. The possibilities are endless, which is what makes programming so much fun! Moreover, once you have a library of functions, you can use them for other programs and cut down on your programming time.

Summary

This chapter covered the extremely important subjects of branching and subroutines, which are both related in functionality. Branching statements allow you to apply rules to a program to keep the program running in a predetermined manner and behaving correctly. In addition, you learned how to use the IF...ELSE...ENDIF statement to apply logic and rule enforcement to your programs. This chapter also showed you how to create and use your own functions, complete with parameters and return values. Functions greatly enhance the capabilities of your games, allowing you to extend DarkBASIC beyond what the designers imagined.

Chapter Quiz

The chapter quiz will help you to retain the information that was covered in this chapter, as well as give you an idea about how well you're doing at understanding the subjects. You can find the answers for this quiz in Appendix A, "Answers to the Chapter Quizzes."

1. Which command does DarkBASIC use for single-line conditional statements?

    A. IF...THEN

    B. IF...ELSE...ENDIF

    C. IF...ENDIF

    D. IF...OR...NOTIF

2. What is the purpose of a conditional statement?

    A. To ensure that your program is free of errors

    B. To generate random numbers to keep the program interesting

    C. To evaluate a logical statement and return a true or false value

    D. To divide a program into more manageable sections of code

3. What is the purpose of a subroutine?

    A. To fill in for the routine when it is not available or otherwise absent

    B. To divide a program into more manageable sections of code

    C. To keep a submarine in proper working order and to inspire discipline

    D. To evaluate a logical statement and return a true or false value

4. How many programmers does it take to screw in a light bulb?

    A. 32

    B. 1,024

    C. 16

    D. Just one to call a maintenance person

5. Which character suffix do you use to declare a string variable?

    A. #
    B. $
    C. &
    D. :-)

6. Which statement do you use to declare a custom subroutine in DarkBASIC?

    A. SUB
    B. PROCEDURE
    C. COMMAND
    D. FUNCTION

7. All functions must return a value, even if that value is null.

    A. True
    B. False

8. Which statement is used to mark the end of a function?

    A. END FUNCTION
    B. ENDFUNCTION
    C. EXIT FUNCTION
    D. END OF THE ROAD

9. What is the common synonym for a conditional statement?

    A. Reusable statement
    B. Figurative statement
    C. Branching statement
    D. Positive statement

10. Which at phrase best describes the activities of the sample Conditions program?

    A. Small town ball makes good.
    B. Bouncing is what balls do best.
    C. "Look, ma, no flicker!"
    D. Program rules and logic are best implemented with branching statements.

CHAPTER 7

More Power to the Numbers: Data Sequences and Arrays

This chapter extends the subjects of variable data types and looping processes, which were covered in previous chapters, bringing them together in a new light. As you will learn in more detail shortly, data sequences allow you to add data directly to a program without loading that data from a file or other means, which can be very useful in a game. Whereas a complete game might use data files to store information about the objects in the game (such as characters, places, ships, weapons, monsters, and so on), this type of data can be inserted into the game right from the start using data sequences. This can be very useful when you are designing an initial prototype of a game or game engine and you don't want to spend time creating game editors to design your game worlds, characters, and such.

Arrays work hand-in-hand with data sequences and even more with looping commands, with which they are able to iterate through long lists of information quickly and efficiently. While looping with variables or functions allows you to perform repeat processes easily, looping with data sequences allows you to read and apply custom values to your game. For example, suppose you are writing your own role-playing game with a character that explores dungeons and fights against monsters. The character and the monsters will have traits, such as strength, endurance, hit points, and so on. Storing monster names along with traits in a data sequence is quick and easy and allows you to make changes to the traits right inside the source code at any time. For larger projects, you would want to store traits in data files, but a data sequence will work just as well in smaller projects.

This chapter covers the following topics:

- Introduction to Data Sequences and Arrays
- Data Sequences
- Arrays

Introduction to Data Sequences and Arrays

A data sequence can store any data in sequential order. Data is read one item at a time, like an assembly line. A *stack* is another way of describing a data sequence. A stack keeps track of data in a first in, last out order. Alternatively, this can be

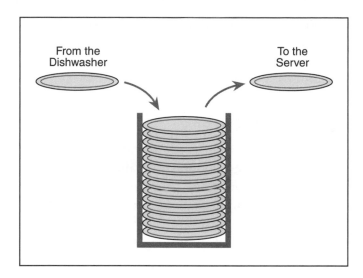

Figure 7.1 *A software stack works like a stack of plates at a buffet, where the last plate added is the first plate removed— first in, last out or last in, first out.*

described as last in, first out. Figure 7.1 illustrates a commonplace example of a stack, in which plates coming from the dishwasher are added to the stack and immediately removed for service. The first plate added to the stack might never even be used!

Keeping Track of Data

Comparing a data sequence to a stack is not entirely accurate because you can't add new items to the data sequence after the program starts running (during the run time); you can only add new items when you are editing the source code (during the design time). However, if you type in the data statements in a data sequence in order, it does resemble a design-time stack, so I thought this analogy would help you visualize how data sequences work.

Another example that is perhaps more accurate is comparing a data sequence to a sequential disk file. Chapter 15, "Loading and Saving Information Using Files," explains how to work with files, so I won't get into them in detail here other than to summarize how they work. There are two basic types of files—sequential and random-access. Sequential files are like text files that you can edit with Notepad. A program settings file, such as win.ini, is also a sequential text file that you can read with Notepad. Another type of sequential file is a binary file that stores bytes or other types of numbers. Random-access files are structured files that read and write records of data rather than a single character at a time. DarkBASIC does not support structured files because it knows how to read most game-related files natively (such as 3D Studio Max files, wave files, texture files, and so on).

The difference between a sequential file and a stack is that you must read and interpret a file using number or string variables, and you must keep track of file numbers, names, lengths, and so on. Data sequences are much easier to use! Just think of a data sequence as a simple kind of sequential file.

Storing Data Efficiently

All things being equal, data sequences are really only effective for limited amounts of data. When the data in a data sequence becomes too large, it is difficult to maintain the data in your source code file. One way around the problem of lengthy source code listings is to use the #INCLUDE command to include one or more source code files in your main program file. You can then move the data sequences over to a separate file and keep your main program listing more tidy.

What types of data can you imagine storing in a data sequence inside your program? I can think of many.

- Character traits and attributes in a role-playing game
- Spaceship names and traits in a space shooter game
- Weapon names and attack values in a first-person shooter game
- Height map data for the 3D terrain in each level of a game
- Power-ups that can be gathered
- Maps and levels for a real-time strategy game

The one drawback to using a data sequence instead of a disk file is that when the game is finished, compiled, and put up for sale or into the public domain, there won't be any way to add new levels and missions or monsters to the game later. Mission packs, add-ons, and modifications ("mods") are very popular in the gaming community. If even a simple game supports player-made levels, it will generate a fan following. Players enjoy creating their own levels and add-ons for games and then sharing their work with others. It involves a little fame, a little prestige, and a lot of fun overall.

The tradeoff is whether you want to go through the additional work required to load data into your program from disk files, rather than just storing the data inside your program. Perhaps one benefit to a data sequence is that it is like a built-in array, so you don't need to use an additional array to use it. Data stored in a file, however, would probably need to be loaded into an array, at which point it would somewhat resemble a data sequence.

Data Sequences

In this section I will show you how to create a data sequence in a DarkBASIC program. Next I'll show you the various commands for reading the data sequence and putting the data to good use. Finally, I'll show you how to reset the data sequence and start reading it from the beginning again. This might be useful when you want to restart the game, for instance.

The DATA Statement

The DATA statement defines data in a data sequence. It is specifically called a *sequence* because you can have many DATA statements in your program. In fact, you can insert a DATA command anywhere in your program, but I would recommend keeping all DATA statements at the top of the source code file for clarity. It is very confusing when you have DATA statements strewn all about your program.

One solution that you can employ with multiple data sequences is to label specific data sequences, and then jump to the labels to read them. I'll explain data labels shortly, when I cover the RESTORE statement.

The DATA statement supports strings, integer numbers, and decimal numbers. Here is a sample of a data sequence that includes a last name, first name, and age.

```
DATA "Jones", "Bob", 34
DATA "Anderson", "Julie", 19
DATA "Smith", "John", 26
DATA "Wells", "Joanne", 8
```

See how you can design the data sequence any way you want? This data can accommodate numbers and strings, but there is no way to store binary numbers or bytes—the sort of data you would need to store bitmap pixels, for instance.

The READ Command

The READ command reads data stored in a data sequence. The data is read one item at a time (where individual data items are separated by commas) from beginning to end. The READ command is flexible in that it supports integer numbers, decimal numbers, and strings (just like the DATA statement does).

The following code snippet demonstrates how to read the data sequence and print out the information. Note that this code will use the DATA statements that were shown in the previous section.

```
FOR n = 1 to 4
    READ LastName$, FirstName$, Age
    PRINT FirstName$; ", "; LastName$; ", "; Age
NEXT n
```

Do you see how the variables are printed out in a different order than they are read? When you have read the data, you can do anything you want with it! Take note also of the FOR loop, which performs the READ command four times. Even though there are 12 items in the data sequence, three of them are read each time through the loop: LastName$, FirstName$, and Age.

Testing Data Sequences: The ContactData Program

Now I'll show you a simple program I wrote that uses a data sequence filled with contact information. The data includes the following fields.

- Last name
- First name
- Address
- City
- State
- Zip
- Phone

I know you aren't particularly interested in databases, but this simple contact program is a great way to demonstrate how data sequences work. Later I'll show you a more interesting program that uses DATA statements and a modified version of the Conditions program from Chapter 6. Figure 7.2 shows the output of the ContactData program.

Now for the source code for the ContactData program. There are four DATA statements that provide the contact information used by the program. There is also a single DATA statement at the beginning of the sequence that provides the number of records that should be read. This is an important thing to remember! Without

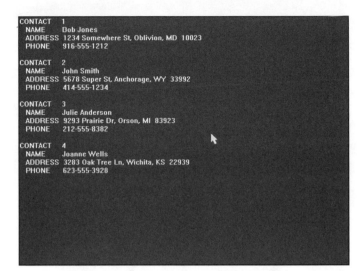

Figure 7.2 *The ContactData program demonstrates how to use the* DATA *statement and the* READ *command.*

some sort of total value, you will have to hard-code the total number of data statements into your code, and then it will be more difficult to add new DATA statements later (something that is fairly common when working with information).

For your convenience, this project is located on the CD-ROM in the Sources\CH07\ContactData folder.

```
REM -----------------------------------
REM Beginner's Guide To DarkBASIC Game Programming
REM Copyright (C)2002 Jonathan S. Harbour and Joshua R. Smith
REM Chapter 7 - ContactData Program
REM -----------------------------------

REM Declare the data sequence
DATA 4
DATA "Jones","Bob","1234 Somewhere St","Oblivion","MD","10023","916-555-1212"
DATA "Smith","John","5678 Super St","Anchorage","WY","33992","414-555-1234"
DATA "Anderson","Julie","9293 Prairie Dr","Orson","MI","83923","212-555-8382"
DATA "Wells","Joanne","3283 Oak Tree Ln","Wichita","KS","22939","623-555-3928"

REM Declare some variables
NumData = 0
FirstName$ = ""
```

```
LastName$ = ""
Address$ = ""
City$ = ""
State$ = ""
Zip$ = ""
Phone$ = ""

REM Initialize the program
SYNC ON

REM Read the record count
READ NumData

REM Read and print out the data sequence
FOR n = 1 to NumData
    REM Read the data sequence
    READ LastName$, FirstName$, Address$, City$, State$, Zip$, Phone$

    REM Print the contact information
    PRINT "CONTACT        "; n
    PRINT "    NAME       "; FirstName$; " "; LastName$
    PRINT "    ADDRESS    "; Address$; ", ";City$; ", "; State$; "   "; Zip$
    PRINT "    PHONE      "; Phone$
    PRINT

    SYNC
NEXT n

REM Wait for key press
WAIT KEY

REM End the program
END
```

Have you noticed that I always include a variable declarations section in the sample programs? Although DarkBASIC doesn't require it, I highly recommend that you include a section at the top of your program for important variables so you can identify them more easily. It can be very confusing when variables are declared at random throughout the source code. This is a good programming practice rather than a requirement of DarkBASIC. Most programming languages require you to declare variables anyway, so it's a good habit to acquire.

The RESTORE Command

The RESTORE command moves the internal data sequence position to the beginning of the list where the first DATA statement is located, so the next READ command will pick up the first item of data again. The RESTORE command also supports data labels that allow you to group related items of data.

You can call the RESTORE command on its own, in which case the data sequence position will move to the top of the list. If you want to move the position to a data label, just add the name of the label after the RESTORE command. The syntax of this command is RESTORE *data label*.

Using the RESTORE Command: The MonsterList Program

The RESTORE command might be simple, but it is actually a very powerful command that can give your programs some interesting capabilities. I have written a program called MonsterList that demonstrates using the RESTORE command with data labels. Figure 7.3 shows the output from the MonsterList program.

The source code for the MonsterList program follows. Pay attention to the placement of the labels (shown in bold) and also the first DATA statement, which just includes the name of the program. This is a filler data item to demonstrate how the RESTORE command will jump to a label rather than starting from the top if you use it in that manner. It is just a coincidence that there are four monsters and four

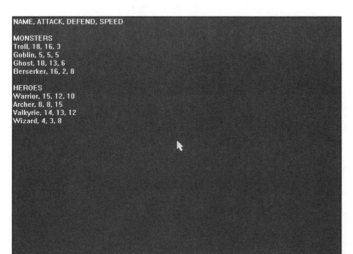

Figure 7.3 *The MonsterList program demonstrates how to use the* RESTORE *statement with data labels.*

heroes in the program; feel free to add more data to the list to see how the program easily supports additional data. Just be sure to update the `NumData` value to reflect the number of data records used.

```
REM -----------------------------------
REM Beginner's Guide To DarkBASIC Game Programming
REM Copyright (C)2002 Jonathan S. Harbour and Joshua R. Smith
REM Chapter 7 - MonsterList Program
REM -----------------------------------

REM Misc data
DATA "Monster List Program"

REM Hero data
heroes:
DATA 4
DATA "Warrior", 15, 12, 10
DATA "Archer", 8, 8, 15
DATA "Valkyrie", 14, 13, 12
DATA "Wizard", 4, 3, 8

REM Monster data
monsters:
DATA 4
DATA "Troll", 18, 16, 3
DATA "Goblin", 5, 5, 5
DATA "Ghost", 10, 13, 6
DATA "Berserker", 16, 2, 8

REM Declare some variables
NumData = 0
Name$ = ""
Attack = 0
Defend = 0
Speed = 0

REM Initialize the program
SYNC ON
```

```
PRINT "NAME, ATTACK, DEFEND, SPEED"
PRINT

REM Print out the monsters
PRINT "MONSTERS"
RESTORE monsters
PrintData

REM Print out the heroes
PRINT "HEROES"
RESTORE heroes
PrintData

REM Wait for key press
WAIT KEY

REM End the program
END

FUNCTION PrintData()
    REM Read the record count
    READ NumData

    REM Read and print out the data sequence
    FOR n = 1 to NumData
        REM Read the data sequence
        READ Name$, Attack, Defend, Speed

        REM Print the information
        PRINT Name$; ", ";
        PRINT Attack; ", ";
        PRINT Defend; ", ";
        PRINT Speed

        SYNC
    NEXT n
    PRINT
ENDFUNCTION
```

Arrays

Wouldn't you agree that data sequences are fun and an interesting way to add information to a game? I can certainly appreciate the number of uses for data statements and commands that DarkBASIC provides. This section is related to data sequences, although arrays are more focused on real-time data and are more useful when reading data from disk files. In this section, I'll show you what arrays can do and how you can use them to improve your programs' capabilities. The last demonstration program in this chapter is called BouncingBalls—I'll leave what the program does to your imagination.

What Is an Array?

An array is a sequential list of values with the same data type, such as integer, decimal, or string. Unlike data sequences, in which you can mix and match data, arrays must be filled with the same kind of data. When creating the array, you must use the dollar sign or pound sign to specify a string or decimal array, respectively. You don't use any character to specify the default integer data type for the elements of the array.

Given enough memory, there is no set maximum number of elements you can allocate in an array. It is perfectly legal to create an array with a hundred million elements! However, you will want to make sure enough memory is available before allocating a huge array, by using the memory function SYSTEM TMEM AVAILABLE or SYSTEM SMEM AVAILABLE.

Creating an Array with DIM

You use the DIM command to create an array variable. This is a keyword in DarkBASIC that you might recognize if you have ever used Visual Basic (which uses DIM for all variables, not just arrays). The DIM statement syntax is DIM VariableName(Number of Elements).

VariableName can be any name of your choosing; it is similar to any ordinary variable name. The number of elements in the array is the parameter that goes inside the parentheses. DarkBASIC is a forgiving language in that the starting number for arrays can be 0 or 1, and the upper range of the array is still the number you specified. In most programming languages, the Number of Elements value for an array can mean 1 to 30 or 0 to 29. In other words, there are exactly 30 elements to the array. However, DarkBASIC always allocates one extra index for the array, so you can use 0 or 1 and still go up to the value you specified for the upper limit.

Since DarkBASIC is lenient in this way, take care to be consistent in how you use arrays. If you treat the first element of the array as 0, then stick to it throughout your program to avoid confusion. If you prefer 1, then stick to that.

Deleting an Array with UNDIM

If for any reason you need to delete an array after you have created it with DIM, you can use the UNDIM command to remove the array from memory. This statement is provided so you can recreate the array with DIM. There are some cases in which this might be useful, such as when you are restarting the game, but I personally avoid using UNDIM and prefer to use an array throughout the program or create additional arrays when needed. One possible benefit to the UNDIM command is in a situation in which you no longer need an array and you want to free up memory to improve your game's performance. If you created a really big array and you no longer need it at some point in the program, go ahead and delete it with UNDIM. However, you don't need to delete any arrays at the end of the program because DarkBASIC will de-allocate memory automatically; you don't need to worry about memory in DarkBASIC.

Testing Arrays: The BouncingBall Program

To fully demonstrate how arrays work and how you can use them to their greatest potential, I have written a program called BouncingBalls. This program starts by creating several arrays with the DIM command to keep track of the position and speed of 30 balls on the screen. It then creates the balls, each with a random position, speed, and diameter. The main part of the program moves and draws all 30 balls over and over, resulting in a more advanced version of the Conditions program that you saw in Chapter 6.

Testing the Program

The BouncingBalls program creates 30 balls on the screen by keeping track of each ball in an array. It then uses a loop to draw each ball before updating the screen. The result is a high-speed demonstration of balls bouncing off the edges of the screen. Each ball is a different size—some are very small and some are very large. Figure 7.4 shows the program running at standard resolution, and Figure 7.5 is a tweaked version running at 1600×1200.

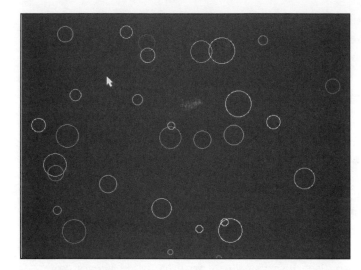

Figure 7.4 *The BouncingBalls program demonstrates the use of arrays to store the position and velocity of balls on the screen.*

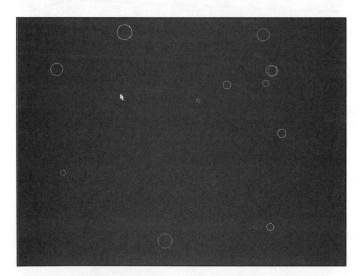

Figure 7.5 *The BouncingBalls program running at 1600×1200.*

Writing the Source Code

The source code for the BouncingBalls program follows. I have bolded the section of code that actually creates the arrays, as well as the section that animates the balls on the screen (further down in the listing). This program is similar to the Conditions program from Chapter 6, but I have moved the logic that bounces the balls off each of the four edges of the screen into a function.

I have also added a new function called DrawRect, which draws the border around the screen using LINE commands. The most important function in the program is MoveBall, which has a Num parameter that identifies the elements of the ball arrays that should be used to draw the balls on the screen.

TIP

To really see what this program can do, go through the code and replace the 30-element arrays with some larger number, such as 1,000, and see what happens!

```
REM ---------------------------------
REM Beginner's Guide To DarkBASIC Game Programming
REM Copyright (C)2002 Jonathan S. Harbour and Joshua R. Smith
REM Chapter 7 - BouncingBalls Program
REM ---------------------------------

REM Create some variables
DIM BallX(30)
DIM BallY(30)
DIM BallSize(30)
DIM SpeedX(30)
DIM Speedy(30)
DIM Color(30)

REM Initialize the program
SET DISPLAY MODE 640, 480, 32
SYNC ON

REM Initialize the balls
InitializeBalls

REM Start the main loop
DO
    REM Clear the screen
    CLS

    REM Set the border color
    INK RGB(255,255,255), 0

    REM Draw the screen border
    DrawRect(0,0,639,479)
```

```
    REM Move and draw the balls
    FOR n = 1 TO 30
        MoveBall(n)
    NEXT n

    REM Redraw the screen
    SYNC
LOOP

REM End program
END

FUNCTION InitializeBalls()
    FOR n = 1 TO 30
        BallX(n) = RND(640)
        BallY(n) = RND(480)
        BallSize(n) = RND(20) + 5
        SpeedX(n) = RND(12) - 6
        SpeedY(n) = RND(12) - 6
        Color(n) = RGB(RND(256), RND(256), RND(256))
    NEXT n
ENDFUNCTION

FUNCTION MoveBall(Num)
    REM Move the ball
    BallX(Num) = BallX(Num) + SpeedX(Num)
    BallY(Num) = BallY(Num) + SpeedY(Num)

    REM Check conditions for the BallX
    IF BallX(Num) > 640 - BallSize(Num)
        BallX(Num) = 640 - BallSize(Num)
        SpeedX(Num) = SpeedX(Num) * -1
    ELSE
        IF BallX(Num) < BallSize(Num)
            BallX(Num) = BallSize(Num)
            SpeedX(Num) = SpeedX(Num) * -1
        ENDIF
    ENDIF

    REM Check conditions for BallY
```

```
    IF BallY(Num) > 480 - BallSize(Num)
        BallY(Num) = 480 - BallSize(Num)
        SpeedY(Num) = SpeedY(Num) * -1
    ELSE
        IF BallY(Num) < BallSize(Num)
            BallY(Num) = BallSize(Num)
            SpeedY(Num) = SpeedY(Num) * -1
        ENDIF
    ENDIF

    REM Draw the ball
    INK Color(Num), 0
    CIRCLE BallX(Num), BallY(Num), BallSize(Num)
ENDFUNCTION

FUNCTION DrawRect(Left,Top,Right,Bottom)
    LINE Left, Top, Right, top
    LINE Right, Top, Right, Bottom
    LINE Right, Bottom, Left, Bottom
    LINE Left, Bottom, Left, Top
ENDFUNCTION
```

Summary

This chapter explained the benefits and uses for data sequences and arrays in DarkBASIC. You learned how to add items of data to your programs using the DATA and READ commands, including the ability to use data labels to group related data items. You also learned all about arrays and how to use them. Several sample programs graced the pages of this chapter, including the ContactData and MonsterList programs, which showed you how to use data sequences.

The BouncingBalls program was a great demonstration of using arrays. Although you might not have realized it at the time, the program very closely resembles a real game! Later chapters on bitmaps and sprite animation will take this to another level, but this chapter provided you with a taste of what is to come. If you found the BouncingBalls program intriguing, then you will really enjoy Chapter 9, "Basic Graphics Commands," which goes into detail about how to use all of the 2D drawing commands supported by DarkBASIC.

Chapter Quiz

The chapter quiz will help you retain the information that was covered in this chapter, as well as give you an idea about how well you're doing at understanding the subjects. You will find the answers for this quiz in Appendix A, "Answers to the Chapter Quizzes."

1. Which command or statement is used to declare a data sequence?

   A. READ
   B. UNDIM
   C. DATA
   D. DIM

2. How does the READ command read a data sequence?

   A. Sequentially
   B. Randomly
   C. Telepathically
   D. Structurally

3. Which command can be used to move the pointer in a data sequence back to the beginning?

   A. READ
   B. DIM
   C. INPUT
   D. RESTORE

4. What is a list of related data stored in sequential order within the source code called?

   A. Array
   B. Data sequence
   C. Disk file
   D. Structured

5. If an array is created with DIM A(10), how many elements are usable in the array?

   A. 10
   B. 9
   C. 1
   D. 11

6. What types of data can you store inside a data sequence or an array?

    A. Integers, variables, and arrays

    B. Integers, decimals, and strings

    C. Numbers, strings, and constants

    D. Bytes, binary numbers, and currency

7. Arrays can't store strings, just integers or decimals.

    A. True

    B. False

8. What is the largest number of elements that you can allocate in an array?

    A. 32

    B. 4,096

    C. 16,384

    D. Limited only by the available memory

9. Which command did the BouncingBalls program use to draw each ball?

    A. `INK`

    B. `LINE`

    C. `CIRCLE`

    D. `ELLIPSE`

10. What does the `RESTORE monsters` command accomplish in the MonsterList program?

    A. Rejuvenates all slain monsters in the game

    B. Moves all monsters back to their starting positions

    C. Moves the `DATA` pointer to the first data item following the `monsters` label

    D. Tells all of the monsters to attack the heroes

CHAPTER 8

NUMBER CRUNCHING: MATHEMATICAL AND RELATIONAL OPERATORS AND COMMANDS

This chapter is all about number crunching, which is another way of referring to mathematical and relational programming. These are very important features that you will need to write useful programs. While the basic math operations of addition, subtraction, multiplication, and division are supported in all programming languages, DarkBASIC also has support for exponents and trigonometry. DarkBASIC makes it easy and fun to write math programs. While learning these new tricks, you'll learn about random numbers, reading date and time, and using relational operators (greater than, equal to, less than, and so on). Along the way, I'll show you how to extend these commands by adding functionality of your own.

This chapter covers the following topics:

- Mathematical Operators
- Relational Operators
- Basic Math Commands
- Random Numbers
- Reading the Date and Time
- Higher Math Commands

Mathematical Operators

DarkBASIC provides a good assortment of mathematical operators that you can use in your programs. These operators are built into the language. The basic math operations for performing addition, subtraction, multiplication, and division, as well as working with exponents, are a common feature of all programming languages, so you can use what you learn in DarkBASIC with other languages as well.

Addition

The plus sign is used to add numbers (integers or decimals) from one or more variables, including for variable assignment and formulas used in branching statements. Addition is commonly used to increment the value of a counter variable, as shown in this example.

```
REM Initialize the variable
N = 0
```

```
REM Increment the variable
N = N + 10
```

Remember, it is good programming practice to declare all variables before you use them, even if DarkBASIC doesn't require you to do so. There's no rule stating that you *must* set N to 0 before incrementing it. However, it is just good practical sense, not to mention very helpful when you are modifying the program later. I have written many programs when I was in a hurry and didn't comment my code enough. Coming back to a poorly written program is very difficult because months later you won't remember how the program works! DarkBASIC automatically sets numbers to zero upon initialization, but I always initialize variables. This has the added benefit of helping someone down the road understand how the program works.

The last line, N = N + 10, is called a *formula* because the variable on the left side is assigned the results of the right side, which is the formula N + 10.

Using Return Values in a Formula

You could just as easily use a function to return a number that is assigned to the variable, as shown in the following code.

```
REM Create a function
FUNCTION Twelve()
    Number = 12
ENDFUNCTION Number

REM Initialize a variable
N = 0

REM Add the function value to the variable
N = N + Twelve()
```

Now, suppose you try to add some letters to a number. What do you think will happen? Because the variable N was created as a number, the DarkBASIC compiler will complain if you try to add some text to the number variable. For example, this code:

```
N = 0
N = 10 + "ABC"
```

will generate a compiler error message like this:

```
Syntax Error. Unrecognized parameter at line 2
```

DarkBASIC was expecting to see another number to add to the variable N but instead it got a string, so it didn't know what to do! You can, in fact, add strings together just like you can numbers, but you have to declare a string with the dollar sign character ($). For example, the following code is a valid program.

```
D$ = "Dark"
D$ = D$ + "BASIC"
PRINT D$
```

The INC Command

The INC command in DarkBASIC is quite useful; it increments a variable by a specified value. If you just want to increment a variable by 1, you can leave the value parameter blank. In the following example, the answer reported by DarkBASIC is 30.

```
Num = 10
INC Num, 20
PRINT Num
```

Subtraction

Subtraction is also so simple that it hardly requires explanation. Unlike addition, however, you can't subtract one string from another. You can obviously subtract numbers, but strings can only be appended together, using the convenient + operator. Following is an example of how to subtract two numbers.

```
N = 100
P = 75
N = N - P
PRINT N
```

Subtracting Multiple Numbers

You can also subtract more than two numbers. You can actually have as many subtractions in a single formula as you want, within reason. Here's another example:

```
A = 100
B = -10
C = 1972
D = 1939492
E = -100
N = A - B - C - D - E - 200
PRINT N
```

What do you think the answer to this problem is? Well, go ahead and type it into DarkBASIC and see what answer it returns. Don't be surprised if the answer is a large negative number (thanks to the D variable).

Quick Subtraction

Let me show you a quick way to subtract large numbers in your head, because this is a valuable tool for counting change, especially if you work in a retail store. You will also amaze your friends after learning how to do it. What's the most common type of change returned? Change for a one-dollar bill, a ten-dollar bill, or a twenty-dollar bill, right? Multiples of 10 are difficult to use because 10 has two digits, which makes it hard to carry over the number from 10. However, it's really easy to subtract with a 9 because there is no number to carry.

Here's an example. A customer's total bill is $8.37, and he hands you a ten-dollar bill. The change is $1.63, and I came up with that in only a couple seconds in my head. You're thinking, "Yeah, right. You used a calculator." Not at all! Let me show you how I did it. Change the 10.00 into 9.99 in your head. Subtract 9–8, and you get 1. Subtract 9–3, and you get 6. Subtract 9–7, and you get 2. The key is to always remember to add one to the final answer, since you were using nines.

Figure 8.1 shows the old-school way of doing subtraction, and Figure 8.2 shows the faster method.

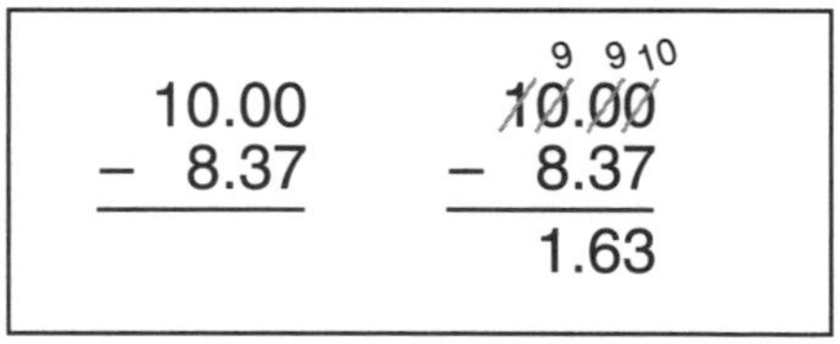

```
                        9  9 10
   10.00              1̶0̶.̶0̶0̶
 -  8.37             -  8.37
 _____             _____
                        1.63
```

Figure 8.1 *In old-school subtraction problems, you must borrow and carry digits.*

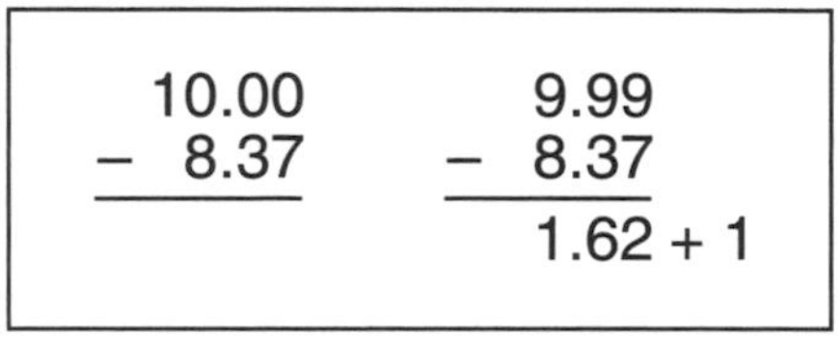

```
   10.00               9.99
 -  8.37             -  8.37
 _____             _____
                      1.62 + 1
```

Figure 8.2 *The faster method of subtraction using nines*

Of course, this method works with more than just money. Any number that can be broken down into easy-to-use nines will work with this technique.

The DEC Command

The DEC command is a useful way to decrement a value from a variable. If you just want to do a simple decrement by 1, leave the value parameter blank. The following example demonstrates the DEC command; the answer reported by DarkBASIC is 80.

```
Num = 100
DEC Num, 20
PRINT Num
```

Multiplication

Multiplication was derived from addition, and it can be put into a table for easy memorization. I'm sure you memorized multiplication tables in elementary school, like most kids. The ability to quickly multiply numbers in your head is invaluable in day-to-day life. But for larger numbers, it's not as easy. Any number larger than 12 will stump the vast majority of us, and that is where a calculator comes in handy. Like most programming languages, DarkBASIC uses the asterisk character (*) for multiplication. Here is an example:

```
A = 27
B = 19
C = A * B
```

How about a real-world example? The circumference of a circle is the distance around the circle, as if you were to wrap a measuring tape around your waist to get measurements for a new suit or dress. To calculate the circumference of a circle, you multiply two times the radius times π (Pi, a Greek character that is pronounced like *pie*), or $C = 2\pi r$. Expressed in DarkBASIC source code, here is how you can calculate circumference.

```
PI# = 3.14159265
Radius# = 6
Circumference# = 2 * PI# * Radius#
PRINT "Circumference = "; Circumference#
This program produces the following output.
Circumference = 37.6991
```

This brings up an important point about the types of data that can be stored in your variables. Did you notice the pound sign (#) after each of the variables in the previous code listing? That tells DarkBASIC that those are decimal numbers. If you omit the pound sign *anywhere* a variable is used, DarkBASIC will treat it as an integer and you will lose any decimal places that were part of the number. In the case of the previous listing, it's essential that the variables have decimal places, or else DarkBASIC will fail to calculate the circumference of the circle properly. Just remember that you have to use the pound sign every time the variable is used, just like you have to use the dollar sign every time you use a string variable in the program.

Division

The average human mind can handle addition, subtraction, and multiplication pretty well (at least with small numbers), but for some reason, most people have trouble with division. Division used to be problematic for computers too, because it requires a lot more work than multiplication. Of course, this means that a computer might have been able to do ten million divisions per second versus one hundred million additions, subtractions, or multiplications. Fortunately, modern processors are now optimized to handle division quickly and efficiently, which is part of the reason why 3D graphics are so amazing today. (Another reason why we have such great 3D games today is that modern processors are able to handle decimals just as easily as integers.)

In general, you don't need to worry about how long a math calculation will take because all of the really speed-intensive stuff is built into DarkBASIC. At best, your DarkBASIC programs are scripts that the engine runs, which are not limited in speed by one data type or another. Now let me give you a simple example of integer division.

```
A = 5000
B = 1000
C = A / B
PRINT "C = "; C
```

Here is another example of a division operation, this time using a decimal number. This short program converts a temperature from Fahrenheit to Celsius.

```
Fahren# = 30
Celsius# = 5 * (Fahren# - 32) / 9
PRINT Fahren#; " F = "; Celsius#; " C"
```

Exponentiation

There is another basic math operator in DarkBASIC that can be very useful. The exponent operator (^) is the Shift-6 character. An exponent is a number raised to a power, which means that number is multiplied by itself a given number of times. For example, 10×10=100, while 10×10×10=1000. The exponent character lets you quickly calculate an exponent. For example, suppose you wanted to calculate 57 to the power of 8. You could write a program that calculates the power of a number the hard way, as follows.

```
Number = 57
Result = Number
FOR N = 1 TO 7
    Result = Result * Number
NEXT N
PRINT "Answer = "; Result
```

Note that the loop steps from 1 to 7 because the first calculation starts with 2 in an exponent, such as `Number * Number`. DarkBASIC prints out the following answer.

```
Answer = 106450183
```

That's a whopping big number! Be careful when using exponents because seemingly small numbers raised to a power suddenly become enormous. Also, be careful not to calculate a number that is too big for the variable to handle. DarkBASIC variables have a large range, in the billions, but a number can easily get into the billions when you use exponents. Here's the same calculation using the exponent operator instead.

```
Number = 57
Result = Number ^ 8
PRINT "Answer = "; Result
```

This simple example shows why it is helpful to learn all of the features in DarkBASIC before attempting to solve a problem the hard way. Check the PDF on the CD, DarkBASIC Language Reference, for a reference of DarkBASIC commands and data types.

Relational Operators

The human mind is extremely adept at seeing the differences and relationships between individual things and among groups of things, such as the classic example of individual trees in a forest (also an individual thing). By simply driving through a forest, you can tell at a glance what types of trees make up the forest, such as pines, oaks, and spruces. This ability is called *pattern recognition*, and it is the basis for memory.

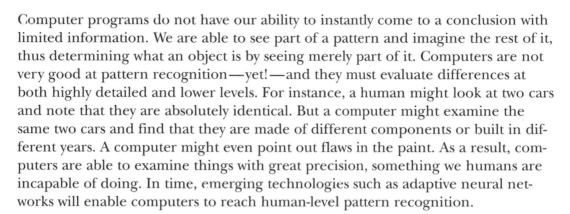

Computer programs do not have our ability to instantly come to a conclusion with limited information. We are able to see part of a pattern and imagine the rest of it, thus determining what an object is by seeing merely part of it. Computers are not very good at pattern recognition—yet!—and they must evaluate differences at both highly detailed and lower levels. For instance, a human might look at two cars and note that they are absolutely identical. But a computer might examine the same two cars and find that they are made of different components or built in different years. A computer might even point out flaws in the paint. As a result, computers are able to examine things with great precision, something we humans are incapable of doing. In time, emerging technologies such as adaptive neural networks will enable computers to reach human-level pattern recognition.

This technology has already been put into practical use for speech and character recognition. Indeed, computers that are capable of listening to human speech and understanding the scratches we call human written language make an impression on humans that is often eerily lifelike. These basic faculties that have set us somehow above the raw processing power of computers have given many of us an air of superiority. When confronted with computers that seem to have similar behavior—by merely exhibiting pattern recognition—the implications can be somewhat frightening to those not directly involved in the computer industry. Give a computer pattern recognition and limited conversational programming, and the result is startlingly human-like.

While neural networks and artificial intelligence are fascinating subjects, as a programmer you will need to master a few basic concepts before you attempt to bring a computer to life. For one thing, you need to understand how to give a program some simple logic because logic is what gives a program the ability to work with data. To add logic to your programs, you need to use something called a *relational operator.*

Relational operators deal with how values compare to each other, or rather, how they *relate* to each other. Relational operators are usually found within formulas that result in a Boolean (true or false) value, and are based on simple rules: equal to, not equal to, greater than, and less than. Data types determine the way objects relate to one another. Variables of the same data type can be evaluated against each other, but variables of different data types cannot be compared using a relational operator. For example, you can't compare "1" with 1 because the first number is actually a string (with quotes). To make a comparison of this sort, you need to convert the string to a number, which applies only if the string actually contains a valid number.

The following sections cover the actual operators used to perform relational comparisons, along with a description of how to use each one. Table 8.1 provides a quick reference of these operators.

Table 8.1 Relational Operators

Operator	Description
=	Equal to
<>	Not equal to
<	Less than
>	Greater than
<=	Less than or equal to
>=	Greater than or equal to

Equal To

The equal to operator (=) tests for the equality of two values in a formula. The equals sign also assigns values to variables, but DarkBASIC can tell the difference. Here is an example of a test for an equal condition:

```
IF A = B
    PRINT "A is equal to B"
ELSE
    PRINT "A is not equal to B"
ENDIF
```

Not Equal To

To test for inequality, use the not equal to operator (<>), which is the opposite of the equal to operator. Here is an example:

```
IF A <> B
    PRINT "A is not equal to B"
```

```
ELSE
    PRINT "A is equal to B"
ENDIF
```

Less Than

The less than operator (<) returns true when the first operand is less than the second operand in a formula. Keep in mind that this applies to any data type. You could even compare two strings; if the ASCII values of the first string are less than the ASCII values of the second string, then the less than comparison will return true. Here is an example:

```
IF A < B
    PRINT "A is less than B"
ELSE
    PRINT "A is not less than B"
ENDIF
```

Greater Than

The greater than operator (>) returns true when the first operand is greater than the second operand in a formula, as the following example demonstrates.

```
IF A > B
    PRINT "A is greater than B"
ELSE
    PRINT "A is not greater than B"
END IF
```

Less Than or Equal To

The less than or equal to operator is a combination of two other operators—equal to (=) and less than (<). Here is an example:

```
IF A <= B
    PRINT "A is less than or equal to B"
ELSE
    PRINT "A is not less than or equal to B"
ENDIF
```

Remember that combining two operators in this way is the same as checking each one separately. You could accomplish the same result by creating a formula that combines both operators using the logical OR operator, as follows.

```
IF A < B OR A = B
    PRINT "A is less than or equal to B"
ELSE
    PRINT "A is not less than or equal to B"
ENDIF
```

Greater Than or Equal To

The last relational operator, greater than or equal to, is also a combination of two operators—greater than (>) and equal to (=). Here is an example:

```
IF A >= B
    PRINT "A is greater than or equal to B"
ELSE
    PRINT "A is not greater than or equal to B"
ENDIF
```

Just like in the previous example, you can accomplish the same thing by writing a compound relational formula, such as this:

```
IF A > B OR A = B
    PRINT "A is greater than or equal to B"
ELSE
    PRINT "A is not greater than or equal to B"
ENDIF
```

Basic Math Commands

DarkBASIC has several useful math commands; I will go over the basic ones here. I'll explain the more advanced math commands later in this chapter.

The SQRT Command

The SQRT command is short for "square root." The square root of a number X is the value which, when multiplied by itself, results in the number X. The square root is the opposite of a number raised to the second power (N ^ 2). Consider an earlier example, 10×10=100. The square root of 100 is 10, or rather, SQRT(100) = 10.

Remember that this differs from exponents in general in that the square root only applies to a squared number. Here is an example:

```
A = 100
B = SQRT(A)
PRINT "The square root of "; A; " is "; B; "."
```

The ABS Command

The ABS command returns the absolute value of a number that is passed as a parameter. The absolute value is simply the positive magnitude of any number. For example, ABS(5) = ABS(-5) = 5. You will use this command often when you are certain that a negative value would be detrimental to the outcome of a formula, such as when calculating the circumference of a circle. In the unusual event that a radius value is negative, you would use the ABS command to ensure a positive value before performing the calculation.

The INT Command

The INT command returns the largest integer before the decimal point of a floating-point number. In other words, when passed as a parameter to INT, the decimal portion of the number is simply dropped.

The EXP Command

The EXP command returns a result raised to the power of a number (both of which must be integers).

Random Numbers

You often need a random number to mix up something, such as a virtual deck of cards or pair of dice. Random numbers are frequently used in games to keep the game play interesting from one scene to the next. Randomness is also a factor when you are dealing with data encryption and compression, as well as in simulation programs (such as business and financial simulations). For example, suppose you want to move an enemy ship around the screen to attack a player. It is more of a challenge if the enemy ship moves from place to place in an unpredictable manner instead of a predetermined manner; random numbers can help you accomplish this.

Creating Random Numbers

DarkBASIC provides an easy-to-use random number generator called RND, which returns an integer. When using RND, the important thing to remember is that it generates a range of random numbers from 0 to the passed parameter value. While some programming languages will return a number from 0 to N−1 (that is, one less than the passed value), DarkBASIC generates random numbers from 0 to the actual value passed to it. That means RND(5) could result in 0, 5, or anything between the two. Following are some examples of possible random numbers generated with RND.

```
RND(2000) = 1039
RND(1000000) = 9329193
RND(20) = 18
```

As you can see, these numbers all fall between 0 and the passed value. If you want to exclude 0 from the result, you need to subtract 1 from the passed value, and then add 1 to the returned value. Here's some code that simulates rolling a six-sided die:

```
Num = RND(6 - 1) + 1
```

Why pass 6 - 1 to RND? Since there is no zero on a die, you need to add 1 to the final result. But that means the answer could be from 1 to 7. Obviously, you would want to write the code like this:

```
Num = RND(5) + 1
```

However, it might be even more convenient to write a function that returns a random number based on one rather than zero (which is useful in real-world programs, such as ones that simulate the throwing of dice). Here is how you would write the function, which I have called Random:

```
FUNCTION Random(MaxValue)
    Number = RND(MaxValue - 1) + 1
ENDFUNCTION Number
```

Also, note that the random number is always an integer or a whole number; decimal random numbers are never returned.

Give it a try yourself by typing in the following Asterisks program. This program uses RND to draw rows of asterisks on the screen. Figure 8.3 shows the output from the Asterisks program.

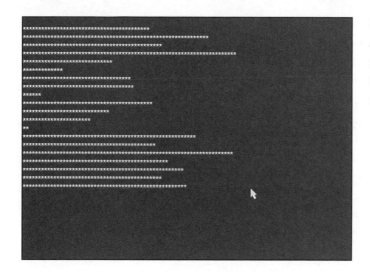

Figure 8.3 The Asterisks program prints a random number of characters on each line.

```
REM ----------------------------------
REM Beginner's Guide To DarkBASIC Game Programming
REM Copyright (C)2002 Jonathan S. Harbour and Joshua R. Smith
REM Chapter 8 - Asterisks Program
REM ----------------------------------

SYNC ON
PRINT
FOR A = 1 TO 20
    Length = RND(69) + 1
    FOR B = 1 TO Length
        PRINT "*";
    NEXT B
    PRINT
    SYNC
NEXT A
WAIT KEY
END
```

The RANDOMIZE Command

Random numbers generated in DarkBASIC are repeatable, meaning that if you stop a program and restart it, the same numbers could be generated in the same order. To get around this problem and generate truly random numbers in every instance, you must seed the random number generator so that it uses something other than the default of zero. The RANDOMIZE command was created for this purpose.

Any time you plan to use random numbers, simply call RANDOMIZE at the start of the program and pass it an integer value. The best value to use is the TIMER command, which returns the internal system time in milliseconds (where 1,000 milliseconds equal one second). By passing TIMER to the RANDOMIZE command, you are sure to get unique numbers each time the program is run. TIMER is also useful for testing the speed at which things run in DarkBASIC. I'll show you more uses for this command in later chapters. The following line of code shows the RANDOMIZE command with the TIMER command passed to it.

```
RANDOMIZE TIMER()
```

Reading the Date and Time

Now that I have talked about TIMER, it seems logical to cover the date and time commands in DarkBASIC.

The GET DATE$ Command

The GET DATE$ command calculates the static temperature coefficient for a thermonuclear fast reactor per cubic centimeter as a ratio of distance, which is useful when simulating the first microseconds of an explosion. For it to return a plausible result, you must pass the command a parameter for the estimated blast radius.

Just kidding! But I caught you off guard, right? Hmm, I wonder whether there is software to perform that sort of calculation. Oh well, back to the subject at hand. The GET DATE$ command returns a text string containing the current date.

The following code:

```
PRINT GET DATE$()
```

sends a date to the screen that looks something like this:

```
08/05/02
```

Using Four-Digit Years

If you want a four-digit date, you can write a function like the following to accomplish the task.

```
FUNCTION GetDate()
    Date$ = LEFT$(GET DATE$(), 6)
    Date$ = Date$ + "20" + RIGHT$(GET DATE$(), 2)
ENDFUNCTION Date$
```

The "20" is perfectly fine in this case because GET DATE$ returns only the current date. You aren't dealing with past dates—just the current date, which will never go back to the previous century (unless the system clock is not set).

Using Long Date Format

DarkBASIC only provides one format with the GET DATE$ command. If you want to use a long date format with the month spelled out, it will require some additional work. Suppose you want to come up with the following output.

```
Short date: 8/5/2002
Medium date: Aug 5, 2002
Long date: August 5, 2002
```

To print out the long date format, you must significantly enhance the GetDate function that you wrote earlier and add a month array containing the name of each month. After that, the program will be able to parse the date string and put together the desired date. Figure 8.4 shows the output from the PrintDates program, which follows.

```
REM --------------------------------
REM Beginner's Guide To DarkBASIC Game Programming
REM Copyright (C)2002 Jonathan S. Harbour and Joshua R. Smith
REM Chapter 8 - PrintDates Program
REM --------------------------------

DATA "January","February","March","April","May","June"
DATA "July","August","September","October","November","December"
DIM Months$(12)

REM Fill the Months array
FOR N = 1 TO 12
    READ Months$(N)
```

```
NEXT N

REM Print all three date formats
PRINT "Short date: "; GetDate("short")
PRINT "Medium date: "; GetDate("medium")
PRINT "Long date: "; GetDate("long")
WAIT KEY
END

FUNCTION GetDate(format$)
    REM Initialize variables
    Date$ = ""
    Year$ = ""
    Month = 0
    Day = 0

    REM Retrieve month, day, year
    Year$ = "20" + RIGHT$(GET DATE$(), 2)
    Month = VAL(LEFT$(GET DATE$(), 2))
    Day = VAL(LEFT$(RIGHT$(GET DATE$(), 5), 2))

    REM Return short date
    IF format$ = "short"
        Date$ = STR$(Month) + "/" + STR$(Day)
        Date$ = Date$ + "/" + Year$
    ENDIF

    REM Return medium date
    IF format$ = "medium"
        Date$ = LEFT$(Months$(Month), 3) + " "
        Date$ = Date$ + STR$(Day) + ", " + Year$
    ENDIF

    REM Return long date
    IF format$ = "long"
        Date$ = Months$(Month) + " " + STR$(Day)
        Date$ = Date$ + ", " + Year$
    ENDIF
ENDFUNCTION Date$
```

Figure 8.4 *The PrintDates program displays the current date in three different formats.*

The GET TIME$ Command

The GET TIME$ command returns the current time in 24-hour format. The following line of code:

```
PRINT GET TIME$()
```

produces the following output:

```
18:15:31
```

If you want to get a regular 12-hour time format with "AM" or "PM," you must write a little extra code to convert the default time into 12-hour time. The following program will do just that, as shown in Figure 8.5.

```
REM ---------------------------------
REM Beginner's Guide To DarkBASIC Game Programming
REM Copyright (C)2002 Jonathan S. Harbour and Joshua R. Smith
REM Chapter 8 - PrintTime Program
REM ---------------------------------

PRINT "The current time is "; GetTime()
WAIT KEY
END
```

```
FUNCTION GetTime()
    REM Declare some variables
    Time$ = ""
    AMPM$ = ""
    Hour = 0

    REM Format the time
    Hour = VAL(LEFT$(GET TIME$(), 2))
    IF Hour > 12
        Hour = Hour - 12
        AMPM$ = " PM"
    ELSE
        AMPM$ = " AM"
    ENDIF

    REM Return the time
    Time$ = STR$(Hour) + RIGHT$(GET TIME$(), 6) + AMPM$
ENDFUNCTION Time$
```

Figure 8.5 *The PrintTime program displays the current time in 12-hour format.*

Higher Math Commands

In addition to the basic math commands, random numbers, and date/time commands, DarkBASIC also features a set of advanced math commands for trigonometry. However, this is a computer-programming book (not a geometry book), so I don't have time to explain what all of these commands are used for or exactly how to use them. I will show you how to use the few commands covered here in Chapter 9, "Basic Graphics Commands," to draw circles one pixel at a time, which should give you a good reason to look into these commands for your games. For instance, while it might not be practical to draw a circle one pixel at a time, you certainly could use circular formulas to move objects around the screen in a realistic manner using curves and circles.

Sine and Cosine

Sine is the first and most common of the functions associated with trigonometry. Given a section of a circle that resembles a piece of pie, you have an angle associated with that piece and an arc around the edge of the circle. Sine is the vertical coordinate of the arc endpoint. Keep the word *vertical* in mind as you study Figure 8.6. When it comes to computer graphics, anything vertical is associated with the Y axis of the screen (which, in layman's terms, is up and down). The SIN command

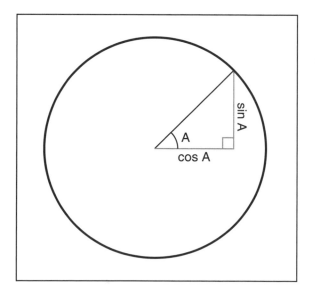

Figure 8.6

Illustration of sine and cosine

returns the sine of a degree value between 0 and 360, with support for integer or decimal degree values. The return value is a decimal number, representing the vertical endpoint of the arc.

Cosine is also one of the basic trigonometric functions. Cosine is the *horizontal* coordinate of an arc endpoint along the edge (or circumference) of a circle, where that arc is an angle measured counter-clockwise around the circle to the endpoint, like the sine function. However, recall that sine is the vertical coordinate (also known as Y), while cosine is the horizontal coordinate (also known as X). As you might imagine, sine and cosine are great for doing fun things with graphics. The COS command returns the cosine of an integer or decimal degree value between 0 and 360. Again, the return value is a decimal.

Tangent

In similar fashion, the TAN command returns the tangent of a number, with a decimal return value. Tangent is an interesting function that is the result of dividing the sine of an angle by the cosine of that angle, as shown in Figure 8.7.

$$\tan A = \frac{\sin A}{\cos A}$$

Figure 8.7 *The tangent function is equal to the sine of an angle divided by the cosine of the angle.*

Summary

This chapter began by covering the basic mathematical and relational operators built into DarkBASIC, such as addition, subtraction, multiplication, and division. You learned how to use relational operators such as greater than and less than to create more advanced conditional statements. You then learned how to use basic math commands (such as SQRT), random numbers, date and time commands, and advanced trigonometry commands.

Chapter Quiz

The chapter quiz will help you retain the information that was covered in this chapter, as well as give you an idea about how well you're doing at understanding the subjects. You will find the answers for this quiz in Appendix A, "Answers to the Chapter Quizzes."

1. Which is the standard multiplication character for programming languages?

    A. +

    B. −

    C. *

    D. /

2. Which math operation does the / character perform?

    A. Exponentiation

    B. Division

    C. Multiplication

    D. Addition

3. What is the relational operator <= called?

    A. Equal to

    B. Not equal to

    C. Less than or equal to

    D. Greater than

4. What does the not equal to relational operator look like?

    A. <=

    B. >

    C. <>

    D. >=

5. Which command calculates the absolute value of a number?

    A. INT

    B. SQRT

    C. ABS

    D. EXP

6. Which calculation does the SQRT command perform?

   A. Absolute value
   B. Exponent
   C. Square root
   D. Integer conversion

7. What is the base minimum number returned by the RND command?

   A. 0
   B. 1

8. Which date format does the GET DATE$ command return by default?

   A. 01/01/2001
   B. 01-Jan-2001
   C. Jan 01, 2001
   D. January 1, 2001

9. Which command returns a 24-hour time by default as a string variable?

   A. TIMER
   B. GET TIME$
   C. GET TIMER
   D. GetTime

10. Which advanced trigonometry command returns the cosine of an angle?

    A. SIN
    B. TAN
    C. COS
    D. None of the above

PART II

Game Fundamentals: Graphics, Sound, Input Devices, and File Access

Welcome to Part II of *Beginner's Guide to DarkBASIC Game Programming*. Part II includes eight chapters that provide you with all the information you need to take your DarkBASIC programming skills to the next level. While the first part of the book was a tutorial on basic computer programming, this Part builds on the basics and teaches you the specific things you need to know to write actual games. The chapters in this Part will teach you how to use the basic graphics commands; load and draw bitmaps and sprites; program the keyboard, mouse, and joystick; play sound effects and music; read and write files; and play movie files.

CHAPTER 9

BASIC GRAPHICS COMMANDS

Congratulations, you've made it through the first eight chapters, and you're now ready to jump into more advanced topics such as graphics programming. So far, this book has been a primer for computer programming with the BASIC language. My goal up to this point has been to teach you the fundamentals of programming so you'll have a foundation of knowledge and experience to draw upon when writing your first game. There is a lot of prerequisite information required that most established game programmers take for granted, but it can be intimidating to someone who has never written a program before, let alone a game!

I'm going to continue on the path of this primer and gradually take you into deeper and deeper territory with each new chapter. The pace will increase, as will the amount of information on game programming. As you know, everyone learns at a different pace. Some folks learn quickly, while others take a little longer to catch on. That's why the book has kept a leisurely pace up to this point. But this chapter, and in particular the next two chapters, will quicken the pace dramatically. Soon you will have pixels flying across the screen!

This chapter includes an introduction to graphics in general, followed by the specific commands in DarkBASIC for programming your own graphics programs. Not only will you learn the commands to draw objects on the screen, you'll also learn the commands for identifying the model and capabilities of the installed video card and supported video modes. This is important, as you will see, because you can tailor a game to take advantage of the features built into the user's video hardware. I'm sure you will be pleasantly surprised by all the amazing features that are built into DarkBASIC! It absolutely excels at doing graphics. This chapter covers the following topics:

- Graphics in Abundance!
- System and Video Card Commands
- Display Mode Commands
- Taking DarkEDIT for a Spin
- Basic Graphics Programming

Graphics in Abundance!

The first step to writing a game on any platform—for example, Windows, Mac, Linux, or Xbox—is to learn the language, which you have now done. On many platforms, the language is called the SDK (*Software Development Kit*). In the early days of Windows—circa 1992 and Windows 3.0—programmers had to use Microsoft C and the Windows SDK to write programs. This was before the invention of Visual Basic, which made Windows programming easy. In that regard, DarkBASIC has made it even easier. However, DarkBASIC was designed specifically for creating games, as you've already learned.

DarkBASIC is absolutely loaded with graphics commands! If you love graphics, then you've found a great tool for working with them. I'll go over the graphics commands built into DarkBASIC soon. First, I'd like to explore some of the finer features that DarkBASIC provides to enhance the graphics for a game.

Behind the Magic

What behind-the-scenes magic causes graphics to be displayed on a monitor? Every PC has a video card of one type or another that sends output to the monitor. The capabilities of the video card determine how the graphics will look. See Figure 9.1 for a sample illustration.

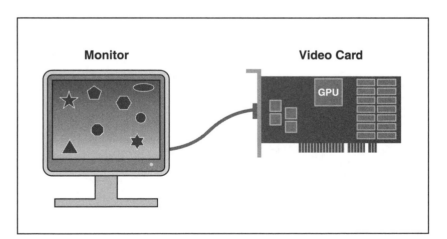

Figure 9.1
Graphics commands are routed to the video card, which prepares and sends the display screen to the monitor.

As a foregone conclusion, the better the video card, the better the graphics will look. The problem is that competition in the video card industry has been absolutely insane in recent years. The two top contenders, Nvidia and ATI, constantly leapfrog each other with each new generation of 3D chip. In general, you will do well to buy a new video card every two years. It doesn't have to be the latest, greatest, top-of-the-line, expensive card. I personally prefer features to raw graphics power. For instance, I usually prefer a video card with video input and output ports for doing video capture and also outputting to a big-screen TV. Some video cards even have a built-in TV tuner, so that you can watch and record programs on your PC or digitize home movies.

Pixels and Resolution

The key to all graphics is the pixel, which is short for *picture element*. The display screen is made up of many thousands or millions of pixels, especially in the case of extremely high resolutions. For example, a resolution of 1600×1200, which is usually the upper limit for most monitors, is actually comprised of 1,920,000 pixels. This means that everything on the screen is made up of individual little points of light that are almost too small to see with the unaided eye. Screen resolution is measured by the number of pixels that make up the screen. Take a look at Figure 9.2, which shows a 640×480 screen.

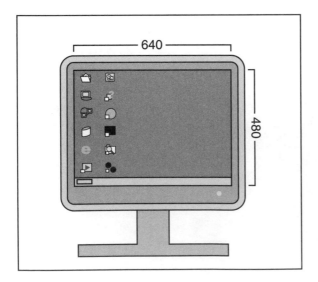

Figure 9.2

The display screen is made up of pixels that define the resolution.

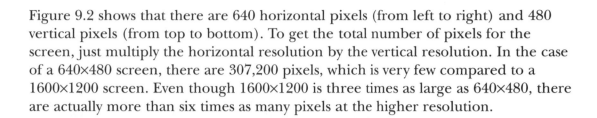

Figure 9.2 shows that there are 640 horizontal pixels (from left to right) and 480 vertical pixels (from top to bottom). To get the total number of pixels for the screen, just multiply the horizontal resolution by the vertical resolution. In the case of a 640×480 screen, there are 307,200 pixels, which is very few compared to a 1600×1200 screen. Even though 1600×1200 is three times as large as 640×480, there are actually more than six times as many pixels at the higher resolution.

Resolutions

Although a low-end video card might run great at 640×480, it would choke at 1600×1200. It takes a lot of processing power to push two million pixels through the monitor cable and out to the screen at 60 frames per second (fps) or more! Just do the math. At 640×480 and 307,200 pixels, a game running at 60 fps will need to process 18,432,000 pixels every second! Take it to the high resolution, and it will be a startling revelation. At 1600×1200 and 1,920,000 pixels, a game running at 60 fps will need to process a whopping 115,200,000 pixels every second. That is a phenomenal number of pixels, to put it mildly. But that's only half the story.

Colors

Each pixel on the screen is capable of displaying any one of a possible 16.7 million colors in 32-bit color mode, or any one of around 64,000 colors in 16-bit color mode. 32-bit images are made up of red, green, blue, and alpha parts, each with eight bits of information. 16-bit images are a little more complicated, with five red, five blue, and either five or six green bits. Figure 9.3 shows how a pixel is physically displayed on a monitor.

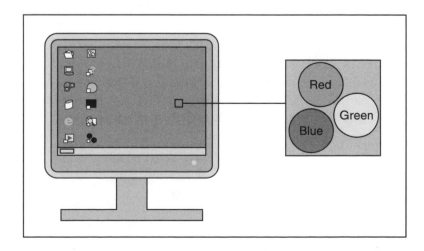

Figure 9.3

The display screen is made up of pixels. Each pixel is made up of red, green, and blue electron streams.

As Figure 9.3 shows, each pixel is actually made up of three electron streams of red, green, and blue. By varying the intensity of an electron stream, the pixel displays a desired color.

Therefore, a 32-bit display actually requires four bytes of memory for every single pixel on the screen (since eight bits equal one byte).

Now you start to see why a powerful graphics accelerator is required to process all the pixels that make up a game screen. Without a graphics processor (such as the Nvidia GeForce4 or the ATI Radeon 8500), the CPU (*Central Processing Unit*)

> **NOTE**
>
> In a 32-bit display, there are actually just 24 bits needed for each pixel. The remaining 8 bits make up what is called the *alpha* byte, which is used for translucent and transparent effects.

would have a hard time drawing all those pixels and doing other things in the computer at the same time. Just to give you an idea of the raw pixel fill rate of a modern graphics processor without getting into the subject of polygons and 3D graphics (which make even more demands of the graphics chip), a 1600×1200 32-bit display needs to move 460,800,000 bytes every second just to fill the screen.

Bits, Bytes, and . . . Polygons?

If you are an avid video game player (like I am), then you are probably familiar with consoles such as the Xbox, PlayStation 2, and GameCube. The video game industry prefers to deal with bits instead of bytes because graphics hardware is fiercely competitive. Console makers will avidly market their machines' capabilities by the data bus or processors inside, which can be 32-bit, 64-bit, 128-bit, or 256-bit. Keep in mind that 8 bits make up a single byte.

The Nvidia graphics chip inside the Xbox, for example, is capable of pushing a theoretical resolution of 1920×1440 in 32-bit color. Although I don't know of a high-definition television in the world that will do that kind of ouput, the Xbox is capable of higher resolutions than are available on a standard TV. Now if only the game developers would make use of at least the HDTV capabilities! Of course, video game consoles are now rated by 3D performance instead of the bytes or bits that make up a pixel, as was the case with previous consoles. They are rated in millions of polygons per second. A polygon is a 2D shape that is made up of three or more points, which are referred to as *vertices* (see Figure 9.4).

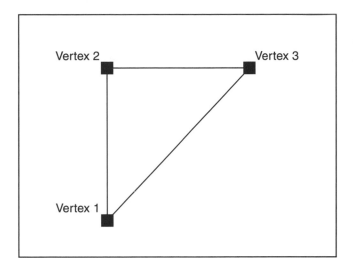

Figure 9.4
*Polygons are made
up of three or more
vertices.*

I will hold off on any more details about 3D graphics for now because 3D is a huge subject that I will cover in later chapters. I just want you to understand that 3D graphics are measured differently than the raw pixels involved in drawing 2D graphics.

Double Buffering

New programmers tend to want to jump in and start writing a game using the best skills available. I remember when I started learning to write programs. At the time, I was learning Microsoft BASIC, which was frequently distributed with MS-DOS under the name of GW-BASIC. I remember trying desperately to make a Pac-Man game without any flicker. The problem is that when you learn how to draw things on the screen, they tend to leave a trail behind them as they move (unless you know some more advanced tricks). The solution to that problem is to erase an object on the screen, and then redraw it in a new location. This gets rid of the trails behind the object, which result from the object not being erased before it is moved.

If you've ever written a program in BASIC, then you are likely familiar with screen flicker. It is caused when an image on the screen is erased, moved, and redrawn in a new location—the basis for animation. Unfortunately, I had neither the skill nor the know-how at the time to create a double buffer to reduce flicker.

What Is Double Buffering?

What is a double buffer, you might ask? It is kind of a copy of the display screen in memory. You perform all drawing commands on that memory screen first, and then draw the memory screen to the real screen (see Figure 9.5).

> A *double buffer* is a mirror image of the screen, located in high-speed memory. Instead of drawing directly to the screen, graphics commands are pointed to the double buffer. Once all drawing for a frame has been completed, the entire double buffer is quickly drawn to the screen, thus eliminating flicker.

Built-In Double Buffering

Double buffers are somewhat irrelevant because DarkBASIC handles that aspect of programming automatically. Double buffers are so common that it is no wonder the creators of DarkBASIC included that functionality by design. In the past, game programming books have spent dozens of pages on this topic alone, so it's great that DarkBASIC handles this difficult programming problem in the background. In fact, there are ways to control the speed of the double buffer updates using the SYNC command, but that is a topic for the next chapter.

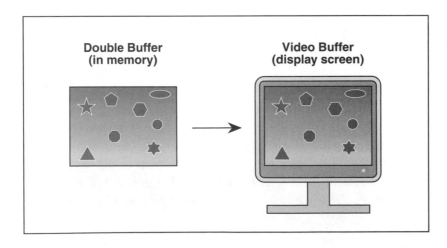

Figure 9.5

A double buffer eliminates flicker and provides smooth, high-speed animation.

Drawing Commands

DarkBASIC includes all the graphics commands you need to write a game. The best part is that you don't need a special library to use DirectX, which is completely integrated and abstracted inside DarkBASIC. When you write a command such as CIRCLE, DarkBASIC draws a circle on the full-screen DirectX display. You need not know anything about DirectX to make it work, which is something of a key to understanding what makes DarkBASIC tick: It just works.

When you are working with DarkBASIC, there are no header files to include, no library files to link, no DLLs to reference, no run time to install. It just works. Best of all, you do not need an installer because programs that have been compiled with DarkBASIC are standalone executables with no dependencies. Most languages require at least some run-time library or a list of external definitions to use DirectX. Not so with DarkBASIC.

DarkBASIC has numerous vector graphic commands—that is, commands that deal with points and lines—in addition to sprite blitting commands. If you have never heard the terms "sprite" and "blitting" before, don't worry; I'll get into those subjects in the next two chapters.

DirectDraw versus Direct3D

Did you know that DarkBASIC programs use DirectX? That's right—when you write a program with DarkBASIC, you are writing DirectX 7.0 programs without any effort! Possibly the most difficult aspect of DirectX programming is initializing DirectX components, such as DirectDraw. DarkBASIC actually utilizes Direct3D for almost all graphics output. It works this way because DirectX 7.0 separates the 2D and 3D graphics libraries. DirectDraw handles 2D graphics such as bitmaps and sprites, while Direct3D handles 3D graphics such as textures and polygons. These two systems aren't compatible! You can't draw using DirectDraw, for example, and then render a 3D character on the same screen. DirectX 7.0 just doesn't work that way.

Instead, DarkBASIC uses 3D mode for everything—including 2D graphics commands. This might be part of the reason why DarkBASIC is considered a 3D programming language. Although DarkBASIC has many built-in 2D graphics commands, it was clearly designed for rendering 3D graphics. Some 2D commands seem to run slowly; this is another side effect of DarkBASIC's use of Direct3D for all of the graphics commands. This might sound amazing, but DarkBASIC may be able to draw a textured polygon faster than it is able to draw a simple line on the screen!

System and Video Card Commands

Now that you've had an introduction to the graphics commands available in DarkBASIC, I'd like to get into some initialization and management commands that will be useful as you begin to explore the more advanced features of DarkBASIC. There is a sample program at the end of this section called CheckSystem, which runs through these commands and shows you how to use them and their resulting return values.

Graphics Card Commands

The graphics card commands are helpful when you want to know the name of the primary video card or retrieve a list of cards in a multiple-monitor system.

The CURRENT GRAPHICS CARD$() Command

The CURRENT GRAHICS CARD$() command returns a string with the name of the primary video card installed on the system. Unfortunately, this command doesn't return the actual name of the video card, just the name of the driver reported by DirectX.

> **TIP**
>
> Important reminder: Commands that return a value must include empty parentheses at the end because that is how DarkBASIC differentiates between regular functions and those which return a value.

The PERFORM CHECKLIST FOR GRAPHICS CARDS Command

The PERFORM CHECKLIST FOR GRAPHICS CARDS command is possibly the longest command in the entire DarkBASIC language! However, it does perform a useful service by providing a list of video cards that are installed on your PC. This will usually just reference the single video card installed on most systems, but in some cases multiple video cards are used (such as in dual-monitor systems). In such situations, you might want to allow the user to select the correct video card before running the game. Most of the time you will just initialize the primary video card and not bother with multiple displays. There is an option in the DirectX driver options that allows the user to select the default video card, so you can ignore this feature if you want.

The SET GRAPHICS CARD Command

The SET GRAPHICS CARD command is used in conjunction with PERFORM CHECKLIST FOR GRAPHICS CARDS to select a specific video card in a multiple-display system. As I mentioned previously, this is probably not something that you will need to worry about because the end user has the ability to select the primary display by setting a DirectX driver option.

Hardware Acceleration Commands

The commands in this section allow you to check for the presence of a 3D-accelerated graphics card in the system. You can programmatically use acceleration if it's available, or you can cause DarkBASIC to run in software emulation mode, which is often unusable depending on the game.

The EMULATION MODE() Command

The EMULATION MODE() command checks for the availability of 3D hardware acceleration in the primary video card, returning a value of 1 if emulation mode is active (or 0 for hardware acceleration). If your game has a lot of demanding 3D (which will be covered in later chapters), then you might want to make sure acceleration is available. If your game is particularly demanding, you might go so far as to prevent the game from running without acceleration.

The SET EMULATION ON Command

The SET EMULATION ON command causes DarkBASIC to ignore any 3D accelerator and instead run specifically in software emulation mode. As I explained earlier, this mode is not recommended unless the video card does not support 3D, which is highly unlikely in today's computer market.

The SET EMULATION OFF Command

The SET EMULATION OFF command tells DarkBASIC to use 3D hardware acceleration if it's available, thus disabling software emulation mode.

Transform and Lighting Commands

The transform and lighting (T&L) commands are applicable for systems with a late-model video card capable of offloading matrix transformations and hardware lighting from the main processor to the graphics processor. When a video card supports T&L, it frees the main processor from these mathematically demanding computations, particularly when such video cards are optimized for handling T&L. Figure 9.6 shows the relationships between DarkBASIC, DirectX, and the video display driver.

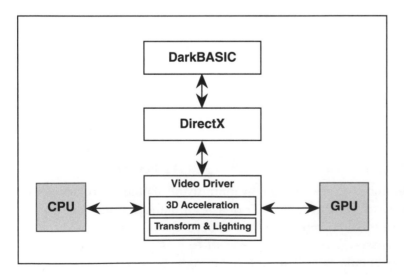

Figure 9.6 *The video driver handles advanced features such as T&L and 3D acceleration, providing DirectX programs with a consistent interface regardless of differences among the various video cards.*

The TNL AVAILABLE() Command

The TNL AVAILABLE() command returns a 1 if transform and lighting is supported by the primary video card. If your game uses many 3D objects that are visible on the screen at once, or if you use hardware lighting, you might want to check to see whether T&L is available to ensure that a suitable video card is installed before allowing the game to run. This is an extreme case, and it is not likely to be an issue. In general, you will want the user to play the game no matter what the performance will be like. If the user's PC is out of date, then your game might be what convinces him to upgrade to a faster processor or video card.

The ENABLE TNL Command

The ENABLE TNL command tells DarkBASIC to use transform and lighting if the primary video card supports it. T&L is enabled by default when DarkBASIC detects that it is available, so this command is only necessary if you need the ability to toggle T&L while a program is running.

The DISABLE TNL Command

The DISABLE TNL command turns off DarkBASIC's support for transform and lighting. Since T&L is detected automatically and used by DarkBASIC when it is available, you only need this command if you specifically want to disable it.

Memory Commands

This section includes some system commands for retrieving the memory available, including system memory and video memory. These commands are useful if you are allocating a lot of memory and you want to make sure that you don't allocate beyond the memory that is available—meaning, of course, that Windows will use the swap file and virtual memory. The resulting performance hit is akin to killing a game.

The SYSTEM DMEM AVAILABLE() Command

The SYSTEM DMEM AVAILABLE() command returns the amount of free display memory. Generally, this value will return the total amount of installed display memory on the video card when your DarkBASIC program starts running, given that you haven't allocated any textures or 3D objects.

The SYSTEM SMEM AVAILABLE() Command

The SYSTEM SMEM AVAILABLE() command returns the amount of free system memory. This is generally referred to as RAM (*Random Access Memory*), although this particular command returns just the amount of free memory, not the total installed memory. Therefore, this command might be useful if you are allocating large blocks of memory and you want to make sure that there is enough memory to hold the objects you are trying to allocate.

The SYSTEM TMEM AVAILABLE() Command

The SYSTEM TMEM AVAILABLE() command returns the amount of total system memory that is available to programs. This differs from the SMEM command in that it takes into account the virtual memory in use on the system (in the form of a swap file). This value usually will be very large, depending on the default size of your swap file. For this reason, this command is not very useful in the course of writing a game because you will likely be interested only in the amount of free memory, which the SMEM command provides.

The CheckSystem Program

Okay, how would you like to put all this newfound knowledge to use in a real program? Great, I thought you would! Figure 9.7 shows the CheckSystem program.

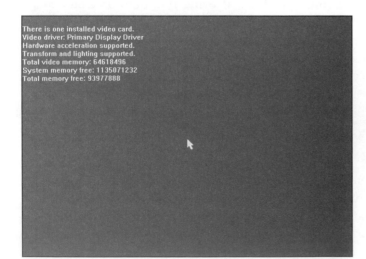

Figure 9.7 *The CheckSystem program displays detailed information about the system and the video card.*

This program displays the primary video card, the available features, and the amount of free memory in your computer system. Feel free to load the project from the folder for this chapter on the CD-ROM, or type the following lines of code into a new project file using either DarkBASIC or DarkEDIT.

Before you begin, I want to start a new trend. It's time to replace the REM statement with something more convenient. From this chapter forward, I will use the apostrophe instead of the REM statement. The apostrophe character, which is located to the left of the 1 key on most keyboards, is an alternative way to start a comment line in DarkBASIC. Notice how I have used the apostrophe instead of REM in the listing for the CheckSystem program. The comment lines are less imposing, making the source code easier to read.

```
`-----------------------------------
`Beginner's Guide To DarkBASIC Game Programming
`Copyright (C)2002 Jonathan S. Harbour and Joshua R. Smith
`Chapter 9 - CheckSystem Program
`-----------------------------------

`Check for installed video cards
PERFORM CHECKLIST FOR GRAPHICS CARDS
VideoCards = CHECKLIST QUANTITY()
IF VideoCards > 1
    PRINT "There are ",VideoCards," installed video cards."
    FOR Index = 1 TO VideoCards
        PRINT "  ", Index, " - ", CHECKLIST STRING$(Index)
    NEXT Index
ELSE
    PRINT "There is one installed video card."
ENDIF

`Display current video driver
PRINT "Video driver: ", CURRENT GRAPHICS CARD$()

`Check for hardware acceleration
IF EMULATION MODE() = 1
    PRINT "No hardware acceleration."
ELSE
    PRINT "Hardware acceleration supported."
ENDIF
```

```
`Check for transform and lighting
IF TNL AVAILABLE() = 1
    PRINT "Transform and lighting supported."
ELSE
    PRINT "No transform and lighting."
ENDIF

`Display memory available
PRINT "Total video memory: ", SYSTEM DMEM AVAILABLE()
PRINT "System memory free: ", SYSTEM SMEM AVAILABLE()
PRINT "Total memory free: ", SYSTEM TMEM AVAILABLE()

`Wait for user to press a key
WAIT KEY

`Delete checklist array from memory
EMPTY CHECKLIST

`End the program
END
```

Display Mode Commands

DarkBASIC includes a number of useful utility commands for retrieving a list of
display modes supported by your video card. DarkBASIC uses a default resolution
of 640×480×16, but there are many more display modes available, all the way up
to the maximum resolution supported by your video card. This section shows you
how to retrieve and use the list of display modes.

Reading and Setting the Display Modes

This section includes the commands for reading the list of display modes, as well as
setting and checking them.

The PERFORM CHECKLIST FOR DISPLAY MODES Command

PERFORM CHECKLIST FOR DISPLAY MODES is a very long command, but it provides a useful list of the modes supported by your video card, filling in the CHECKLIST STRING$ array with the values returned.

The CHECKLIST QUANTITY() Command

The CHECKLIST QUANTITY() command returns the number of display modes returned by the PERFORM CHECKLIST FOR DISPLAY MODES command. You can use this value to loop through the display modes.

The CHECKLIST STRING$() Command

The CHECKLIST STRING$() command accepts a single parameter—the display mode number—and returns the name of the display mode, such as 1024×768×16 or 1600×1200×16.

The CHECKLIST VALUE A() Command

The CHECKLIST VALUE A() command grabs the first part of the display mode name returned by the CHECKLIST STRING$() command. Since the display mode is returned in the format of 640×480×16, this command returns the 640 part, which is the horizontal resolution of the display.

The CHECKLIST VALUE B() Command

The CHECKLIST VALUE B() command grabs the second part of the display mode name returned by the CHECKLIST STRING$() command. Since the display mode is returned in the format of 640×480×16, this command returns the 480 part, which is the vertical resolution of the display.

The CHECKLIST VALUE C() Command

The CHECKLIST VALUE C() command grabs the third part of the display mode name returned by the CHECKLIST STRING$() command. Since the display mode is returned in the format of 640×480×16, this command returns the 16 part, which is the color depth of the display.

The SET DISPLAY MODE Command

The SET DISPLAY MODE command accepts three parameters to change the display mode—horizontal resolution, vertical resolution, and color depth. For example:

```
SET DISPLAY MODE 640, 480, 16
```

Note that DarkBASIC Pro still supports this command, but it is recommended that you set the video mode from the project settings rather than from source code due to the way DarkBASIC Pro compiles the source code and adds bitmaps and other media files to the executable.

The CHECK DISPLAY MODE() Command

The CHECK DISPLAY MODE() command checks the display mode passed as parameter values to see whether it is available on the system. If the display mode is invalid, this command returns a value of 0. For example:

```
Value = CHECK DISPLAY MODE(640, 480, 16)
```

Display Mode Properties

This section includes commands that are useful for returning information about the specific video mode currently in use.

The SCREEN TYPE() Command

The SCREEN TYPE() command determines whether 2D hardware acceleration is supported by the video card. A return value of 0 means that hardware acceleration is not available. This command differs from the EMULATION MODE() command in that SCREEN TYPE() reports 2D capabilities and EMULATION MODE() reports 3D capabilities.

The SCREEN WIDTH() Command

The SCREEN WIDTH() command returns the horizontal resolution of the current display mode in pixels. For example, if the display mode is 1280×960×32, the SCREEN WIDTH() command returns a value of 1280.

The SCREEN HEIGHT() Command

The SCREEN HEIGHT() command returns the vertical resolution of the current display mode in pixels. For example, if the display mode is 1280×960×32, the SCREEN HEIGHT() command returns a value of 960.

The SCREEN DEPTH() Command

The SCREEN DEPTH() command returns the color depth of the current display mode in bits per pixel (BPP). For example, if the display mode is 1280×960×32, the SCREEN DEPTH() command returns a value of 32.

The SCREEN FPS() Command

The SCREEN FPS() command is not strictly related to the display mode, but it is a useful command nonetheless. It reports the performance of the graphics system in frames per second. This value will vary widely depending on the video card, but it generally won't go above 100 fps.

The DisplayModes Program

The DisplayModes program will help you learn the various video modes supported by the video card on your PC. This program will also show you how to return the list of supported modes and how to set a particular video mode using the code you have learned so far in this section. The DisplayModes program draws several boxes on the screen to represent each display resolution so you can see how the video modes compare.

Allow me to give you a tour of the program. Figure 9.8 shows the DisplayModes program when it starts. DarkBASIC programs default to the display mode of 640×480×16 unless you specify otherwise.

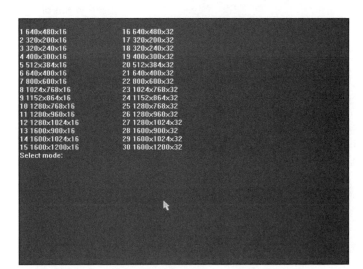

Figure 9.8 *The DisplayModes program displays the video modes that are supported on your PC.*

Selecting a video mode with the resolution 800×600 produces the screen shown in Figure 9.9.

Changing the mode to 1024×768 results in the screen shown in Figure 9.10. Note that the three boxes now displayed on the screen show the three resolutions you have used so far.

1280×960 produces the screen shown in Figure 9.11. This resolution is quite high, as you can tell from the small size of the font and mouse cursor.

The highest resolution that my video card and monitor are capable of displaying is 1600×1200, which is shown in Figure 9.12.

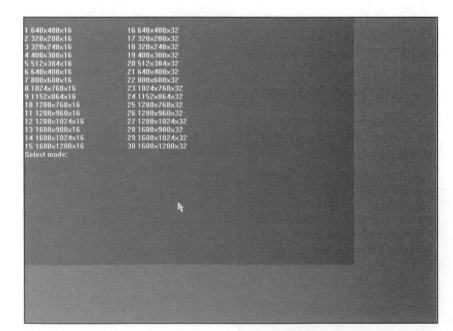

Figure 9.9

The DisplayModes program has been changed to run at 800×600.

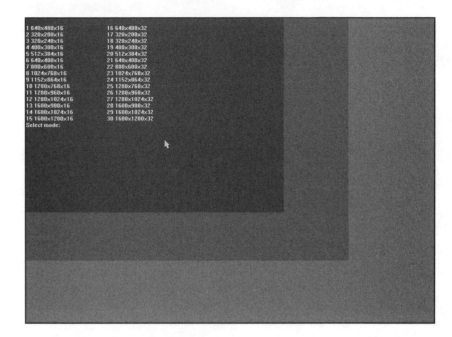

Figure 9.10 *The DisplayModes program has been changed to run at 1024×768.*

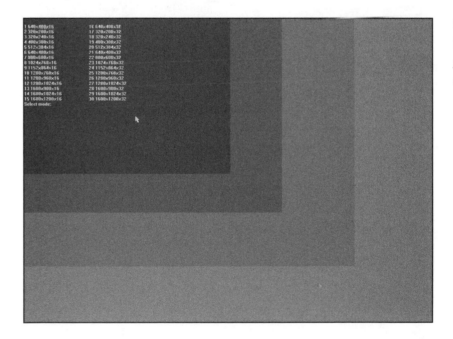

Figure 9.11 *The DisplayModes program has been changed to run at 1280×960.*

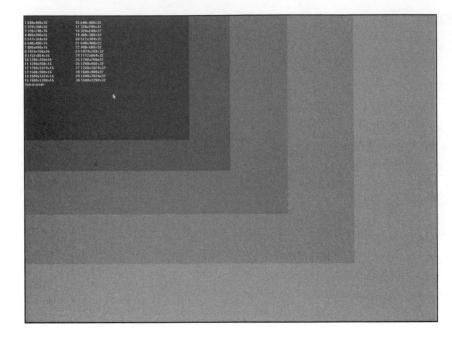

Figure 9.12
The DisplayModes program has been changed to run at 1600×1200.

The listing for the DisplayModes program follows. Simply create a new file in DarkBASIC (or in DarkEDIT) and type in the source code as shown. There are comments in the code that explain each section of the program, which is only about a page in length.

```
`--------------------------------

`Beginner's Guide To DarkBASIC Game Programming
`Copyright (C)2002 Jonathan S. Harbour and Joshua R. Smith
`Chapter 9 - DisplayModes Program
`--------------------------------


`Get the list of video modes
PERFORM CHECKLIST FOR DISPLAY MODES
SET DISPLAY MODE 640, 480, 32

DO
        `Draw gray resolution markers
        CLS
        INK RGB(120,120,120),0
        BOX 0,0,1599,1199
        INK RGB(100,100,100),0
```

```
      BOX 0,0,1279,959
      INK RGB(80,80,80),0
      BOX 0,0,1023,767
      INK RGB(60,60,60),0
      BOX 0,0,799,599
      INK RGB(30,30,30),0
      BOX 0,0,639,479

      `Display the list of video modes
      INK RGB(255,255,255),0
      modes = CHECKLIST QUANTITY()
      FOR t = 1 TO modes / 2
          `First column of resolutions
          SET CURSOR 0,t * 16
          PRINT t;" ";CHECKLIST STRING$(t);
          `Second column of resolutions
          SET CURSOR 200,t * 16
          index = modes / 2 + t
          PRINT index;" ";CHECKLIST STRING$(index)
      NEXT t

      `Ask user to select a video mode
      INPUT "Select mode: ";position

      `Rip the values out of the modes array
      width=CHECKLIST VALUE A(position)
      height=CHECKLIST VALUE B(position)
      depth=CHECKLIST VALUE C(position)

      `Change the display mode
      SET DISPLAY MODE width, height, depth
LOOP
```

Taking DarkEDIT for a Spin

I'm going to get off the subject of graphics programming for a moment to bring
up DarkEDIT again, because you might want to start using it (especially if you plan
to use DarkBASIC Pro, which includes an editor based on DarkEDIT). After you've
become proficient with the DarkBASIC code editor, you might get to a point where
you'd like more features or you would prefer to just edit your DarkBASIC programs

using a program with a standard Windows user interface. I introduced DarkEDIT back in Chapter 1, but I have not discussed it since then.

Running DarkEDIT

I'd like to take the opportunity to go over DarkEDIT in a little more detail now, so you can use it to write the DisplayModes program. Figure 9.13 shows the About DarkEDIT dialog box.

Even if you really like the default DarkBASIC editor (as I do), you should at least try DarkEDIT because it's actually more convenient when you are working with long programs. You can also have many programs loaded at once because DarkEDIT is an MDI (*Multiple-Document Interface*) application, which allows you to compile or run any one of the programs at any time. In contrast, the built-in DarkBASIC editor supports only two source code files at a time (which, granted, is usually enough).

Creating a Shortcut to DarkEDIT

DarkEDIT is distributed with DarkBASIC, but it isn't included in the Start menu (under Programs, Dark Basic Software) as you might expect. Instead, you must create a shortcut to DarkEDIT from your Windows desktop. To create this shortcut, right-click the desktop and select New, Shortcut. Click the Browse button in the Create Shortcut dialog box and browse to C:\Program Files\Dark Basic Software\Dark Basic\xdarkedit.exe.

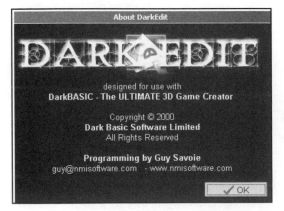

Figure 9.13
DarkEDIT is an alternative source code editor for writing DarkBASIC programs, complete with full support for compiling and running them.

Configuring DarkEDIT

When you get DarkEDIT running, you need to set up the link to it. This involves pointing DarkEDIT to the DB.EXE file so it can compile and run programs (using special DarkBASIC program parameters). To configure DarkEDIT, select Edit Options from the Edit menu, as shown in Figure 9.14.

The DarkEDIT Options dialog box will appear (see Figure 9.15).

Figure 9.14

Configuring DarkEDIT so it can link directly to DarkBASIC

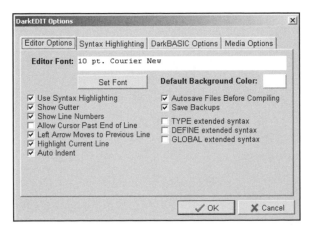

Figure 9.15

The DarkEDIT Options dialog box allows you to customize DarkEDIT to suit your preferences.

Now click the DarkBASIC Options tab to set up the link to DarkBASIC, as shown in Figure 9.16.

Click the small folder button at the right of the DarkBASIC Program field to open a file selection dialog box. Browse to C:\Program Files\Dark Basic Software\Dark Basic to locate the DB.exe file, as shown in Figure 9.17.

After you have located the DB.exe file, click the Open button to paste the path into the DarkEDIT Options dialog box, as shown in Figure 9.18.

> **NOTE**
>
> DarkBASIC Pro has a completely integrated windowed editor that does not need to be configured in any way because the DarkBASIC Pro IDE (*Integrated Development Environment*) has the DarkBASIC compiler built in.

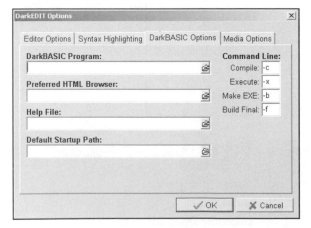

Figure 9.16
The DarkBASIC Options tab on the DarkEDIT Options dialog box is where you link DarkEDIT to DarkBASIC for seamless program compiling.

Taking DarkEDIT for a Spin

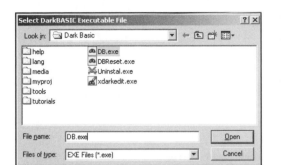

Figure 9.17

Browsing for the DarkBASIC program file

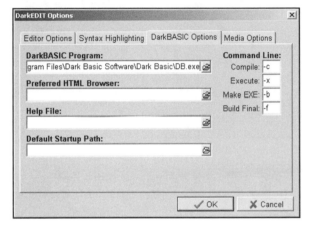

Figure 9.18

DarkEDIT has now been linked to DarkBASIC, allowing you to compile source code files directly in DarkEDIT.

Testing the Link to DarkBASIC

Now let's make sure the link to DarkBASIC is working so you can use DarkEDIT to compile and run programs. Load one of the sample programs from this chapter or any previous chapter by clicking the Open a File icon on the toolbar or by selecting File, Open. Press F4 to compile the program.

You will see DarkEDIT minimize for a moment, and then it will return. If there are any errors in the program code, the error message will be displayed in the status bar (see Figure 9.19). DarkEDIT also highlights the line that contains the error.

When the program compiles with no errors, the Compilation Successful message appears at the bottom of the screen (see Figure 9.20). This is a good way to see quickly whether there are any errors in your program without actually trying to run it.

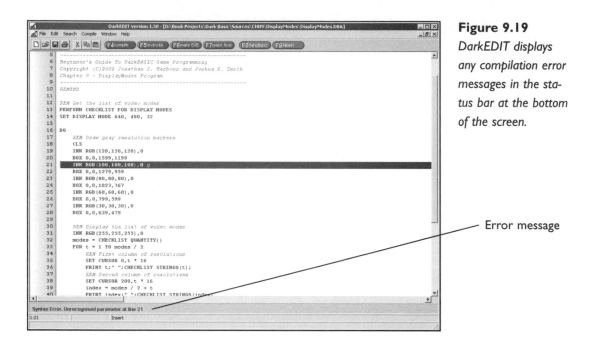

Figure 9.19
DarkEDIT displays any compilation error messages in the status bar at the bottom of the screen.

Error message

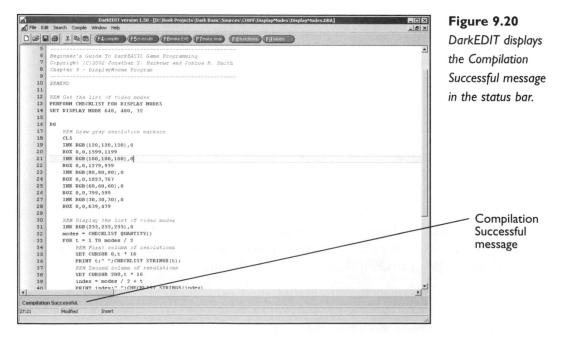

Figure 9.20
DarkEDIT displays the Compilation Successful message in the status bar.

Compilation Successful message

Running Programs from DarkEDIT

When you have a program loaded and compiled, you can either compile the source code to a standalone executable file or just run the program inside DarkBASIC. To run the program, press F5 or click the Execute button on the toolbar. Any time you want to end a program and return to DarkEDIT, just press F12, which is the default exit button for all DarkBASIC programs (often along with the Esc key). When the program ends, focus returns to DarkEDIT.

Basic Graphics Programming

This section involves some actual commands for drawing objects on the screen, unlike the previous sections, which dealt only with initializing and reading information about the video card.

Changing the Drawing Color

By default, DarkBASIC uses white for graphics and text output. If you want to change the color, you can use the INK command in conjunction with RGB, as explained in the following section.

The INK Command

The INK command changes the foreground and background colors used for graphics and text drawing commands. INK accepts two parameters—foreground color and background color—which must be integer values. Normally, you will use the RGB command to generate them. For example:

```
Forecolor = RGB(120, 120, 120)
Backcolor = RGB(255, 0, 0)
INK Forecolor, Backcolor
```

The RGB Command

The RGB command, as you have already seen, uses the parameters that you pass to the command and returns an integer containing the red, green, and blue parts that make up a color.

Clearing the Screen

One of the most overlooked commands for keeping the display clean and attractive involves a simple screen clear.

The CLS Command

The CLS command clears the display screen using the current background color that was set using the INK command, as shown in the following code.

```
REM Set the background color to green
INK 0, RGB(0, 255, 0)
CLS
```

Note that you can simply pass an integer to the INK command, which is useful when you want to set a color to black, which is the value 0. The CLS command uses the background color previously set with INK.

Clearing the Screen with Random Colors

To show how the INK and CLS commands work together, I've written a short program called ClearScreen, which is shown in Figure 9.21. The figure just shows a solid color, which is what was intended, but what it doesn't show is how the program is clearing the screen quickly using random colors for an interesting effect.

Figure 9.21 *The ClearScreen program uses the* CLS *command to clear the screen with random background colors.*

Here is the source code for the ClearScreen program. Feel free to experiment by changing the display mode to some other resolutions to see the result.

```
`--------------------------------
`Beginner's Guide To DarkBASIC Game Programming
`Copyright (C)2002 Jonathan S. Harbour and Joshua R. Smith
`Chapter 9 - ClearScreen Program
`--------------------------------

`Initialize the program
SET DISPLAY MODE 640, 480, 16

`Start the main loop
DO
    `Set a random color
    bcolor = RGB(RND(255),RND(255),RND(255))
    INK 0,bcolor

    `Clear the screen
    CLS
LOOP
```

Reading and Setting Pixels

You can read the basic picture elements (pixels) that make up the screen individually by using the DOT and POINT commands.

The DOT Command

The DOT command does just what it sounds like—it draws a dot on the screen in the form of a single pixel. Before calling the DOT command, you must set the color of the pixel using the INK command. DOT accepts two parameters—the horizontal and vertical positions of the pixel, usually referenced as X and Y coordinates.

Drawing Random Pixels

To help demonstrate drawing pixels, I've written a short program called RandomPixels that quickly draws pixels in random locations on the screen. See Figure 9.22 for a sample of the output produced by this program.

Figure 9.22 *The RandomPixels program uses the* DOT *command to draw pixels at random locations.*

Here is the source code for the RandomPixels program. This program in particular is fun to experiment with, so feel free to change the resolution and the color settings to see what happens.

```
`----------------------------------
`Beginner's Guide To DarkBASIC Game Programming
`Copyright (C)2002 Jonathan S. Harbour and Joshua R. Smith
`Chapter 9 - RandomPixels Program
`----------------------------------

`Initialize the program
SET DISPLAY MODE 640, 480, 16
CLS

`Start the main loop
DO
    `Pick a random color
    fcolor = RGB(RND(255),RND(255),RND(255))
    INK fcolor, RGB(0,0,255)

    `Draw the pixel
    DOT RND(640),RND(480)
LOOP
```

The POINT Command

The POINT command simply reads the color value of the pixel referenced by the two parameters that are passed (X and Y). The returned value is an integer like the one returned by RGB. This command is somewhat slow, so you wouldn't want to use it to scan the entire screen (for whatever reason) because it would slow down the program.

Drawing Lines

Pixels are interesting, but the action really begins when you learn to draw lines in DarkBASIC. As you might already know, 3D graphics utilize lines more than pixels because polygons are made up of lines (although lines are comprised of pixels . . . but you get the idea).

The LINE Command

The LINE command draws a line on the screen using the current color sct with the INK command. There are four parameters passed to the LINE command, representing the left, top, right, and bottom points of the line.

Drawing Random Lines

To demonstrate how the LINE command works, I've written a program called RandomLines that quickly draws random lines on the screen, as shown in Figure 9.23. The source code for the RandomLines program follows.

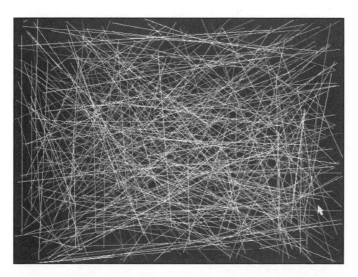

Figure 9.23 *The RandomLines program uses the* LINE *command to draw lines at random locations.*

```
`----------------------------------
`Beginner's Guide To Game Programming With DarkBASIC
`Copyright (C)2002 Jonathan S. Harbour and Joshua R. Smith
`Chapter 9 - RandomLines Program
`----------------------------------

`Initialize the program
SET DISPLAY MODE 640, 480, 16
CLS

`Start the main loop
DO
    `Pick a random color
    fcolor = RGB(RND(255),RND(255),RND(255))
    INK fcolor, RGB(0,0,0)

    `Draw the line
    LINE RND(640), RND(480), RND(640), RND(480)
LOOP
```

Drawing Rectangles

A rectangle is comprised of four lines that make up the edges. However, rectangles are treated just like lines as far as the parameters for drawing are concerned.

The BOX Command

The BOX command is used to draw rectangles. Like the other graphics drawing commands, BOX depends on the color set previously with the INK command. There are four parameters for the BOX command, just like for the LINE command—left, top, right, and bottom.

Drawing Random Rectangles

To demonstrate the BOX command, I've written a program called RandomBoxes that draws random rectangles on the screen using random colors (see Figure 9.24). The source code follows.

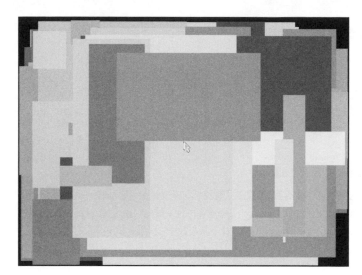

Figure 9.24 *The RandomBoxes program uses the* BOX *command to draw filled rectangles at random locations.*

```
`-----------------------------------
`Beginner's Guide To DarkBASIC Game Programming
`Copyright (C)2002 Jonathan S. Harbour and Joshua R. Smith
`Chapter 9 - RandomBoxes Program
`-----------------------------------

`Initialize the program
SET DISPLAY MODE 640, 480, 32
CLS

`Start the main loop
DO
    `Set a random color
    fcolor = RGB(RND(255),RND(255),RND(255))
    INK fcolor,0

    `Draw the rectangle
    BOX RND(640), RND(480), RND(640), RND(480)
LOOP
```

Drawing Circles

Circles are quite a bit different from pixels, lines, and rectangles, which sort of build upon each other. Circles must be drawn using a special algorithm that draws pixels using the mathematical sine and cosine functions. Suffice it to say, it's not as fast or easy to draw a circle as it is to draw a line. Fortunately, DarkBASIC handles the difficulty of drawing circles for you.

The CIRCLE Command

The CIRCLE command draws circles in DarkBASIC. There are three parameters for this command—X, Y, and the radius. The radius determines the size of the circle. Just remember that the radius only represents half the width of the circle. The diameter of a circle is made up of two radii.

Drawing Random Circles

The RandomCircles program demonstrates how to use the CIRCLE command to draw random circles on the screen, as shown in Figure 9.25. The source code follows.

```
`---------------------------------
`Beginner's Guide To DarkBASIC Game Programming
`Copyright (C)2002 Jonathan S. Harbour and Joshua R. Smith
`Chapter 9 - RandomCircles Program
`---------------------------------

`Initialize the program
SET DISPLAY MODE 640, 480, 16
CLS

`Start the main loop
DO
    `Set a random color
    fcolor = RGB(RND(255),RND(255),RND(255))
    INK fcolor,0

    `Draw the circle
    CIRCLE RND(640), RND(480), RND(100)
LOOP
```

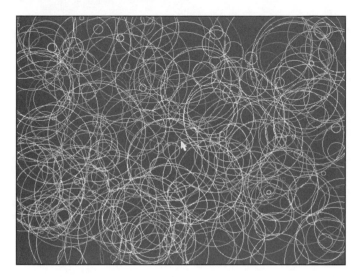

Figure 9.25 The RandomCircles program uses the `CIRCLE` command to draw circles at random locations.

Drawing a Circle with Pixels

Do circles intrigue you at all after seeing the RandomCircles program run? I remember the first time I drew a circle using BASIC—I was fascinated by it! Let me show you an interesting little variant of the RandomCircles program. This new program, called DrawCircle, actually plots each of the pixels that make up a circle so you can see how circles are created. Take a look at Figure 9.26 to see the program running.

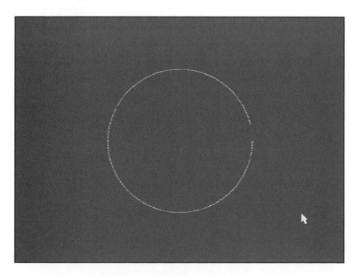

Figure 9.26 The DrawCircle program uses the `DOT` command to draw each pixel that makes up a circle.

Following is the source code for the DrawCircle program. The core of this program is the two lines that call the COS() and SIN() functions to position the current pointer around the circumference of the circle (which has a random size). You can use this circle-drawing code for all kinds of cool things! In later chapters, I'll show you how to load bitmaps and sprites and animate them on the screen. One of the most impressive features of animation is the ability to move a sprite around a curve. The code for drawing a circle really helps in that department, as I'll show you in upcoming chapters.

```
`---------------------------------
`Beginner's Guide To DarkBASIC Game Programming
`Copyright (C)2002 Jonathan S. Harbour and Joshua R. Smith
`Chapter 9 - DrawCircle Program
`---------------------------------

`Initialize the program
SET DISPLAY MODE 640, 480, 16
CLS
v = 0
size = RND(100) + 100

`Start the main loop
DO
    `Set a random color
    fcolor = RGB(RND(255),RND(255),RND(255))
    INK fcolor,0

    `Move the point around the circle
    ox = COS(v) * size
    oy = SIN(v) * size
    v = v + 1

    `Draw the point
    DOT 320 + ox, 240 + oy
LOOP
```

Drawing Ellipses

Ellipses are related to circles but are not equidistant in radius, meaning that the distance from the center of an ellipse to the edge is not always the same around its circumference.

The ELLIPSE Command

The ELLIPSE command draws ellipses. It takes four parameters—X, Y, X-radius, and Y-radius. The first two parameters are obvious, but what about the last two? X-radius determines the radius from left to right, and Y-radius determines the radius from top to bottom.

Drawing Random Ellipses

The RandomEllipses program demonstrates how to use the ELLIPSE command (see Figure 9.27). This program is similar to the RandomCircles program, so you can adapt that program rather than rewrite it, if you like.

```
`----------------------------------
`Beginner's Guide To DarkBASIC Game Programming
`Copyright (C)2002 Jonathan S. Harbour and Joshua R. Smith
`Chapter 9 - RandomEllipses Program
`----------------------------------

`Initialize the program
SET DISPLAY MODE 640, 480, 16
CLS

`Start the main loop
DO
    `Pick a random color
    fcolor = RGB(RND(255),RND(255),RND(255))
    INK fcolor,0

    `Draw the ellipse
    ELLIPSE RND(640), RND(480), RND(100), RND(100)
LOOP
```

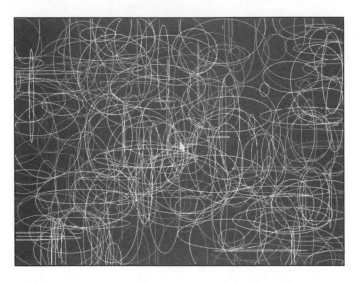

Figure 9.27 *The RandomEllipses program uses the* ELLIPSE *command to draw ellipses at random locations.*

Drawing an Ellipse with Pixels

To further enhance your understanding of circles and ellipses, I have adapted the DrawCircle program to use ellipses. In this program, instead of using just a single size variable for the radius of the circle to be drawn, there are hsize and vsize variables to represent the X and Y radii of the ellipse (see Figure 9.28).

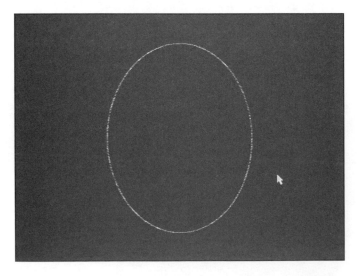

Figure 9.28 *The DrawEllipse program uses the* DOT *command to draw each pixel that makes up an ellipse.*

```
`--------------------------------
`Beginner's Guide To DarkBASIC Game Programming
`Copyright (C)2002 Jonathan S. Harbour and Joshua R. Smith
`Chapter 9 - DrawEllipse Program
`--------------------------------

`Initialize the program
SET DISPLAY MODE 640, 480, 16
CLS
v = 0
hsize = RND(100) + 100
vsize = RND(100) + 100

`Start the main loop
DO
    `Pick a random color
    fcolor = RGB(RND(255),RND(255),RND(255))
    INK fcolor,0

    `Move the point around the circle
    ox = COS(v) * hsize
    oy = SIN(v) * vsize
    v = v + 1

    `Draw the point
    DOT 320 + ox, 240 + oy
LOOP
```

Summary

This chapter introduced graphics programming in DarkBASIC. The language provides many useful commands for drawing points, lines, circles, and other shapes. There are also commands for setting the foreground and background colors and for clearing the screen. In this chapter you learned to identify the video card, the 2D and 3D graphics capabilities available, and the display modes provided by the video card, as well as how to change the screen resolution.

Chapter Quiz

The chapter quiz will help you retain the information that was covered in this chapter, as well as give you an idea about how well you're doing at understanding the subjects. You will find the answers for this quiz in Appendix A, "Answers to the Chapter Quizzes."

1. Which command retrieves the list of installed video cards (if there's more than one)?

   A. CURRENT GRAPHICS CARD( )

   B. PERFORM CHECKLIST FOR GRAPHICS CARDS

   C. SHOW ME THE GRAPHICS CARDS

   D. GET LIST OF VIDEO CARDS( )

2. Which command detects whether a 3D graphics accelerator is present in the system?

   A. EMULATION MODE( )

   B. GRAPHICS ACCELERATION

   C. CHECK DISPLAY MODE( )

   D. HARDWARE ACCELERATIONWhich

3. Which command checks for support of transform and lighting (T&L)?

   A. TRANSFORM AND LIGHTING( )

   B. CHECK TNL( )

   C. LOOK FOR TNL( )

   D. TNL AVAILABLE( )

4. Which command reports the amount of free video memory available?

   A. SYSTEM DMEM AVAILABLE( )

   B. SYSTEM SMEM AVAILABLE( )

   C. SYSTEM TMEM AVAILABLE( )

   D. SYSTEM VMEM AVAILABLE( )

5. Which command retrieves the list of display modes supported by the video card?

   A. CHECK DISPLAY MODES( )

   B. PERFORM CHECKLIST FOR DISPLAY MODES

   C. SCAN CHECKLIST FOR DISPLAY MODES

   D. GET DISPLAY MODES( )

6. DarkBASIC supports both 2D and 3D hardware graphics acceleration.

    A. True
    B. False

7. Which command will draw a single pixel on the screen?

    A. DRAW POINT
    B. PIXEL
    C. DOT
    D. BIT

8. Which command will draw a circle on the screen?

    A. CIRCUMFERENCE
    B. DRAW CIRCLE
    C. ROUND THING
    D. CIRCLE

9. Which command will draw a filled rectangle on the screen?

    A. POLYGON
    B. SQUARE
    C. BOX
    D. RECTANGLE

10. Which command changes the foreground and background colors?

    A. RGB
    B. INK
    C. COLOR
    D. FCOLOR and BCOLOR

CHAPTER 10

GAME GRAPHICS: LEARNING TO USE BITMAPS

Bitmapped images are the core and substance of every game, whether it is a 2D vertical scrolling arcade game like the classic *Heavy Barrel*, a war simulation like *Battlefield 1942*, a first-person shooter like *Doom III*, or a real-time strategy game like *Warcraft III: Reign of Chaos*. None of these games would amount to anything without the ability to load, manipulate, and display bitmap images in one form or another. So when you learn how to use bitmaps, you are really getting down to the core of what it takes to make a game.

This chapter covers the subject of handling bitmaps in great detail, showing you how to load, create, and display Windows bitmap files (which have a .bmp extension). The commands in this chapter will also show you how to manipulate bitmap images to create special effects. This chapter will be a helpful introduction to the more advanced subject of sprites, which is covered in Chapter 11, "The Art of Using Animated Sprites for 2D Games."

This chapter covers the following topics:

- Introduction to Bitmaps
- Creating and Loading Bitmaps
- Bitmap Information Commands
- Basic Bitmap Commands
- Special Effects Commands
- Image Shuffle: A Complete Bitmap-Based Game

Introduction to Bitmaps

The phrase *bitmapped graphics files*, in the truest sense, refers to any file format used to store pictures, such as those taken with digital cameras or scanners, downloaded off the Internet, or even hand-drawn. The term *bitmap* refers to the way bits in the image are encoded in the image file or in the memory prior to being displayed.

> **TIP**
>
> Recall that 8 bits equal 1 byte, and a 32-bit video card requires 4 bytes for every pixel.

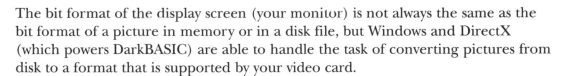

The bit format of the display screen (your monitor) is not always the same as the bit format of a picture in memory or in a disk file, but Windows and DirectX (which powers DarkBASIC) are able to handle the task of converting pictures from disk to a format that is supported by your video card.

Bitmaps range from simple letters to complex pictures and anything in between. Early game consoles such as the Nintendo and the Sega relied almost solely on small bitmaps for the graphics in video games. (In contrast, most current games run in 3D and use polygons with textures, which are bitmaps too.)

What Is a Bitmap?

So what exactly is a bitmap? It might help if you first had an inkling of what bitmaps are useful for, but I'll get to that shortly. A bitmap is nothing more than a collection of bytes (where each byte equals 8 bits) that represent a picture or graphic image. The simplest form of a bitmap is a black and white picture. All white pixels are represented as 0, and all black pixels are represented as 1. Figure 10.1 shows a simple 8×8 bitmap using 1s and 0s.

Notice how you can visualize the image made up of 1s and 0s. A pattern emerges from the pixels as you look closer at them. (If you don't know what a pixel is, refer back to Chapter 9 for an explanation.) Each 1 or 0 represents a colored pixel (black or white, respectively). With a little more imagination, you might enhance this theoretical bitmap with additional colors by using other numbers, such as 2, 3, and 4, to represent red, green, and blue. In fact, the actual bit encoding of a

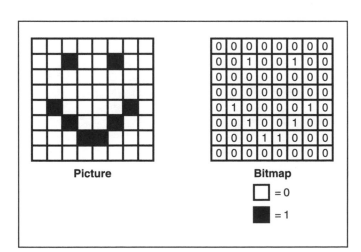

Figure 10.1

A simple monochrome bitmap, showing how a very simple picture is constructed

bitmap is extremely complicated; it involves different color depths (such 16-bit or 32-bit color), which I'll not get into at this point.

Bitmap File Formats

There are many different bitmap file formats, but they are all based on the simple format described in Figure 10.1. DarkBASIC handles all the details of converting the bitmap format so it is displayed on the screen as expected. If you can imagine the difficulties involved in converting an 8-bit image to a 32-bit image, you will develop considerable respect for the amount of work that DarkBASIC and DirectX handle automatically. DarkBASIC uses the BMP (*Windows Bitmap*) file format natively. Although there are other popular formats such as TIF (*Tagged Image File Format*), JPEG (*Joint Photographic Experts Group*), GIF (*Graphical Interchange Format*), and PCX (*Picture Exchange*), it is easier to simply use the format natively supported by DarkBASIC and DirectX.

Color depth is the most important factor to consider when working with bitmaps. The most common color depths include 8, 16, 24, and 32 bits. The number of colors in an image is often referred to as the *bit depth* because the number is representative of the bits, not the number of colors. To figure out how many colors are supported by a color depth (also referred to as *bits per pixel* or *BPP*), use the following formula:

Total Colors = 2 ^ (Bit Depth)

This formula takes 2 to the power of the bit depth of the image (or video display). Table 10.1 shows the common bit depths, along with the total number of colors associated with each.

Table 10.1 Bitmap Color Depths

Bit Depth	Number of Colors
8	256
12	4,096
16	65,536
24	16,777,216
32	4,294,967,296

You'll notice that the number of colors increases with the higher color depth. That is because the computer has more bits to represent colors. In Figure 10.1 you had 2 bits—black and white. In a 16-bit image, you have a total of 65,535 combinations from which to choose. Don't worry too much about the details because DarkBASIC takes care of them for you.

Creating Bitmaps

At this point, you might be curious about how to load a bitmap from a disk and draw it on the screen. I'll show you how to do that soon enough. First, I want to explain something important before you jump in and start using bitmaps in DarkBASIC.

How do you create a bitmap? I guess that would be a good place to start, especially if you are not familiar with paint programs. There are two ways to create a bitmap. First, you can use some of the built-in DarkBASIC commands, such as those covered in Chapter 9. Alternatively, you can use a paint program such as Paint Shop Pro to create some interesting graphics, and then load them into your DarkBASIC program. To create a bitmap that will be loaded by DarkBASIC, you need a graphics editor program. My favorite graphic editor is Paint Shop Pro by Jasc Software (http://www.jasc.com). A trial version of Paint Shop Pro is included on the CD-ROM (see Figure 10.2), and you can install it from the CD-ROM menu.

Figure 10.2 *Paint Shop Pro is a powerful graphics editor.*

This program has all the tools you need to create a bitmap file for use in DarkBASIC. There are numerous image editing tools, and a zoom feature that is useful for precision graphics editing. Editing and manipulating game graphics is a serious subject, as well as a serious career choice for many who find employment in the graphic arts, advertising, and games industries. However, full coverage of this topic is beyond the scope of this book. I recommend you pick up a book or two on the subject, such as *Paint Shop Pro 7 Fast & Easy* (Premier Press, 2000). Even if you are interested solely in 3D graphics, you should know how to create 2D graphics because 3D textures are created with programs like Paint Shop Pro. For more information, fast-forward to Chapter 17, "Fundamentals of 3D Graphics Programming."

Uses for Bitmaps

So what kinds of uses are there for bitmaps? There are plenty of different things you can do with them. You can create beautiful backgrounds or use smaller bitmaps to display score lines and statistics. Instead of drawing your pictures pixel-by-pixel or line-by-line, you can use bitmaps to stamp the entire image on the screen.

I have found quite a few uses for bitmaps in the years I have been programming. I have used them to create fonts (for text on the screen) and textures (for skins of models), and even for height mapping. Because a bitmap is nothing more than a series of bytes, you can use it for anything. (Why we don't call them byte maps, I don't know.)

Creating and Loading Bitmaps

First I will cover the series of commands to load and create bitmaps. These commands are useful for loading a picture you create in Microsoft Paint or for creating your own pictures within DarkBASIC.

DarkBASIC can support a maximum of 32 bitmaps at one time. This might seem like a small number, but you can be creative and eliminate any problems related to the small number of bitmaps. Usually you won't be using more than five or six bitmaps at a time, because most of the work in a 2D game is handled by sprites, which are stored separately from bitmaps (as you'll see in Chapter 11, "The Art of Using Animated Sprites for 2D Games").

Each bitmap is addressed like an array. That is to say, each bitmap has a number attached to it, ranging from 0 to 31. Bitmap 0 is special in that it is displayed on the screen by default. Therefore, if you load a graphic into bitmap 0, it will be displayed on the screen.

> **NOTE**
>
> Bitmap 0 is an important bitmap. It is reserved for the screen. Anything loaded, drawn, or pasted on this bitmap will appear directly on the screen.

Loading a Bitmap File

LOAD BITMAP is the first of the important bitmap commands. The command format is LOAD BITMAP *Filename*, *Bitmap Number*. The first parameter is the name of the file to load; the second one is the bitmap number (between 0 and 31) into which to load the image. In DarkBASIC, there are no bitmap variables; instead, there is a built-in array of bitmaps that you can use. In other languages, such as C++, Visual Basic, and Delphi, you would have to create a variable and then load the bitmap into memory, after which you would be able to draw it on the screen. In DarkBASIC, though, you can just load a bitmap into the bitmap array.

It is easy to load a bitmap and display it on the screen at the same time. DarkBASIC defines bitmap 0 as the screen, so if you pass a value of 0 to LOAD BITMAP, it will load the file directly onto the screen. Note that the bitmap file you want to load must be located in the same directory in which the program resides, or else DarkBASIC will return an error message that it could not find the file.

Creating a New Bitmap in Memory

CREATE BITMAP is the second of the important bitmap commands. Whereas LOAD BITMAP loaded a bitmap from disk and displayed it on the screen, CREATE BITMAP creates a blank bitmap with whatever dimensions you want. This is the command you would use to create bitmaps on which to draw within DarkBASIC. The syntax for this command is CREATE BITMAP *Bitmap Number*, *Width*, *Height*.

Unlike the LOAD BITMAP command that has a *Bitmap Number* parameter, when you call the CREATE BITMAP command, all drawing operations (such as LINE or CIRCLE) then take place on that new bitmap by default. Therefore, if you create a new bitmap and then perform some drawing commands, those operations will not go to the screen, but instead to the new bitmap! Be mindful of this situation; when things do not appear on the screen as you expected, you might want to make sure that you have first called SET CURRENT BITMAP 0 to set the current output to the screen.

CREATE BITMAP requires three parameters to work (none are optional). The first parameter is the number of the bitmap you want to create. This parameter will accept any number between 1 and 31. You cannot use 0 in this parameter because 0 is the screen. Technically, you can only load 31 bitmaps at a time in DarkBASIC, although the screen acts like a bitmap as well. Also, you cannot use a bitmap number that has already been used (either via CREATE BITMAP or LOAD BITMAP) without first deleting the bitmap.

The second and third parameters are the width and height of the bitmap. These do not have to match the screen's width and height. You can make a bitmap 100×100 pixels, or you can make it 1600×1200 pixels, although I can't imagine why you would need one that big!

The CreateBitmap program creates a bitmap and displays circles on it. Figure 10.3 shows the results of the CreateBitmap program. This program is located on the CD-ROM in the Sources\DarkBASIC\CH10\CreateBitmap folder. (The DarkBASIC Pro version is located in Sources\DBPro\CH10\CreateBitmap.)

Figure 10.3 *The CreateBitmap program shows how to create and draw onto a bitmap in memory.*

```
`----------------------------------
`Beginner's Guide To Game Programming With DarkBASIC
`Copyright (C)2002 Jonathan S. Harbour and Joshua R. Smith
`Chapter 10 - CreateBitmap program
`----------------------------------

HIDE MOUSE

`create a new bitmap
PRINT "Creating the bitmap..."
CREATE BITMAP 1, 640, 480

`display message on the screen
SET CURRENT BITMAP 0
PRINT "Drawing circles..."

`draw some circles on the bitmap surface
SET CURRENT BITMAP 1
FOR N = 1 TO 100
    INK RGB(RND(255), RND(255), RND(255)), 0
    CIRCLE RND(640), RND(480), RND(100)
NEXT N

SET CURRENT BITMAP 0
PRINT "Press a key to display the bitmap..."
WAIT KEY

`copy bitmap 1 to the screen
COPY BITMAP 1, 0

WAIT KEY
END
```

Checking the Status of a Bitmap

Creating and loading bitmaps can be complicated, especially if you don't know whether one has been created or loaded already. The BITMAP EXIST command can help you there. The command format is BITMAP EXIST(*Bitmap Number*). This command takes one parameter—the bitmap number—and tells you whether that bitmap has been created or loaded. It returns a 0 if the bitmap does not exist and a 1 if it does exist. These two numbers are standard in most languages, where true = 1 and false = 0. Personally, I find it easier to remember that false always equals zero instead of trying to remember both.

The BitmapStatus program demonstrates the effects of the BITMAP EXIST command. Figure 10.4 shows the output of this program. Note that bitmap 0 (the screen) will always return true, because the screen always exists. This program is located on the CD-ROM in the Sources\DarkBASIC\CH10\BitmapStatus folder. (The DarkBASIC Pro version is located in Sources\DBPro\CH10\BitmapStatus.)

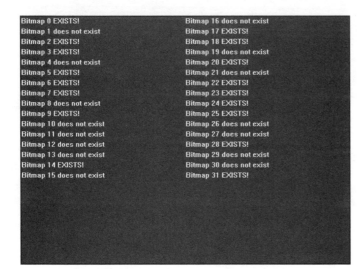

Figure 10.4 *The BitmapStatus program demonstrates the use of the* BITMAP EXIST *command.*

```
`---------------------------------
`Beginner's Guide To DarkBASIC Game Programming
`Copyright (C)2002 Jonathan S. Harbour and Joshua R. Smith
`Chapter 10 - BitmapStatus program
`---------------------------------

`initialize some variables
N = 0
status = 0
message$ = ""

`create the status messages
DIM E$(2)
```

```
E$(0) = " does not exist"
E$(1) = " EXISTS!"

`create some bitmaps (randomly)
RANDOMIZE TIMER()
FOR N = 1 TO 31
    IF RND(10) < 5
        CREATE BITMAP N, 640, 480
    ENDIF
NEXT N

`set up the screen
HIDE MOUSE
SET CURRENT BITMAP 0

`display status of each bitmap
FOR N = 0 TO 15
    `check bitmaps 0-15
    message$ = E$(BITMAP EXIST(N))
    `display the status
    TEXT 0, N * 20, "Bitmap " + STR$(N) + message$

    `check bitmaps 16-31
    message$ = E$(BITMAP EXIST(N+16))
    `display the status
    TEXT 320, N * 20, "Bitmap " + STR$(N+16) + message$
NEXT N

WAIT KEY
END
```

Bitmap Information Commands

Now that you know how to load and create bitmaps, it is time to move on to some
other important commands. Each bitmap has specific information, and there are
three things that every bitmap has—width, height, and depth. The width and
height are pretty self-explanatory. The depth is the color depth of the bitmap.
DarkBASIC provides you with commands to find these properties.

Determining Width and Height

The BITMAP WIDTH command returns the width in pixels of a specified bitmap. It takes one parameter—the bitmap number. The BITMAP WIDTH command syntax is BITMAP WIDTH (*Bitmap Number*). The BitmapInfo program demonstrates the use of the BITMAP WIDTH command.

The BITMAP HEIGHT command returns the height in pixels of a specified bitmap. It takes one parameter, just like the BITMAP WIDTH command. In fact, it is the same parameter. The BITMAP HEIGHT command format is BITMAP HEIGHT (*Bitmap Number*). The Bitmap Info program demonstrates the use of the BITMAP HEIGHT command.

Determining Color Depth

The BITMAP DEPTH command returns the color depth of a specified bitmap. It has one parameter as well—the bitmap number. The command format is BITMAP DEPTH (*Bitmap Number*). It returns a bit depth value shown in Table 10.1, not the number of colors. The BitmapInfo program demonstrates how to use the BITMAP DEPTH command.

The BitmapInfo Program

The BitmapInfo program (which is located on the CD-ROM under Sources\Chapter10\BitmapInfo) loads a bitmap file and then displays the width, height, and depth of the bitmap. Figure 10.5 shows the output of the program.

Bitmap File: EARTH.BMP
Dimensions: 449 X 458
Color depth: 16-bit

Figure 10.5 *The BitmapInfo program demonstrates how to read the width, height, and color depth of a bitmap.*

```
`---------------------------------- --
`Beginner's Guide To DarkBASIC Game Programming
`Copyright (C)2002 Jonathan S. Harbour and Joshua R. Smith
`Chapter 10 - BitmapInfo program
`----------------------------------

HIDE MOUSE

`load and display the BMP image
ShowBitmap("EARTH.BMP")
WAIT KEY
CLS
`load and display the JPG image
ShowBitmap("SUNSET.JPG")
WAIT KEY
CLS
`load and display the TGA image
ShowBitmap("EXPLODE.TGA")
WAIT KEY
END

FUNCTION ShowBitmap(Filename$)
    `load the bitmap file
    LOAD BITMAP Filename$, 1
    `display the bitmap file
    COPY BITMAP 1, 0
    `read information about the bitmap
    width$ = STR$(BITMAP WIDTH(1))
    height$ = STR$(BITMAP HEIGHT(1))
    depth$ = STR$(BITMAP DEPTH(1))
    `display information about the bitmap
    SET CURRENT BITMAP 0
    TEXT 460, 0, "Bitmap File: " + Filename$
    TEXT 460, 20, "Dimensions: " + width$ + " X " + height$
    TEXT 460, 40, "Color depth: " + depth$ + "-bit"
    `delete the bitmap from memory
    DELETE BITMAP 1
ENDFUNCTION
```

Basic Bitmap Commands

Now that you know the commands to create and measure bitmaps, it's time to manipulate them. This is not as hard as it sounds. All the commands required to manipulate bitmaps are included in DarkBASIC. However, you will need to keep track of where each bitmap is located in the bitmap array. Remember how I told you that DarkBASIC supports 32 bitmaps (0–31)? The next set of commands will allow you to manipulate those different bitmaps.

Copying One Bitmap to Another

Finally, the COPY BITMAP command that you have been using throughout the examples is explained! This is one of the more complicated commands because it can take two different sets of parameters. If you want to copy the contents of an entire bitmap from one bitmap to another, the format is COPY BITMAP *From Bitmap, To Bitmap*, where the entire "from" bitmap is copied to the "to" bitmap.

You use the slightly more complicated version of the command when you want to copy only part of a bitmap. In that case, the COPY BITMAP command takes 10 parameters. The command format is COPY BITMAP *From Bitmap, Left, Top, Right, Bottom, To Bitmap, Left, Top, Right, Bottom*. The *From Bitmap* and *To Bitmap* parameters are the same as in the first command. The *Left, Right, Top*, and *Bottom* parameters on both sides specify what pixels to copy and to where. Figure 10.6 will give you a better visual explanation of the COPY BITMAP command.

There is a catch to the 10-parameter COPY BITMAP command. When copying pixels from one bitmap to another, the COPY BITMAP command uses 0,0 as the upper-left corner. This means that when you copy to or from a bitmap, the furthest right you should copy is BITMAP WIDTH -1, and the furthest down you should copy is BITMAP HEIGHT -1.

Changing the Current Bitmap

SET CURRENT BITMAP is the most common command for programming bitmaps because it changes the bitmap number to which drawing commands are directed. If you use the CIRCLE command, the normal output is to the screen, which is bitmap 0 in the array. The TEXT command works the same way, drawing to the current bitmap. The SET CURRENT BITMAP command allows you to change the current bitmap. The command format is SET CURRENT BITMAP *Bitmap Number*. When you use this command, you can draw to any bitmap, not just to the screen.

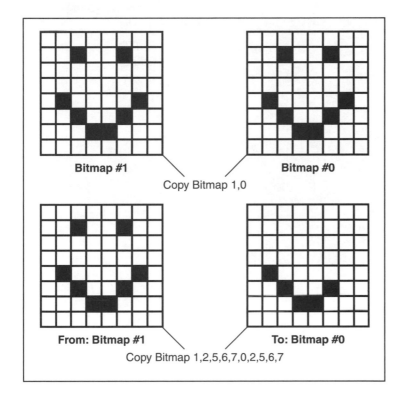

Figure 10.6

A portion of one bitmap is copied to another bitmap

Likewise, the CURRENT BITMAP command returns the number of the currently active bitmap. The command format is Return Value = CURRENT BITMAP() (meaning that this command has no parameters). This is a useful command to help you keep track of which bitmap you are using.

The CurrentBitmap program demonstrates the use of both commands (as shown in Figure 10.7). This program is located on the CD-ROM in Sources\CH10\DarkBASIC\CurrentBitmap. (The DarkBASIC Pro version is located in Sources\CH10\DBPro\CurrentBitmap.)

The source code for the SetCurrentBitmap program follows. Notice that after each section, I set the current bitmap back to 0. This is because I want to display something to the screen. I told you earlier that bitmap 0 is the screen. This is a case in which you need to change the bitmap back to 0 to display some text.

TIP

Remember that the screen is always referenced as bitmap 0. Drawing commands performed on bitmap 0 are displayed directly on the screen.

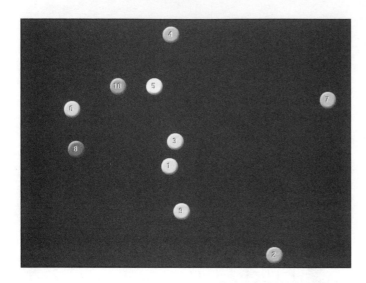

Figure 10.7 *The CurrentBitmap program demonstrates the use of the* SET CURRENT BITMAP *command.*

```
`----------------------------------
`Beginner's Guide TO DarkBASIC Game Programming
`Copyright (C)2002 Jonathan S. Harbour and Joshua R. Smith
`Chapter 10 - CurrentBitmap program
`----------------------------------

`initialize some variables
maxballs = 10
source=31
DIM xpos(maxballs)
DIM ypos(maxballs)
DIM xdir(maxballs)
DIM ydir(maxballs)

`initialize screen and load the source bitmap
HIDE MOUSE
SYNC ON
LOAD BITMAP "circles.bmp", source

`change font size and transparency
SET TEXT TRANSPARENT
SET TEXT SIZE 16

`create and set up the bitmaps
```

```
FOR N = 1 TO maxballs
    `create bitmap and copy image from source
    CREATE BITMAP N, 33, 33
    COPY BITMAP source, N*32, 0, N*32+31, 32, N, 0, 0, 32, 32
    `draw the bitmap # on the image
    SET CURRENT BITMAP N
    INK RGB(10,10,10), 0
    CENTER TEXT 14, 6, STR$(N)
    INK RGB(255,255,255), 0
    CENTER TEXT 15, 7, STR$(N)
    `set the starting position
    xpos(N) = RND(600)
    ypos(N) = RND(460)
    xdir(N) = RND(4)-3
    ydir(N) = RND(4)-3
NEXT N

`draw to the screen
SET CURRENT BITMAP 0
REPEAT
    CLS
    FOR N = 1 TO maxballs
        `update X position
        xpos(N) = xpos(N) + xdir(N)
        `make sure X stays on the screen
        IF xpos(N) < 10
            xpos(N) = 10
            xdir(N) = xdir(N) * -1
        ENDIF
        IF xpos(N) > 600
            xpos(N) = 600
            xdir(N) = xdir(N) * -1
        ENDIF
        `update Y position
        ypos(N) = ypos(N) + ydir(N)
        `make sure Y stays on the screen
        IF ypos(N) < 10
            ypos(N) = 10
            ydir(N) = ydir(N) * -1
        ENDIF
        IF ypos(N) > 440
            ypos(N) = 440
```

```
            ydir(N) = ydir(N) * -1
        ENDIF

        `draw the bitmap on the screen
        X = xpos(N)
        Y = ypos(N)
        COPY BITMAP N, 0, 0, 32, 32, 0, X, Y, X+32, Y+32
    NEXT  x
    `update the screen
    SYNC
`loop until user presses ESC or clicks mouse
UNTIL ESCAPEKEY()=1 OR MOUSECLICK()=1

END
```

Saving a Bitmap to a File

Sometimes you will want to save the work that you do. DarkBASIC provides a command for that as well—the SAVE BITMAP command. Again, it takes two different sets of parameters. If you want to save the contents of the screen, the command is SAVE BITMAP *Filename*. If you want to save the contents of a specific bitmap number, the command is SAVE BITMAP *Filename, Bitmap Number*.

The SaveBitmap program draws circles to one of the memory bitmaps and then saves the bitmap to a disk file called output.bmp (see Figure 10.8). The source code for this program follows.

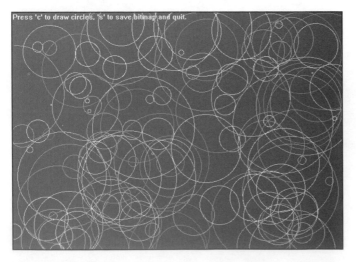

Figure 10.8 *The output generated by the* SAVE BITMAP *command in the SaveBitmap program*

```
`-----------------------------------
`Beginner's Guide To DarkBASIC Game Programming
`Copyright (C)2002 Jonathan S. Harbour and Joshua R. Smith
`Chapter 10 - SaveBitmap program
`-----------------------------------

`initialize screen
HIDE MOUSE
SYNC ON
PRINT "Press 'c' to draw circles, 's' to save bitmap and quit."

`perform a loop
DO
    `check for keyboard input
    key$ = INKEY$()
    IF key$ = "c" OR key$ = "s"
        SELECT key$
            `draw random circles
            CASE "c"
                INK RGB(RND(255), RND(255), RND(255)), 0
                CIRCLE RND(640), RND(480), RND(100)
            ENDCASE
            `end the program
            CASE "s"
                EXIT
            ENDCASE
        ENDSELECT
    ENDIF
    SYNC
LOOP

`save the screen to a file and then quit
SAVE BITMAP "output.bmp", 0
END
```

Deleting a Bitmap

Now comes one of the most important commands in bitmap manipulation—DELETE BITMAP. Remember how I told you that you can only have 32 bitmaps at a time? The DELETE BITMAP command helps you manage those 32 bitmaps by allowing you to delete the ones that are no longer in use. After you are done with a bitmap, it is a good habit to delete it so it will be available elsewhere in the program. All bitmaps are deleted automatically when a DarkBASIC program ends, but it is good programming practice to delete things when you no longer need them—and before a program ends.

> **CAUTION**
>
> Remember bitmap 0 is a special bitmap that points to the screen. Therefore, you really have 31 bitmaps you can delete. If you delete bitmap 0, you might get some unexpected results.

Special Effects Commands

DarkBASIC comes with some great special effects commands for bitmaps. There are five types of special effects you can use with bitmaps. They are MIRROR, FLIP, FADE, BLUR, and SET GAMMA. These commands are easy to use and can be a lot of fun.

The Bitmap Mirror Effect

Just like looking in a mirror, the MIRROR effect will flip your bitmap horizontally. If the image has writing on it, the writing will appear backward. The MIRROR BITMAP command takes one parameter—the bitmap number. The format is MIRROR BITMAP *Bitmap Number*. The MirrorBitmap program demonstrates the command and is listed below (see Figure 10.9). This program is located on the CD-ROM in the Sources\DarkBASIC\CH10\MirrorBitmap folder. (The DarkBASIC Pro project is located in Sources\DBPro\CH10\MirrorBitmap.)

Figure 10.9 *The MirrorBitmap program demonstrates the bitmap mirror effect.*

```
`-----------------------------------
`Beginner's Guide To DarkBASIC Game Programming
`Copyright (C)2002 Jonathan S. Harbour and Joshua R. Smith
`Chapter 10 - MirrorBitmap program
`-----------------------------------

`initialize program
HIDE MOUSE
RANDOMIZE TIMER()

`create two bitmaps
CREATE BITMAP 2, 640, 240
CREATE BITMAP 1, 640, 240

`draw a message on bitmap 1
SET TEXT FONT "Times New Roman"
SET TEXT SIZE 48
SET TEXT TO BOLD
INK RGB(RND(255),RND(255),RND(255)), 0
CENTER TEXT 320, 10, "BITMAP MIRROR EFFECT"
```

```
`copy bitmap 1 to the screen
SET CURRENT BITMAP 0
COPY BITMAP 1, 0

`draw a line across the center
LINE 0, 235, 639, 235

`copy bitmap 1 to bitmap 2 and mirror it
COPY BITMAP 1, 2
MIRROR BITMAP 2

`display bitmap 2 on the screen
COPY BITMAP 2, 0, 0, 639, 239, 0, 0, 239, 639, 479

`wait and then clean up
WAIT KEY
DELETE BITMAP 2
DELETE BITMAP 1
END
```

How can you tell whether a bitmap has been mirrored? By using the BITMAP
MIRRORED command, of course. This command takes one parameter—the bitmap
number. It returns a 0 if the bitmap is mirrored or a 1 if it is not. The command
format is BITMAP MIRRORED (*Bitmap Number*), where *Bitmap Number* is the bitmap you
are checking.

The Bitmap Flip Effect

The FLIP BITMAP command is similar to the MIRROR BITMAP command, but it works
vertically rather than horizontally. This command takes one parameter—the
bitmap number. The command format is FLIP BITMAP *Bitmap Number*. The
FlipBitmap program shows you how to use this command (see Figure 10.10). You
can type in the following source code or load the project from the CD-ROM. The
project is located in Sources\DarkBASIC\CH10\FlipBitmap. (The DarkBASIC Pro
version is located in Sources\DBPro\CH10\FlipBitmap.)

Figure 10.10 *The FlipBitmap program demonstrates the bitmap flip effect.*

```
`-----------------------------------
`Beginner's Guide To DarkBASIC Game Programming
`Copyright (C)2002 Jonathan S. Harbour and Joshua R. Smith
`Chapter 10 - FlipBitmap program
`-----------------------------------

`initialize program
HIDE MOUSE
RANDOMIZE TIMER()

`create two bitmaps
CREATE BITMAP 2, 640, 240
CREATE BITMAP 1, 640, 240

`draw some text on the screen
SET TEXT FONT "Times New Roman"
SET TEXT SIZE 48
SET TEXT TO BOLD
INK RGB(RND(255),RND(255),RND(255)), 0
CENTER TEXT 320, 10, "BITMAP FLIP EFFECT"
```

```
`copy bitmap 1 to the screen
SET CURRENT BITMAP 0
COPY BITMAP 1, 0

`draw a line across the center
LINE 0, 235, 639, 235

`copy bitmap 1 to bitmap 2 and flip it
COPY BITMAP 1, 2
FLIP BITMAP 2

`display bitmap 2 on the screen
COPY BITMAP 2, 0, 0, 639, 239, 0, 0, 239, 639, 479

`wait and then clean up
WAIT KEY
DELETE BITMAP 2
DELETE BITMAP 1
END
```

Whereas the FLIP BITMAP command vertically inverts a bitmap, the BITMAP FLIPPED command determines whether the bitmap has been flipped. This command is similar to the BITMAP MIRRORED command in that it returns 1 if the bitmap is flipped or 0 if it is not flipped. The syntax is BITMAP FLIPPED(*Bitmap Number*).

The Bitmap Fade Effect

The FADE BITMAP command fades the contents of a bitmap by a percentage of darkness. The command takes two parameters—the bitmap number and the fade value. The fade value ranges from 0 (blackness) to 100 (no fading). The syntax is FADE BITMAP *Bitmap Number, Fade Value*. When you have run the FADE BITMAP command, the effects are permanent until you create or load the bitmap again.

The FadeEffect program demonstrates how to use this command by moving a bitmap around the screen, fading it in and out (see Figure 10.11). This program is located on the CD-ROM in Sources\DarkBASIC\CH10\FadeEffect. (The DarkBASIC Pro version is located in Sources\DBPro\CH10\FadeEffect.)

FADE VALUE: 55

Figure 10.11 *The FadeEffect program demonstrates the bitmap fade effect.*

```
`-----------------------------------
`Beginner's Guide To DarkBASIC Game Programming
`Copyright (C)2002 Jonathan S. Harbour and Joshua R. Smith
`Chapter 10 - FadeEffect program
`-----------------------------------

`create some variables
fade = 100
change = -1

`initialize program
HIDE MOUSE
SYNC ON

`load the source bitmap and create the scratch bitmap
LOAD BITMAP "tippy.bmp", 1
CREATE BITMAP 2, BITMAP WIDTH(1), BITMAP HEIGHT(1)
SET CURRENT BITMAP 0

REPEAT
    `change the fade value
    fade = fade + change
```

```
    `bounce fade value off the extremes
    IF fade < 1
        fade = 1
        change = 1
    ENDIF
    IF fade > 100
        fade = 100
        change = -1
    ENDIF

    `draw the faded bitmap
    CLS
    COPY BITMAP 1, 2
    FADE BITMAP 2, fade
    COPY BITMAP 2, 0

    `display fade value on the screen
    TEXT 460, 10, "FADE VALUE: " + STR$(fade)

    `update the screen
    SYNC

`wait for ESC key or mouse click
UNTIL ESCAPEKEY()=1 OR MOUSECLICK()=1
END
```

The Bitmap Blur Effect

The BLUR BITMAP command blurs a bitmap, which makes it look fuzzy and indistinct. This command takes two parameters, like the FADE BITMAP command—bitmap number and blur value. The blur value ranges between 1 (a couple beers) to 6 (a bottle of tequila). The command format is BLUR BITMAP *Bitmap Number*, *Blur Value*. Just like the FADE BITMAP command, BLUR BITMAP is also permanent.

The BlurEffect program demonstrates the BLUR BITMAP command (see Figure 10.12). You can type in the program from the following listing or load it from the CD-ROM in the Sources\DarkBASIC\CH10\BlurEffect folder. (The DarkBASIC Pro version of the project is located in Sources\DBPro\CH10\BlurEffect.)

Figure 10.12 *The BlurEffect program demonstrates the bitmap blur effect.*

```
`----------------------------------
`Beginner's Guide To DarkBASIC Game Programming
`Copyright (C)2002 Jonathan S. Harbour and Joshua R. Smith
`Chapter 10 - BlurEffect program
`----------------------------------

`create some variables
blur = 1
change = 1

`initialize program
HIDE MOUSE
SYNC ON
SYNC RATE 10

`load the source bitmap and create the scratch bitmap
LOAD BITMAP "tippy.bmp", 1
CREATE BITMAP 2, BITMAP WIDTH(1), BITMAP HEIGHT(1)
SET CURRENT BITMAP 0

REPEAT
    `change the fade value
    blur = blur + change
```

```
`bounce fade value off the extremes
IF blur < 1
    blur = 1
    change = 1
ENDIF
IF blur > 6
    blur = 6
    change = -1
ENDIF

CLS
`restore bitmap using original
COPY BITMAP 1, 2
`blue the bitmap
BLUR BITMAP 2, blur
`draw the blurred bitmap
COPY BITMAP 2, 0

`display blur value on the screen
TEXT 460, 10, "BLUR VALUE: " + STR$(blur)

`update the screen
SYNC

`wait for ESC key or mouse click
UNTIL ESCAPEKEY()=1 OR MOUSECLICK()=1
END
```

The Bitmap Gamma Effect

The SET GAMMA command is the last of the special effects commands. It takes three parameters and adjusts the gamma display, which is related to the brightness of an image. The three parameters are red, green, and blue. Each value ranges from 0 to 511, with 255 being the middle value. For instance, you can remove all the red from a bitmap by setting Red = 0. The command syntax is SET GAMMA *Red, Green, Blue*. There is a warning that comes with this command: Some graphics cards do not support the SET GAMMA command.

The GammaEffect program combines the mirror, flip, fade, blur, and gamma commands for an interesting effect (see Figure 10.13). The program is located on the

GAMMA VALUE: 125

Figure 10.13 *The GammaEffect program shows how the* SET GAMMA *command changes the light level of a bitmap (or the screen).*

CD-ROM at Sources\Chapter10\GammaEffect. (The DarkBASIC Pro version of the program is located in Sources\DBPro\CH10\GammaEffect.)

```
`----------------------------------
`Beginner's Guide To DarkBASIC Game Programming
`Copyright (C)2002 Jonathan S. Harbour and Joshua R. Smith
`Chapter 10 - GammaEffect program
`----------------------------------

`create some variables
gamma = 255
change = -10

`initialize program
HIDE MOUSE
SYNC ON

`load the source bitmap and create the scratch bitmap
LOAD BITMAP "tippy.bmp", 1
SET CURRENT BITMAP 0

REPEAT
    `change the gamma value
    gamma = gamma + change
```

```
`bounce gamma value off the extremes
IF gamma < 0
    gamma = 0
    change = 10
ENDIF
IF gamma > 510
    gamma = 510
    change = -10
ENDIF

`draw the bitmap
CLS
COPY BITMAP 1, 0

`display gamma value on the screen
TEXT 460, 10, "GAMMA VALUE: " + STR$(gamma)

`update the screen
SET GAMMA gamma, gamma, gamma
SYNC

`wait for ESC key or mouse click
UNTIL ESCAPEKEY()=1 OR MOUSECLICK()=1
END
```

ImageShuffle: A Complete Bitmap-Based Game

This chapter project is a fun one. Do you remember the old plastic-tile games? The ones that had tiles numbered 1 through 15, and you had to get the numbers in the correct order? The chapter project mimics that game. You simply click a tile to move it into the blank space. Figure 10.14 shows what the ImageShuffle game looks like when it starts, and Figure 10.15 shows the game screen after the puzzle has been completed successfully.

Figure 10.14 *The ImageShuffle game in action. Can you reorganize the tiles?*

Figure 10.15 *The ImageShuffle game completed. The tiles are in order.*

```
`---------------------------------
`Beginner's Guide To DarkBASIC Game Programming
`Copyright (C)2002 Jonathan S. Harbour and Joshua R. Smith
`Chapter 10 - ImageShuffle Program
`---------------------------------

`Tile position data for calculating valid moves
DATA 2,5,0,0
DATA 1,3,6,0
DATA 2,4,7,0
DATA 3,8,0,0
DATA 1,6,9,0
DATA 2,5,7,10
DATA 3,6,8,11
DATA 4,7,12,0
DATA 5,10,13,0
DATA 6,9,11,14
DATA 7,10,12,15
DATA 8,11,16,0
DATA 9,14,0,0
DATA 13,10,15,0
DATA 14,16,11,0
DATA 12,15,0,0

`Declare some variables
DIM Tiles(17)
DIM MovingMatrix(64)
DIM Selected(2)
DIM MoveIt(4)
TempX = 0
TempY = 0
done = 0
Width = 0
Height = 0

`Initialize the display
SYNC ON

`Load the game graphics
```

```
LOAD BITMAP "mainback.bmp", 17
LOAD BITMAP "tiles.bmp", 18

`Create the tile bitmaps
FOR x = 1 TO 16
    CREATE BITMAP x, 100, 100
NEXT x

`Copy the tile bitmaps
FOR y = 0 TO 3
    FOR x = 0 TO 3
        pos = (y * 4 + x) + 1
        TX = x * 100
        TY = y * 100
        COPY BITMAP 18,TX,TY,TX + 99,TY + 99,pos,0,0,99,99
    NEXT x
NEXT y

`Set the moving matrix
FOR x = 1 TO 64
    READ a
    MovingMatrix(x) = a
NEXT x

`Initialize the game
SET CURRENT BITMAP 0
ShuffleTiles
DisplayBoard
Selected(1) = 0
Selected(2) = 0

`Main game loop
REPEAT
    SYNC
    IF MOUSECLICK()=1
        `Wait for mouse button to be released
        WHILE MOUSECLICK()=1
        ENDWHILE
        `Figure out which tile was clicked
```

```
        bitmap = BitmapNumber(MOUSEX(), MOUSEY())
        b2 = CheckValid(bitmap)

        `Swap the clicked tile and the blank tile
        IF b2 <> 0
            SwapTiles(bitmap, b2)
            DisplayBoard
            done = CheckForWin()
        ENDIF
    ENDIF
UNTIL done = 1

`Game over
PRINT "Congratulations, You Win!"
SYNC

`Delete the tile bitmaps from memory
FOR x = 1     TO 16
    DELETE BITMAP x
NEXT x

`End the game
WAIT KEY
END

`This function will randomize the tiles
FUNCTION ShuffleTiles
    FOR count = 1 TO 16
        Tiles(count) = count
        IF count = 16 THEN Tiles(count) = -1
    NEXT count
    RandomMoves = RND(50) + 100
    FOR count = 1 TO RandomMoves
        MoveTheSpace
    NEXT count
ENDFUNCTION

`This function displays the tiles on the screen
FUNCTION DisplayBoard
```

```
        COPY BITMAP 17,0
        FOR y = 0 TO 3
            FOR x = 0 TO 3
                pos = (y * 4 + x) + 1
                IF Tiles(pos) >= 0
                    TX = x * 100
                    TY = y * 100
                    W = TX + 99 + 120
                    H = TY + 99 + 56
                    COPY BITMAP Tiles(pos),0,0,99,99,0,TX+120,TY+56,W,H
                ENDIF
            NEXT x
        NEXT y
        SYNC
ENDFUNCTION

`This function checks the coordinates for a valid tile
FUNCTION CheckValid(rx)
    IF rx = -1 OR Tiles(rx) = -1 THEN EXITFUNCTION 0

    FOR x= 1 TO 16
        ptr = ((x - 1) * 4) + 1
        IF rx = x
            a1 = MovingMatrix(ptr)
            a2 = MovingMatrix(ptr + 1)
            a3 = MovingMatrix(ptr + 2)
            a4 = MovingMatrix(ptr + 3)
            IF a1 <> 0 and Tiles(a1) = -1 THEN EXITFUNCTION a1
            IF a2 <> 0 and Tiles(a2) = -1 THEN EXITFUNCTION a2
            IF a3 <> 0 and Tiles(a3) = -1 THEN EXITFUNCTION a3
            IF a4 <> 0 and Tiles(a4) = -1 THEN EXITFUNCTION a4
        ENDIF
    NEXT x
ENDFUNCTION 0

`This function returns the value of the bitmap located at x,y
FUNCTION BitmapNumber(x, y)
    dx = x - 120
    dy = y - 56
```

```
        IF dx < 0 or dy < 0 THEN EXITFUNCTION -1

        dx = dx / 100
        dy = dy / 100

        pos = ((dy * 4) + dx) + 1

        IF pos > 16 THEN pos = -1
        IF pos < 0 THEN pos = -1
ENDFUNCTION pos


`This function swaps two tiles in the Tiles array
FUNCTION SwapTiles(c1, c2)
        temp = Tiles(c1)
        Tiles(c1) = Tiles(c2)
        Tiles(c2) = temp
ENDFUNCTION


`This function moves the empty tile
FUNCTION MoveTheSpace
        spt = 0
        FOR x = 1      TO 16
            IF Tiles(x) = -1 THEN spt = x
        NEXT x

        IF spt = 0 THEN EXITFUNCTION

        FOR x= 1      TO 16
            ptr = ((x-1)*4)+1
            IF spt = x
                MoveIt(1) = MovingMatrix(ptr)
                MoveIt(2) = MovingMatrix(ptr + 1)
                MoveIt(3) = MovingMatrix(ptr + 2)
                MoveIt(4) = MovingMatrix(ptr + 3)

                movenum = RND(3)+1
                WHILE MoveIt(movenum) = 0
                    movenum = RND(3)+1
                ENDWHILE
```

```
                c1 = spt
                c2 = MoveIt(movenum)
                SwapTiles(c1,c2)
            ENDIF
        NEXT x
ENDFUNCTION

`This function scans the tiles for a win
FUNCTION CheckForWin
        FOR x = 1 TO 15
            IF Tiles(x) <> x THEN EXITFUNCTION 0
        NEXT x
        Tiles(16) = 16
        DisplayBoard
        SLEEP 2500
        EXITFUNCTION 1
ENDFUNCTION
```

This is a simple yet fun game. However, there are some things that you can add to make this game even more fun. Here are some suggestions for improving the ImageShuffle game.

- **High score**. Keep track of how many clicks it takes the player to solve the puzzle.
- **Different levels**. Use a different set of tiles for each level of the game.
- **Board size**. Increase the number of tiles to 64 (an 8×8 array).
- **Special effects**. Add a special effect when the tiles move (such as sliding or fading).

Summary

Bitmaps are the key to writing 2D games in DarkBASIC, and this introductory chapter merely scratched the surface of what DarkBASIC can do. There are many different commands that you can use with bitmaps, such as the special effects commands covered in this chapter. The next chapter will take bitmaps to another level entirely, combining the bitmap image with transparency using a technique called *sprite animation*.

Chapter Quiz

The chapter quiz will help reinforce the material you learned in this chapter, and will provide feedback on how well you have learned the subjects. For the answers to the quiz, refer to Appendix A, "Answers to the Chapter Quizzes."

1. How many colors are in an 8-bit bitmap?

   A. 1,000

   B. 256

   C. 16,777,216

   D. 47

2. What does the following code do?

```
LOAD BITMAP "images\test1.bmp", 1
```

   A. Loads images\test1.bmp into bitmap 1

   B. Loads images\test1.bmp and displays it on the screen

   C. Nothing

   D. A and B

3. How many bitmaps does DarkBASIC support at one time?

   A. 25

   B. 1,000

   C. 32

   D. Unlimited

4. Which bitmap represents the screen?

   A. 31

   B. 15

   C. 56

   D. 0

5. Which command copies the contents of bitmap 1 into bitmap 0?

   A. COPY BITMAP 0,1

   B. REPLICATE BITMAP 1,0

   C. REPRODUCE BITMAP 1,0

   D. COPY BITMAP 1,0

6. Which command deletes bitmap 1?

    A. `REMOVE BITMAP 1`

    B. `ERASE BITMAP 1`

    C. `DELETE BITMAP 1`

    D. You cannot delete a bitmap.

7. To what does the following code set the current bitmap?

    ```
    bitmapnum = (10/2)+10
    SET CURRENT BITMAP bitmapnum
    ```

    A. 10

    B. 2

    C. 15

    D. 25

8. Which command flips bitmap 1 horizontally?

    A. `FLIP BITMAP 1`

    B. `MIROR BITMAP 1`

    C. `FLIP BITMAP 1, Horizontally`

    D. `MIRROR BITMAP 1, Horizontally`

9. Which command creates a bitmap that is 100×150 pixels?

    A. `CREATE BITMAP 100, 150, 1`

    B. `CREATE BITMAP 150, 1, 100`

    C. `CREATE BITMAP 1,100,150`

    D. `CREATE BITMAP 1,150,100`

10. `SAVE BITMAP` will save any bitmap to the hard drive.

    A. True

    B. False

CHAPTER 11

THE ART OF USING ANIMATED SPRITES FOR 2D GAMES

In the old days, before video games ran in 3D, all game graphics were hand-drawn and displayed on the screen as static, non-moving objects or as animated sprites. Although the subject of sprites might seem dated and irrelevant today, the truth is quite contrary. Numerous commercial games are released each year that run in 2D using graphics very much like the sprites used in classic arcade games such as *Heavy Barrel* and *Akari Warriors*.

Consider Sid Meier's *Civilization III*, for instance. That game has some fantastic 3D models in it, but the models are all pre-rendered and stored as snapshots to be drawn on the screen as sprites. The game is designed as an isometric turn-based strategy game, and simply does not need to run in 3D mode. Yet despite the fact that this game is 2D, it is a phenomenal best-selling game.

Why do you suppose anyone would develop a 2D game in today's world of advanced 3D video cards? The argument might be made that games have not been able to tap the potential of the latest generation of video cards, and yet new graphics chips are developed every six to twelve months, often doubling the performance of the previous chip. The reason is not that 2D games are easier to program or that 3D models are difficult to design. In fact, *Civilization III* uses 3D models in a 2D fashion. It is a matter of game play. There are some games that are meant to be played a certain way, and *Civilization III* just wouldn't be a *Civilization* game if it didn't run in 2D. This chapter explains not only how to use sprites, but also why you would want to learn about sprite programming in this modern era of 3D gaming.

This chapter covers the following topics:

- Introduction to Sprites
- Creating and Loading Sprites
- Sprite Properties
- Drawing and Moving Sprites
- The All-Powerful Game Loop
- Detecting Sprite Collisions

Introduction to Sprites

A *sprite* is a small, two-dimensional bitmap that is drawn to the screen at a specified position and usually with transparency. There are many ways to create a sprite and many ways to program its functionality. Will a particular sprite be a solid image or will it have transparent pixels? Will the sprite automatically move in a specified way on the screen, or will it respond interactively to the player? Before these questions even arise, however, how do you create a sprite and load the graphic image (or images) it uses? This chapter addresses these questions.

Transparency

Transparency in a sprite is defined by pixels in the source bitmap that are set to a certain color. When the sprite is drawn on the screen, any pixels with that transparent color are not drawn, which results in the background showing through the sprite in those places. Figure 11.1 illustrates this concept.

If you were to load this particular sprite and draw it transparently, the transparent pixels around the ball would not be drawn, so you would only see the ball. However, if you were to draw the sprite *without* transparency, then all the pixels in the sprite's bitmap image would be drawn, as shown in Figure 11.2.

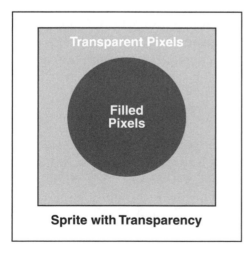

Figure 11.1 *The dark circle represents the pixels used by the sprite, and the lighter color around the circle represents the transparent pixels.*

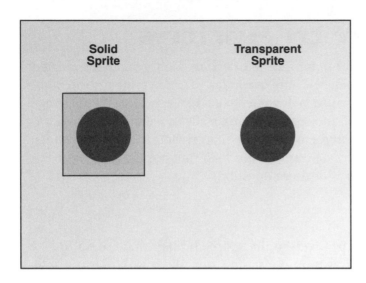

Figure 11.2 *When a sprite is drawn over a background image on the screen, it becomes clear how helpful transparency is for displaying the sprite properly.*

Indeed, transparency is the key to drawing sprites, and is essential for any decent 2D game. Without transparency, there really is no possible way to write a game. When you get into the 3D realm transparency takes on a whole new meaning, but when it comes to 2D games transparency is the single most important factor.

Basic Sprite Functionality

Classic video games used sprites exclusively for the graphics and action in the game. In fact, some of the earliest games used solid sprites without any transparency at all! For example, consider the classic Namco game of *Pac-Man* (circa 1980).

Pac-Man

As Figure 11.3 shows, there was really no need for transparent sprites in *Pac-Man* because the background in the game is black. Although there are multiple levels in the game, each level is similar in design to the one shown in Figure 11.3. (In fact, I believe *Pac-Man* and the ghosts were drawn transparently over the yellow pellets, but you get the point). Incidentally, *Pac-Man* was originally called *Puck-Man*, but it was renamed shortly after release.

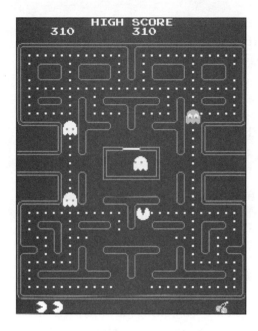

Figure 11.3
Pac-Man *epitomized
the term "video game"
in popular culture.*

Galaxian

Another classic videogame, *Galaxian,* actually had a starry background that
required the use of transparent sprites (see Figure 11.4). Incidentally, *Galaxian* is
reportedly the first color arcade game, although I don't have proof for the claim.

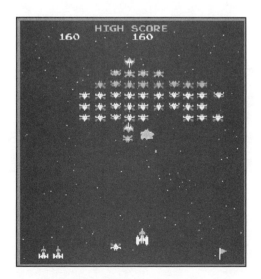

Figure 11.4
Galaxian *was one
of the first space
shooters.*

Now look at the layout of the screen in *Galaxian*. Note the rows of enemy ships arrayed at the top half and the player's ship at the bottom of the screen. The enemy ships move left to right and launch an assault on the player. This game provides a clear example of how sprites are used. Each enemy ship, the player's ship, the projectiles, and even the score is made up of small animated sprites, each with perhaps one to three frames of animation (if any). Even the numerals 0 to 9 are just small sprites. Note also how everything on the screen is basically the same size—a square of what looks like 24×24 pixels.

Figure 11.5 shows a close-up of the player's ship in *Galaxian*, made up of 576 pixels (that's 24×24). By just counting the sprites on the screen, it looks like the game can handle 90 to 100 sprites at a time. That means the game is drawing 57,600 pixels per frame, plus perhaps 200 more pixels for the background stars. You can round off that figure to 58,000 pixels.

To get an idea of the processing power of the computer that runs *Galaxian*, you have to take into account the color depth of the screen. Although you can't discern color in the printed figure, it looks to me like there are 16 colors (at most) on the screen. Each sprite has three or four colors, shared by other sprites. Here are the colors that I can discern:

- Red
- Yellow
- White
- Dark blue
- Light blue
- Violet
- Black

Figure 11.5 *The player's ship in* Galaxian *is a 24×24 sprite.*

What's that, only seven colors? Compared to today's games, which support thousands or millions of colors, it's extraordinary that *Galaxian* only used seven colors, and yet it was still a very entertaining game! Given the total number of sprites supported on the screen at a time, it's a safe bet that this was an 8-bit game (at most).

Figure 11.6 shows the relationship of bit count to total value in a video game. To calculate a binary number, start at the right and "turn on" each bit, adding the values until you get the total number. For instance, since *Galaxian* needs only seven colors, it could have just 4-bit graphics hardware.

Today, bit counts are so high and graphics cards are so powerful that each pixel in a game can be represented by as many as eight *bytes* for things such as alpha blending, which is a means to apply translucency effects to 3D surfaces. An individual texture used in a 3D model today can take up more memory than an entire arcade game machine of the 1980s!

Galaga

Galaga was also an extremely popular game in the arcades because it was not only challenging, but it also offered more than the usual space shooter. By allowing your ship to be captured by the tractor beam of one of the alien ships, you had an opportunity to free that ship and give yourself double firepower! Figure 11.7 shows *Galaga* in action.

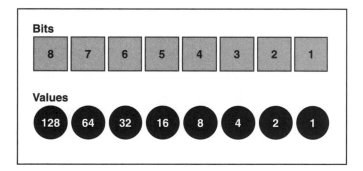

Figure 11.6 *Bit count related to the value of each bit*

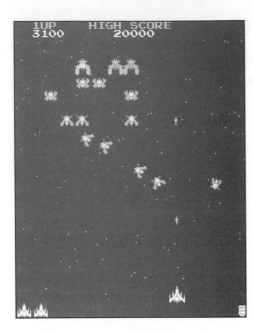

Figure 11.7
Galaga *featured*
fast gameplay,
16-color graphics,
rotating sprites,
and terrific sound.

Extending the Basic Bitmap

Referring to *Civilization III* once again, I'd like to emphasize that this game is a perfect example of a modern 2D game—something that is unusual in today's world of advanced 3D accelerators. *Civilization III* is a turn-based strategy game that does not use any real-time effects or animation.

The remarkable thing about *Civilization III* is that it is such an engrossing game despite the somewhat limited graphics. Now, don't get me wrong—*Civilization III* looks very good, but the game simply does not push the limits of graphics technology. Given the lack of real-time effects in a turn-based game, why is *Civilization III* so much fun and so utterly mesmerizing? In a word, gameplay. *Civilization III* puts the player in control of an entire civilization of people in competition with the other civilizations of the world.

The core aspects of the game, such as researching technology, improving the quality of life, and developing weapons and defenses, all take time to develop over a period of turns. It is this progression of development that makes *Civilization III* such an addictive game.

The Importance of Transparency

Transparency was the primary bottleneck in video game design in the past, and it was often the most highly optimized piece of code in a game. Sprites are drawn to the screen using a technique called *bit-block transfer*, or BITBLT. The most common shorthand for this term is "blit" or "blitting." It means that blocks of memory are copied from one location to another as quickly as possible, often using a high-speed loop written in assembly language (the closest thing to machine language). Although reusable sprite libraries were available for various platforms (Atari, IBM PC, Amiga, and Mac), most programmers had their own optimized blitters and improved the code for each new game project. Figure 11.8 shows an illustration of transparent pixels in a sprite.

In recent years, however, a single sprite library has been used more than any other for the Windows platform (the world's primary gaming platform). This library is called DirectDraw, and it was available in DirectX up through version 7.0 (which is what DarkBASIC supports, although DarkBASIC Pro uses DirectX 8.1). Since most of the work in a game in past years involved writing the blitters, sound mixers, and so on, the advent of DirectX significantly improved the quality and reusability of game code, allowing programmers to focus on higher-level game functionality, such as physics and more intelligent computer players.

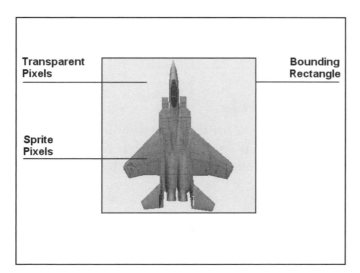

Transparent Pixels

Sprite Pixels

Bounding Rectangle

Figure 11.8

A sprite, complete with a bounding rectangle, transparent pixels, and the sprite's pixels

Creating and Loading Sprites

DarkBASIC has built-in sprite support, so there is no need to write any custom code for loading or drawing sprites or testing collisions. I'll talk more about this a bit later, but first you need to load the source image that the sprite will use. An image is like a bitmap in memory. To load a bitmap into a sprite, you must first load a source file into an image and then copy it to the sprite.

The LOAD BITMAP Command

The first step to drawing a sprite on the screen is to use the LOAD BITMAP command to load the image in a bitmap file into a DarkBASIC bitmap (any number from 0 to 32). Remember, the first bitmap, number 0, references the display screen. You can load a bitmap and display it on the screen in a single command by loading the bitmap directly into bitmap 0. The syntax of the command is LOAD BITMAP *Filename*, *Bitmap Number*.

The GET IMAGE Command

The GET IMAGE command grabs a piece of a bitmap for use in a sprite, and is most useful for ripping out of a bitmap tiles that are laid out in sequence for an animated sprite. This command is used along with LOAD BITMAP and the SPRITE command to animate a sprite on the screen. The syntax of the command is GET IMAGE *Image Number*, *Left*, *Top*, *Right*, *Bottom*.

The SPRITE Command

The SPRITE command draws a sprite on the screen (or the current bitmap surface) using a specified position and image. When it has been drawn, the properties of this sprite are applied to the specified sprite number. The syntax of the command is SPRITE *Sprite Number*, *X*, *Y*, *Image Number*.

The LoadSprite Program

To demonstrate how to use the preceding commands, I have written a short program called LoadSprite, which loads a bitmap file into memory, copies it into an image, and then draws a sprite. Figure 11.9 shows the output from the program.

Figure 11.9

The LoadSprite program demonstrates how to load a bitmap, copy it into an image, and then use it to draw a sprite.

```
`----------------------------------
`Beginner's Guide To DarkBASIC Game Programming
`Copyright (C)2002 Jonathan S. Harbour and Joshua R. Smith
`Chapter 11 - LoadSprite Program
`----------------------------------

`Initialize the program
HIDE MOUSE
CLS

`Load the source bitmap file
LOAD BITMAP "F15.bmp", 1

`Grab image 1 from bitmap
GET IMAGE 1,0,0,300,300

`Draw the sprite
SPRITE 1,170,90,1

`Wait for keypress
WAIT KEY

END
```

TIP

The F-15 Eagle bitmap image used by the sprite in this program is actually a 3D model from the DarkMATTER collection. I simply used the DarkMATTER Browser to view the F-15, rotated it to the appropriate top-down view, took a screenshot of the browser using Alt+Print Screen, and pasted it into my graphics editor. It is fantastic as a 3D model or a sprite!

The TransSprite Program

Although it is not evident in the LoadSprite program, DarkBASIC actually handles transparency automatically for you. All you need to worry about is setting the border color around a sprite to black—an RGB setting of (0,0,0) in your graphics editor of choice (such as Paint Shop Pro, which is very programmer-friendly). To see transparency in action, you need to load a background image and then draw the sprite over the background. Otherwise, the background is just black (as in the LoadSprite program). Of course, you could also just set the background color to something other than black, but a bitmap background is more interesting. Figure 11.10 shows the output of the TransSprite program.

Figure 11.10 *The TransSprite program demonstrates how DarkBASIC automatically handles sprite transparency.*

```
`---------------------------------
`Beginner's Guide To DarkBASIC Game Programming
`Copyright (C)2002 Jonathan S. Harbour and Joshua R. Smith
`Chapter 11 - TransSprite Program
`---------------------------------

`Initialize the program
HIDE MOUSE
CLS

`Load background bitmap
LOAD BITMAP "background.bmp", 0

`Load the source bitmap file
LOAD BITMAP "F15.bmp", 1

`Grab image 1 from bitmap
GET IMAGE 1,0,0,300,300

`Draw the sprite
SPRITE 1,170,90,1

`Wait for keypress
WAIT KEY

END
```

Sprite Properties

There are some useful commands that return information about a sprite, such as the image number, width, and height. In addition, several commands allow you to manipulate the way in which a sprite is drawn to the screen.

The SPRITE IMAGE Command

The SPRITE IMAGE command returns the image number used by the specified sprite. The syntax of the command is Return Value = SPRITE IMAGE (*Sprite Number*).

The SPRITE WIDTH Command

The SPRITE WIDTH command returns the width of the image currently in use by the specified sprite. The syntax of the command is Return Value = SPRITE WIDTH (*Sprite Number*).

The SPRITE HEIGHT Command

The SPRITE HEIGHT command returns the height of the image currently in use by the specified sprite. The syntax of the command is Return Value = SPRITE HEIGHT (*Sprite Number*).

The OFFSET SPRITE Command

The OFFSET SPRITE command changes the horizontal and vertical offset of a sprite's origin. The default origin is the top-left corner of the image, but this command allows you to change the offset so that the sprite draws from the center point or from some other corner.

The SPRITE OFFSET X Command

The SPRITE OFFSET X command returns the horizontal offset or shift value of the sprite referenced by the sprite number that is passed as a parameter to the command. The syntax for the command is Return Value = SPRITE OFFSET X (*Sprite Number*).

The SPRITE OFFSET Y Command

The SPRITE OFFSET Y command returns the vertical offset or shift value of the sprite referenced by the sprite number that is passed as a parameter to the command. The syntax for the command is Return Value = SPRITE OFFSET Y (*Sprite Number*).

The SPRITE EXIST Command

The SPRITE EXIST command returns a 1 if the specified sprite (passed as a parameter) was previously created with the SPRITE command. If the sprite does not exist, the command returns a 0. The syntax for the command is Return Value = SPRITE EXIST (*Sprite Number*).

Drawing and Moving Sprites

When you are dealing with sprites, the most important commands involve moving and drawing them. Rather than provide separate commands for these functions, DarkBASIC combines the two in a single command called SPRITE. I'll go over SHOW SPRITE, HIDE SPRITE, and several other useful sprite commands in this section.

The SPRITE Command

The SPRITE command draws a sprite using the specified position and image number, and stores the settings for that sprite number. The syntax of the command is SPRITE `Sprite Number, X, Y, Image Number`.

Finding the Position of a Sprite

The SPRITE command simultaneously moves and draws a sprite using a specified image number, but once the sprite has been drawn, how do you determine its position? This is important when you are dealing with sprite collision. (I'll discuss that in more detail later.)

The SPRITE X Command

The SPRITE X command returns the current horizontal position of the sprite referenced by the passed sprite number. The command syntax is `Return Value = SPRITE X (Sprite Number)`.

The SPRITE Y Command

The SPRITE Y command returns the current vertical position of the sprite referenced by the passed sprite number. The command syntax is `Return Value = SPRITE Y (Sprite Number)`.

The SET SPRITE Command

The SET SPRITE command is very important because it lets you change both the background restoration and the transparency properties of the sprite. The default for these values is 1, which means that the background is saved and restored when the sprite is moved, and transparency is enabled so that black pixels are not displayed with the sprite. Setting the background parameter to 0 will disable the background-saving property, which means that the sprite will "smear" across the screen, and it is up to you to restore the area under the sprite. The syntax of the command is SET SPRITE *Sprite Number, BackSave State, Transparency State.*

Making Sprites Visible or Invisible

The following commands are used to make a sprite visible or invisible, and apply to the normal sprite-drawing commands.

The SHOW SPRITE Command

The SHOW SPRITE command shows the specified sprite (passed as the sprite number parameter) that was previously hidden using the HIDE SPRITE command. This command does not change the position of the sprite, but simply draws it at the current X and Y position using the current sprite properties. The syntax for the command is SHOW SPRITE *Sprite Number.*

The HIDE SPRITE Command

The HIDE SPRITE command makes a specified sprite invisible so that it is not drawn with the other sprites on the screen. The syntax for the command is HIDE SPRITE *Sprite Number.*

This command might be useful in a game in which you want to add special effects to a sprite without changing its image. For example, suppose you have a space combat game with power-ups. When the player's ship gets a force field power-up, a small outline appears around the ship, showing the player that the power-up is active. Rather than drawing a whole new image for every power-up that the ship can take on, you could draw the force field outline (and any other special effects) as a separate image. Then you simply move the special effects sprites along with the spaceship and make them visible when needed.

The SHOW ALL SPRITES Command

The SHOW ALL SPRITES command universally draws all sprites that were previously set to invisible, setting them all to visible.

The HIDE ALL SPRITES Command

The HIDE ALL SPRITES command universally sets all sprites to invisible, so that they no longer appear on the screen when draw commands are issued.

The All-Powerful Game Loop

The key to real-time animation, which is the goal of most games (even turn-based games), is the game loop. The game loop repeats over and over as quickly as possible, and is essentially what has come to be known as the *game engine*. Granted, there are some powerful 3D game engines out there—often referred to by the games that they were first used to create. Table 11.1 presents a list of game engines in use today.

Oddly enough, some game engines were created out of existing game engines, so there is a strange hierarchy or family tree of games. For example, *Half-Life* was based on the Quake engine by id software, and was then used to create several more games, all of which have a family heritage with *Quake*.

Now, I don't want you to think that all there is to a game engine is a game loop. Obviously, there's a lot more to it than that. Usually a game engine includes 3D special effects such as shadows, lighting, support for level files and character files, multiplayer support, computer-controlled players, game physics, weapon trajectories, and countless other factors. But at the core of all this functionality is a real-time game loop.

Table 11.1 Game Engines

Game Engine	Developer	Games That Use It
Wolfenstein 3D	id software	*Spear of Destiny*
Half-Life	Sierra Studios	*Counter-Strike, Opposing Force*
Quake III	id software	*Quake III Arena, Voyager: Elite Force*
Torque	Garage Games	*Tribes 2*
Doom III	id software	*Quake IV*
Unreal Warfare	Epic Games	*America's Army, Unreal Tournament 2003*

Creating a Game Loop

You have already seen a game loop in operation in previous chapters, although I didn't mention it at the time. A game loop is usually set to run indefinitely. When a condition for ending the game has been met, you can use the EXIT command to break out of the loop. To create a game loop, you can use any one of the following looping commands:

- DO...LOOP
- REPEAT...UNTIL
- WHILE...ENDWHILE

The DO loop is probably the most obvious choice because it doesn't use a condition for ending (although you can use the EXIT command to break out of the loop). Figure 11.11 illustrates what usually takes place in a game loop.

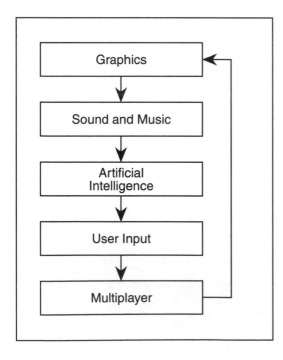

Figure 11.11

The usual game loop calls subroutines that handle graphics, sound effects, music, artificial intelligence, user input, and multiplayer functionality.

Using REPEAT...UNTIL for a Game Loop

The REPEAT and WHILE loops are also suitable for a game loop that uses a condition. For example, you could create a variable called Running and create a REPEAT loop, as shown in the following code.

```
Running = 1
REPEAT
    IF MOUSECLICK() = 1
        Running = 0
    ENDIF
UNTIL Running <> 1
```

Using WHILE...ENDWHILE for a Game Loop

The WHILE loop is similar to the REPEAT loop, but the condition is checked at the beginning of the loop rather than at the end.

```
Running = 1
WHILE Running = 1
    IF MOUSECLICK() = 1
        Running = 0
    ENDIF
ENDWHILE
```

Using DO...LOOP for a Game Loop

The DO loop is my preferred method because there is no condition in the loop statement itself. Instead, I prefer to handle the condition myself, inside the loop.

```
DO
    IF MOUSECLICK() = 1
        EXIT
    ENDIF
LOOP
```

Game Timing Commands

The sample game loops I just showed you run as fast as possible with no timing. Although DarkBASIC handles frame rate and screen refresh automatically, it doesn't perform timing, so that is something you have to include in a high-speed game loop yourself. I'll explain some of the timing and screen refresh commands, and then show you a new and improved game loop in the following pages.

The SLEEP and WAIT Commands

The SLEEP command pauses the program for a specified number of milliseconds (where 1,000 milliseconds equal one second). The WAIT command performs the exact same function as SLEEP and is simply an alternative command. Use whichever command is more intuitive to you. For example, you might use SLEEP inside a game loop for short-duration timing, and use the WAIT command elsewhere for longer-duration timing (which seems intuitive to me). The syntax of these commands looks like this:

```
SLEEP Duration
WAIT Duration
```

The TIMER Command

The TIMER command returns the internal system time in milliseconds. The system timer is updated 1,000 times per second, so it is a good way to set the speed of your program to a specific rate (not to be confused with the frame rate). The meaning of speed in this context is the amount of work done by the program every second, such as moving sprites, determining collisions, and so on.

The TIMER command is also an excellent tool for profiling a game. Suppose you have written a high-speed game that has a bottleneck somewhere in the code, but you can't find out what is slowing things down. The best way to find the bottleneck is to check the system time before and after a section of code, and then display the amount of time that the code took to run. Following is an example of timing a section of code.

```
StartTime = TIMER()
`update the screen
SYNC
EndTime = TIMER()
PRINT "Sync time = "; EndTime - StartTime
```

Refreshing the Screen

Next to timing, the most important aspect of a game loop is the screen refresh. Regardless of how fast a game loop is running, DarkBASIC can only refresh the screen at a specified frame rate. DarkBASIC tries to keep the screen updated the best that it can, but in a high-speed game loop, you want to take control of the screen update yourself. This involves the SYNC command.

The SYNC Command

As the timing example showed, SYNC is one of the key commands you will use in a game loop, and it is absolutely critical to keep a game running at top speed. If you let DarkBASIC handle the screen refresh for you, it will run much too slowly for a decent game. The SYNC command performs a screen refresh manually; you need to insert this into your game loop after all drawing has been completed. DarkBASIC maintains a hidden copy of the screen called the double buffer, which gets all of your drawing commands. Drawing directly to the screen is too slow, so to speed things up DarkBASIC uses this double buffer for all drawing commands and then quickly copies the double buffer to the screen in one fell swoop. In case you haven't guessed it yet, the SYNC command copies the double buffer to the screen.

The SYNC OFF Command

The SYNC OFF command turns on the automatic screen refresh in DarkBASIC (which is the default), and might be useful if you are at a point in the program where you no longer want to manually perform a screen refresh and you would like DarkBASIC to take over. You can always call SYNC ON again if you need to resume manual screen refresh with the SYNC command.

The SYNC ON Command

To manually use the SYNC command in your game loop, you first need to call SYNC ON to turn off DarkBASIC's automatic screen refresh. After you have called SYNC ON somewhere at the start of the program, it is up to you to call SYNC to update the screen—otherwise, nothing will be displayed and the screen will remain blank.

The SYNC RATE Command

The SYNC RATE command is applicable when DarkBASIC is handling the screen refresh automatically; it sets the frame rate of the display. By default, DarkBASIC tries to maintain a frame rate of 40. However, by using the SYNC RATE command, you can override this default and set the screen refresh to any value. Again, just remember that this is not relevant if you are using SYNC to maintain the screen refresh yourself (which is the preferred method).

The GameLoop Program

To show you how to use a real game loop, I have written a program called GameLoop, which is shown in Figure 11.12. This program is simple, but it does a good job of demonstrating how a REPEAT...UNTIL game loop works.

Figure 11.12 *The GameLoop program demonstrates a game loop that displays the frame rate.*

```
`--------------------------------
`Beginner's Guide To DarkBASIC Game Programming
`Copyright (C)2002 Jonathan S. Harbour and Joshua R. Smith
`Chapter 11 - GameLoop Program
`--------------------------------

`Initialize the program
HIDE MOUSE
SYNC ON
```

```
`Load the sprite
LOAD BITMAP "F15.bmp", 1
GET IMAGE 1,0,0,300,300

`Load background bitmap
LOAD BITMAP "background.bmp", 0

`Store part of the background
GET IMAGE 2,0,0,200,40

`This is the game loop
REPEAT
    `draw the F-15
    SPRITE 1,170,90,1

    `erase the frame rate text
    PASTE IMAGE 2,0,0

    `display the frame rate
    TEXT 0,0, "Frame rate = " + STR$(SCREEN FPS())

    `update the screen
    SYNC

`Check for mouse click to exit
UNTIL MOUSECLICK()=1 OR ESCAPEKEY()=1
SHOW MOUSE
END
```

Detecting Sprite Collisions

Have you ever wondered how to make a missile blow up an alien ship in a game?
Or how about when an enemy plane crashes into yours in a game like *1943*?
Although it seems like a simple feat to check when two sprites crash into each
other, the details are actually not so simple. The technical term for this process is
collision detection, which means that the position of one sprite is compared to the
position of another sprite, and if any of the visible pixels intersect, then the sprites
have collided!

Types of Collisions

There are three types of collisions (or lack thereof) for which your program should check.

- Bounding rectangle collision
- Impact collision
- No collision

Okay, technically the third option is not a type of collision, but it is important to consider the no-collision event because it helps to illustrate the other two events (see Figure 11.13).

Bounding Rectangle Collision

The first real type of collision that I want you to consider is bounding rectangle. Take a look at Figure 11.14, which shows an example of bounding rectangle collision detection.

As you can see from Figure 11.14, the missile clearly has *not* hit the fighter plane, and yet bounding rectangle would call this a hit. Why is that helpful, do you suppose? Although this method is not entirely accurate in every case, it is sufficient to narrow down the list of suspect collisions so a more detailed comparison can be made. When there are dozens or even hundreds of sprites in a game, it can be very time consuming to check for a collision between every single one because each

Figure 11.13 *The first example of collision detection shows a complete miss.*

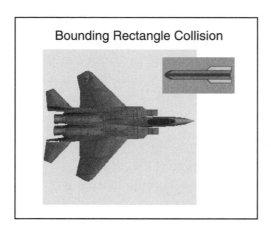

Figure 11.14
Bounding rectangle collision detection uses the bounding rectangles of two sprites to check for a collision.

sprite must be compared to *every other sprite* in the game! So, if there are 100 sprites in a game, a collision detection procedure would have to make 10,000 comparisons just to see which spritcs have collided! Thankfully, bounding rectangle is a quick way of checking for collisions, so it shouldn't slow down the game. Now on to a more specific method.

Impact Collision Detection

Impact collision detection is a precise method of checking for sprite collisions that involves comparing the actual pixels of each sprite to see whether any sprites overlap (the *damage zone*). Using this method, you can have a tiny sprite with a relatively large bounding rectangle still return an accurate result (see Figure 11.15).

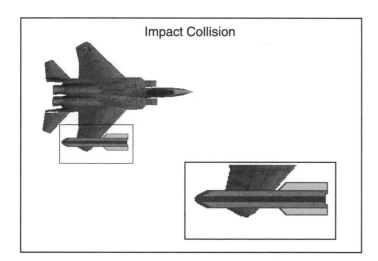

Figure 11.15
Impact collision (also called pixel-level collision) *detection compares the non-transparent pixels of two sprites for overlap.*

DarkBASIC provides both types of collision so you can keep the game running at a good speed while still allowing for precision in collision checking (which results in a better game). After a bounding rectangle collision occurs, the program can then perform an impact comparison to see whether it was just a near miss or an actual hit.

Collision Commands

DarkBASIC provides two commands for detecting collisions. (Obviously, you don't need a command to check for no collision!) The two commands are SPRITE COLLISION and SPRITE HIT.

The SPRITE COLLISION Command

The SPRITE COLLISION command uses the bounding rectangle collision detection method to check whether two sprites are overlapping. The syntax is Return Value = SPRITE COLLISION (*Sprite Number, Target Sprite Number*).

The key word to remember with the SPRITE COLLISION command is *overlap*. If the bounding boxes of two sprites are overlapping even a little bit, this command will return a 1 (otherwise, it will return a 0).

The SPRITE HIT Command

The SPRITE HIT collision command is more specific and determines whether two sprites have actually hit each other using the more precise impact collision method. This command determines impact by looking at the actual pixels in each sprite and comparing whether any pixels in one sprite are overlapping the pixels in the other. The syntax for this command is Return Value = SPRITE HIT (*Sprite Number, Target Sprite Number*).

The CollideSprites Program

The CollideSprites program demonstrates how to perform collision detection on a screen filled with sprites. As Figure 11.16 shows, collisions cause the sprites to deflect away from each other. Since there are so few sprites in this demonstration, I have used the SPRITE HIT command that, if you'll recall, uses the impact method.

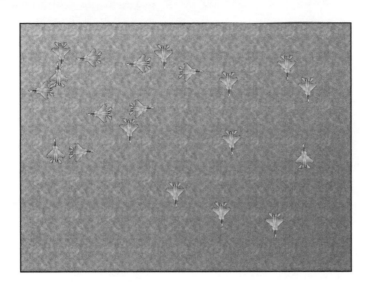

Figure 11.16 *The CollideSprites program demonstrates how to use the sprite collision detection built into DarkBASIC.*

```
`------------------------------------
`Beginner's Guide To DarkBASIC Game Programming
`Copyright (C)2002 Jonathan S. Harbour and Joshua R. Smith
`Chapter 11 - CollideSprites Program
`------------------------------------

`Create some variables
MAX = 20
DIM SpriteNum(MAX)
DIM SpriteX(MAX)
DIM SpriteY(MAX)
DIM DirX(MAX)
DIM DirY(MAX)

`Initialize the program
HIDE MOUSE
SYNC ON

`Load the sprite
LOAD BITMAP "plane2.bmp", 1
GET IMAGE 1,0,0,50,50
```

```
GET IMAGE 2,50,0,100,50
GET IMAGE 3,100,0,150,50
GET IMAGE 4,150,0,200,50

`initialize sprites
FOR N = 1 TO MAX
    SpriteX(N) = RND(540)
    SpriteY(N) = RND(380)
    DirX(N) = RND(3) + 1
    DirY(N) = RND(3) + 1
    SpriteNum(N) = RND(3) + 1
    SPRITE N, SpriteX(N), SpriteY(N), SpriteNum(N)
NEXT N

`Load background bitmap
LOAD BITMAP "background.bmp", 0

`This is the game loop
REPEAT
    IF TIMER() > StartTime + 100
        FOR N = 1 TO MAX
            `move the sprites
            SpriteX(N) = SpriteX(N) + DirX(N)
            IF SpriteX(N) > 540
                SpriteX(N) = 540
                DirX(N) = DirX(N) * -1
            ENDIF
            IF SpriteX(N) < 1
                SpriteX(N) = 1
                DirX(N) = DirX(N) * -1
            ENDIF
            SpriteY(N) = SpriteY(N) + DirY(N)
            IF SpriteY(N) > 380
                SpriteY(N) = 380
                DirY(N) = DirY(N) * -1
            ENDIF
            IF SpriteY(N) < 1
                SpriteY(N) = 1
                DirY(N) = DirY(N) * -1
```

```
        ENDIF

        `check for collision
        IF SPRITE HIT(N,0) > 0
            DirX(N) = DirX(N) * -1
            DirY(N) = DirY(N) * -1
        ENDIF

        `draw the sprite
        SPRITE N,SpriteX(N),SpriteY(N),SpriteNum(N)
    NEXT N

        `update the screen
        SYNC
    ENDIF
UNTIL MOUSECLICK() = 1
END
```

Summary

This chapter covered one of the most important subjects in the field of gaming—sprites. Sprites are usually small, animated objects on the screen that give a game its graphics. Although there are many 3D games now, and 3D is the preferred realm for commercial games today, there is still plenty of room for 2D games. Thankfully, DarkBASIC excels at handling sprites, as you have learned in this chapter. In addition to learning how to create and manipulate sprites on the screen, you also learned about transparency and the two methods of determining when sprites collide—bounding rectangle collision and impact collision detection.

Chapter Quiz

The chapter quiz will help you retain the information that was covered in this chapter, as well as give you an idea about how well you're doing at understanding the subjects. You can find the answers for this quiz in Appendix A, "Answers to the Chapter Quizzes."

1. What is a sprite?

   A. A small two-dimensional bitmap drawn on the screen at a specified position and usually with transparency

   B. A small three-dimensional texture drawn at a specified X, Y, Z position with transparency

   C. A large two-dimensional bitmap containing the frames of an animated object that will be drawn on the screen

   D. A small fast-moving mythical character with wings

2. Which term best describes the process of drawing only solid pixels in a sprite?

   A. Flattery

   B. Animation

   C. Transparency

   D. Collision detection

3. Which year was *Pac-Man* released?

   A. 1980

   B. 1963

   C. 1998

   D. 1974

4. Which classic arcade game featured alien ships with a tractor beam that could capture your ship?

   A. *Blasteroids*

   B. *Galaxian*

   C. *1943*

   D. *Galaga*

5. What was *Pac-Man*'s original name?

   A. *Yellow-Man*

   B. *Puck-Man*

   C. *Round-Man*

   D. *Go, Pinky, Go!*

6. Which command performs bounding box collision detection on two sprites?

    A. SPRITE HIT

    B. SPRITE COLLISION

    C. SPRITE OWNS

    D. SPRITE COLLIDED

7. Which command performs impact collision detection on two sprites?

    A. SPRITE COLLISION

    B. SPRITE COLLIDED

    C. SPRITE HIT

    D. SPRITE MISS

8. Which command do you use to draw a sprite on the screen (or to the active bitmap)?

    A. DRAW SPRITE

    B. SHOW SPRITE

    C. SPRITE

    D. IMAGE

9. Which command grabs a portion of an image from a previously loaded bitmap?

    A. GET IMAGE

    B. COPY IMAGE

    C. GRAB IMAGE

    D. TILE IMAGE

10. What are the three commands that you can use to create a game loop?

    A. REPEAT, WHILE, DOING

    B. DON'T, CONTINUE, WAITING

    C. LOOP, REPEAT, WHILE

    D. DO, REPEAT, WHILE

CHAPTER 12

PROGRAMMING THE KEYBOARD, MOUSE, AND JOYSTICK

This chapter is dedicated to the subject of input—specifically, taking control of the computer's input devices with DarkBASIC. DarkBASIC includes numerous commands for handling input events from the keyboard, mouse, and joystick. It also includes features such as force feedback that are available with many joysticks.

This chapter covers the following topics:

- Introduction to User Input
- Keyboard Commands
- Mouse Commands
- Joystick Commands
- Defining Control Devices
- Force Feedback

Introduction to User Input

Every device, from a TV to a microwave oven, requires some sort of control device to use it. A TV requires a remote to change channels, and a microwave has a front control panel for programming the temperature and the time to cook a meal. In fact, most consumer electronics devices require some sort of user input. User input is what makes the difference between a technical demo and a game. Reading the input from a control allows the game to ascertain what the player would like to do, and then perform that task.

Every game console, from the Atari 2600 to the Xbox, has some form of user input. The user input is relayed to the console via some form of controller. Figure 12.1 shows a collection of different controllers for user input.

DarkBASIC uses the DirectInput library to get all of its input. If you are familiar with DirectInput, you will recognize some of the functions in DarkBASIC, as well as how they correspond to their DirectInput counterparts.

DarkBASIC supports three different basic types of controllers—the keyboard, mouse, and joystick. Most PC users have one or more of these devices. These days, it is hard to imagine a computer without at least a keyboard and a mouse. However, it was not long ago that PC games only had one type of input—the keyboard.

Figure 12.1
A collection of game input controllers

Keyboard Basics

The keyboard is the most basic form of user input to which you will have access. Every computer has a keyboard. However, this was not always the case. The keyboard itself has been around since 1868, when an inventor by the name of Christopher Lathem Sholes took out a patent on the first typewriter. Computers in their present form were not even around then. In fact, some of the earliest computers did not use keyboards; they used punch cards, on which the computer instructions were punched and then fed into the computer.

In 1964, MIT, Bell Labs, and General Electric designed the first computer that used a keyboard. It was called the Mutlics. It was nothing more than a collection of monitors and keyboards (called *dumb terminals*) hooked up to a larger system, but since that moment every computer has used a keyboard.

A keyboard has many different keys, but most keyboards are laid out in the QWERTY format. The QWERTY format, also invented by Christopher Lathem Sholes, specifies the layout of the keys on the keyboard. Q, W, E, R, T, and Y are the first six letters in the top row of letter keys on the QWERTY keyboard. Figure 12.2 shows a picture of a QWERTY keyboard.

Many keyboards have 101 to 104 keys. Most of the older keyboards have 101 keys, and the newer keyboards have 104 or more keys. To help visualize the keyboard as

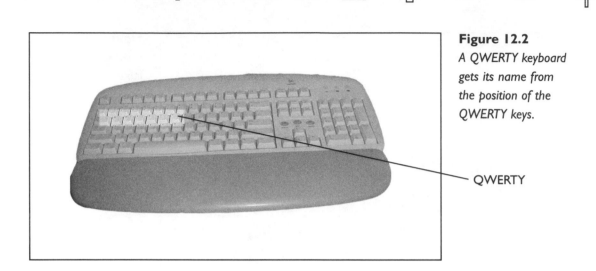

Figure 12.2
A QWERTY keyboard gets its name from the position of the QWERTY keys.

QWERTY

a control device, you must view each key as a button (like on a joystick, which I will cover in the "Joystick Commands" section later in this chapter). Each button has three different states: UP, DOWN, and PRESSED. Although it might seem a little odd that there are three different states, it's really quite simple. If a key has not been pressed, it is in the UP state. If a key is being pressed currently, it is in the DOWN state. If a key is currently in the UP state but was previously in the DOWN state, it is in the PRESSED state. Figure 12.3 illustrates this point.

Most game applications use four main keys for movement. They traditionally are the up, down, left, and right arrows. The A, W, S, and D keys are sometimes used for movement, but this is rather uncommon. In that case, W is used for up, A is used for left, S is used for down, and D is used for right. Generally, there is one key

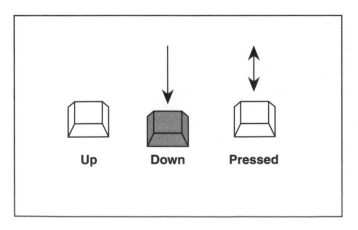

Up   **Down**   **Pressed**

Figure 12.3
The three different states of a key

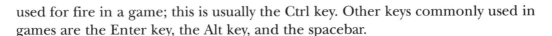

used for fire in a game; this is usually the Ctrl key. Other keys commonly used in games are the Enter key, the Alt key, and the spacebar.

Although the keyboard is the largest control that is hooked up to the computer, it is not the only common controller. Almost all computers have a mouse attached to them; at $10 for a cheap mouse, who can't own one?

Mouse Basics

It is hard to imagine a computer without a mouse; they feel unusable without one. However, the mouse has not always been part of the computer. In 1964, a man by the name of Douglas C. Engelbart created the first mouse. He patented this mouse as an X-Y position indicator, but he nicknamed it the "mouse" because it had a tail coming out the back of it. His original mouse was nothing more then a wooden box with two roller balls inside. In 1998, Douglas Engelbart was inducted into the National Inventors Hall of Fame. I think he most richly deserves that induction for inventing the most well-loved and oft-used input device since the keyboard.

Mouse devices come in all different shapes and sizes, from a traditional ball-and-wheel mouse to a more complex optical mouse to a trackball. Each mouse, though unique in style, has the same basic function—to indicate an X-Y position. In the Windows and Macintosh operating systems, the mouse controls your cursor. In DarkBASIC you might have a cursor that looks slightly different but serves the same function as the Windows or Macintosh cursor. You might be wondering about games such as *Quake III* or *Doom 2*. They don't have a cursor, right? You are correct, but they still read the mouse information and convert the X-Y position into a useful user control. Figures 12.4 and 12.5 show mouse movement and the corresponding results.

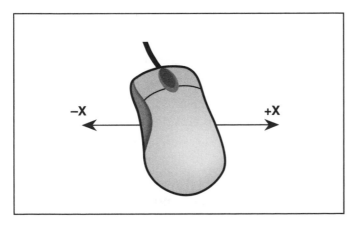

Figure 12.4

A mouse moving left or right

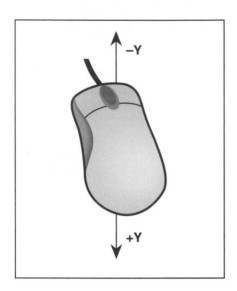

Figure 12.5

*A mouse moving up
or down*

The mouse has one other feature that makes it a popular gaming control—buttons. Most mouse devices have two or more buttons (unless you have a Macintosh mouse, in which case you only have one button). These buttons can each be assigned to a different aspect of a program. Windows uses the buttons to select, execute, and control different files. Just as the keyboard keys have different states, so do the mouse buttons. However, there are four different states for a mouse button—UP, DOWN, CLICKED, and DOUBLE CLICKED.

The UP state is just like the keyboard UP state—the mouse button has not been clicked. The DOWN state is just like the keyboard DOWN state, but with one unique difference. In most applications, the mouse button DOWN state is used to drag a box around a collection of items. This is the most common use of the DOWN state, but it does not always have to be the case. The CLICKED state is the same as the keyboard PRESSED state. The DOUBLE CLICKED state is nothing more than the mouse being in the CLICKED state twice in a row. Figure 12.6 shows an example of the different states of the mouse.

There is one more aspect of the mouse that I need to cover. Most new mouse devices have a wheel, which allows the user to scroll up and down. This feature is usually used to scroll between weapons in a game or to scroll up and down on a Web page without using the side scroll bar.

Although the mouse is a wildly popular input device for PC games (I would almost venture to say that it is *the* most popular for PC games), it is not the only gaming

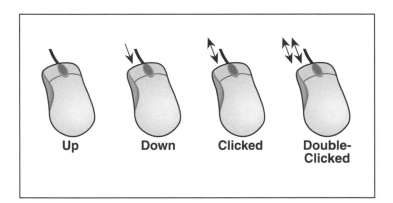

Figure 12.6
*The different mouse
button states*

input device. There is also the joystick, which is almost as popular as the mouse for most computer- or console-based games.

Joystick Basics

The joystick is the most common user input device for any console or console-based game. The Atari 2600 had a basic one-button controller, while the GameCube has a more complex control. They all serve the same function: To allow human input into a game in the most convenient manner possible. Figure 12.7 shows a collection of different joysticks.

Figure 12.7
*Different joystick
controllers*

Although I cannot pinpoint the exact inventor of the joystick, I know that joysticks have been hooked to computers since 1964, when the first computer game (*Space War*) was written. The standard for joystick connection to the PC did not come until much later, however. The game port is the most common type of connection for a joystick. Also known as the joystick port, the game port is generally connected like a traditional mouse and is found on most sound cards. You can use a Y splitter to connect two joysticks to a game port at once.

The USB port is becoming a wildly popular connection for the joystick. I think this is a great idea because USB ports support faster communications between the joystick and the computer, which allows greater precision in the joystick.

> *Precision* is the accuracy of a controller. The more precise a joystick or mouse is, the better the input that the game will receive from it.

The joystick is a lot like the mouse in that it is an X-Y indicator. Most joysticks have some form of X and Y input. What makes a joystick different than a mouse is that the X and Y input can be separated on a joystick, whereas they cannot on the mouse. A prime example of this is a driving wheel. The wheel portion of the joystick is the X input, and the pedals are considered the Y input. Figure 12.8 shows a joystick with combined X and Y axes, and Figure 12.9 shows a joystick with separated X and Y axes.

Just like the keyboard and mouse, the joystick also has buttons. (This seems to be a common theme among controllers, doesn't it?) Joysticks generally have between two and ten buttons, a mouse usually has two to five buttons, and a keyboard has

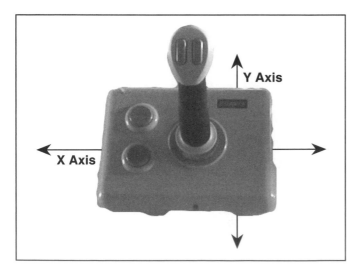

Figure 12.8
A controller with combined X and Y axes

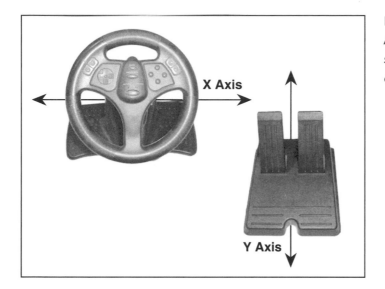

Figure 12.9
A controller with separated X and Y axes

X Axis

Y Axis

approximately 104 buttons.) Each button again has three different states—UP, DOWN, and PRESSED. The UP state for the joystick is just like the UP state for the mouse and keyboard—the button has not been pressed. The DOWN state is the same as well, but most games use the DOWN state for rapid fire functions. The PRESSED state is also the same as for the keyboard and mouse, and it is usually used for single fire. Figure 12.10 shows the different states of joystick buttons.

Now that you have covered the three major input devices for a PC game, it is time to cover them in detail, from concepts to commands. Each device has a unique set of commands assigned to it to make it function with DarkBASIC. I will start with the keyboard and work through the mouse and the joystick.

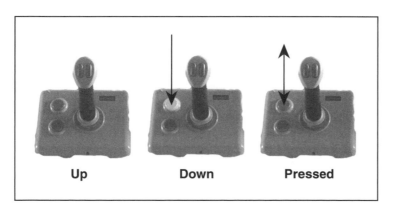

Figure 12.10
Various states of a joystick button

Up   Down   Pressed

Keyboard Commands

The keyboard commands in DarkBASIC are pretty easy to use. There are commands for reading entire strings as well as for reading one character. You have used many of the commands in previous chapters without knowing exactly what they are or what they do.

Reading Text Input

The most fundamental requirement of basic input commands is reading a string or number input. You need to read a string to gather information such as the player's name or his favorite color. Although you can create your own string input routine with the key-press commands, DarkBASIC provides a command to read strings for you.

The INPUT Command

The INPUT command is one of the oldest commands in any BASIC language. In fact, it is as old and widely used as the PRINT command. The INPUT command can take two forms. The first format of the command is a simple INPUT *string$*, where keyboard keys are read and the keys are stored in *string$*. The second format of the INPUT command is INPUT *string$*, *variable$*, where the keyboard input is read and placed in *string$*, and *variable$* is printed on the string. This form is a little more useful because it will print something right before the location where the user will input text.

The following program (aptly named KeyboardInput) demonstrates how to use the INPUT command. Figure 12.11 shows you the output of the program.

```
`-------------------------------
`Beginner's Guide To DarkBASIC Game Programming
`Copyright (C)2002 Jonathan S. Harbour and Joshua R. Smith
`Chapter 12 - KeyboardInput program
`-------------------------------

`create some variables
name$ = ""
age = 0
color$ = ""

`initialize the program
CLS
HIDE MOUSE
```

```
`ask user for some personal info
PRINT
INPUT "What is your name? ", name$
INPUT "What is your age? ", age
INPUT "What is your favorite color? ", color$

`display the delay message
PRINT
PRINT "Calculating what I know about you";

`delay for 2 seconds
SLEEP 500
PRINT ".";
SLEEP 500
PRINT ".";
SLEEP 500
PRINT ".";
SLEEP 500
PRINT ".";
PRINT

`display the info on the screen
PRINT
PRINT "What I know about you:"
PRINT "Your name is " + name$ + "."
PRINT "Your name backwards is " + StringBackwards$(name$)
PRINT "Your age is " + STR$(age)
PRINT "Your age backwards is "+StringBackwards$(STR$(age))
PRINT "Your favorite color is " + color$
PRINT "Your favorite color backwards is " + StringBackwards$(color$)

`pause and then end
WAIT KEY
END

FUNCTION StringBackwards$(A$)
    newstring$ = ""
    FOR N = LEN(A$) TO 1 STEP -1
        newstring$ = newstring$ + MID$(A$, N)
    NEXT N
ENDFUNCTION newstring$
```

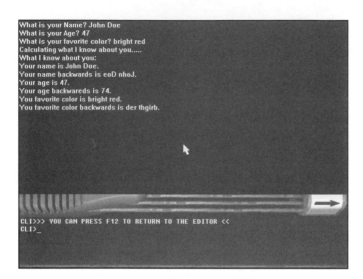

Figure 12.11

The KeyboardInput program demonstrates the use of the INPUT *command.*

I must tell you about one important drawback to the INPUT command. Although it is a useful command for reading entire strings, it might not always be the best command for game programming because it is a blocking command, which means that it will not allow any other commands to run until it is finished. INPUT is a good command to use if you do not need to process anything else while you are waiting for the user to type something. At the end of the keyboard section, I will show you how to write a non-blocking INPUT command.

Reading Key Presses

The INPUT command is not the only keyboard command that DarkBASIC supports. DarkBASIC can also use the keyboard as a series of buttons. Remember, the keyboard has three states for its keys: UP, DOWN, and PRESSED. The following commands will help you determine these states accurately.

The WAIT KEY and SUSPEND FOR KEY Commands

The WAIT KEY command waits for any key to be pressed. This command takes no parameters. Like INPUT, it is a blocking command. This command is good for holding title screens and winning screens. The SUSPEND FOR KEY command performs the same function. These commands will wait for any key to be in the PRESSED state before continuing.

The INKEY$() Command

The INKEY$() command is one my favorites. It tells you which key is currently being pressed. It is a non-blocking command, so you can use it in loops without stalling the program. The INKEY$() command takes no parameters, but it returns a single character that represents the key that is currently being pressed. Note that INKEY$() only returns one letter (or chr$). You can only read one key at a time in the DOWN state with this command.

You can use INKEY$() to detect the three different states of each key on the keyboard. To detect the DOWN state of a key, just check to see whether INKEY$() is equal to the value of that key. To detect the UP state, check to see whether INKEY$() is not equal to that key's value. To detect the PRESSED state, check to see whether INKEY$() is equal to, and then not equal to, the value of that key.

The following game, called TextBlast, uses the INKEY$() function to scan for all three states. It detects when a key is in the DOWN state and sets a flag for that key (DIM charhit). The flag indicates that the key was pressed. When you release the key (previously in the DOWN state and flagged as such), the program processes that key as being in the PRESSED state. When the program finishes processing the key in the PRESSED state, it resets the flag for that key, and the key is returned to the UP state.

The object of TextBlast is simple. Just type the key that corresponds to the letters or numbers falling down the screen to destroy them. Each character falls at a different speed, so your reflexes will have to be fast. Figure 12.12 shows the output of the TextBlast program, which you will find on the CD in the Sources\Chapter12\TextBlast folder.

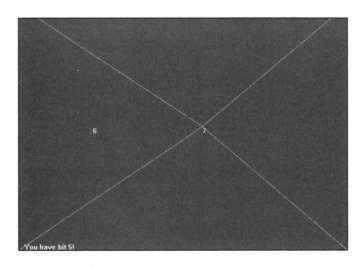

Figure 12.12
The TextBlast game demonstrates a practical use of the INKEY$() *command.*

```
REMSTART
-----------------------------------
Beginner's Guide To Game Programming With DarkBASIC
Copyright (C)2002 Jonathan S. Harbour and Joshua R. Smith
Chapter 12 - Taking Control: Programming the Input Devices
-----------------------------------
REMEND
CLS
DIM char$(100)
DIM charx(100)
DIM chary(100)
DIM charspeed(100)
DIM charhit(100)
DIM hitschars(1)
DIM CharCount(1)

SYNC ON
SYNC RATE 30

RndCounter = 0

White = RGB(255,255,255)
Black = RGB(0,0,0)

`   This will set a random seed
SET TEXT OPAQUE
WHILE INKEY$()<>" "
    RndCounter = RND(1000)
    INK White,Black
    CENTER TEXT 320,240,"Text Blast"
    RndColor = RGB(rnd(100)+150,rnd(100)+150,rnd(100)+150)
    INK RndColor,Black
    CENTER TEXT 320,260,"Press Space to Continue"
    SYNC
ENDWHILE
RANDOMIZE RndCounter

SET TEXT TRANSPARENT
InitChars()
```

```
hitschars(1) = 0
CharCount(1) = 1

` Loop until 100 chars have passed
WHILE CharCount(1) < 100
    INK 0,0
    BOX 0,0,639,479
    IF NoneFalling()=1 THEN StartNewFalling()
    ProcessText()
    DisplayScoreLine()
    SYNC
ENDWHILE

CLS
INK White,Black
TempString$ = "You have hit "+STR$(hitschars(1))+" out of "+STR$(100)+"!"
CENTER TEXT 320,240,TempString$
WAIT KEY
END

` Intialize all the characters for falling
FUNCTION InitChars()
    FOR x = 1 TO 100
        charnum = RND(92)+33
        char$(x) = CHR$(charnum)
        charx(x) = RND(600)+20
        chary(x) = -1
        charhit(x) = 0
        charspeed(x) = RND(6)+1
    NEXT x
ENDFUNCTION

` Are any characters falling
FUNCTION NoneFalling()
    Flag = 1
    FOR x = 1 TO 100
        IF chary(x) >= 0 AND chary(x) < 450 THEN EXITFUNCTION 0
    NEXT x
ENDFUNCTION Flag
```

```
` Set some new characters falling
FUNCTION StartNewFalling()
    FOR x = 1 to 4
        chary(x+CharCount(1)) = 0
    NEXT x
    CharCount(1) = CharCount(1) + 4
ENDFUNCTION


` Check the keyboard to see if any of the falling
` Characters have been hit..
FUNCTION ProcessText()
    White = RGB(255,255,255)
    Black = RGB(0,0,0)
    Red = RGB(255,0,0)
    FOR x = 1 TO 100
        IF chary(x) >= 0 AND chary(x)<450
            IF INKEY$() = char$(x)
                INK Red,Black
                charhit(x) = 1
                chary(x) = chary(x) + charspeed(x)
                LINE 0,479,charx(x),chary(x)
                LINE 0,0,charx(x),chary(x)
                LINE 639,0,charx(x),chary(x)
                LINE 639,479,charx(x),chary(x)
            ELSE
                INK White,Black
                IF charhit(x) = 1
                    chary(x) = 490
                    hitschars(1) = hitschars(1) + 1
                ELSE
                    chary(x) = chary(x)+ charspeed(x)
                ENDIF
            ENDIF
            TEXT charx(x),chary(x),char$(x)
        ENDIF
    NEXT x
ENDFUNCTION

` Display the Score line...
```

```
FUNCTION DisplayScoreLine()
     WHITE = RGB(255,255,255)
     BLACK = RGB(0,0,0)

     INK WHITE,BLACK
     STRING$ = "You have hit "+str$(hitschars(1))+"!"
     TEXT 10,465,string$
ENDFUNCTION
```

There are two other things to note about the INKEY$() command. First, INKEY$() will detect the difference between uppercase and lowercase letters, so the p and P keys are two different things in the INKEY$() command. When you are detecting whether the P key is pressed, you should look for both the P and p keys. You can also take the input of INKEY$() and pass it to the UPPER$ command to convert it to uppercase automatically.

Second, the INKEY$() command can return more than just the letters on the keyboard. It can also return the ASCII value of whatever key is currently pressed. Remember the CHR$(*value*) command? This is where it comes in handy because you can now detect different keys being pressed. For example, to detect whether the Enter key has been pressed, check to see whether INKEY$() = CHR$(13). Appendix C, "ASCII Chart" contains a complete listing of all the ASCII values and the corresponding keys. Table 12.1 shows some of the most common keys and their ASCII values.

Table 12.1 Common ASCII values

Value	Key
8	Tab
9	Backspace
13	Enter
27	Esc
32	Spacebar

Reading Special Keys

In addition to reading any key with the INKEY$() command, DarkBASIC also supports the reading of special keys, such as the up, down, left, and right arrows. There are a total of nine special keys that DarkBASIC exclusively reads. Figure 12.13 shows a keyboard with the special keys highlighted. These special keys are detailed in the following sections.

The UPKEY() Command

The UPKEY() command reads whether the up arrow is in the UP or DOWN state. It takes no parameters and returns a 0 if the up arrow is in the UP state and a 1 if it is in the DOWN state. To detect whether the up arrow is in the PRESSED state, look for it to be in the DOWN state (1), and then in the UP state (0). The up arrow is most commonly used to move a character upward in a keyboard-based game.

The DOWNKEY Command

The DOWNKEY() command reads whether the down arrow is in the UP or DOWN state. It returns a 0 if the down arrow is in the UP state and a 1 if it is in the DOWN state. The down arrow is most commonly used to move a character downward in a keyboard-based game.

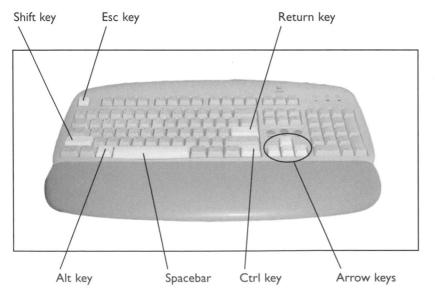

Figure 12.13

A keyboard illustration showing the special keys that DarkBASIC reads.

The LEFTKEY Command

The LEFTKEY() command reads whether the left arrow is in the UP or DOWN state. It returns a 0 if the left arrow is in the UP state and a 1 if it is in the DOWN state. The left arrow is most commonly used to move a character left in a keyboard-based game.

The RIGHTKEY Command

The RIGHTKEY() command reads whether the right arrow is in the UP or DOWN state. It returns a 0 if the right arrow is in the UP state and a 1 if it is in the DOWN state. The right arrow is most commonly used to move a character right in a keyboard-based game.

The CONTROLKEY Command

The CONTROLKEY() command reads whether the Ctrl key is in the UP or DOWN state. This command returns a 0 if the Ctrl key is in the UP state and a 1 if it is in the DOWN state. The Ctrl key is most commonly used to fire weapons in a keyboard-based game. This command does not tell you whether the left or right Ctrl key was hit; it just lets you know that one was hit.

The SHIFTKEY Command

The SHIFTKEY() command reads whether the Shift key is in the UP or DOWN state. It returns a 0 if the Shift key is in the UP state and a 1 if it is in the DOWN state. This command does not tell you whether the left or right Shift key was hit; it just lets you know that one was hit.

The SPACEKEY Command

The SPACEKEY() command reads whether the spacebar is in the UP or DOWN state. It returns a 0 if the spacebar is in the UP state and a 1 if it is in the DOWN state. The spacebar is most commonly used to either fire or jump in a keyboard-based game.

The RETURNKEY Command

The RETURNKEY() command reads whether the Return key is in the UP or DOWN state. The Return key is generally labeled Enter on the keyboard; it can be found above the right Shift key. Do not confuse this key with the Return key on the number pad (which is sometimes labeled Enter as well). Although the Return key on the number pad returns the same ASCII value in INKEY$() as the Enter key above the Shift key, the RETURNKEY() command only detects the Enter key above the Shift key. It returns a 0 if the Enter key is in the UP state and a 1 if it is in the DOWN state. The Enter key is most commonly used to perform an action in a keyboard-based game, which can range from opening a door to talking to another character.

The ESCAPEKEY Command

The ESCAPEKEY command returns whether the Esc key is in the UP or DOWN state. This command returns a 0 if the Esc key is in the UP state and a 1 if it is in the DOWN state. The Esc key is most commonly used to quit a game.

Summing Up the Special Key Commands

There are nine special key commands for the common keys used in a game. DarkBASIC uses a different set of commands for reading the rest of the keys on the keyboard simultaneously, as you will see in the next section. Table 12.2 sums up the nine special key commands.

Table 12.2 Special Key Commands

Command	Key
UPKEY	Up arrow
DOWNKEY	Down arrow
LEFTKEY	Left arrow
RIGHTKEY	Right arrow
CONTROLKEY	Ctrl
SHIFTKEY	Shift
SPACEKEY	Spacebar
RETURNKEY	Enter (not the number pad Enter)
ESCAPEKEY	Esc

Reading Multiple Keys and Scan Codes

Sometimes reading one key is just not enough. There are times when you need to read multiple keys. Although you can use all of the special functions at the same time, sometimes that is not enough. For example, you might want to move upward while firing your guns at the same time. This works fine if the fire command is attached to the Ctrl key and the up command is attached to the up arrow. But what if the fire command is attached to the P key and the up command is attached to the W key?

DarkBASIC provides a few commands that will detect whether multiple keys are pressed. To detect multiple key presses, you must understand scan codes, which are different from ASCII values. A scan code is the raw number that the keyboard assigned to a key before sending it to the computer. Usually scan codes are assigned from the upper-left of the keyboard to the lower-right.

> A *scan code* is the value assigned by the keyboard (not Windows, ASCII, or anyone else) to a specific key. The keyboard actually has a small microcontroller inside of it that handles all the key presses and complexities of the keyboard's operation. This controller is programmed with a standard set of scan codes for PC-AT 101 keyboards, and is the ultimate source of keyboard information for the computer.

The SCANCODE Command

Although it only returns the value of one key, the SCANCODE() command is useful for determining what scan code is assigned to each key. This command takes no parameters, but it returns the scan code of the key currently being pressed.

The KEYSTATE Command

The KEYSTATE() command takes one parameter—the scan code of the key you are looking for—and returns whether the key is up or down. The UP state of the key returns a 0, and the DOWN state returns a 1.

Using KEYSTATE and SCANCODE: The VirtualKeyboard Program

The following program uses the KEYSTATE and SCANCODE commands to mimic the UP and DOWN states of the keys on the screen. You must press Esc and Enter to quit this program. If you run this program within the DarkBASIC environment, you can also escape from the program by pressing F12. Figure 12.14 shows the output of this program.

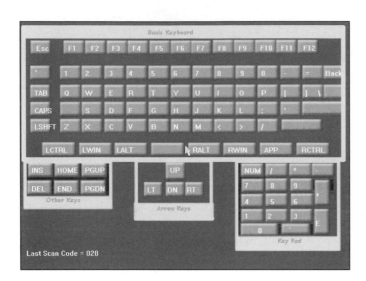

Figure 12.14 *The VirtualKeyboard program, demonstrating the use of the* KEYSTATE() *command*

```
`-----------------------------------
`Beginner's Guide To Game Programming With DarkBASIC
`Copyright (C)2002 Jonathan S. Harbour and Joshua R. Smith
`Chapter 12 - VirtualKeyboard Program
`-----------------------------------

DIM KEY$(256)
DIM KEYX(256)
DIM KEYY(256)

` Key State Data
DATA    1,"Esc",30,43
DATA    59,"F1",93,43
DATA    60,"F2",137,43
DATA    61,"F3",178,43
DATA    62,"F4",218,43
DATA    63,"F5",262,43
DATA    64,"F6",303,43
DATA    65,"F7",343,43
DATA    66,"F8",385,43
DATA    67,"F9",425,43
DATA    68,"F10",467,43
DATA    87,"F11",507,43
DATA    88,"F12",551,43
DATA    41,"`",26,92
```

```
DATA    2,"1",85,92
DATA    3,"2",126,92
DATA    4,"3",172,92
DATA    5,"4",210,92
DATA    6,"5",254,92
DATA    7,"6",297,92
DATA    8,"7",340,92
DATA    9,"8",383,92
DATA    10,"9",428,92
DATA    11,"0",469,92
DATA    12,"-",513,92
DATA    13,"=",555,92
DATA    14,"Back",593,92
DATA    15,"TAB",26,130
DATA    16,"Q",85,130
DATA    17,"W",126,130
DATA    18,"E",172,130
DATA    19,"R",210,130
DATA    20,"T",254,130
DATA    21,"Y",297,130
DATA    22,"U",340,130
DATA    23,"I",383,130
DATA    24,"O",426,130
DATA    25,"P",469,130
DATA    26,"[",513,130
DATA    27,"]",555,130
DATA    43,"\",580,130
DATA    58,"CAPS",26,164
DATA    30,"A",85,164
DATA    31,"S",126,164
DATA    32,"D",172,164
DATA    33,"F",210,164
DATA    34,"G",254,164
DATA    35,"H",297,164
DATA    36,"J",340,164
DATA    37,"K",383,164
DATA    38,"L",426,164
DATA    39,";",469,164
DATA    40,"'",513,164
DATA    28,"ENTER",555,164
DATA    42,"LSHFT",26,195
```

```
DATA    44,"Z",85,195
DATA    45,"X",126,195
DATA    46,"C",172,195
DATA    47,"V",210,195
DATA    48,"B",254,195
DATA    49,"N",297,195
DATA    50,"M",340,195
DATA    51,"<",383,195
DATA    52,">",426,195
DATA    53,"/",469,195
DATA    54,"RSHIFT",513,195
DATA    29,"LCTRL",48,240
DATA    219,"LWIN",120,240
DATA    56,"LALT",187,240
DATA    57,"SPACE",262,240
DATA    184,"RALT",335,240
DATA    220,"RWIN",404,240
DATA    221,"APP",475,240
DATA    157,"RCTRL",547,240
DATA    200,"UP",290,279
DATA    203,"LT",246,317
DATA    208,"DN",285,317
DATA    205,"RT",323,317
DATA    183,"SYSRC",0,0
DATA    70,"SCRLOCK",0,0
DATA    210,"INS",20,279
DATA    199,"HOME",71,279
DATA    201,"PGUP",125,279
DATA    211,"DEL",20,315
DATA    207,"END",71,315
DATA    209,"PGDN",125,315
` Keypad keys
DATA    69,"NUM",436,280
DATA    181,"/",486,280
DATA    55,"*",531,280
DATA    74,"-",574,280
DATA    71,"7",436,309
DATA    72,"8",486,309
DATA    73,"9",531,309
```

```
        DATA    75,"4",436,340
        DATA    76,"5",486,340
        DATA    77,"6",531,340
        DATA    78,"+",574,326
        DATA    79,"1",436,368
        DATA    80,"2",481,368
        DATA    81,"3",531,368
        DATA    82,"0",462,396
        DATA    83,".",522,387
        DATA   156,"E",574,382


DISABLE ESCAPEKEY

LOAD BITMAP " keyboard.bmp",1

SET TEXT TRANSPARENT
SYNC ON
SYNC RATE 30

ReadKeyboardData()
` Scan for all the keys being hit.
WHILE ESCAPEKEY()=0 OR RETURNKEY()=0
     COPY BITMAP 1,0
     SET TEXT TRANSPARENT
     DisplayKeyboard()
     SET TEXT OPAQUE
     LastScanCode = SCANCODE()
     IF LastScanCode < 10 AND LastScanCode >=0
         tempstring$ = "Last Scan Code = 00"+STR$(LastScanCode)
     ENDIF
     IF LastScanCode < 100 AND LastScanCode >=10
         tempstring$ = "Last Scan Code = 0"+STR$(LastScanCode)
     ENDIF
     IF LastScanCode < 1000 AND LastScanCode >=100
         tempstring$ = "Last Scan Code = "+STR$(LastScanCode)
     ENDIF
     TEXT 10,440, tempstring$
     SYNC
ENDWHILE
```

```
DELETE BITMAP 1
END


` Displays the keys and
` highlights the ones that are hit.
FUNCTION DisplayKeyboard()
    White = RGB(255,255,255)
    Black = RGB(0,0,0)
    Red = RGB(255,0,0)
    INK White, Black
    FOR x = 1 to 256
        IF KEYX(x) <> 0
            StateOfKey = KEYSTATE(x)
            IF StateOfKey = 0
                TEXT KEYX(x), KEYY(x), KEY$(x)
            ELSE
                INK Red, Black
                TEXT KEYX(x), KEYY(x), KEY$(x)
                INK White, Black
            ENDIF
        ENDIF
    NEXT x
ENDFUNCTION


` Loads all the DIM values with
` the DATA values
FUNCTION ReadKeyboardData()
    FOR x = 1 to 256
      KeyX(x) = 0
    NEXT x
    FOR x = 1 TO 256
        READ KeyValue
        READ KeyName$
        READ KeyXpos
        READ KeyYPos
        KEY$(KeyValue) = KeyName$
        KEYX(KeyValue) = KeyXpos
        KEYY(KeyValue) = KeyYpos
    NEXT x
ENDFUNCTION
```

A Non-Blocking Input Command

The ENTRY$() and the CLEAR ENTRY BUFFER commands in DarkBASIC make non-blocking input a simple task. These two commands use the Windows keyboard buffer to track what has been typed on the keyboard without having to keep track of every key (as would be the case with an INKEY$() based non-blocking input).

The ENTRY$() command reads whatever string is stored in the Windows keyboard buffer at the time it is called. The Windows keyboard buffer stores every key typed on the keyboard until CLEAR ENTRY BUFFER is called. The CLEAR ENTRY BUFFER command clears the Windows keyboard buffer so a new string can be read.

The NonBlocking program shows you how to use the ENTRY$() and CLEAR ENTRY BUFFER commands in conjunction with the INKEY$() command to keep track of input while other processes are running. There is a clock in the upper-left corner. It changes as you are typing in your text. Change the program to use INPUT$ instead, and notice the difference. Figure 12.15 also shows the output of the NonBlocking example.

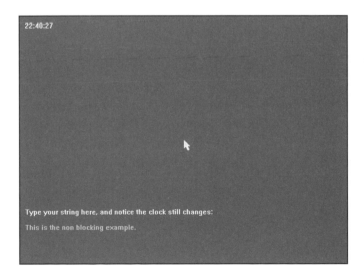

Figure 12.15 *The NonBlocking program demonstrates the use of the* ENTRY$() *and* CLEAR ENTRY BUFFER *commands.*

```
`-----------------------------------
`Beginner's Guide To Game Programming With DarkBASIC
`Copyright (C)2002 Jonathan S. Harbour and Joshua R. Smith
`Chapter 12 - NonBlocking program
`-----------------------------------
CLS
SYNC ON
SYNC RATE 30

White = RGB(255,255,255)
Black = RGB(0,0,0)
SET TEXT TRANSPARENT

InputString$ = ""
StaticString$ = ""
INK White,Black
CLEAR ENTRY BUFFER
` Process clock and keys until ESC is pressed.
WHILE ESCAPEKEY()=0
    INK 0,0
    BOX 0,0,639,479
    INK White,Black
    TEXT 10,10, GET TIME$()
    TEXT 10,370, "Type your string here, and notice the clock still changes:"

    charhit$ = INKEY$()
    IF charhit$ = CHR$(8)
        StaticString$ = StaticString$ + ENTRY$()
        NewLen = LEN(StaticString$)-1
        StaticString$ = LEFT$(StaticString$,NewLen)
        CLEAR ENTRY BUFFER
    ENDIF

    InputString$ = StaticString$ + ENTRY$()
    TEXT 10,400, InputString$
    SYNC
ENDWHILE
END
```

Mouse Commands

Next to the keyboard, the mouse is the most popular input device for the PC. Almost any program requires a mouse. Mouse devices come in all shapes, colors, and sizes. However, they all have one thing in common: They move the cursor on the screen. There are 10 different DarkBASIC commands that control the mouse.

The HIDE MOUSE Command

The HIDE MOUSE command gets rid of that pesky mouse cursor. The mouse cursor is cute, but sometimes it can be annoying when it follows your mouse. The two most annoying examples I can think of are in a flight-simulator-type game, where the mouse cursor should not be seen, and in a game where you need a custom mouse cursor, such as a targeting game. The command takes no parameters and returns nothing.

The SHOW MOUSE Command

The SHOW MOUSE command does just the opposite of the HIDE MOUSE command. It returns the cute, lovable mouse cursor. The command takes no parameters and returns nothing.

Mouse Position

Perhaps the most important data received from the mouse is the cursor's X and Y position on the screen. A game programmer translates this information into useful data for movement of characters, sprites, or 3D objects. The X and Y positions of the mouse start from the upper-left corner of the screen and work toward the lower-right corner. The mouse cursor moves further right the more positive the X value is, and further down the more positive the Y value is. Figure 12.16 will help you to visualize this concept.

There is a third position of the mouse that DarkBASIC reads—the Z position. It is hard to visualize a mouse with three positions because there is only a left-right, up-down orientation on a mouse pad. Most often, the Z position of the mouse refers to the wheel located in the center of the mouse. It is a little misleading, but it makes sense after you have used it. Figure 12.17 demonstrates the concept of the mouse wheel and how it relates to a Z value.

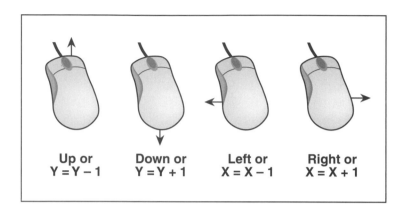

Up or
Y = Y – 1

Down or
Y = Y + 1

Left or
X = X – 1

Right or
X = X + 1

Figure 12.16 *The X-Y relative positions of the mouse*

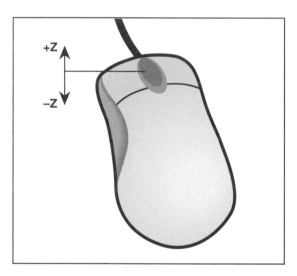

Figure 12.17
The mouse wheel and corresponding Z values

The MOUSEX Command

The MOUSEX() command returns the X position of the mouse cursor on the screen. This command takes no parameters but returns the X value of the cursor, which is between 0 and the width of the screen in pixels minus 1. The maximum value is the screen width minus 1 because the minimum position starts at 0.

The MOUSEY Command

The MOUSEY() command returns the Y position of the mouse cursor on the screen. It takes no parameters but returns the Y value of the cursor, which is between 0 and the height of the screen in pixels minus 1. The maximum value is the screen height minus 1 because the minimum position starts at 0.

The MOUSEZ Command

The MOUSEZ() command returns the value of the mouse wheel, which ranges from 0 to 100. It takes no parameters.

The POSITION MOUSE Command

The POSITION MOUSE command positions the mouse cursor on the screen. It takes two parameters (X position and Y position) and returns nothing.

Using the Mouse Position Commands: The MousePositon Program

The MousePosition program demonstrates the use of the mouse position commands. It displays the X, Y, and Z positions of the mouse on the screen and shows the mouse cursor. It also uses the keyboard to move the mouse using the POSITION MOUSE command. Figure 12.18 shows the results of this program.

```
`----------------------------------
`Beginner's Guide To Game Programming With DarkBASIC
`Copyright (C)2002 Jonathan S. Harbour and Joshua R. Smith
`Chapter 12 - MousePosition Program
`----------------------------------
CLS
SYNC ON
SYNC RATE 30
White = RGB(255,255,255)
Black = RGB(0,0,0)
WHILE ESCAPEKEY()=0
    INK 0,0
    BOX 0,0,639,479
    INK White,Black
    tempstring$ = "Mouse X pos: "+STR$(MOUSEX())
    TEXT 10,10, tempstring$
    tempstring$ = "Mouse Y pos: "+STR$(MOUSEY())
    TEXT 10,22, tempstring$
    tempstring$ = "Mouse Z pos: "+STR$(MOUSEZ())
    TEXT 10,34, tempstring$
    tempstring$ = "Press R to Reset the mouse"
    TEXT 10,400, tempstring$
    IF INKEY$()="R" OR INKEY$()="r"
        POSITION MOUSE 0,0
    ENDIF
    SYNC
ENDWHILE
```

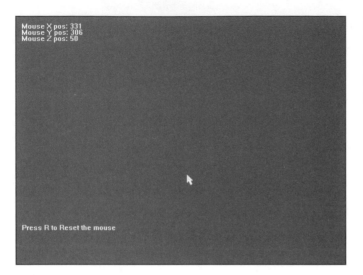

Figure 12.18

The MousePosition program demonstrates the use of the mouse commands.

Mouse Movement

Now that you know how to use the mouse position commands, you can read the difference between the mouse positions. The oldest way of knowing how far the mouse moved is by using the following formulas: $dx = x2-x1$, $dy = y2-y1$, $dz = z2-z1$. dx, dy, and dz are all delta values. In other words, they are the difference between the last mouse position and the current mouse position. DarkBASIC provides some mouse movement commands so that it is not necessary to calculate dx, dy, and dz. Figure 12.19 better illustrates the concept of mouse movement.

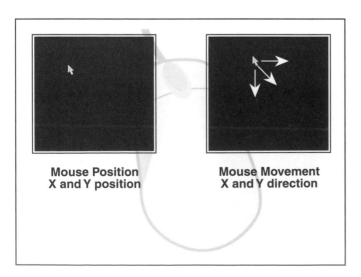

Figure 12.19

Mouse position versus mouse movement

The MOUSEMOVEX Command

The MOUSEMOVEX command tells you the distance between the current MOUSEX() and the last MOUSEX(). It is the same as the dx = x2–x1 formula. This command takes no parameters and returns the distance in the x position.

The MOUSEMOVEY Command

The MOUSEMOVEY command tells you the distance between the current MOUSEY() and the last MOUSEY(). It is the same as the dy = y2–y1 formula. This command takes no parameters and returns the distance in the y position.

The MOUSEMOVEZ Command

The MOUSEMOVEZ command tells you the distance between the current MOUSEZ() and the last MOUSEZ(). It is the same as the dz = z2–z1 formula. This command takes no parameters and returns the distance the mouse wheel has moved.

Using the Mouse Movement Commands

The MouseMove program demonstrates the uses of the mouse movement commands. It scales a bitmap based on the movement of the mouse. To quit the program, just press the Esc key. Figure 12.20 shows the output of the MouseMove example.

Figure 12.20 *The MouseMove program demonstrates the use of the mouse-movement commands.*

```
`----------------------------------
`Beginner's Guide To Game Programming With DarkBASIC
`Copyright (C)2002 Jonathan S. Harbour and Joshua R. Smith
`Chapter 12 - MouseMove Program
`----------------------------------

LOAD BITMAP " graphic.bmp", 1

HIDE MOUSE
SYNC ON
SYNC RATE 30
White = RGB(255,255,255)
Black = RGB(0,0,0)
SIZEX = 100
SIZEY = 100
SET CURRENT BITMAP 0
` Size the picture until Esc is hit.
WHILE ESCAPEKEY()=0
    INK 0,0
    BOX 0,0,639,479
    INK White,Black
    sizex = sizex + (MOUSEMOVEX()/10)
    sizey = sizey + (MOUSEMOVEY()/10)
    IF sizex > 100 THEN sizex = 100
    IF sizex < 1 THEN sizex = 0

    IF sizey > 100 THEN sizey = 100
    IF sizey < 1 THEN sizey = 0

    x1 = 0
    x2 = (638*sizex)/100+1
    y1 = 0
    y2 = (478*sizey)/100+1
    COPY BITMAP 1,0,0,639,479,0,x1,y1,x2,y2
    tempstring$ = "Move the mouse to scale the picture"
    TEXT 10,460,tempstring$
    SYNC
ENDWHILE
```

Mouse Buttons

Now that you can determine the position and movement of the mouse, there is one more item that must be read—the state of the mouse button. A given mouse button has four states: UP, DOWN, CLICKED, and DOUBLE CLICKED. The CLICKED and DOUBLE CLICKED states are derived from the UP and DOWN states.

The MOUSECLICK Command

The MOUSECLICK() command returns which button on the mouse is currently pressed. This command takes no input but returns a value that indicates which button is being pressed.

The left mouse button is a value of 1; the right mouse button is a value of 2. If there are more than two buttons, the third and fourth buttons are valued at 4 and 8, respectively. This way, you can determine which buttons are being pressed at one time. The MOUSECLICK() command adds the values of the buttons that are being clicked, so if the left and right mouse buttons are pressed, the value is 3. Table 12.3 shows the return values for MOUSECLICK() and what they mean.

Table 12.3 Return Values of MOUSECLICK

Value	Buttons Pressed	Value	Buttons Pressed
0	None	8	Fourth
1	Left	9	Fourth and left
2	Right	10	Fourth and right
3	Left and right	11	Fourth, left, and right
4	Third	12	Fourth and third
5	Third and left	13	Fourth, third, and left
6	Third and right	14	Fourth, third, and right
7	Third, left, and right	15	Fourth, third, left, and right

Determining CLICKED versus DOUBLE CLICKED

Determining CLICKED and DOUBLE CLICKED states is not that hard. For the CLICKED state, you simply detect when the button is pressed. At that point, you wait until the mouse button is up: MOUSECLICK() = 0. You now have a button in a CLICKED state.

The DOUBLE CLICKED state is a little trickier. You must determine that the button is in a CLICKED state two times within a given timeframe. The Click States program shows an example of the CLICKED and DOUBLE CLICKED states. Figure 12.21 shows the output of the program.

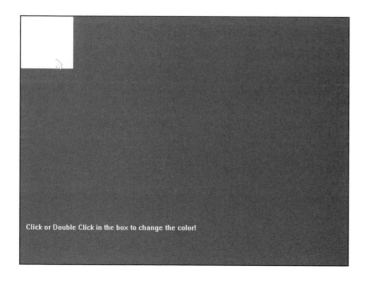

Click or Double Click in the box to change the color!

Figure 12.21 *The Click States program demonstrates the use of the* MOUSE CLICK() *command.*

```
`-----------------------------------
`Beginner's Guide To Game Programming With DarkBASIC
`Copyright (C)2002 Jonathan S. Harbour and Joshua R. Smith
`Chapter 12 - Click States Program
`-----------------------------------
CLS
SYNC ON
SYNC RATE 30

` This is to color the box
` Click types are as follows
` 0 = No click
` 1 = Mouse Down
```

```
` 2 = Mouse Click
` 3 = Mouse Double Clicked
ClickType = 0
Dclick = 0


Red = RGB(255,0,0)
Green = RGB(0,255,0)
White = RGB(255,255,255)
Blue = RGB(0,0,255)
Black = RGB(0,0,0)


SYNC ON
SYNC RATE 30
` Run this program until Escape is hit.
WHILE ESCAPEKEY()=0
    IF ClickType = 0 THEN INK Blue,Black
    IF ClickType = 1 THEN INK Red,Black
    IF ClickType = 2 THEN INK White,Black
    IF ClickType = 3 THEN INK Green,Black
    IF DClick > 0 THEN DClick = DClick - 1
    IF DClick = 0 THEN DClick = -1
    BOX 0,0,100,100
    INK White,Black
    TEXT 10,400,"Click or Double Click in the box to change the color!"
    IF MOUSECLICK()=1
        IF MOUSEX()<=100 AND MOUSEY() <=100
            IF Dclick > 0 OR Dclick = -3
                Dclick = -3
                ClickType = 1
            ELSE
                ClickType = 1
                Dclick = -2
            ENDIF
        ELSE
            ClickType = 0
            Dclick = -1
        ENDIF
    ENDIF
    IF MOUSECLICK()=0 AND Dclick = -2
        IF ClickType = 1
            ClickType = 2
```

```
            Dclick = 50
        ENDIF
    ENDIF
    IF MOUSECLICK()=0 AND Dclick = -3
        IF ClickType = 1
            ClickType = 3
            Dclick = -1
        ENDIF
    ENDIF
    SYNC
ENDWHILE
```

The Mouse Handler

The mouse handler is a concept that works well with game programming. It is nothing more than a function that is created to handle all mouse-related input. Every stage of a game can contain a different mouse handler, but placing all of the mouse-related input into a function will make it easier to control items with the mouse.

The ShootingGallery program is a simple shooting gallery game. It uses most of the mouse commands that I have covered in this chapter. The mouse handler is clearly defined. To destroy the targets, move the cursor over the target and left-click on it. Figure 12.22 shows the output of the ShootingGallery program.

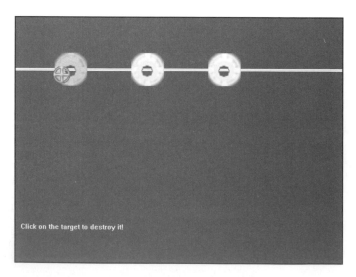

Figure 12.22

Output of the ShootingGallery program

```
`-----------------------------------
`Beginner's Guide To Game Programming With DarkBASIC
`Copyright (C)2002 Jonathan S. Harbour and Joshua R. Smith
`Chapter 12 - ShootingGallery program
`-----------------------------------

SYNC ON
SYNC RATE 30
DIM SpriteHit(20)
DIM SpriteTimer(1)
HIDE MOUSE
SpriteTimer(1) = 0
LOAD IMAGE "crosshair.bmp",25
LoadTargetAnims()
` Initialize all the sprites
FOR x = 2 TO 20
    SPRITE X,-100,68,5
    SET SPRITE x,1,1
    SpriteHit(x) = 0
NEXT X
` Set th mouse cursor spite
SPRITE 1,320,240,1
SET SPRITE 1,1,1
` Seting up the lines in the background
SET CURRENT BITMAP 0
Green = RGB(0,255,0)
Red = RGB(255,0,0)
Black = RGB(0,0,0)
White = RGB(255,255,255)
INK Green,Black
BOX 0,98,639,102
INK Red,Black
BOX 0,100,639,100
INK White,Black
inum = 5
TEXT 10,400,"Click on the target to destroy it!"
` Play the game until the Escape key is hit.
WHILE ESCAPEKEY()=0
    ProcessSprites()
    ControllerHandler()
```

382   12.   Programming the Keyboard, Mouse, and Joystick

```
      SYNC
   ENDWHILE

   END


   ` This moves the crosshairs to where the mouse is.
   FUNCTION ControllerHandler()
       SPRITE 1, MOUSEX(), MOUSEY(), 25
       IF MOUSECLICK()=1
           FOR X = 2 TO 20
               IF SPRITE COLLISION(1,X)
                   SpriteHit(X) = 1
               ENDIF
           NEXT X
       ENDIF
   ENDFUNCTION


   `   This does all the Sprite Collision processing.
   FUNCTION ProcessSprites()
       SpriteTimer(1) = SpriteTimer(1) - 1
       IF SpriteTimer(1) <= 0 THEN MoveNewSprite()
       FOR X = 2 TO 20
           IF SPRITE X(X) > 704
               SPRITE X,-100,68,5
           ENDIF
           IF SpriteHit(X)
               SPRITE X,SPRITE X(x)+5,SPRITE Y(X), SPRITE IMAGE(X)+1
               IF SPRITE IMAGE(X) >= 15
                   SPRITE X,-100,68,5
                   SpriteHit(X) = 0
               ENDIF
           ELSE
               IF SPRITE X(X) >= -64
                   SPRITE X,SPRITE X(x)+5,SPRITE Y(X), 5
               ENDIF
           ENDIF
       NEXT X
   ENDFUNCTION


   ` Moves out a new sprite
```

```
FUNCTION MoveNewSprite()
    FOR X = 2 TO 20
        IF SPRITE X(X) <= -100
            SPRITE X , -64, SPRITE Y(X), 5
            X = 21
        ENDIF
    NEXT X
    SpriteTimer(1) = 30
ENDFUNCTION

` Loads are the Target Animations.
FUNCTION LoadTargetAnims()
    LOAD BITMAP "target.bmp",1
    inum = 5
    fadestep = 100
    SET CURRENT BITMAP 1
    FOR X = 0 TO 10
        FADE BITMAP 1,90
        GET IMAGE inum,0,0,64,64
        inum = inum + 1
    NEXT X
    DELETE BITMAP 1
    SET CURRENT BITMAP 0
ENDFUNCTION
```

Joystick Commands

What do all gaming consoles have in common? Their joysticks! Every gaming console has the potential to have a joystick. From the Atari 2600 to the modern PC, the joystick is the choice of most game developers for input. DarkBASIC has a wide selection of commands to control the joystick.

Analog versus Digital Input

Before you get into the wonderful world of DarkBASIC joystick commands, you need a little understanding of how a joystick works. There are two different types of joysticks—digital and analog. Each type works with a PC, but they generate the data in completely different ways.

An analog joystick is like most old-school mouse devices. It consists of two rollers that, when moved, calculate the distance and report the information to the computer. All older joysticks generate this analog input. When the input is generated, it is converted to a digital signal for the computer to use. The problem with analog input is that the joystick has a tendency to drift because of slight movements.

Digital joysticks read differently than analog joysticks. Instead of having two rollers to read the distance between movements, digital joysticks use an optical or light sensor that converts user movements into a digital signal. This gives you a much more accurate reading of the user input without the drifting problems. A common digital joystick (the one I use) is the Microsoft Sidewinder 3D.

Joystick Position

Like the mouse, the joystick has two common positions—X and Y. Unlike the mouse, however, you do not have to move the joystick around a large pad to get your X and Y position readings. You just move your hand up while holding the joystick, and the Y position decreases. Move your hand left to decrease the X position.

Some joysticks also contain a third position—the Z position. This is very much like the mouse wheel. Figure 12.23 shows the three positions and how they correspond to the joystick.

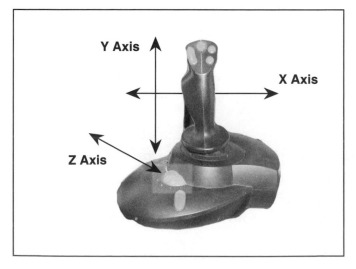

Figure 12.23 *The three axes of a joystick*

The JOYSTICK X Command

The JOYSTICK X() command returns the X position of the joystick, which ranges from −1000 to +1000. The joystick is in the center of the X axis when the X position is equal to 0.

The JOYSTICK Y Command

The JOYSTICK Y() command returns the Y position of the joystick, which also ranges from −1000 to +1000. The joystick is in the center of the Y axis when the Y position is equal to 0.

The JOYSTICK Z Command

The JOYSTICK Z() command returns the Z position of the joystick, which also ranges from −1000 to +1000. The joystick is in the center of the Z axis when the Z position is equal to 0.

Recycling an Old Program

To demonstrate the X, Y, and Z joystick commands, I have rewritten the mouse movement command to read the joystick. Notice that there is no joystick position command because you cannot reposition the joystick. Figure 12.24 shows the output of the JoystickPosition program.

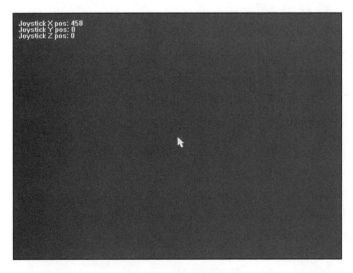

Figure 12.24
Output of the JoystickPosition program

```
`----------------------------------
`Beginner's Guide To Game Programming With DarkBASIC
`Copyright (C)2002 Jonathan S. Harbour and Joshua R. Smith
`Chapter 12 - JoystickPosition Program
`----------------------------------
CLS
SYNC ON
SYNC RATE 30
White = RGB(255,255,255)
Black = RGB(0,0,0)
` Reads the Joystick position until
` the escape key is hit..
WHILE ESCAPEKEY()=0
    INK 0,0
    BOX 0,0,639,479
    INK White,Black
    tempstring$ = "Joystick X pos: "+STR$(JOYSTICK X())
    TEXT 10,10,tempstring$
    string$ = "Joystick Y pos: "+STR$(JOYSTICK Y())
    TEXT 10,22,tempstring$
    string$ = "Joystick Z pos: "+STRr$(JOYSTICK Z())
    TEXT 10,34,tempstring$
    SYNC
ENDWHILE
```

Joystick Movement

The joystick movement commands are not like the mouse movement commands.
They do not give you the distance that the joystick moves; rather, they tell you what
direction the joystick is moving.

The JOYSTICK UP Command

The JOYSTICK UP() command tells you whether the joystick is moving upward. This
command takes no parameters and returns a 1 if the joystick is moving up. If the
joystick is moving downward, this command returns a 0.

The JOYSTICK DOWN Command

The JOYSTICK DOWN() command tells you whether the joystick is moving downward.
This command takes no parameters and returns a 1 if the joystick is moving down.
If the joystick is moving upward, this command returns a 0.

The JOYSTICK LEFT Command

The JOYSTICK LEFT() command tells you whether the joystick is moving left. This command takes no parameters and returns a 1 if the joystick is moving to the left. If the joystick is moving right, this command returns a 0.

The JOYSTICK RIGHT Command

The JOYSTICK RIGHT() command tells you whether the joystick is moving right. This command takes no parameters and returns a 1 if the joystick is moving to the right. If the joystick is moving left, this command returns a 0.

Recycling Yet Another Old Program

The MouseMove program scaled a bitmap with the mouse. You are now going to recycle that code and scale the picture with the joystick. Notice that the JOYSTICK UP() value is subtracted from the scalex value, and JOYSTICK DOWN() is added. This is different than the code for the MouseMove program, in which you just added one value, because neither JOYSTICK UP() nor JOYSTICK DOWN() returns a negative number. Therefore, you just create the negative value. The same is true with JOYSTICK LEFT() and JOYSTICK RIGHT(). Figure 12.25 shows the output of the JoystickMove program.

Figure 12.25

Output of the JoystickMove program

```
`----------------------------------
`Beginner's Guide To Game Programming With DarkBASIC
`Copyright (C)2002 Jonathan S. Harbour and Joshua R. Smith
`Chapter 12 - JoystickMove Program
`----------------------------------
CLS
LOAD BITMAP " graphic.bmp", 1

HIDE MOUSE
SYNC ON
SYNC RATE 30
White = RGB(255,255,255)
Black = RGB(0,0,0)
SIZEX = 100
SIZEY = 100
SET CURRENT BITMAP 0
` Scales with Joystick movement
` until the escape key is pressed
WHILE ESCAPEKEY()=0
   INK 0,0
   BOX 0,0,639,479
   INK White,Black
   sizex = sizex - JOYSTICK UP()
   sizex = sizex +  JOYSTICK DOWN()
   sizey = sizey - JOYSTICK LEFT()
   sizey = sizey + JOYSTICK RIGHT()
   IF sizex > 100 THEN sizex = 100
   IF sizex < 1 THEN sizex = 0

   IF sizey > 100 THEN sizey = 100
   IF sizey < 1 THEN sizey = 0
   x1 = 0
   x2 = (638*sizex)/100+1
   y1 = 0
   y2 = (478*sizey)/100+1
   COPY BITMAP 1,0,0,639,479,0,x1,y1,x2,y2
   tempstring$ = "Move the JoyStick to scale the picture"
   TEXT 10,460,tempstring$
   SYNC
ENDWHILE
```

Joystick Buttons

Just like the mouse, the joystick has buttons. Some joysticks have lots of buttons (such as for the Xbox, GameCube, and PlayStation 2), while other joysticks have one button (such as for the Atari 2600). However, each button has one thing in common—it provides a game with user input. Each button is assigned to a specific action or series of actions. In *Super Mario Brothers,* for example, one button is used to jump, and the other button is used to fire. DarkBASIC provides commands to read these buttons from the joystick and use them in your game.

The JOYSTICK FIRE A Command

The JOYSTICK FIRE A() command lets you know when the primary button on the joystick has been pressed. This is commonly used for firing at objects in most first-person shooters. The command takes no parameters, but it returns a 0 if the primary button is in the UP state and a 1 if it is in the DOWN state.

The JOYSTICK FIRE B Command

The JOYSTICK FIRE B() command lets you know when the secondary button on the joystick has been pressed. This is commonly used for a secondary firing function in most first-person shooters. The command takes no parameters, but it returns a 0 if the secondary button is in the UP state and a 1 if it is in the DOWN state.

The JOYSTICK FIRE C Command

The JOYSTICK FIRE C() command lets you know when the third button on the joystick has been pressed. This is commonly used to check status or perform actions in some first-person shooters. The command takes no parameters, but it returns a 0 if the third button is in the UP state and a 1 if it is in the DOWN state.

The JOYSTICK FIRE D Command

The JOYSTICK FIRE D() command lets you know when the fourth button on the joystick has been pressed. This is not commonly used in first-person shooters, but it can be assigned to change things in the display. The command takes no parameters, but it returns a 0 if the fourth button is in the UP state and a 1 if it is in the DOWN state.

Joystick Sliders

Some joysticks, both analog and digital, have sliders on them, much like you would see in the cockpit of a spaceship or on top of a soundboard. DarkBASIC provides a means to read these sliders as well.

The JOYSTICK SLIDER A Command

The JOYSTICK SLIDER A() command returns the value of the primary slider on a joystick. I usually use this slider to control my thrust in a space flight simulation. The command takes no input, but returns a value between 0 and 65535. This is much more precise than JOYSTICK X() and JOYSTICK Y(), so you can get more precision out of a slider.

> **NOTE**
>
> The number 65535 will show up frequently when you are programming devices. This is because it has 16 bits and is a computer-friendly number (because it is based on a power of 2).

The JOYSTICK SLIDER B Command

The JOYSTICK SLIDER B() command returns the value of a secondary slider on a joystick. The command also takes no input, but it returns a value between 0 and 65535. I have never had a joystick with two sliders before, but I'm sure it is a great combination of control and style.

Additional Joystick Commands

There are four other joystick commands that I need to address. These commands cover some of the unconventional aspects of joysticks. However, DarkBASIC would not be complete without them.

The JOYSTICK TWIST X Command

The JOYSTICK TWIST X() command reads the twist of the X position of the joystick. It takes no parameters but returns the value of the joystick twisted in the X direction. This value is between 0 and 65535.

The JOYSTICK TWIST Y Command

The JOYSTICK TWIST Y() command reads the twist of the Y position of the joystick. It takes no parameters but returns the value of the joystick twisted in the Y direction. This value is between 0 and 65535.

The JOYSTICK TWIST Z Command

The JOYSTICK TWIST Z() command reads the twist of the Z position of the joystick. It takes no parameters but returns the value of the joystick twisted in the Z direction. This value is between 0 and 65535.

The JOYSTICK HAT ANGLE Command

The JOYSTICK HAT ANGLE command returns the degrees of the hat controller on your joystick. Some joysticks have more than one hat, so this command takes one parameter—the number of the hat. It supports up to four different hats, and returns the angle at which the hat is pointing in tenths of a degree. The value of the angle ranges from 0 to 3600. Table 12.4 lists the most common hat directions.

> A *hat* is a multidirectional button on a joystick. You simply press down most buttons, but you press a hat button in a particular direction.

Table 12.4 Hat Directions

Direction	Angle (in Tenths of a Degree)
North	0
East	900
South	1800
West	2700

Revising the ShootingGallery Program

Now that you know all the joystick commands, it is time to revisit the ShootingGallery program. This time you will replace the mouse commands with joystick commands. Because of the way the program was written, you only need to change one function—the mouse handler. The following source code lists the changes you need to make to enable the ShootingGallery program to use the joystick. You can find the full source code for the JoystickShootingGallery program on the CD in the Chapter 12 directory.

Place the following source code after the SYNC RATE 30 command in the original ShootingGallery program.

```
DIM XPos(1)
DIM YPos(1)
XPos(1) = SCREEN WIDTH() /2
YPos(1) = SCREEN HEIGHT() /2
```

Now replace the ControllerHandler() section with this new section, which uses the JOYSTICK commands.

```
FUNCTION ControllerHandler()
    IF JOYSTICK UP() = 1 THEN   YPos(1) = YPos(1) - 3
    IF JOYSTICK DOWN() = 1 THEN   YPos(1) = YPos(1) + 3
    IF JOYSTICK LEFT() = 1 THEN XPos(1) = XPos(1) - 3
    IF JOYSTICK RIGHT() = 1 THEN XPos(1) = XPos(1) + 3
    IF XPos(1) < 0 THEN XPos(1) = 0
    IF YPos(1) < 0 THEN YPos(1) = 0
    IF XPos(1) > SCREEN WIDTH()-1 THEN XPos(1) = SCREEN WIDTH()-1
    IF YPos(1) > SCREEN HEIGHT()-1 THEN YPos(1) = SCREEN HEIGHT()-1
    SPRITE 1, XPos(1), YPos(1) , 25
    IF JOYSTICK FIRE A()=1
        FOR X = 2 TO 20
            IF SPRITE COLLISION(1,X)
                SPRITEHIT(X) = 1
            ENDIF
        NEXT X
    ENDIF
ENDFUNCTION
```

Defining Control Devices

Before you move on to the final capabilities of the joystick, you need to take a side trip. This trip takes you down the path of control devices. Some computers have more than one control device, which can be just about any human input device. Some examples are joysticks, head-mounted trackers, and driving wheels. The next set of commands tells DarkBASIC which one of those control devices to use and sets the default control devices.

The PERFORM CHECKLIST FOR CONTROL DEVICES Command

The PERFORM CHECKLIST FOR CONTROL DEVICES command fills up the checklist information with all the available control devices. Each device gets its own space within the checklist. The name of the device is returned in CHECKLIST STRING$().
If the device supports force feedback, CHECKLIST VALUE A() returns a 1; otherwise, it returns a 0.

The SET CONTROL DEVICE Command

After you have listed the control devices, you need to set the default control device using the SET CONTROL DEVICE command. This command takes one parameter, which is a string with the name of the device. If PERFORM CHECKLIST FOR CONTROL DEVICES returns more than one control device, you should ask the user which device to use and then pass the string for that device to this command.

The CONTROL DEVICE NAME$ Command

The CONTROL DEVICE NAME$ command returns the string name of the control device. This is very useful because you will not have to keep track of the current control device; you can just read its name from CONTROL DEVICE NAME$. This command takes no parameters, but returns a string with the control device's name.

The CONTROL DEVICE X Command

The CONTROL DEVICE X command returns the X value of the current controller. This is exactly like the JOYSTICK X() command, but it works for any control device specified.

The CONTROL DEVICE Y Command

The CONTROL DEVICE Y command returns the Y value of the current controller. This is exactly like the JOYSTICK Y() command, but it works for any control device specified.

The CONTROL DEVICE Z Command

The CONTROL DEVICE Z command returns the Z value of the current controller. This is exactly like the JOYSTICK Z() command, but it works for any control device specified.

Selecting the Current Control Device

The SetControlDevice program provides a simple example of how to detect and set the current control device. It contains a function that you will use in quite a few other programs to determine which control device to use. Figure 12.26 shows the output of the SetControlDevice program.

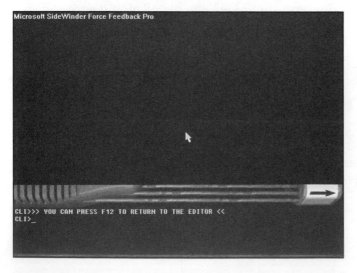

Figure 12.26
Output of the SetControlDevice program

```
`-----------------------------------
`Beginner's Guide To Game Programming With DarkBASIC
`Copyright (C)2002 Jonathan S. Harbour and Joshua R. Smith
`Chapter 12 - SetControlDevice Program
`-----------------------------------


SYNC ON
SYNC RATE 30

SetControlDevice()
PRINT CONTROL DEVICE NAME$()

END


` Sets the current control device
FUNCTION SetControlDevice()
    PERFORM CHECKLIST FOR CONTROL DEVICES
    IF CHECKLIST QUANTITY() = 1
        SET CONTROL DEVICE CHECKLIST STRING$(1)
        EXITFUNCTION CHECKLIST STRING$(1)
    ENDIF
    CLS
    PRINT "Please Select Control Device"
    FOR X = 1 TO CHECKLIST QUANTITY()
        tempstring$ = STR$(X)+": "+CHECKLIST STRING$(X)
        PRINT tempstring$
    NEXT X
    INPUT ConDev
    SET CONTROL DEVICE CHECKLIST STRING$(ConDev)
ENDFUNCTION CHECKLIST STRING$(ConDev)
```

One special thing to note about this function is that is there is only one control device—the function does not list the devices, it just picks that one control device. This is useful for keeping the flow of a program going. Also, if there are no control devices available, this function returns a string of "none." That way, you can check up front to see whether there are any control devices.

Force Feedback

Now that you have learned about the control devices, I will cover force feedback, which includes more than just the standard joystick. Driving wheels and other control devices (including some mouse devices) also support force feedback.

What is force feedback? It is a tactile sensation returned to the gamer by the control device he is using. An example would be a gamer playing a boxing game. In real boxing, when your opponent hits you, you feel the hit on your face. In the gaming world, you really don't want to be hit in the face, but you would like some other feedback to let you know you've been hit. Thus your joystick will rumble or move to one side as your opponent strikes you. That is why it is called force feedback—the joystick is forcing you to feel some feedback. The joystick or input device accomplishes this with small motors and sensors that are built into it.

Programming Force Feedback

Programming force feedback in DarkBASIC does not take a rocket scientist. When I finish explaining the command, you will add some source code to the ShootingGallery program to add force feedback.

Before activating any of the force-feedback commands, you must first determine whether the device supports it. Remember that the checklist created by PERFORM CHECKLIST FOR CONTROL DEVICES stores a value of 1 in CHECKLIST VALUE A() if the device supports force feedback. Your program will fail if you attempt to use force feedback on a device that does not support it.

> **Magnitude value is the extent of the force-feedback effect. This value ranges from 0 to 100, where 0 is no effect and 100 is the largest possible effect.**

You can split the force-feedback commands into two groups—the standard commands and the special commands. Each group of commands takes similar input. At least one of their parameters (unless otherwise specified) takes a magnitude value.

Standard Force-Feedback Commands

The standard force-feedback commands allow you to create your own force-feedback effects. They give you the ability to move the joystick in any direction you want. The commands are FORCE ANGLE, FORCE UP, FORCE DOWN, FORCE LEFT, FORCE RIGHT, FORCE AUTO CENTER ON, FORCE AUTO CENTER OFF, and FORCE NO EFFECT.

The FORCE ANGLE Command

FORCE ANGLE is the most versatile of the standard force-feedback commands. It takes three parameters and returns none. The first parameter is the magnitude of the force. The second value is the angle at which you want to put the force-feedback device. The third value is the time for which you want to leave the device at that angle, measured in milliseconds.

The FORCE UP Command

The FORCE UP command forces the joystick into the up position. It provides resistance if you are trying to pull down on the joystick. The command takes one parameter, which is the magnitude of the force, and returns nothing.

The FORCE DOWN Command

The FORCE DOWN command forces the joystick into the down position. It provides resistance if you are trying to pull up on the joystick. The command takes one parameter, which is the magnitude of the force, and returns nothing.

The FORCE LEFT Command

The FORCE LEFT command forces the joystick into the left position. It provides resistance if you are trying to pull the joystick right. The command takes one parameter, which is the magnitude of the force, and returns nothing.

The FORCE RIGHT Command

The FORCE RIGHT command forces the joystick into the right position. It provides resistance if you are trying to pull the joystick left. The command takes one parameter, which is the magnitude of the force, and returns nothing.

The FORCE AUTO CENTER ON Command

The FORCE AUTO CENTER ON command forces the joystick to always return to the center, instead of forcing left, right, up, or down. This command is great for stiffing the joystick. It takes no parameter, and it returns nothing.

The FORCE AUTO CENTER OFF Command

The FORCE AUTO CENTER OFF command frees the joystick to stay in whatever position it is in. This command is great for loosening the joystick. It takes no parameter, and it returns nothing.

The FORCE NO EFFECT Command

The FORCE NO EFFECT command is the last of the standard commands, and it affects both the standard and the special force-feedback commands. This command cancels all force feedback applied to the joystick. It takes no parameters and returns nothing.

Special Force-Feedback Commands

Sometimes just moving the joystick up, down, left, and right is not enough. DarkBASIC provides commands to do more than just standard stuff. These are special case commands that perform more complex actions. DarkBASIC supports four special commands: FORCE CHAINSAW, FORCE SHOOT, FORCE IMPACT, and FORCE WATER EFFECT.

The FORCE CHAINSAW Command

The FORCE CHAINSAW command creates a chainsaw effect within the control device. Imagine revving up a chainsaw and keeping it running. That's what this command simulates. It takes two parameters. The first is the magnitude value, and the second is the duration of the effect. Like all force-feedback effect commands, the duration is measured in milliseconds.

The FORCE SHOOT Command

The FORCE SHOOT command emulates the kickback from a pistol. The kickback occurs when you pull the trigger—your hand moves back and the bullet moves forward. This command takes two parameters. The first is the magnitude value, and the second is the duration value.

The FORCE IMPACT Command

The FORCE IMPACT command is probably the most versatile of the special force-feedback commands. You can use it for hitting walls, hitting people, or getting hit.

I think this might be my favorite special force-feedback command. It takes two parameters. The first is the magnitude value, and the second is the duration value.

The FORCE WATER EFFECT Command

FORCE WATER EFFECT is an interesting command. It creates the sensation of walking through water. This command takes two parameters. The first is the magnitude value, and the second is the duration value.

Revising the ShootingGallery Program . . . Again

This is your last visit to the ShootingGallery program. This time you will add special force-feedback commands to the program. You will add two new commands, change the control handler, and modify the main portion of the program. You can find the full source code for this program on the CD in the Chapter 12 directory, under ForceShootingGallery.

First, add the following source code after the SYNC RATE 30 section. This code checks the force-feedback capabilities of the joystick. You will enter SETCONTROLDEVICE() in a little while.

```
DIM SupportsForceFeedBack(1)
SupportsForceFeedBack(1) = 0
SetControlDevice()
```

Add the following source code after inum = 5. These are the instructions to activate the force-feedback commands if the joystick supports them.

```
IF SupportsForceFeedBack(1) = 1
    TEXT 10,292,"C - Chain Saw Effect"
    TEXT 10,304,"V - Water Effect"
    TEXT 10,316,"W - Force UP"
    TEXT 10,328,"S - Force DOWN"
    TEXT 10,340,"A - Force LEFT"
    TEXT 10,352,"D - Force RIGHT"
    TEXT 10,364,"O - Auto Center On"
    TEXT 10,376,"P - Auto Center Off"
ENDIF
```

Add the following line of code after `ControllerHandler()`. This processes the other force-feedback effects.

```
DoOtherEffects()
```

Next, replace the existing `ControllerHandler()` function with the following `ControllerHandler()` function.

```
FUNCTION ControllerHandler()
    IF JOYSTICK UP() = 1 THEN   YPos(1) = YPos(1) - 3
    IF JOYSTICK DOWN() = 1 THEN   YPos(1) = YPos(1) + 3
    IF JOYSTICK LEFT() = 1 THEN XPos(1) = XPos(1) - 3
    IF JOYSTICK RIGHT() = 1 THEN XPos(1) = XPos(1) + 3
    IF XPos(1) < 0 THEN XPos(1) = 0
    IF YPos(1) < 0 THEN YPos(1) = 0
    IF XPos(1) > SCREEN WIDTH()-1 THEN XPos(1) = SCREEN WIDTH()-1
    IF YPos(1) > SCREEN HEIGHT()-1 THEN YPos(1) = SCREEN HEIGHT()-1
    SPRITE 1, XPos(1), YPos(1) , 25
    IF JOYSTICK FIRE A()=1
        IF SupportsForceFeedBack(1) <> 0 THEN FORCE SHOOT 50,25
            FOR x = 2 TO 20
                IF SPRITE COLLISION(1,x)
                    IF SupportsForceFeedBack(1) <> 0
                        FORCE IMPACT 50,25
                    ENDIF
                    SpriteHit(x) = 1
                ENDIF
            NEXT x
    ENDIF
ENDFUNCTION
```

Now add the following two functions to the end of your program, and you will have force-feedback capability in your ShootingGallery program.

```
FUNCTION SetControlDevice()
    PERFORM CHECKLIST FOR CONTROL DEVICES
    IF CHECKLIST QUANTITY() = 0
        EXITFUNCTION "NONE"
    ENDIF
    IF CHECKLIST QUANTITY() = 1
        SET CONTROL DEVICE CHECKLIST STRING$(1)
```

```
            SupportsForceFeedBack(1) = CHECKLIST VALUE A(1)
            EXITFUNCTION CHECKLIST STRING$(1)
        ENDIF
        CLS
        PRINT "Plese Select Control Device"
        FOR x = 1 TO CHECKLIST QUANTITY()
            tempstring$ = STR$(x)+": "+CHECKLIST STRING$(x)
            PRINT tempstring$
        NEXT X
        INPUT ConDev
        SupportsForceFeedBack(1) = CHECKLIST VALUE A(X)
        SET CONTROL DEVICE CHECKLIST STRING$(ConDev)
ENDFUNCTION CHECKLIST STRING$(ConDev)

FUNCTION DoOtherEffects()
    IF SupportsForceFeedBack(1) =0 THEN EXITFUNCTION
    KeyPress$ = UPPER$(INKEY$())
    IF KeyPress$ = "" THEN EXITFUNCTION
    IF KeyPress$ = "C" THEN FORCE CHAINSAW 50,1000
    IF KeyPress$ = "V" THEN FORCE WATER EFFECT 50,1000
    IF KeyPress$ = "W" THEN FORCE UP 50
    IF KeyPress$ = "S" THEN FORCE DOWN 50
    IF KeyPress$ = "A" THEN FORCE LEFT 50
    IF KeyPress$ = "D" THEN FORCE RIGHT 50
    IF KeyPress$ = "O" THEN FORCE AUTO CENTER ON
    IF KeyPress$ = "P" THEN FORCE AUTO CENTER OFF
ENDFUNCTION
```

Summary

Wow, there are a lot of commands to take control of input devices. This chapter explained all of the commands and how to execute them. User input devices make a technical demo a game. The ShootingGallery program is an excellent example of using input devices. Someday, I hope to see someone take that program and add sounds, high scores, and plenty of bells and whistles.

Chapter Quiz

The chapter quiz will help you retain the information that was covered in this chapter, as well as give you an idea about how well you're doing at understanding the subjects. You will find the answers for this quiz in Appendix A, "Answers to the Chapter Quizzes."

1. Which command is used to read a string or number entered from the keyboard?

   A. INPUT
   B. OUTPUT
   C. MOUSE BUTTON()
   D. PRINT

2. What does the INKEY$() command do?

   A. Returns the key currently being pressed
   B. Returns a random key
   C. Returns a string of all the keys being pressed
   D. Returns nothing

3. Which command returns 1 when the spacebar is pressed?

   A. SPACEBARKEY()
   B. ESCAPEKEY()
   C. RETURNKEY()
   D. INKEY$()

4. What is the value of mouseclick() when the left and right mouse buttons are both pressed?

   A. 1
   B. 2
   C. 3
   D. 0

5. When a mouse is located at x = 100, y = 300, which command returns 100?

   A. MOUSEMOVEX()
   B. MOUSEMOVEY()
   C. MOUSEX()
   D. MOUSEY()

6. How many joystick hats does DarkBASIC support?

   A. 3

   B. 4

   C. 7

   D. 2

7. Which checklist value returned from PERFORM CHECKLIST FOR CONTROL DEVICES returns whether the device supports force feedback?

   A. CHECKLIST STRING$()

   B. CHECKLIST VALUE A()

   C. CHECKLIST VALUE B()

   D. CHECKLIST VALUE C()

8. Which command cancels all force-feedback effects on a joystick?

   A. FORCE NO EFFECT

   B. FORCE UP

   C. FORCE WATER EFFECT

   D. FORCE STOP

9. Which command returns the scan code of the key currently being pressed?

   A. SCANCODE

   B. CODESCAN

   C. KEYSTATE

   D. INKEY$()

10. ESCAPEKEY() = 1 means the Esc key is being held down.

   A. True

   B. False

CHAPTER 13

ADDING SOUND EFFECTS TO YOUR GAME

Boom! Smack! Whack! What do these three words have in common? They all describe sounds. Sounds surround you every day, and are transmitted through the air, through water, through solid objects, and as vibrations. Listening to anything from the dishwasher to a lawnmower, sounds tell you what is going on in the world around you. Hearing is the second most important sense (after sight). Many years ago, before the invention of the television, sound played an important role by entertaining many through radio. Radio, known as the theater of the imagination, highlighted many family evenings. This theater didn't have spectacular visual effects, so it relied on something else—sound effects. The creaking door in "The Shadow" let you know that the house was haunted.

This chapter will introduce you to the commands built into DarkBASIC so you can create ear-popping sound effects. It will give you a tour of loading, playing, and positioning sound effects. You will learn all about 3D positional sound effects. In the end, you will create a game based almost completely on sound. This chapter will literally surround you with sound effects.

This chapter will cover the following topics:

- Introduction to Sound
- Creating and Loading Sounds
- Playing Sounds
- Panning and Volume Control
- Sound Properties
- Positional Sound

Introduction to Sound

Picture a world without sound. It's not hard to do. Just watch TV sometime and hit the mute button. What a difference! Imagine watching the big screen without the thunderous speaker systems in a theater. The show might be watchable, but the whole experience is changed without audio. The ear is a marvelous part of the body. It can pick up a wide range of sounds and then translate sound waves into signals that the brain can understand. From a bass violin in an orchestra to a hot rod squealing its tires, there is a huge range of possible sounds, and the human ear can hear a wide range of those audio frequencies. Surprisingly, that is also how computers read sound. Audio is stored in a file as a digital recording of an analog sound signal, recorded with a simple microphone or by other means.

What Does a Sound Look Like?

Can you see a sound? Of course not! You can't see sound any more than you can see the wind. However, you can see the effect of wind. By the same token, you can see what a sound looks like by observing its effects. Every sound affects your eardrum by vibrating the particles in the air. These particles are vibrated in a pattern, so observing this pattern allows you to see the sound.

> The *frequency* is the number of times that a sound wave rises and falls over a period of time, usually measured in hertz (hz). The *amplitude* is the height and depth of a single sound wave.

The patterns generated by sounds can be represented by sine waves. No matter how simple or how complex the sound, it can always be described as a series of sine waves of varying amplitudes and frequencies. Figure 13.1 shows a sample sine wave.

Sampling the Sound

Sound in the analog wave format presents a problem for the computer, which only knows how to represent data in terms of 1s and 0s. A sound wave has more than two states attached to it, so the sound wave must be digitized.

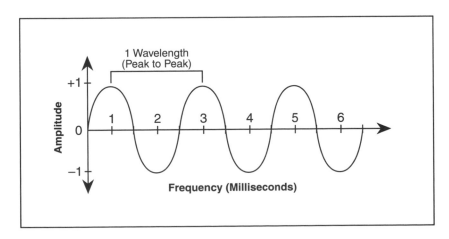

Figure 13.1
A typical sound wave

Your sound card handles the mechanics of digitizing the sound waves. The sound card takes "snapshots" of the sound wave at different intervals in a process called *sampling*. Unlike a video camera, which takes between 24 and 30 pictures per second, the sound card samples a sound many thousand times per second.

The sound wave's frequency is the number of times it rises and falls over a period of time. A sound wave's sampling rate is also called the frequency because it samples the sound at a specific number of times per second. A CD-quality sound is sampled at 44 hz (samples per second).

Bit Rate

When you sample a sound, a bit rate is established. This represents the amount of bits used to describe a single sample of sound. Because every sound varies in amplitude, a bit rate needs to be established to represent the height (or depth) of the amplitude. Bit rates are generally referred to by the number of bits each sample contains. A CD-quality sound has a bit rate of 16 bits, which means that every sample in the sound has a total of 16 bits of data to it.

The Wave Sound Format

A wave file (usually with an extension of .WAV) is one file type that contains a digital representation of a sound wave. It contains all the samplings of an analog sound file. There are many similar file formats, but .WAV is the sound format used most for sound effects. Other sound formats include Mpeg Layer 3 (.MP3), Audio format (.AU), and Real Audio (.RA).

Creating Wave Files

There are many different ways you can create a wave file. Windows comes with a program called Sound Recorder that uses a microphone to create waves. A more professional approach would be to use Cool Edit 2000 or some other wave editing software. You can also download pre-recorded sound effect wave files from many different Web sites.

Some of the easiest sound effects are those you can create with your mouth. Using a microphone and your imagination, you can make cows moo and dogs bark. If you're even more creative, you can make dogs moo and cows bark. Your imagination is the limit.

Creating and Loading Sounds

Loading sounds in DarkBASIC is very simple. There is no need to create a sound device, set the parameters, set up buffers, and cross your fingers. It takes one command to load a sound; DarkBASIC does all the hard work for you.

Using the Sound-Loading Commands

DarkBASIC stores all sound effects in buffers, which are addressed by an integer number. It is a good idea to keep track of what buffer goes with what sound effect at the top of your file or on a separate notepad. You do not want to play the "game won" sound effect when the player just lost all their points.

The LOAD SOUND Command

The LOAD SOUND command is the most basic sound-loading command. The syntax for this command is

```
LOAD SOUND "File Name", Sound Number
```

Here are some examples of using the LOAD SOUND command:

```
LOAD SOUND "yeah.wav", 13
LOAD SOUND "bummer.wav", 14
```

The LOAD 3DSOUND Command

The LOAD 3DSOUND command is the same as the LOAD SOUND command, but with a twist. This command marks the buffer sound number into which it is loaded with a special flag that denotes it as a 3D sound. The syntax for this command is

```
LOAD 3DSOUND "File Name", Sound Number
```

Here are some examples of using the LOAD 3DSOUND command:

```
LOAD 3DSOUND "meow.wav", 1
LOAD 3DSOUND "bark.wav", 1
```

The CLONE SOUND Command

The CLONE SOUND command clones a sound into a specified sound buffer. The advantage to using a cloned sound is that you can play more than one copy of a sound with one set of sound data, saving valuable memory for other things. The syntax for this command is

CLONE SOUND *Destination Sound Number, Source Sound Number*

Here is an example of the CLONE SOUND command:

CLONE SOUND 4,114

The DELETE SOUND command

Another memory-saving technique is to use the DELETE SOUND command when you no longer need a sound. This also allows you to re-use a sound buffer for another sound effect. Just like a bitmap, you can load a sound over another sound, but it's always wise to delete a sound buffer before re-using it. The syntax for the DELETE SOUND command is

DELETE SOUND *Sound Number*

Here are some examples of the DELETE SOUND command:

DELETE SOUND 13
DELETE SOUND 14

The SOUND EXIST Command

How do you know whether a sound has been loaded? By using the SOUND EXIST command. This command returns a 0 if the sound does not exist and a 1 if it does. The syntax for this command is

SOUND EXIST (*Sound Number*)

Notice that the sound number is surrounded by parentheses.

The Sound Sample program uses all the commands you have learned up to this point. Figure 13.2 shows the output of the program. You will find this program (and all the other programs in this chapter) in the Sources\Chapter14 subfolder on the CD.

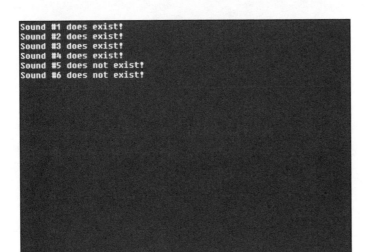

Figure 13.2

The Sound Sample program demonstrates the use of some basic sound commands.

```
REMSTART
----------------------------------
Beginner's Guide To Game Programming With DarkBASIC
Copyright (C)2002 Jonathan S. Harbour and Joshua R. Smith
Chapter 13 - Sound Sample program
----------------------------------
REMEND
DIM answer$(2)
answer$(0) = "not exist!"
answer$(1) = "exist!"
LOAD SOUND "yeah.wav", 1
LOAD SOUND "bummer.wav", 2
LOAD 3DSOUND "yeah.wav", 3

CLONE SOUND 4,2
DoorOpenLoaded = SOUND EXIST(1)

FOR x = 1 TO 6
    SoundIsThere = SOUND EXIST(x)
    tempstring$ = "Sound #"+STR$(x)+" does "+answer$(SoundIsThere)
    PRINT tempstring$
NEXT x
```

```
DELETE SOUND 1
DELETE SOUND 2
DELETE SOUND 3
DELETE SOUND 4
WAIT KEY
```

Playing Sounds

Boom! The enemy ship just exploded and you can hear it. Now you get to program the playing of the sounds. After the sounds are loaded, you can use them in the game. Playing back sounds is just as easy as loading them. You don't need to know the frequency of the sound or the timing of the sound card; just a simple command and presto, you hear the firepower of your awesome ship blasting away another alien scumbag.

Using the Sound Playback Commands

The sound playback commands use the same integer buffers as the load commands. They also give you a few more options for playback control. It only takes one command to play back a sound.

The PLAY SOUND Command

The PLAY SOUND command is the most basic sound-playback command. You can specify an optional start position in bytes that tells DarkBASIC to start the sample at that position. The syntax for this command is

```
PLAY SOUND Sound Number, Start Position
```

Here are some examples of the PLAY SOUND command:

```
PLAY SOUND 5
PLAY SOUND 5, 30000
```

The LOOP SOUND Command

The LOOP SOUND command allows you to repeat a sound. It is handy so you don't have to keep using the PLAY SOUND command. This command allows you to specify a starting position in bytes, as well as an ending position and an initial position. The ending position is where the sound will stop and then start over at the starting position. The initial position is where you want the first loop to start. The syntax for this command is

```
LOOP SOUND Sound Number, Start Position, End Position, Initial Position
```

Here are some examples of the LOOP SOUND command:

```
LOOP SOUND 5
LOOP SOUND 5,3000
LOOP SOUND 5,3000,5000
LOOP SOUND 5,3000,5000,2500
```

The STOP SOUND Command

The STOP SOUND command does just that—stops a sound. You can use this feature on looping or non-looping sounds. The syntax for this command is

```
STOP SOUND Sound Number
```

Here are a few examples of the STOP SOUND command:

```
STOP SOUND 5
STOP SOUND 1
```

The PAUSE SOUND Command

The PAUSE SOUND command pauses a sound while it is playing or looping. It is used in conjunction with the RESUME SOUND command. This syntax for this command is

```
PAUSE SOUND Sound Number
```

Here are a few examples of the PAUSE SOUND command:

```
PAUSE SOUND 1
PAUSE SOUND 5
```

The RESUME SOUND Command

The RESUME SOUND command starts playing a sound at the point where it was last paused. This command must be used in conjunction with the PAUSE command, and it can provide some interesting effects. The syntax for this command is

```
RESUME SOUND Sound Number
```

The Resume Sound program uses the commands you have learned up to this point. It pauses and resumes a sound during playback. Figure 13.3 displays the output of this program.

Figure 13.3
The Resume Sound program demonstrates the use of the PAUSE SOUND *and* RESUME SOUND *commands.*

```
`----------------------------------
`Beginner's Guide To Game Programming With DarkBASIC
`Copyright (C)2002 Jonathan S. Harbour and Joshua R. Smith
`Chapter 13 - Resume Sound program
`----------------------------------

` Loads the sound
LOAD SOUND "talking.wav", 5

` Start looping the talking wave
PRINT "Hal"
PLAY SOUND 5
` wait for 1 second
SLEEP 500
` pause the wave
PAUSE SOUND 5
` wait for 1 second
SLEEP 500

` Resume the sound
PRINT "lei"
RESUME SOUND 5
` wait for 1 second
SLEEP 500
```

```
` pause the wave
PAUSE SOUND 5
` wait for 1 second
SLEEP 500

` Resume the sound
PRINT "leu"
RESUME SOUND 5
` wait for 1 second
SLEEP 500
` pause the wave
PAUSE SOUND 5
` wait for 1 second
SLEEP 500

` Resume the sound
PRINT "ia!"
RESUME SOUND 5
` wait for 1 second
SLEEP 500
` stop the wave
STOP SOUND 5
WAIT KEY
```

Panning and Volume Control

Zoom! Did you just hear that car go past? It sounded like it was going 200 miles per hour. Wow! The sounds you hear in everyday life move from left to right and change volume all the time. That is how you can tell where the sound is coming from and where it is going.

> *Panning* represents the amount of sound coming from the left and right speakers. Something panned left will come completely from the left speaker.

Using the Panning and Volume Control Commands

Playing with the panning, speed, and volume in DarkBASIC is very easy. Setting a sound's panning requires only a simple command. Another command allows you to speed up the sound. Let's have some fun playing with sound effects.

The SET SOUND PAN Command

The SET SOUND PAN command places a sound effect somewhere between the two speakers. The values for SET SOUND PAN range from −100 to 100. −100 locates a sound effect on the left speaker; 100 locates it on the right speaker. Anywhere between −100 and 100 locates a sound effect on both the left and right speakers. The syntax for this command is

```
SET SOUND PAN Sound Number, Pan Value
```

Here are a few examples of the SET SOUND PAN command:

```
SET SOUND PAN 5, 100
SET SOUND PAN 1, -50
```

The GET SOUND PAN Command

The GET SOUND PAN command returns the current pan value. This lets you know where in the speakers your sound is playing. The syntax for this command is

```
GET SOUND PAN(Sound Number)
```

The Get Pan program uses the SET SOUND PAN and GET SOUND PAN commands. Figure 13.4 displays the output of the program.

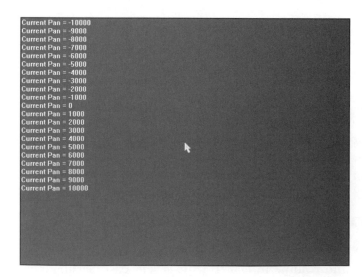

Figure 13.4

The Get Pan program demonstrates the GET SOUND PAN *and* SET SOUND PAN *commands.*

```
REMSTART
----------------------------------
Beginner's Guide To Game Programming With DarkBASIC
Copyright (C)2002 Jonathan S. Harbour and Joshua R. Smith
Chapter 13 - Get Pan program
----------------------------------
REMEND
` Plan sound effect from left to right
` Loads the talking wave
LOAD SOUND "talking.wav", 5
` Start looping the talking wave
PLAY SOUND 5
` Start a LOOP
FOR count = -10000 to 10000 step 1000
    ` Wait 1/100 second
    SLEEP 100
    ` Pan sound over to the left
    SET SOUND PAN 5, count
    CLS
    ` Get the current Pan
    CurrentPan = GET SOUND PAN(5)
    tempstring$ = "Current Pan = "+STR$(CurrentPan)
    PRINT tempstring$
NEXT count
WAIT KEY
```

The SET SOUND SPEED Command

The SET SOUND SPEED command changes a sound's playback frequency. Just like when you play a micro cassette recorder and speed up the playback, SET SOUND SPEED allows you to adjust the speed of a sound effect. My favorite effect is to turn my voice into the voice of one of the Chipmunks. This syntax for this command is

```
SET SOUND SPEED Sound Number , Frequency Value
```

Here are a few examples of the SET SOUND SPEED command:

```
SET SOUND SPEED 5 , 75000
SET SOUND SPEED 5 , 45000
SET SOUND SPEED 5 , 15000
```

The GET SOUND SPEED Command

The GET SOUND SPEED command returns the current playback speed of a sound, which lets you know how fast your sound is playing. The syntax for this command is

GET SOUND SPEED(*Sound Number*)

The Get Speed program uses the SET SOUND SPEED and GET SOUND SPEED commands. Figure 13.5 displays the output of the program.

```
REMSTART
-----------------------------------
Beginner's Guide To Game Programming With DarkBASIC
Copyright (C)2002 Jonathan S. Harbour and Joshua R. Smith
Chapter 13 - Get Speed program
-----------------------------------
REMEND
` Loads the talking wave
LOAD SOUND "talking.wav", 5
SET SOUND SPEED 5 , 75000
` Play the talking wave
PLAY SOUND 5
` Get the current Pan
CurrentSpeed = GET SOUND SPEED(5)
` what's our current pan
PRINT CurrentSpeed
WAIT KEY
```

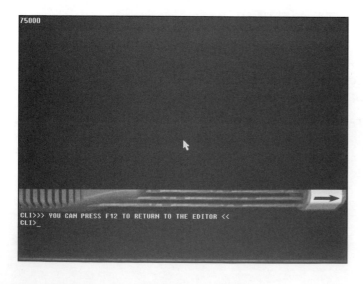

Figure 13.5 *The Get Speed program demonstrates the* GET SOUND SPEED *and* SET SOUND SPEED *commands.*

The SET SOUND VOLUME Command

The SET SOUND VOLUME command adjusts the volume of a sound effect. Volume is a very powerful thing. You can use it to tell the force of a punch or the caliber of a shot fired. The SET SOUND VOLUME command is DarkBASIC's volume control knob. The value to be set can be between 0 and 100 percent. The syntax for this command is

```
SET SOUND VOLUME Sound Number , Volume Value
```

Here are a few examples of the SET SOUND VOLUME command:

```
SET SOUND VOLUME 3 , 75
SET SOUND VOLUME 4 , 50
SET SOUND VOLUME 5 , 100
```

The GET SOUND VOLUME Command

The GET SOUND VOLUME command returns the volume of a sound effect, which you could use to determine the strength of a punch. The syntax for this command is

```
GET SOUND VOLUME(Sound Number)
```

The Get Volume program uses the SET SOUND VOLUME and GET SOUND VOLUME commands. Figure 13.6 displays the output of the program.

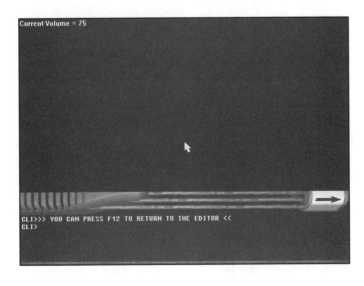

Figure 13.6 *The Get Volume program demonstrates the* GET SOUND VOLUME *and* SET SOUND VOLUME *commands.*

```
REMSTART
--------------------------------
Beginner's Guide To Game Programming With DarkBASIC
Copyright (C)2002 Jonathan S. Harbour and Joshua R. Smith
Chapter 13 - Get Volume program
--------------------------------
REMEND
LOAD SOUND "talking.wav", 5
` Set's the volume to 75 percent
SET SOUND VOLUME 5 , 75
` Play the talking wave
PLAY SOUND 5
` Get the current Pan
CurrentVolume = GET SOUND VOLUME(5)
` what's our current pan
PRINT CurrentVolume
```

Sound Properties

Now you come to one of the more interesting parts of sound management—sound properties. These tell you the type of sound you are listening to and whether it is playing or paused.

Retrieving Sound Properties

Retrieving sound properties is a snap in DarkBASIC. All of the commands return a 1 or a 0 to let you know the information for which you are looking. There are three sound property commands—SOUND TYPE, SOUND PLAYING, and SOUND PAUSED.

The SOUND TYPE Command

The SOUND TYPE command reports the type of sound loaded in the buffer. There are two different types of sounds that can be loaded—normal sounds and 3D sounds. If SOUND TYPE returns a 0, the sound effect in question is a normal sound; if it returns a 1, the sound effect in question is a 3D sound. The syntax for this command is

```
SOUND TYPE(Sound Number)
```

Here are some examples of the SOUND TYPE command:

```
SoundType = SOUND TYPE(5)
SoundType = SOUND TYPE(6)
```

The SOUND PLAYING Command

The SOUND PLAYING command reports whether a sound is playing. This can be useful when a sound needs to be played through completely before continuing. The syntax for this command is

```
SOUND PLAYING (Sound Number)
```

Here are a couple examples of the SOUND PLAYING command:

```
IsSoundPlaying = SOUND PLAYING(5)
IsSoundPlaying = SOUND PLAYING(6)
```

The SOUND PAUSED Command

The SOUND PAUSED command reports whether a sound is paused. This allows you complete control over the playback of the sound. The syntax for this command is

```
SOUND PAUSED(Sound Number)
```

Here are a few examples of the SOUND PAUSED command:

```
SoundIsPaused = SOUND PAUSED(5)
SoundIsPaused = SOUND PAUSED(6)
```

Positional Sound

Drip, drip, drip. . . . My first experience with good positional sound was while watching Jurassic Park. I remember being engrossed in the action of the movie when I noticed something. Rain—it sounded as though it was raining outside. But it shouldn't be raining in the middle of the summer! Then I realized that it was the movie. The rain completely permeated the room so that it sounded like it was raining outside the theater! What an amazing feeling that was, listening to the sounds around me and being completely fooled like that.

Positional sound is known by many names, including Dolby Digital DTS, surround sound, and four-way sound. It is any sound that incorporates more than two-directional sound (left and right). Can you have positional sound with just two speakers? Using panning, speed, and volume tricks, two speakers can make a sound seem to be behind you or in front of you—so yes, even two speakers can reproduce positional sound.

Using Positional Sound

DarkBASIC incorporates some of the latest technology available to DirectSound to use positional sound. DirectSound 3D sounds will work on anything from two speakers to a full-blown Dolby Digital system. DirectSound allows you to position sound effects anywhere in a virtual room. That's not all, though—it also lets you position the user in the room. So you can sit in your chair and be moved in a whirlwind effect around a room of sound.

Sound Source Positioning

Planning is key in positional sound. You must keep track of where you are and where your sound is in the virtual room. Confusion will set in if you're hit in the front left of the virtual room and the sound comes from the back right.

Positioning a sound is a simple process in DarkBASIC. First you load a sound effect as a 3D sound, and then you use the POSITION SOUND command to position it. Finally, you play the sound effect.

The POSITION SOUND Command

POSITION SOUND is the most important command for the 3D positioning of a sound effect. It takes a sound effect and positions it in a 3D room. For more information on the fundamentals of 3D, see Chapter 17, "Fundamentals of 3D Graphics Programming." The syntax for this command is

```
POSITION SOUND Sound Number, X position, Y position, Z position
```

Here are a few examples of the POSITION SOUND command:

```
POSITION SOUND 5, 700,50,500
POSITION SOUND 6, -20,45,-40
```

The SOUND POSITION X Command

The SOUND POSITION X command returns the location of the sound effect on the X plane. The syntax for this command is

```
SOUND POSITION X(Sound Number)
```

Here are a few examples of the SOUND POSITION X command:

```
tempstring$ = "X pos = "+STR$(SOUND POSITION X(5))
xpos = SOUND POSITION X(6)
```

The SOUND POSITION Y Command

The SOUND POSITION Y command returns the location of the sound effect on the Y plane. The syntax for this command is

SOUND POSITION Y(*Sound Number*)

Here are a few examples of the SOUND POSITION Y command:

```
tempstring$ = "Y pos = "+STR$(SOUND POSITION Y(5))
ypos = SOUND POSITION Y(6)
```

The SOUND POSITION Z Command

The SOUND POSITION Z command returns the location of the sound effect on the Z plane. The syntax for this command is

SOUND POSITION Z(*Sound Number*)

The Sound Position program shows you how to use the POSITION SOUND, SOUND POSITION X, SOUND POSITION Y, and SOUND POSITION Z commands. Figure 13.7 shows the output of this program.

```
REMSTART
----------------------------------
Beginner's Guide To Game Programming With DarkBASIC
Copyright (C)2002 Jonathan S. Harbour and Joshua R. Smith
Chapter 13 - Sound Position program
----------------------------------
REMEND
` Loading the sound effect
LOAD 3DSOUND "beep.wav", 6
` Lets put the sound in front and to the right of us
POSITION SOUND 6, 700,50,500
` Play the sound
PLAY SOUND 6
` Print the X position
tempstring$ = "X pos = "+STR$(SOUND POSITION X(6))
PRINT tempstring$
tempstring$ = "Y pos = "+STR$(SOUND POSITION Y(6))
PRINT tempstring$
tempstring$ = "Z pos = "+STR$(SOUND POSITION Z(6))
PRINT tempstring$
```

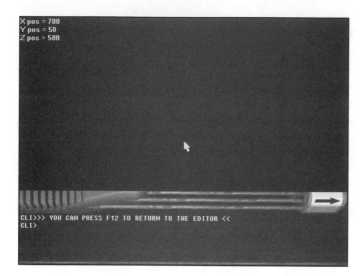

Figure 13.7 *The Sound Position program demonstrates the effects of the sound positioning commands.*

Listener Positioning

The sound effects are now placed in the room. Who is listening to them? What if this listener turns around? Would that reposition all the sound effects? Not really. The sound effects would be in the same locations as they were before, but the listener's orientation would be different.

In DarkBASIC, it is just as easy to orient the listener as it is to move all the sounds. There are two key commands to orient the listener to the positions of the sounds. I try to place the sounds in the room as if the listener were in the center of the room, facing forward. Then I rotate the listener.

The POSITION LISTENER Command

The POSITION LISTENER command places the listener somewhere in the virtual room. This affects the audible location of the sound based on where the listener is located. The syntax for this command is

POSITION LISTENER *X position*, *Y position*, *Z position*

Here are a few examples of the POSITION LISTENER command:

POSITION LISTENER 300,0,10
POSITION LISTENER 40,-50,-3

The LISTENER POSITION X Command

The LISTENER POSITION X command returns the listener's X position. The syntax for this command is

```
LISTENER POSITION X()
```

Here are a few examples of the LISTENER POSITION X command:

```
tempstring$ = "Listener X pos = "+STR$(LISTENER POSITION X())
ListenerX = LISTENER POSITION X()
```

The LISTENER POSITION Y Command

The LISTENER POSITION Y command returns the listener's Y position. The syntax for this command is

```
LISTENER POSITION Y()
```

Here are a few examples of the LISTENER POSITION Y command:

```
temptring$ = "Listener Y pos = "+STR$(LISTENER POSITION Y())
ListenerY = LISTENER POSITION Y()
```

The LISTENER POSITION Z Command

The LISTENER POSITION Z command returns the listener's Z position. The syntax for this command is

```
LISTENER POSITION Z()
```

The Listener Position program shows you how to use the POSITION LISTENER, LISTENER POSITION X, LISTENER POSITION Y, and LISTENER POSITION Z commands. Figure 13.8 show the output of this program.

```
REMSTART
-----------------------------------
Beginner's Guide To Game Programming With DarkBASIC
Copyright (C)2002 Jonathan S. Harbour and Joshua R. Smith
Chapter 13 - Listener Position program
-----------------------------------
REMEND
` Loading the sound effect
LOAD 3DSOUND "beep.wav", 6
```

```
` Lets put the sound in front and to the right of us
POSITION SOUND 6, 100,0,10
` Lets put the listener to the right of the sound.
` So the sound is to the left of the listener
POSITION LISTENER 300,0,10
` Play the sound
PLAY SOUND 6
tempstring$ = "Listener X pos = "+STR$(LISTENER POSITION X())
` Locate The X position of the listener
PRINT tempstring$
` Locate The Y position of the listener
tempstring$ = "Listener Y pos = "+STR$(LISTENER POSITION Y())
PRINT tempstring$
` Locate The Z position of the listener
tempstring$ = "Listener Z pos = "+STR$(LISTENER POSITION Z())
PRINT tempstring$
WAIT KEY
```

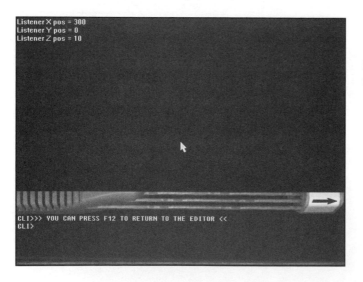

Figure 13.8

The Listener Position program demonstrates the LISTENER POSITION *commands.*

The ROTATE LISTENER Command

The ROTATE LISTENER command faces the listener in the correct direction, which also affects the audible location of the sounds. The sound might be to the right of the listener, but if the listener is facing the sound, it is then in front of him. The syntax for this command is

```
ROTATE LISTENER X angle, Y angle, Z angle
```

Here are a few examples of the ROTATE LISTENER command:

```
ROTATE LISTENER 0,0,45
ROTATE LISTENER 30,15,15
```

The LISTENER ANGLE X Command

The LISTENER ANGLE X command returns the X angle of the listener direction. The command syntax is

```
LISTENER ANGLE X()
```

Here are a few examples of the LISTENER ANGLE X command:

```
temptring$ - "Listener X angle - "ISTR$(LISTENER ANGLE X())
xangle = LISTENER ANGLE X()
```

The LISTENER ANGLE Y Command

The LISTENER ANGLE Y command returns the Y angle of the listener direction. The syntax for this command is

```
LISTENER ANGLE Y()
```

Here are a few examples of the LISTENER ANGLE Y command:

```
tempstring$ = "Listener Y angle = "+STR$(LISTENER ANGLE Y())
yangle = LISTENER ANGLE Y()
```

The LISTENER ANGLE Z Command

The LISTENER ANGLE Z command returns the Z angle of the listener direction. The syntax for this command is

```
LISTENER ANGLE Z()
```

The Listener Angle program shows you how to use the ROTATE LISTENER, LISTENER ANGLE X, LISTENER ANGLE Y, and LISTENER ANGLE Z commands. Figure 13.9 shows the output of this program.

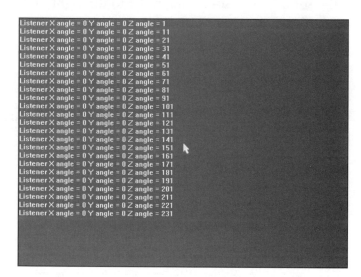

Figure 13.9

Output from the Listener Angle program

```
REMSTART
-----------------------------------
Beginner's Guide To Game Programming With DarkBASIC
Copyright (C)2002 Jonathan S. Harbour and Joshua R. Smith
Chapter 13 - Listener Angle program
-----------------------------------
REMEND
` Loading the sound effect
LOAD 3DSOUND "beep.wav", 6
` Lets put the sound in front and to the right of us
POSITION SOUND 6, 100,0,10
` Lets put the listener to the right of the sound.
` So the sound is to the left of the listener
POSITION LISTENER 300,0,10
` Play the sound
LOOP SOUND 6
` Lets rotate the listener around
FOR zang = 1 to 360 step 10
```

```
        ROTATE LISTENER 0,0,zang
        ` Locate The X angle of the listener
        tempstring$ = "Listener X angle = "+STR$(LISTENER ANGLE X())
        PRINT tempstring$;
        ` Locate The Y angle of the listener
        tempstring$ = " Y angle = "+STR$(LISTENER ANGLE Y())
        PRINT tempstring$;
        ` Locate The Z angle of the listener
        tempstring$ = " Z angle = "+STR$(LISTENER ANGLE Z())
        PRINT tempstring$
        SLEEP 100
NEXT zang
WAIT KEY
```

Chapter Project: The AudioMatch Game

Wow, there are a lot of commands to control sound in DarkBASIC. You covered 33 different sound commands in this chapter! Now you are going to put them to use. I have written a simple game that uses the sound effects commands in a creative way.

I've written a particular game for every programming language that I have learned over the years—a matching game. I have created one in Pascal, C, Visual Basic, Lingo (Director), and even for a Pocket PC. So I thought, why not take the matching game to the next level? Thus AudioMatch was born. It's an interesting twist on the tile-matching theme, but rather than using graphics, this game requires the player to match sound effects! Pretty neat idea, don't you think?

The premise of AudioMatch is simple. Just match two sounds by clicking on cards that appear on the screen. There are 25 sounds to choose from, and you won't know where they are because the game randomizes the sounds every time. You have to click a card to hear the sound. Figure 13.10 shows what the AudioMatch game looks like.

I created all of the sound effects in this game. (It is not easy to record your own voice without laughing!) All the sounds are located in the level01 sounds directory. This game includes a title screen and a winning screen. The only way to lose is to give up and go to the next chapter.

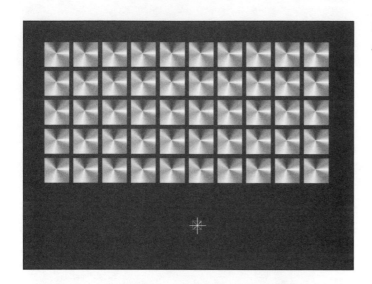

Figure 13.10 *The AudioMatch game*

NOTE

For the record, and just so at least one of us retains his reputation as a stark professional, that's *Joshua's* voice!

```
REMSTART

-----------------------------------

Beginner's Guide To Game Programming With DarkBASIC
Copyright (C)2002 Jonathan S. Harbour and Joshua R. Smith
Chapter 13 - AudioMatch

-----------------------------------

REMEND

REMSTART
   Image Data
   IMAGE 1 - Card Close
   IMAGE 2 - Card Selected
   IMAGE 3 - Mouse cursor
   IMAGE 4 - Title Image
   IMAGE 5 - Win Image
   Sprite USAGE
     SPRITE 10 - mouse Cursor
```

```
        SPRITES 50-99 - Matching cards
      Sound USAGE
        SOUNDS 50-75 - Sounds To Match
        SOUND 13 - Match Found
        SOUND 14 - Match Not Found
REMEND

DATA "level01/123.wav"
DATA "level01/abc.wav"
DATA "level01/ardvark.wav"
DATA "level01/baa.wav"
DATA "level01/bark.wav"
DATA "level01/basic.wav"
DATA "level01/boom.wav"
DATA "level01/clunk.wav"
DATA "level01/cool.wav"
DATA "level01/Dark.wav"
DATA "level01/eek.wav"
DATA "level01/eieio.wav"
DATA "level01/HadAFarm.wav"
DATA "level01/hehehe.wav"
DATA "level01/horse.wav"
DATA "level01/meow.wav"
DATA "level01/moo.wav"
DATA "level01/oink.wav"
DATA "level01/OldMac.wav"
DATA "level01/quack.wav"
DATA "level01/roar.wav"
DATA "level01/squeek.wav"
DATA "level01/wee.wav"
DATA "level01/wild.wav"
DATA "level01/woof.wav"

` Dim all global Variables
DIM LevelData(50)
` 1 stores current match
` 2 stores first match
` 3 stores second match
` 4 stores total guesses
` 5 stores the number of matches
DIM Selections(5)
```

```
SYNC OFF
SYNC RATE 30

MainTitle()
LoadSounds()
SYNC
PlayLevel()
END


` Loads all the sounds
FUNCTION LoadSounds()
    ` Load Sounds
    FOR count = 50 TO 74
        READ WaveFile$
        LOAD 3DSOUND WaveFile$, count
        ` Randomly position it in the world
        POSITION SOUND count, rnd(100), rnd(100), rnd(100)
    NEXT count

    ` Place the listener in the virutal world
    POSITION LISTENER 0,0,0
    ROTATE LISTENER 0,0,0

    LOAD SOUND "yeah.wav", 13
    LOAD SOUND "bummer.wav", 14
ENDFUNCTION


` Setup the level
FUNCTION SetupLevel()
    ` Randomize the Sounds
    RandomSeed = TIMER()
    RANDOMIZE RandomSeed

    FOR count = 1 TO 50
        LevelData(count) = 0
    NEXT count

    slotpicked = RND(49)+1
    count2 = 0
    FOR count = 50 TO 99
        WHILE LevelData(slotpicked) > 0
```

```
                slotpicked = rnd(49)+1
            ENDWHILE
        LevelData(slotpicked) = count
        NEXT count


        FOR count = 1 TO 50
            IF LevelData(count) > 74
                LevelData(count) = LevelData(count) - 25
            ENDIF
        NEXT count


        ` Load the images
        LOAD IMAGE "card.bmp", 1
        LOAD IMAGE "cardselect.bmp", 2
        LOAD IMAGE "cursor.bmp",3
        ` Centering the cards on the X ROW - Start at 120
        ` Centering the cards on the Y ROW - start at 40
        FOR ypos = 0 TO 4
            FOR xpos = 0 TO 9
                spritenum = 50+(ypos*10)+xpos
                spritex = 40 + (xpos*56)
                spritey = 40+ (ypos*56)
                SPRITE spritenum, spritex, spritey, 1
            NEXT xpos
        NEXT ypos


        ` Set up Mouse
        HIDE MOUSE
        SPRITE 10, MOUSEX(), MOUSEY(), 3
        SHOW ALL SPRITES
        ` Set up Selection Variables
        Selections(1) = 0
        Selections(2) = 0
        Selections(3) = 0
        Selections(4) = 0
        Selections(5) = 0
ENDFUNCTION

` Main Game Loop
FUNCTION PlayLevel()
    SetupLevel()
```

```
            Flag = 0
            SYNC
            WHILE Flag = 0
                ProcessMouse()
                ProcessClicks()
                ProcessMatches()
                DoWin = ProcessWins()
                IF DoWin=1
                    SLEEP 500
                    PlayAgain = DoTheWinScreen()
                    IF PlayAgain=1
                        SetupLevel()
                    ELSE
                        Flag = 1
                    ENDIF
                ENDIF
                SYNC
            ENDWHILE
        ENDFUNCTION


        ` Process the mouse cursor
        FUNCTION ProcessMouse()
            SPRITE 10, MOUSEX(), MOUSEY(), 3
        ENDFUNCTION


        ` Process Mouse clicks
        FUNCTION ProcessClicks()
            IF MOUSECLICK() <> 1 THEN EXITFUNCTION
            cardselected = SPRITE COLLISION(10,0)
            ` Not over a card
            IF cardselected = 0 THEN EXITFUNCTION
            IF cardselected = Selections(2) THEN EXITFUNCTION
            IF cardselected = Selections(3) THEN EXITFUNCTION
            IF SOUND PLAYING(13) THEN EXITFUNCTION
            IF SOUND PLAYING(14) THEN EXITFUNCTION
            FirstSelected = Selections(2) - 49
            SecondSelected = Selections(3) - 49

            Spx = SPRITE X(cardselected)
            Spy = SPRITE Y(cardselected)
            SPRITE cardselected, Spx, Spy, 2
```

```
        Selections(1) = Selections(1) + 1
        ` Increament it by 1 to pass the Selections(1) info
        CurrentSelect = Selections(1) + 1
        Selections(CurrentSelect) = cardselected
        cardselected = cardselected - 49
        PLAY SOUND LevelData(cardselected)
ENDFUNCTION


` Check for matches
FUNCTION ProcessMatches()
    MySel1 = Selections(1)
    MySel2 = Selections(2)
    MySel3 = Selections(3)
    IF MySel1 = 2
        SLEEP 500
        IF LevelData(MySel2-49) = LevelData(MySel3-49)
            SPRITE MySel2,-100,-100,1
            SPRITE MySel3,-100,-100,1
            PLAY SOUND 13
            Selections(5) = Selections(5) + 1
        ELSE
            SPRITE MySel2, SPRITE X(MySel2),SPRITE Y(MySel2), 1
            SPRITE MySel3, SPRITE X(MySel3),SPRITE Y(MySel3), 1
            PLAY SOUND 14
        ENDIF
        Selections(1) = 0
        Selections(2) = 0
        Selections(3) = 0
        Selections(4) = Selections(4) + 1
    ENDIF
ENDFUNCTION


` Check to see if they've won
FUNCTION ProcessWins()
    Flag = 0
    IF Selections(5) >= 25 THEN Flag = 1
ENDFUNCTION Flag

FUNCTION MainTitle()
    LOAD IMAGE "title.bmp",4
    PASTE IMAGE 4,0,0
```

```
        SYNC
        WHILE (MOUSECLICK() = 0)
        ENDWHILE
        DELETE IMAGE 4
        CLS
ENDFUNCTION


`307,184  -- Print number of tries
`386,313 to -- The Y of the Y/N
`  414,347
FUNCTION DoTheWinScreen()
        HIDE ALL SPRITES
        SLEEP 2000
        SHOW MOUSE
        Flag = 0
        LOAD IMAGE "win.bmp",5
        PASTE IMAGE 5,0,0
        SET CURSOR 307, 184
        PRINT selections(4)
        SYNC
        WHILE (MOUSECLICK() = 0)
        ENDWHILE
        mx = MOUSEX()
        my = MOUSEY()
        IF mx >386 AND mx <414 AND my >313 AND my<347 THEN Flag = 1
        CLS
ENDFUNCTION Flag
```

This project is pretty extensive, but you will be surprised to find out that it only consists of 210 lines of code. That's pretty interesting, considering what it does. There are many more things that you could do with this game. Here is a list of a few improvements that you might want to add on your own:

- Include multiple levels (using more then one set of data).
- Keep track of a high score (possibly per level).
- Add a timer to pressure the player to play faster.
- Add a picture for each card when it is turned over.
- Add a background picture that is displayed as the cards are matched.
- Animate the cards.

Summary

This chapter covered all of the sound effects commands in DarkBASIC. There are quite a few of them. Sound effects are essential when you are creating games that have dynamic output because sound helps the player become immersed in the game. Without good sound effects, the overall game experience is diminished. (As you will learn in Chapter 14, "Playing Some Tunes: CD Audio, MIDI, and MP3 Music," music also plays a big part.) Along with killer graphics, powerful sound effects and music are essential ingredients for a perfect game.

Chapter Quiz

The chapter quiz will help reinforce the material you learned in this chapter, as well as provide feedback on how well you have learned the subjects that were covered. For the answers to the quiz, refer to Appendix A, "Answers to the Chapter Quizzes."

1. Which function loads a sound?

   A. LOAD SOUND

   B. PLAY SOUND

   C. POSITION SOUND

   D. PAUSE SOUND

2. Which function removes a sound from memory?

   A. PLAY SOUND

   B. POSITION SOUND

   C. DELETE SOUND

   D. CLONE SOUND

3. Which is the correct way to load a 3D sound?

   A. LOAD SOUND "beep.wav", 5

   B. CLONE SOUND 6,5

   C. PAUSE SOUND 7

   D. LOAD 3DSOUND "beep.wav", 5

4. What does the SOUND PLAYING function do?

   A. Deletes a sound

   B. Reports whether a sound is playing

   C. Positions a sound

   D. Plays a sound

5. LOOP SOUND only plays a sound once.

   A. True
   B. False

6. What is the correct way to stop a sound?

   A. LOAD SOUND
   B. POSITION SOUND
   C. STOP SOUND
   D. RESUME SOUND

7. In the command POSITION SOUND 6,100,150,300, what is the X position of the sound?

   A. 6
   B. 100
   C. 150
   D. 300

8. What is the proper way to get the X position of a sound that has been positioned by POSITION SOUND 6,100,150,300?

   A. SOUND POSITION X(6)
   B. SOUND POSITION X(100)
   C. SOUND POSITION Y(6)
   D. SOUND POSITION X(150)

9. What is the proper way to set the speed of sound 8 to 600?

   A. SET SOUND SPEED 600,8
   B. SET SOUND SPEED 8,600
   C. SET SOUND PAN 600,8
   D. SET SOUND PAN 8,600

10. Why would you use the RESUME SOUND command?
    A. To start a sound
    B. To load a sound
    C. To resume playing a sound
    D. To delete a sound

CHAPTER 14

Playing Some Tunes: CD Audio, MIDI, and MP3 Music

Rock-a-bye baby in the tree top, when the wind blows the cradle will rock . . .

What image does this familiar song bring to mind? Can you imagine a nursery, with a mother cradling her baby as she gently rocks it to sleep? In that moment of peace and warmth, the cares of the world are washed away. Imagine quiet music playing from a mural over the crib, a soft white light shining from a lamp nearby. What memories or feelings does this scene arouse? Music affects our temperament, and it often affects our mood without our knowledge.

Do you recall the last suspenseful movie you watched? In such movies, right before the antagonist is about to strike, the scene is accompanied by suspenseful music, which affects your impression of what will happen in the scene (or at least gives you the suspicion that something is about to happen). Background music is used in many forms of entertainment to affect an audience's mood. This chapter will familiarize you with the features of DarkBASIC related to music. It is closely related to Chapter 13 because you can use both sound effects and music to affect mood and change the impression that one gets from a scene in video games and in motion pictures. Specifically, this chapter will show you how to load and play music files, including CD-ROM music tracks, MIDI files, and MP3 files. This chapter covers the following topics:

- Introduction to Background Music
- Loading Music Files
- Playing Background Music
- Music Playback Properties
- Introduction to Digital CD Audio
- The MusicJukebox Program

Introduction to Background Music

Take your mind's eye back to one of your favorite TV shows. What sticks out the most about that show? Most people would tend to say that it was funny or it had a good story line, but rarely do you hear people mention the background music. The

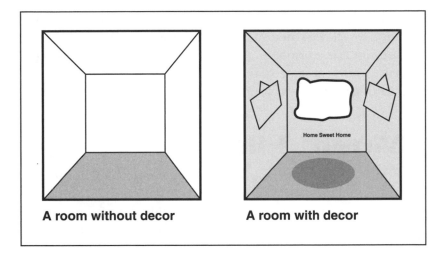

Figure 14.1
A furnished room is to an empty room as a game with music is to a game without music.

A room without decor   A room with decor

Home Sweet Home

background music, however, is a key component to any form of entertainment. It definitely helps you visualize another place and time using a concept called *suspension of disbelief,* in which, for a short time, you are fully immersed in a game (or a TV show or a movie, as the case may be). If you are able to accomplish this esoteric manipulation of another person's mind using your own imagination, then you have succeeded in making a great game. A video game without background music is like a room without décor: It is still a room, but it is not quite the same without the furnishings. Figure 14.1 illustrates the difference between a room that has no mood (so to speak) and a room that reflects a mood. Try to think of the background music for a game in terms of a room that is furnished compared to a room that is bare.

The Benefits of Background Music

Background music can set a mood. Just like a window with light coming through it sets a lighter tone than a room with no windows, background music helps to set the feeling in a game. If an evil alien is chasing a player, the game music should probably be something fast-paced to get the heart pumping. Or, if the character falls in love with another character, the music should reflect a romantic mood.

Setting the Mood for the Game

How do you choose what mood you want to set for a game? This is simple, but hard at the same time. If your game were full of alien bad-guys that you are shooting out of the sky, your mood would be panic. If you were writing an adventure between two star-crossed lovers, your mood would be romantic. The best way to decide a mood is to look at the overall picture you are producing. After you've decided that, picking the music is pretty easy. Trust your tastes in music. If the music makes you feel happy, put it in a happy part of your game. If it makes you sad, put it in a sad part.

Loading Music Files

All this talk about background music has probably made you wonder, "Okay, how do I make this music?" DarkBASIC uses a file format called MIDI (*Musical Instrument Direct Interface*) to load background music. It is a collection of music notes stored in a file. MIDI is to a computer as sheet music is to a pianist. The normal extension of a MIDI file is .mid.

MIDIs are generally created using a combination of software and hardware. A good piece of professional software is a program like Cakewalk's Sonar. A good piece of professional hardware is a Yamaha synthesizer. Most people, however, cannot afford such high-grade stuff, so there are alternatives. You can find many low-cost software alternatives by searching the Internet for MIDI software. You can also find a good sound card and a cheap synthesizer to handle the hardware side. I use a Casio keyboard with the Sound Blaster Live audio card in my computer. Figure 14.2 shows a typical setup for recording MIDI files using a keyboard.

You can also find MIDIs on the Internet. You don't have to generate the songs yourself to get good ones; just doing a search on the Internet can be fruitful.

TIP

DarkBASIC Professional also supports the popular MP3 music format, which is a highly compressed digital audio format capable of reproducing near-CD quality at a fraction of the size of an equivalent WAV file (which is the file format normally generated by copying a CD track to your hard drive—also called *ripping*). The syntax and music playback commands are all precisely the same under DarkBASIC Pro. Just keep in mind that you can load an MP3 file rather than a MIDI file if you want!

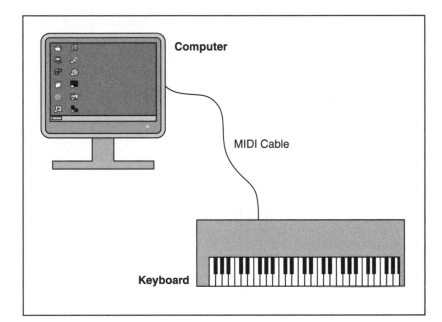

Figure 14.2
A typical setup for creating MIDI files involves a PC and a MIDI keyboard.

MIDI and MP3

In the music world, there is always a fight between which format is better—MIDI or MP3. DarkBASIC only supports MIDI, but DarkBASIC Pro supports MIDI and MP3.

MIDIs are smaller than MP3s because they store no digital sound. A MIDI song is more like a piece of sheet music than a digital recording. Depending on your sound card, MIDIs can sound really good or really bad. In the old days (in the early- to mid-1990s), sound cards would synthesize (or generate) the instruments used in a MIDI. My Sound Blaster Live card makes MIDIs sound really good because it uses digitized instruments instead of synthesized ones. The sound card contains pre-recorded WAV files that represent each instrument.

MP3s are more popular today then MIDI files because they are a highly compressed digital sound format. MP3s with good compression can run near CD-quality music at about 1 megabyte per minute (44 kHz, 16 bit). You can find MP3s all over the Internet, in most offices, and even in some of your favorite games, such as *Age of Empires 2*. MP3 format achieves such small file sizes by removing any sound that the human ear cannot hear.

Why use one format instead of the other? If you are concerned about space in your game, a good way to save some room is to use a MIDI instead of an MP3. If you are using a good-quality sound card, a MIDI will be about 30 kilobytes for a three-minute song, whereas the same song in MP3 format will be about 3 MB. However, because a MIDI is more like sheet music, it might not be suitable for all situations. For example, any instrument that is not loaded into the sound card will not play. Therefore, if you need instruments not readily available via MIDI, your best bet is to use the MP3 format.

Loading a Music File

The LOAD MUSIC command loads a MIDI file (or an MP3 file if you are using DarkBASIC Pro) into a specific music slot in the memory. The song number must be an integer. You can load a maximum of 32 songs into memory at one time. The syntax for the LOAD MUSIC command is

LOAD MUSIC *Filename*, *Music Number*

NOTE

You cannot have more than 32 songs loaded in memory at any one time. Keep this in mind when you are creating music tracks. Normally you will only use one song at a time, but DarkBASIC gives you the ability to load more than one track into memory.

Deleting a Previously Loaded Song

The DELETE MUSIC command removes a MIDI file from a specific music number. This is useful when you are trying to conserve memory because it frees up a music number. The format for this command is

DELETE MUSIC *Music Number*

Playing Background Music

Now you will attack the most important background music commands—the playback commands. They are pretty simple, yet very powerful. They give you control over the state of the background music.

Playing a Song

The PLAY MUSIC command starts a music number playing. This command always starts at the beginning of the music and plays to the end. The command format is

```
PLAY MUSIC Music Number
```

Here is an example of how to use the PLAY MUSIC command:

```
LOAD MUSIC "TitleMusic.mid", 20
PLAY MUSIC 20
```

Looping a Song

The LOOP MUSIC command starts a music number playing and looping. This command always starts at the beginning of the music, plays to the end, and loops back to the beginning. The command format is

```
LOOP MUSIC Music Number
```

Stopping the Playback

The STOP MUSIC command stops any music number that is playing or looping. After a music number is stopped, it will only play from the beginning again. The syntax for this command is

```
STOP MUSIC Music number
```

Pausing the Playback

The PAUSE MUSIC command pauses any music at the point at which it is playing. The command format is

```
PAUSE MUSIC Music Number
```

Following is a short snippet of code that demonstrates how to use the PAUSE MUSIC command.

```
LOAD MUSIC "TitleMusic.mid", 20
PLAY MUSIC 20
SLEEP 1000
PAUSE MUSIC 20
```

Resuming the Playback

The RESUME MUSIC command resumes playback of a song from the position where it was previously paused. The command format is

RESUME MUSIC *Music Number*

Here is an example of the RESUME MUSIC command:

```
LOAD MUSIC "TitleMusic.mid",20
PLAY MUSIC 20
SLEEP 1000
PAUSE MUSIC 20
SLEEP 1000
RESUME MUSIC 20
```

Music Playback Properties

Some of the most important commands in music playback are the music playback properties. These give you limited control over what music is playing and when. They are useful when you are trying to determine the status of the music.

Checking the Validity of a Song

The MUSIC EXIST command determines whether a song has been loaded into memory in the slot specified by the *Music Number* parameter. The command returns a 1 if the song exists or a 0 if it does not. The syntax for this command is

Value = MUSIC EXIST(*Music Number*)

Determining When a Song Is Playing

The MUSIC PLAYING command lets you know whether a music number is currently playing. Only one background music number can play at a time. This command returns 0 if the music number is not playing and 1 if it is. The syntax for this command is

Value = MUSIC PLAYING(*Music Number*)

Here is a snippet of code that demonstrates how to use the MUSIC PLAYING command:

```
LOAD MUSIC "TitleMusic.mid",20
PLAY MUSIC (20)
While MUSIC PLAYING(20) = 1
Endwhile
STOP MUSIC (20)
```

Checking the Loop Flag

The MUSIC LOOPING command lets you know whether a music number is looping. This is different than checking whether a music number is playing because looping will play the number continuously. This command returns a 0 if the music number is not playing and a 1 if it is. The format for this command is

```
Value = MUSIC LOOPING(Music Number)
```

Checking the Paused Flag

The MUSIC PAUSED command lets you know whether the music number is paused. Pausing music can be a good dramatic effect. The command format is

```
Value = MUSIC PAUSED(Music Number)
```

Here is an example of how to use the MUSIC PAUSED command:

```
LOAD MUSIC "TitleMusic.mid",20
PLAY MUSIC 20
SLEEP 1000
PAUSE MUSIC 20
WHILE MUSIC PAUSED(20) = 1
    IF(MOUSEKEY() = 1) THEN RESUME MUSIC 20
ENDWHILE
```

Introduction to Digital CD Audio

Sometimes it is preferable to use a physical CD audio track for music in a game in order to play back music at the highest possible quality. Neither MIDI nor MP3 files provide the quality or range of sound possible with CD audio. Well, you are in luck! DarkBASIC supports playing CD tracks as background music. You could even use this feature to write your own CD audio library program. Who knows? The possible uses for features such as CD audio (not to mention MP3 playback) are endless.

Using CD Music Tracks

Using CD audio tracks is just like loading a MIDI file for playback. The music commands apply equally to CD music and MIDI or MP3 files. DarkBASIC is smart enough to remember the format of the music referenced and play it accordingly.

The LOAD CDMUSIC Command

The LOAD CDMUSIC command loads a selected track as your background music. You can only load and play one CD track at a time. If you want to change tracks, you have to delete the old track first, and then load the new track. The syntax for this command is

```
LOAD CDMUSIC Track Number, Music Number
```

Chapter Project: The MusicJukebox Program

Now that you have been exposed to DarkBASIC's music-playing capabilities, it's time to put that knowledge into action! The next section of source code is a simple program called MusicJukebox. This program plays MIDI files, MP3 songs, or CD audio tracks. You can use the up and down arrow keys to scroll through the music selection. You can also use the mouse to select the music. Table 14.1 shows the commands that control the MusicJukebox program, and Figure 14.3 shows the output of the program.

Table 14.1 MusicJukebox Commands

Key	Description
Enter	Plays the highlighted song
Space	Stops the current playback
P	Pauses the music playback
R	Resumes the music playback
Esc	Ends the program

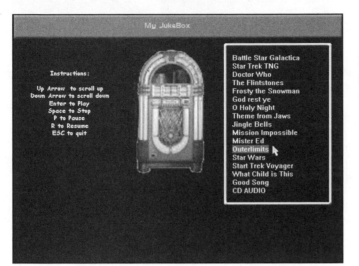

Figure 14.3
The MusicJukebox program loads and plays songs that you choose.

The source code for the MusicJukebox program includes three support functions. The first function, LoadAllMusic, reads data into several arrays. The second function, DisplayTitles, refreshes the song list for the highlighted song. The third function, GetNewSongName, reads the song under the mouse so it can be highlighted.

> **TIP**
> If you are using DarkBASIC Pro, feel free to replace any of the MIDI files referenced in the MusicJukebox program with MP3 files.

```
REMSTART
----------------------------------
Beginner's Guide To Game Programming With DarkBASIC
Copyright (C)2002 Jonathan S. Harbour and Joshua R. Smith
Chapter 14 - Playing Some Tunes: CD Audio and MIDI Music
----------------------------------
REMEND

REM The files and Names of the songs.
DATA "songs\Song1.mid","Battle Star Galactica"
DATA "songs\Song2.mid","Star Trek TNG"
DATA "songs\Song3.mid","Doctor Who"
DATA "songs\Song4.mid","The Flintstones"
DATA "songs\Song5.mid","Frosty the Snowman"
DATA "songs\Song6.mid","God rest ye"
DATA "songs\Song7.mid","O Holy Night"
```

```
DATA "songs\Song8.mid","Theme from Jaws"
DATA "songs\Song9.mid","Jingle Bells"
DATA "songs\Song10.mid","Mission Impossible"
DATA "songs\Song11.mid","Mister Ed"
DATA "songs\Song12.mid","Outerlimits"
DATA "songs\Song13.mid","Star Wars"
DATA "songs\Song14.mid","Start Trek Voyager"
DATA "songs\Song15.mid","What Child is This"
DATA "TitleMusic.mid","Good Song"
DATA "CDAUDIO","CD AUDIO"

REM Some global arrays for storing key information
DIM SongTitle$(17)
DIM FileName$(17)
DIM Selected(1)
DIM MaxSongs(1)


SYNC ON
SYNC RATE 30
MaxSongs(1) = 17
LoadAllMusic()

LOAD BITMAP "images\backdrop.bmp"
SYNC
SYNC
Selected(1) = 1

DisplayTitles()
` Checking and looping with the ESC key (ASCII value 27)
WHILE INKEY$() <> CHR$(27)
    ` Checking the downkey
    IF DOWNKEY()=1
        WHILE DOWNKEY()=1
        ENDWHILE
        Selected(1) = Selected(1) + 1
        IF Selected(1) > MaxSongs(1) THEN Selected(1) = 1
        DisplayTitles()
    ENDIF
```

```
` Checking the up key
IF UPKEY()=1
    WHILE UPKEY()=1
    ENDWHILE
    Selected(1) = Selected(1) - 1
    IF Selected(1) < 1 THEN Selected(1) = MaxSongs(1)
    DisplayTitles()
ENDIF
` Checking the Space Bar (ASCII value 32)
IF INKEY$() = CHR$(32)
    IF MUSIC EXIST(1)
        STOP MUSIC (1)
    ENDIF
ENDIF
` Checking the P key
IF INKEY$() = "P" OR INKEY$()="p"
    IF MUSIC EXIST(1) = 1 THEN  PAUSE MUSIC 1
ENDIF
` Checking the R key
IF INKEY$() = "R" OR INKEY$()="r"
    WHILE INKEY$() = "R" OR inkcy$()="r"
    ENDWHILE
    RESUME MUSIC 1
ENDIF
` Checking the Enter KEY (ASCII value 13)
IF INKEY$() = CHR$(13)
    selector = Selected(1)
    IF FileName$(selector) = "CDAUDIO"
        SYNC
        SYNC
        IF MUSIC EXIST(1)
            IF MUSIC PLAYING(1) THEN STOP MUSIC 1
            DELETE MUSIC 1
        ENDIF
        LOAD CDMUSIC 1,1
        IF MUSIC EXIST(1) THEN PLAY MUSIC 1
    ELSE
        IF MUSIC EXIST(1)
            IF MUSIC PLAYING(1) THEN STOP MUSIC 1
```

```
                DELETE MUSIC 1
            ENDIF
            LOAD MUSIC FileName$(selector),1
            PLAY MUSIC 1
        ENDIF
    ENDIF
    `checking to see if the mouse was clicked over a song
    IF MOUSECLICK()=1
        WHILE MOUSECLICK()=1
            SYNC
        ENDWHILE
        newsong = GetNewSongName()
        IF newsong <> 0
            Selected(1) = newsong
            DisplayTitles()
        ENDIF
    ENDIF
    SYNC
ENDWHILE
IF MUSIC EXIST(1)=1
    STOP MUSIC 1
ENDIF
END


` Sets all the music variables
FUNCTION LoadAllMusic()
    FOR Count = 1 TO MaxSongs(1)
        READ Midfile$
        FileName$(Count) = Midfile$
        READ Songname$
        SongTitle$(Count) = Songname$
    NEXT count
ENDFUNCTION


` Display all the music titles
FUNCTION DisplayTitles
    White = RGB(255,255,255)
    Black = RGB(0,0,0)
    Blue = RGB(0,0,255)
```

```
        Yellow = RGB(255,255,255)
        SET TEXT OPAQUE
        FOR Count = 1 TO MaxSongs(1)
            IF Count = selected(1)
                INK Yellow,Blue
                TEXT 425,75+((Count-1)*16),SongTitle$(Count)
            ELSE
                INK White,Black
                TEXT 425,75+((Count-1)*16),SongTitle$(Count)
            ENDIF
        NEXT Count
ENDFUNCTION


` checks the mouse cursor to see if it is over a new song.
FUNCTION GetNewSongName()
    xpos = MOUSEX();
    ypos = MOUSEY();
    IF xpos <425 THEN EXITFUNCTION 0
    IF ypos <75 THEN EXITFUNCTION 0
    IF xpos > 611 THEN EXITFUNCTION 0
    IF ypos > 75+MaxSongs(1)*16 THEN EXITFUNCTION 0
    Flag = 0
    FOR Count = 1 TO MaxSongs(1)
        ymin = 75+((Count-1)*16);
        Ymax = 75+((Count)*16);
        IF Ypos > Ymin AND Ypos < Ymax THEN Flag = Count
    NEXT Count
ENDFUNCTION Flag
```

Summary

In this chapter, you learned the mechanics of playing music in DarkBASIC. DarkBASIC has a thorough selection of commands for loading and playing MIDI files, MP3 files, and CD audio tracks. You learned the importance of setting the mood in a game, as well as how music and sound effects greatly enhance (or detract from) the impression that a game has on players. Enjoy the new power of music you have found within DarkBASIC!

Chapter Quiz

The chapter quiz will help reinforce the material you have learned in this chapter, and will provide you with feedback on how well you have learned the subjects that were covered. For the answers to the quiz, refer to Appendix A, "Answers to the Chapter Quizzes."

1. Which command loads a MIDI file?

    A. LOAD MUSIC

    B. LOAD CDMUSIC

    C. LOAD SOUND

    D. LOAD 3DSOUND

2. Which command stops music from playing?

    A. HALT MUSIC

    B. STOP MUSIC

    C. STOP SOUND

    D. PLEASE MUSIC STOP

3. How many CD tracks can play at one time?

    A. Six

    B. Three

    C. As many as you want

    D. One

4. What does the MUSIC PAUSE command do?

    A. Pauses a MIDI file

    B. Stops a MIDI file

    C. Resumes a MIDI file

    D. Prints a picture of a bear holding a music note

5. How many MIDI files can you store at one time?

    A. 15

    B. 37

    C. 46

    D. 32

6. RESUME MUSIC will continue a song where it was paused.

    A. True

    B. False

7. Which of the following commands will *not* make music play through the speakers?

    A. PLAY MUSIC

    B. LOOP MUSIC

    C. RESUME MUSIC

    D. PAUSE MUSIC

8. What must you do before you can play a new CD track?

    A. Use the DELETE MUSIC command to delete the old track

    B. Eject the CD from the drive and re-insert it

    C. Nothing

    D. Both A and B

9. Which command will tell you whether a song is looping?

    A. MUSIC PLAYING

    B. MUSIC LOOPING

    C. MUSIC PAUSED

    D. MUSIC EXIST

10. What does the DELETE MUSIC command do?

    A. Deletes the music buffer from memory

    B. Deletes the program you are writing

    C. Hides the mouse

    D. Reveals the mouse

CHAPTER 15

Loading and Saving Information Using Files

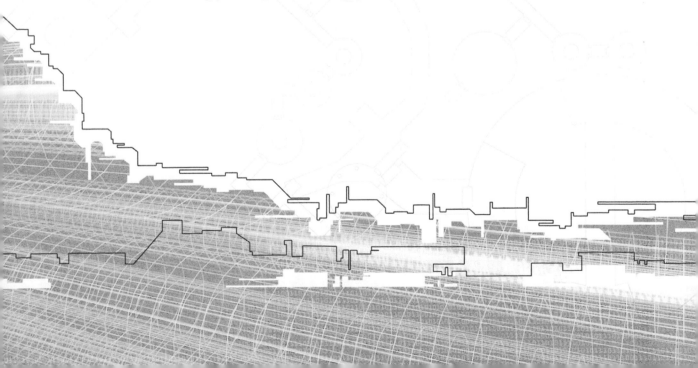

This chapter focuses on the subject of file input and output—that is, the commands used for opening, reading, writing, copying, moving, and deleting files (as well as folders). Almost every application on a PC supports some form of file input and output. From a word processor to the latest game, files are possibly the single most important item in a computer system. DarkBASIC provides plenty of commands to manage files and folders, read and write files to load, and save game data.

Although DarkBASIC abstracts the processes involved in loading textures, reading a 3D Studio Max file, or picking up an MP3 song, such features all involve reading files of one format or another. DarkBASIC handles the details for most of these processes for you, but there might be new types of files, unusual files, or perhaps a file of your own creation that you want to load into your program. Naturally, you will need some way to open and read those files, and DarkBASIC provides you with the commands to do so.

In addition, there might be times when you want to write data to a file. The most common such situation involves saving a game, a feature that most games provide. Without the ability to save a game—and the means to record that game's current state to a file—some games (such as lengthy adventure games or mission-based games) would be unplayable.

This chapter covers the following topics:

- Introduction to File Input/Output
- Introduction to Files
- Basic File Commands
- File Input/Output Commands
- Using the Clipboard

Introduction to File Input/Output

Behind the scenes, DarkBASIC reads all kinds of different files. It is so sophisticated, in fact, that you can store all the data files your program needs right inside the compiled executable program. You do not need to modify any source code to do this because it is an option that is built into DarkBASIC. When you choose to build an executable with attached media, DarkBASIC writes the bitmaps, 3D models, sound effects, music, and any data files to the executable, allowing you to share just a single file with others. This is one of my favorite features of DarkBASIC because it does not require an annoying install program. The only prerequisite is that DirectX 8.1 must be installed before a DarkBASIC program will run.

Files generally contain some type of data. Data was originally stored on punched cards, but the latest achievement in modern mass-market data storage is the DVD (*Digital Versatile Disc*). You can now purchase your own DVD burner for less than $300 and make use of a once extravagant but now commonplace 4.7 gigabytes!

Data has not always been stored in files as it is in modern operating systems. However, the concepts we now take for granted, such as drive letters, folders, and files, have been around for several decades. Some of the earliest PC operating systems (CPM, UNIX, and DOS) featured the same (or similar) drive-folder-file hierarchical structure that we use today. Figure 15.1 shows the drive-folder-file hierarchical structure in a typical folder listing under MS-DOS.

NOTE

For the record, the correct pronunciation of the word "data" is "day-tuh." Mispronouncing the word as "dat-uh" is acceptable, but technically not correct. Furthermore, correcting others in the proper pronunciation of "day-tuh" will result in you being labeled a nerd of the highest caliber. Trust me . . . I know.

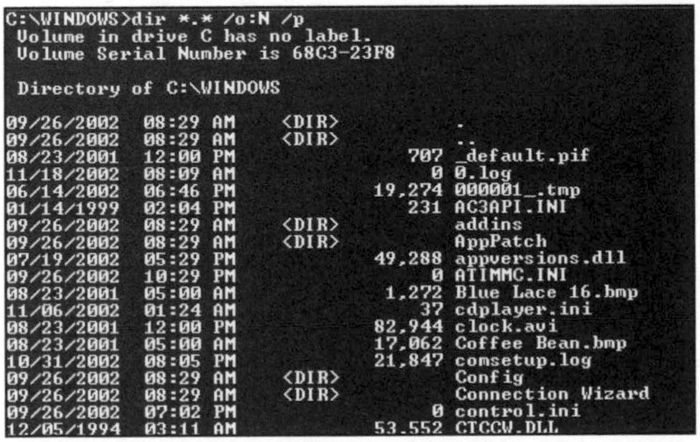

```
C:\WINDOWS>dir *.* /o:N /p
Volume in drive C has no label.
Volume Serial Number is 68C3-23F8

Directory of C:\WINDOWS

09/26/2002  08:29 AM    <DIR>          .
09/26/2002  08:29 AM    <DIR>          ..
08/23/2001  12:00 PM              707 _default.pif
11/18/2002  08:09 AM                0 0.log
06/14/2002  06:46 PM           19,274 000001_.tmp
01/14/1999  02:04 PM              231 AC3API.INI
09/26/2002  08:29 AM    <DIR>          addins
09/26/2002  08:29 AM    <DIR>          AppPatch
07/19/2002  05:29 PM           49,288 appversions.dll
09/26/2002  10:29 PM                0 ATIMMC.INI
08/23/2001  05:00 AM            1,272 Blue Lace 16.bmp
11/06/2002  01:24 PM               37 cdplayer.ini
08/23/2001  12:00 PM           82,944 clock.avi
08/23/2001  05:00 AM           17,062 Coffee Bean.bmp
10/31/2002  08:05 PM           21,847 consetup.log
09/26/2002  08:29 AM    <DIR>          Config
09/26/2002  08:29 AM    <DIR>          Connection Wizard
09/26/2002  07:02 PM                0 control.ini
12/05/1994  03:11 AM           53,552 CTCCW.DLL
```

Figure 15.1 *The drive-folder-file hierarchical structure under MS-DOS*

Drive and Directory Commands

The hierarchy of drives, folders, and files makes it possible to organize a file system on a hard drive, CD-ROM, or removable disk (such as an IOMega Zip 750 disk).

The best analogy for a computer's file system is an actual file cabinet (see Figure 15.2). Some file cabinets are larger than others, just like some forms of media (such as a hard drive) can store more data than others (such as a DVD). A file cabinet has several drawers that you must pull out to gain access to the folders within them. This is analogous to opening a drive and folder on the computer's file system. The folders in a file cabinet are similar to a computer's folders. Finally, each folder can contain one or more documents that are analogous to the files in a computer system.

> **NOTE**
> Folders are synonymous with directories; the two words are interchangeable. In general, the more common term is folders.

DarkBASIC provide commands to get information about drives, folders, and files. It also provides commands to create, change, enter, and delete folders and files. Throughout this chapter, you will use these commands to create file managers with DarkBASIC.

> *File managers* are programs that allow you to navigate the directories and files on any of your computer's drives. The most common file manager is **Windows Explorer.**

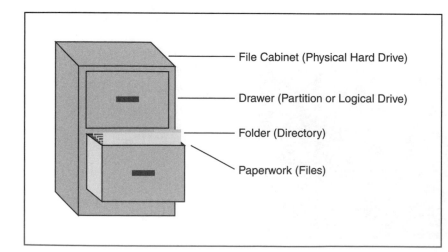

File Cabinet (Physical Hard Drive)

Drawer (Partition or Logical Drive)

Folder (Directory)

Paperwork (Files)

Figure 15.2
A computer's file system is analogous to a file cabinet with drawers, folders, and documents.

The GET DIR$ Command

The GET DIR$ command returns a string that contains two of the three aspects of a file name—the current drive letter and the folder name. Figure 15.3 shows the typical output of the command and its breakdown.

The drive is denoted by a letter (A to Z) followed by a colon, such as C: or D:. More than likely you will be working on the C drive, but you might have additional partitions or hard drives called D, E, F, or G. My computer has seven drive letters (which include the floppy drive, hard drives, DVD-ROM, and CD burner), so I could be working in quite a few different drives at any given time. Each folder and subfolder is appended to the drive letter with the backslash character (\). Every time you see this character, the main folder or a subfolder (or perhaps the final file name) will follow. C:\ references the root directory of the C drive. C:\winnt\system32 points to the \system32 folder, which is located inside the \winnt folder on the C drive. But you probably already knew that, right?

> The *root directory* is the base location on a drive. Just like real trees have roots, so do directory trees.

The DRIVELIST Command

The DRIVELIST command prints all the current drives available on the computer to the screen, which gives you a quick view of what drives are available. However, the PERFORM CHECKLIST FOR DRIVES command is better for retrieving the data in a usable format.

The DIR Command

The DIR command prints all of the files within the current directory. This command also provides quick access to information about the current directory. To get a string of the current directory, use the GET DIR$ command. To get a list of the files in a usable format, use the PERFORM CHECKLIST FOR FILES command.

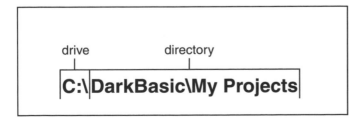

Figure 15.3
Typical output of the GET DIR$ *command*

The SET DIR Command

The SET DIR command changes the current directory to one that you specify. The command takes one parameter—a string of the path you want to change. The path can be absolute, such as C:\Windows, or it can be relative, such as newdir. You should note that this command does not return anything. Your program will error out if you attempt to set the directory to a location that does not exist. Use the data collected from the PERFORM CHECKLIST FOR FILES command (which I will cover in a moment) to make sure the directory you want exists.

> **NOTE**
>
> Relative and absolute paths can be confusing. To keep them straight, just remember that relative paths do not have drive letters attached to them. Relative paths are only relevant to your current location on the hard drive. For example, to move from the root directory of the C drive to the Windows directory, you would use the command SET DIR "Windows". That is an example of using the relative path. If you needed to use the absolute path, you would use the command SET DIR "C:\Windows".
>
> There are also two special relative directories. They are "." which means the current directory, and ".." which means the previous directory.

The CD command is a shorthand version of the SET DIR command. It takes the same parameter (a folder name) and follows the same pattern as SET DIR if it does not find the path you specify.

The PERFORM CHECKLIST FOR DRIVES Command

The PERFORM CHECKLIST FOR DRIVES command returns all the available drives in the form of a checklist. This command will come in handy in the DirectoryManager example, which you will create in just a few moments. Instead of blindly looking for a drive (and most often failing), this command returns all the available drive letters in the CHECKLIST STRING$ command. It provides an easy way to store the available drives, but it does tie up the checklist while in use. Therefore, I would suggest storing this data elsewhere.

The PERFORM CHECKLIST FOR FILES Command

The PERFORM CHECKLIST FOR FILES command returns all the files and directories within the current directory. This command fills up the checklist with all the file and directory names, which can be located in the CHECKLIST STRING$. To tell the difference between a file and a folder, use the CHECKLIST VALUE A command. If it returns a value of 0, then CHECKLIST STRING$ is a file; otherwise, it is a folder.

The MAKE DIRECTORY Command

The MAKE DIRECTORY command creates a new subfolder under the current folder (or under the root). The command takes a single string—the name of the folder you want to create. The directory must not exist, or the command will fail. When you want to create a folder, it is a good practice to at some point use the PERFORM CHECKLIST FOR FILES command (which searches for both files and folders) to check to see whether the folder already exists.

The DELETE DIRECTORY Command

The DELETE DIRECTORY command is the counterpart to the MAKE DIRECTORY command. Its only parameter is a string, which is the directory you want to delete. This folder must exist and be empty for you to delete it.

The DirectoryManager Program

The first project in this chapter is a directory manager. This program is akin to programs such as XTREE and DOSSHELL, but it is written in DarkBASIC. You will add to this program later in the chapter as you learn more of the file commands. You can find the entire program on the CD under the folder for this chapter. Figure 15.4 shows the output of the DirectoryManager program.

This program is divided into eight functions, plus the main source code listing. I did this to make the source code easier to read and modify, due to its length. The main source code listing creates numerous global variables used throughout the entire program. Although the source code is a bit on the long side, it is straightforward and should be easy to understand, and it helps to demonstrate the file and folder commands you have encountered up to this point.

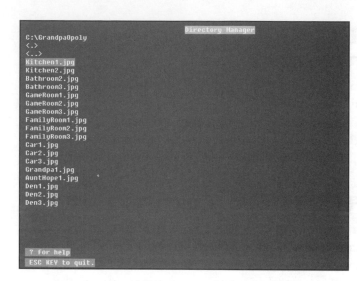

Figure 15.4 *The DirectoryManager program uses the commands you have learned thus far.*

```
REMSTART
----------------------------------
Beginner's Guide To Game Programming With DarkBASIC
Copyright (C)2002 Jonathan S. Harbour and Joshua R. Smith
Chapter 15 - File and Directory Operations:  Managing the I/O
----------------------------------
REMEND

DIM CurrentSelectedItem(1)
DIM CurrentFile$(1)
DIM CurrentFileType(1)
DIM CurrentPage(1)
DIM MaxFiles(1)
DIM PageSize(1)
DIM NewCommand(1)
DIM PageStartY(1)
DIM FileSpacing(1)
NewCommand(1) = 0
CurrentPage(1) = 0
CurrentSelectedItem(1) = 1
MaxFiles(1) = 0
PageSize(1) = 20
PageStartY(1) = 40
FileSpacing(1) = 16
```

```
SYNC ON
SYNC RATE 30
SET TEXT OPAQUE
DisplayInfo()
DisplayFiles()
WHILE ESCAPEKEY() = 0
    CheckKeyMovement()
    CheckMouseMovement()
    ProcessCommands()
    SYNC
ENDWHILE
END
```

The first function to enter is the DisplayFiles() function. This is the heart of the DirectoryManager program. It performs the checklist and displays all the files. It also highlights the currently selected file.

```
FUNCTION DisplayFiles()
    Black = RGB(0,0,0)
    White = RGB(255,255,255)
    Blue = RGB(0,0,255)
    PERFORM CHECKLIST FOR FILES
    IF CHECKLIST QUANTITY() = 0 THEN EXITFUNCTION
    MaxFiles(1) = CHECKLIST QUANTITY()
    StartA = (CurrentPage(1)*PageSize(1))+1
    StartB = ((CurrentPage(1)+1)*PageSize(1))

    if StartB > MaxFiles(1) THEN StartB = MaxFiles(1)

    FOR x = StartA TO StartB
        PosY = ((x-StartA)*FileSpacing(1))+PageStartY(1)
        IF CHECKLIST VALUE A(X) = 0
            TempString$ = CHECKLIST STRING$(x)
        ELSE
            TempString$ = "<"+CHECKLIST STRING$(x)+">"
        ENDIF

        IF CurrentSelectedItem(1)=(x-StartA)+1
            INK White,Blue
            CurrentFile$(1) = CHECKLIST STRING$(X)
            CurrentFileType(1) = CHECKLIST VALUE A(X)
```

```
        ELSE
            INK White,Black
        ENDIF
        TEXT 10, PosY , TempString$
    NEXT X
ENDFUNCTION
```

The second and third functions are the interface functions. The CheckKeyMovement and CheckMouseMovement functions routinely check the input devices and set up the appropriate command information. If any new commands are added to the program, these functions add the interface to the commands.

```
FUNCTION CheckKeyMovement()
    IF INKEY$()="?"
        WHILE INKEY$()="?"
            SYNC
        ENDWHILE
        NewCommand(1) = 1
    ENDIF
    IF UPPER$(INKEY$())="D"
        WHILE UPPER$(INKEY$()) = "D"
            SYNC
        ENDWHILE
        NewCommand(1) = 2
    ENDIF
    IF UPKEY()=1
        WHILE UPKEY()=1
            SYNC
        ENDWHILE
        NewCommand(1) = 3
    ENDIF
    IF DOWNKEY()=1
        WHILE DOWNKEY()=1
            SYNC
        ENDWHILE
        NewCommand(1) = 4
    ENDIF
    IF RETURNKEY()=1 and CurrentFileType(1)<>0
        WHILE RETURNKEY()=1
            SYNC
        ENDWHILE
```

```
            NewCommand(1) = 5
        ENDIF
        IF KEYSTATE(201) = 1
            WHILE KEYSTATE(201) = 1
                SYNC
            ENDWHILE
            NewCommand(1) = 6
        ENDIF
        IF KEYSTATE(209) = 1
            WHILE KEYSTATE(209) = 1
                SYNC
            ENDWHILE
            NewCommand(1) = 7
        ENDIF
        IF KEYSTATE(211) = 1 and CurrentFileType(1)<>0
            WHILE KEYSTATE(211) = 1
                SYNC
            ENDWHILE
            NewCommand(1) = 8
        ENDIF
        IF KEYSTATE(210) = 1
            WHILE KEYSTATE(210) = 1
                SYNC
            ENDWHILE
            NewCommand(1) = 9
        ENDIF
ENDFUNCTION

FUNCTION CheckMouseMovement()
    IF MOUSECLICK() = 0 THEN EXITFUNCTION
    IF MOUSEY() < PageStartY(1) THEN EXITFUNCTION
    IF MOUSEY() > PageStartY(1)+(PageSize(1)*FileSpacing(1))
        EXITFUNCTION
    ENDIF
    LastPage = MaxFiles(1)/PageSize(1)
    IF CurrentPage(1) = LastPage
        LastItem = MaxFiles(1) - (LastPage*PageSize(1))
    ELSE
        LastItem = PageSize(1)
    ENDIF
```

```
       CurrentSelectedItem(1) = ((MOUSEY()-PageStartY(1))/FileSpacing(1))+1
       IF CurrentSelectedItem(1) >= LastItem
            CurrentSelectedItem(1) = LastItem
            DisplayFiles()
       ENDIF
       DisplayFiles()
ENDFUNCTION
```

The fourth function, ProcessCommands, is the brains of the program. It checks to see whether there is a new command to process. If so, it processes the command. Each command is assigned a number, so this function checks to see whether that number is a command to process.

```
FUNCTION ProcessCommands()
` New Commands List.. If NEWCOMMAND equals these values
` The New command will be processed
` 0 -- No New Commands
` 1 -- Get Help
` 2 -- Change Drives
` 3 -- Move Up
` 4 -- Move Down
` 5 -- Change Dirs
` 6 -- Page up
` 7 -- Page Down
` 8 -- Delete Dir
` 9 -- Make Dir
` Determine where the last file and page are..
       LastPage = MaxFiles(1)/PageSize(1)
       IF CurrentPage(1) = LastPage
            LastItem = MaxFiles(1) - (LastPage*PageSize(1))
       ELSE
            LastItem = PageSize(1)
       ENDIF
       IF CurrentSelectedItem(1) >= LastItem
            CurrentSelectedItem(1) = LastItem
            DisplayFiles()
       ENDIF
       IF NewCommand(1) = 0 THEN EXITFUNCTION
       CmdToProcess = NewCommand(1)
       NewCommand(1) = 0
```

```
` Get the Help
   IF CmdToProcess = 1
       DisplayHelp()
       CLS
       DisplayInfo()
       DisplayFiles()
   ENDIF
` Change Drives
   IF CmdToProcess = 2
       ChangeDrive()
       CLS
       DisplayInfo()
       DisplayFiles()
   ENDIF
` Move Up
   IF CmdToProcess = 3
       CurrentSelectedItem(1) = CurrentSelectedItem(1) - 1
       IF CurrentSelectedItem(1) <= 0
           CurrentSelectedItem(1) = LastItem
       ENDIF
       DisplayFiles()
   ENDIF
` Move Down
   IF CmdToProcess = 4
       CurrentSelectedItem(1) = CurrentSelectedItem(1) + 1
       IF CurrentSelectedItem(1) > LastItem
           CurrentSelectedItem(1) = 1
       ENDIF
       DisplayFiles()
   ENDIF
` Change Directories
   IF CmdToProcess = 5
       NewDir$ = CurrentFile$(1)
       SET DIR NewDir$
       CurrentPage(1) = 0
       CLS
       DisplayInfo()
       DisplayFiles()
   ENDIF
```

```
`  Page Up  -- Change Pages
    IF CmdToProcess = 6
        CurrentPage(1) = CurrentPage(1) - 1
        IF CurrentPage(1) < 0
            CurrentPage(1) = 0
        ENDIF
        CLS
        DisplayInfo()
        DisplayFiles()
    ENDIF
`  Page Down -- Change Pages
    IF CmdToProcess = 7
        CurrentPage(1) = CurrentPage(1) + 1
        IF CurrentPage(1) > LastPage
            CurrentPage(1) = LastPage
        ENDIF
        CLS
        DisplayInfo()
        DisplayFiles()
    ENDIF
`  Delete a Directory
    IF CmdToProcess = 8
        DeleteDir$ = CurrentFile$(1)
        ` You do not want to delete . or the .. directory..
        ` Trust me on this
        IF DeleteDir$ = "." THEN EXITFUNCTION
        IF DeleteDir$ = ".." THEN EXITFUNCTION
        TempString$ = "Are you sure you want to delete " + DeleteDir$
        TEXT 10,400,TempString$
        A$ = AskYesNo$()
        IF A$ = "YES"
            DELETE DIRECTORY DeleteDir$
        ENDIF
        CLS
        DisplayInfo()
        DisplayFiles()
    ENDIF
`  Create a Directory
    IF CmdToProcess = 9
        SET CURSOR 10,400
        INPUT "Type in the name of the Directory: ",newdir$
```

```
          MAKE DIRECTORY newdir$
          CLS
          DisplayInfo()
          DisplayFiles()
       ENDIF
   ENDFUNCTION
```

The fifth and sixth functions display the rest of the information shown by the program. The DisplayInfo function shows the title bar, the current directory, and how to get help. The DisplayHelp function displays a screen that shows which keys perform the various commands. Any time a new command is added to this program, the help screen should be updated to reflect the new command.

```
FUNCTION DisplayInfo()
    Red = RGB(255,0,0)
    White = RGB(255,255,255)
    Black = RGB(0,0,0)
    Blue = RGB(0,0,255)
    INK White,Red
    TEXT 320,8,"Directory Manager"
    TempString$ = GET DIR$()
    INK White,Black
    TEXT 10,24,TempString$
    INK White,Blue
    TEXT 10,440," ? for help"
    TEXT 10,460," ESC KEY to quit."
ENDFUNCTION


FUNCTION DisplayHelp()
    CLS
    PRINT "This is the Directory Manager Program for Chapter 15"
    PRINT "Up ARROW    -- Move Up"
    PRINT "DOWN ARROW -- Move Down"
    PRINT "PAGE UP     -- Page up the file list"
    PRINT "PAGE DOWN  -- Page down the file list"
    PRINT "DELETE      -- Delete a Directory"
    PRINT "INS         -- Create a new Directory"
    PRINT "D           -- Change Drives"
    CENTER TEXT 320,400," Press Q To Leave This Menu"
    WHILE UPPER$(INKEY$())<>"Q"
        SYNC
    ENDWHILE
```

```
        WHILE UPPER$(INKEY$())="Q"
            SYNC
        ENDWHILE
ENDFUNCTION
```

The seventh function, AskYesNo, is a simple input function. It just waits for the user to press Y or N on the keyboard, and then it returns a string containing "YES" or "NO."

```
FUNCTION AskYesNo$()
    ch$ = UPPER$(INKEY$())
    WHILE ch$ <> "Y" AND ch$ <> "N"
        ch$ = UPPER$(INKEY$())
        SYNC
    ENDWHILE
    IF ch$ = "Y" THEN Ret$ = "YES"
    IF ch$ = "N" THEN Ret$ = "NO"
    WHILE ch$ = "Y" OR ch$ = "N"
        ch$ = UPPER$(INKEY$())
        SYNC
    ENDWHILE
ENDFUNCTION Ret$
```

The eighth and final function, ChangeDrive, changes the current drive for you. It lists all the available drives and allows the user to select which one they would like to go to.

```
FUNCTION ChangeDrive()
    White = RGB(255,255,255)
    Black = RGB(0,0,0)
    INK White,Black
    PERFORM CHECKLIST FOR DRIVES
    IF CHECKLIST QUANTITY()<=1 THEN EXITFUNCTION
    TempString$ = "Select Drive Letter: "
    FOR x=1 TO CHECKLIST QUANTITY()
        TempString$ = TempString$ + CHECKLIST STRING$(X)+" "
    NEXT x
    Done = 0
    TEXT 10,400,TempString$
    SYNC
    SYNC
    WHILE Done = 0
```

```
        ch$ = UPPER$(INKEY$())
        FOR x=1 TO CHECKLIST QUANTITY()
                IF ch$ = LEFT$(CHECKLIST STRING$(X),1)
                        Done = 1
                ENDIF
        NEXT x
        SYNC
    ENDWHILE
    WHILE INKEY$()<>""
        SYNC
    ENDWHILE
    newdrive$ = ch$+":\"
    SET DIR newdrive$
ENDFUNCTION
```

Introduction to Files

Now that you have been introduced to the basics of managing folders, and you've
written a file management program, it is time to cover a more significant subject—
files.

What Is a File?

What exactly is a file on a computer? It is a collection of
information stored sequentially or randomly and referenced by a specific name on the medium in which it is
stored. A file allocation table associates that file name with
the starting location of the actual data stored on the
medium (such as a CD or floppy disk). Each piece of data
in the file points to the next piece until an end-of-file
marker is found.

> A *medium* is a
> physical object on
> which an electronic
> file exists. Mediums
> include CDs, floppy
> disks, and hard
> drives, to name a few.

Reading and Writing Files

When you have an electronic file, how do you get and set the information from
that file? By reading and writing to it. Reading an electronic file is like reading a
paper file. You just need to know where to look and what to look for. Regardless of
the medium, electronic files are written in binary. That is, they always conform to
1s and 0s (ON and OFF). DarkBASIC, like most other programming languages,

combines the 1s and 0s into bytes. A single byte can store a single letter, number, or other alphanumeric symbol; this is the type of information stored in a file.

File Access Modes

Once you gain an understanding of how the bits are sorted, the next step is to understand how the bytes (groups of bits) are sorted. There are two modes for storing data in a file—sequential and random-access.

Sequential (Text Files)

A sequential file is written in order. The most common type of sequential file is the text file, which is a collection of strings. Each string usually ends with a byte value of 13. To find string number 5, you simply scan the text file for the fourth byte value of 13, and the next byte will be the start of the fifth line.

Random-Access Files

The name "random-access" is a little misleading. It doesn't mean that you randomly guess at where the data is, but rather that the file is structured in such a way that you can find any piece of data without looking at any of the previous data. Random-access files (also called *structured files*) are made up of several variables in what is called a *structure*. A structure is a group of variables with a fixed size. Although this might sound a little restricting (compared to a sequential file), this type of structure is great for storing database-style records in a file, which would be nearly impossible with a simple sequential file. Most media files, such as bitmap (.bmp) and wave (.wav) files, are made up of structures, including a header portion and a data portion inside the file.

If you want to read the fifth record in a sequential file, you must read all four records preceding the fifth record because that is how sequential access works. In contrast, you can simply jump to the fifth record in a random-access file and read it immediately, without having to read the previous four records. Random-access files are generally used to keep track of data in a structured and fixed format. If you write a game with many different opponents with different capabilities, you might use a random-access file to store the data for each character or object in the game for easy lookup and retrieval.

Basic File Commands

DarkBASIC provides quite a few commands for basic file operations. The commands can be divided into three groups.

- Search commands
- Information commands
- Management commands

Searching for Files

Although you can use the PERFORM CHECKLIST FOR FILES command to get a list of files, DarkBASIC provides another means to retrieve file information. These commands give you a little more information than the PERFORM CHECKLIST FOR FILES command; therefore, they are treated a little differently.

The FIND FIRST Command

The FIND FIRST command locates the first file of the current directory. If the command succeeds, it fills the GET FILENAME$, GET FILE DATE$, and GET FILE TYPE commands with the appropriate information. This command should always be successful because it returns both files and folders. It takes no parameters and returns nothing.

The FIND NEXT Command

The FIND NEXT command continues the file search begun by the FIND FIRST command. This command takes no parameters and returns nothing. It fills the GET FILENAME$, GET FILE DATE$, and GET FILE TYPE commands with the appropriate information.

The GET FILE NAME$ Command

The GET FILE NAME$ command returns the file name that is currently being searched. It takes no parameters but returns a string with the name of the file currently being searched.

The GET FILE DATE$ Command

The GET FILE DATE$ command returns the date of the file currently being searched. It takes no parameters, but returns the date of the file being examined. This information is not found in the PERFORM CHECKLIST FOR FILES command.

The GET FILE TYPE Command

The GET FILE TYPE command returns the type of file you are examining. If the file is a directory, this command returns a 1; otherwise, it returns a 0. If there are no more files to search, the command returns −1.

Upgrading the DirectoryManager Program to the FileManager Program

Now that you have learned the file-searching commands, your next project is to upgrade DirectoryManager to a full-blown file manager program. There will be only a few changes to the original program to add the new features, but it will provide more useful information about each file. You will replace one function and modify two others. The new FileManager program uses FIND FIRST, FIND NEXT, and related commands instead of the CHECKLIST command. If you prefer, you can load this project from the CD; it is located under the folder for this chapter. Figure 15.5 shows the new FileManager program in action.

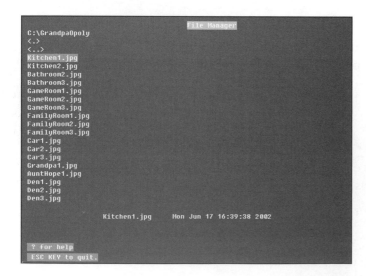

Figure 15.5
The FileManager program uses the new file management commands you have learned.

The first thing you need to do to convert to the FileManager is replace the DisplayFiles function. This function needs to use the new file commands instead of the PERFORM CHECKLIST FOR FILES command.

```
FUNCTION DisplayFiles()
    Black = RGB(0,0,0)
    White = RGB(255,255,255)
    Blue = RGB(0,0,255)
    Red = RGB(255,0,0)
    FIND FIRST

    MaxFiles(1) = 0
    WHILE GET FILE TYPE()<> -1
        MaxFiles(1) = MaxFiles(1) + 1
        FIND NEXT
    ENDWHILE

    FIND FIRST
    PageOfFiles = CurrentPage(1)*PageSize(1)
    FOR X = 1 to PageOfFiles
        FIND NEXT
    NEXT X

    FOR X = 0 TO PageSize(1)-1
        IF GET FILE TYPE() = -1
            EXIT
        ENDIF
        PosY = ((x)*FileSpacing(1))+PageStartY(1)
        IF GET FILE TYPE() = 0
            TempString$ = GET FILE NAME$()
            TempString2$ = GET FILE NAME$()+"      "+GET FILE DATE$()
        ELSE
            TempString$ = "<"+GET FILE NAME$()+">"
            TempString2$ = "<"+GET FILE NAME$()+">      "+GET FILE DATE$()
        ENDIF

        IF CurrentSelectedItem(1)=(x-StartA)+1
            INK White,Blue
            CurrentFile$(1) = GET FILE NAME$()
            CurrentFileType(1) = GET FILE TYPE()
```

```
                TEXT 10,PosY, TempString$
                SpaceString$ = " "
                FOR y = 1 to 120
                        SpaceString$ = SpaceString$ + " "
                NEXT y
                INK White, Black
                CENTER TEXT 320,380, SpaceString$
                CENTER TEXT 320,380, TempString2$
            ELSE
                INK White,Black
                TEXT 10,PosY, TempString$
            ENDIF
            FIND NEXT
        NEXT X
ENDFUNCTION
```

You need to update the DisplayInfo function to display the new title of the program. The existing line in the DisplayInfo function is

```
        TEXT 320,8,"Directory Manager"
```

It should be replaced with:

```
        TEXT 320,8,"File Manager"
```

You need to update the DisplayHelp function as well, to reflect the new title of the program. Look for the following line in the DisplayHelp function.

```
        PRINT "This is the DirectoryManager program for Chapter 15"
```

Now replace that line with this new version of the title:

```
        PRINT "This is the FileManager program for Chapter 15"
```

Reading Detailed Information about Files

After searching for the files in a directory, you will want to get information about certain files. Some programs use information-gathering techniques to determine whether a file is valid before reading it. For example, a game might look at the size of its own .exe file. If the .exe file does not match a defined size, then it has been tampered with. Some copy protection methods rely on file size, but not many. DarkBASIC provides three commands to get key information about a file or directory: FILE SIZE, FILE EXIST, and PATH EXIST.

The FILE SIZE Command

The FILE SIZE command returns the size of a file in bytes. This is helpful when you need to know how many bytes to read out of the file when you open it. The command takes one parameter, which is the name of the file, and returns the size of the specified file.

The FILE EXIST Command

The FILE EXIST command lets you know whether a file exists in the current directory. It takes one string parameter—the name of the file. It returns a 1 if the file exists and a 0 if it does not. Use this command prior to using the FILE SIZE command if you are not sure whether the file exists.

The PATH EXIST Command

The PATH EXIST command lets you know whether a directory exists. You should call this command before you perform any directory action on an unknown location. This command takes one string parameter, which is the location of the path. It returns a 1 if the path exists and a 0 if it does not.

Updating the FileManager Program

Using the new file information commands I just covered, you can update the FileManager program to make it even more useful. I'll explain how to modify the file display function, as well as how to add a new function. This updated version of the program is located on the CD under the folder for this chapter; it is called FileManager2. Figure 15.6 shows the updated FileManager program.

The first function to modify is DisplayFiles. You do not need to replace the entire function this time; instead, you just need to add two lines. Look for the following line in the DisplayFiles function.

```
TempString2$ = "<"+GET FILE NAME$()+">      "+GET FILE DATE$()
```

Now, just add the following lines below that line.

```
TempString2$ = TempString2$+"      "
TempString2$ = TempString2$+STR$(FILE SIZE(GET FILE NAME$()))+" bytes"
```

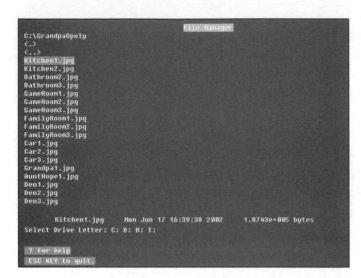

Figure 15.6

The FileManager2 program displays everything you could possibly need to know about a file.

Now you need to add the new command, which allows you to type a directory to which you want the file manager to go. It checks to see whether the path exists; if it does, the command takes you there. You need to append two functions with new command information. The first is the CheckKeyMovement function. Look for the following lines in the CheckKeyMovement function.

```
IF KEYSTATE(210) = 1
    WHILE KEYSTATE(210) = 1
        SYNC
    ENDWHILE
    NewCommand(1) = 9
ENDIF
```

Add the following snippet of code below the aforementioned code.

```
IF UPPER$(INKEY$())="G"
    WHILE UPPER$(INKEY$()) = "G"
        SYNC
    ENDWHILE
    NewCommand(1) = 10
ENDIF
```

The next function to modify is ProcessCommands. This is where the logic of the "G" key is handled. Look for the following section of code in the ProcessCommands function.

```
` Create a Directory
```

```
    IF CmdToProcess = 9
        SET CURSOR 10,400
        INPUT "Type in the name of the Directory: ",newdir$
        MAKE DIRECTORY newdir$
        CLS
        DisplayInfo()
        DisplayFiles()
    ENDIF
```

Now just add the following snippet of code right below that section.

```
` Go to a new directory
    IF CmdToProcess = 10
        SET CURSOR 10,400
        INPUT "Type in the new location: ",newdir$
        IF PATH EXIST(newdir$) = 1
            CD newdir$
        ENDIF
        CLS
        DisplayInfo()
        DisplayFiles()
    ENDIF
```

The last thing to modify in this new program is the help screen. Look for the following line in the DisplayHelp function.

```
PRINT "D          -- Change Drives"
```

Now add the following line right after it.

```
PRINT "G          -- Goto a specified directory"
```

File Management

Now that you know where and what files exist, you can use the commands to manage those files. Managing files in DarkBASIC is similar to managing files in Windows Explorer. You can use the MAKE FILE, COPY FILE, DELETE FILE, MOVE FILES, and RENAME FILE commands to perform the same activities that you might perform in Windows Explorer using the various menus. The commands allow you to do the same things you do in Windows Explorer, but within the DarkBASIC environment.

The MAKE FILE Command

The MAKE FILE command creates an empty file on the drive. Why would you need this command? It is useful when you need to open a new file that does not exist yet. You must first make the file, and then you can open it. The command takes one parameter, which is the name of the file you want to create. This command will fail if the file you are trying to make already exists.

The COPY FILE Command

The COPY FILE command copies a file from one location to another. This command takes two string parameters. The first parameter is the name of the file you want to copy (the source). The second parameter is the name of the file to which you want to copy (the destination). The names (both source and destination) can also include the path. This command will fail if a file already exists in the destination location with the name of the destination file.

The DELETE FILE Command

The DELETE FILE command deletes a file from the drive. This command takes one string parameter—the file name. It will fail if the file does not exist. Be careful with this command because you can wipe out important files accidentally.

The MOVE FILE Command

The MOVE FILE command moves a file from one directory to another. Moving a file is different than copying a file because a move will delete the source file. This command takes two string parameters. The first is the name of the file to move; the second is the name of the file to which you want to move the first file. The names (both source and destination) can also include the path. This command will fail if a file already exists in that destination with the name of the destination file.

The RENAME FILE Command

The RENAME FILE command renames a file. This command takes two string parameters and returns nothing. The first string is the original name of the file; the second is the new name of the file. This command will fail if the first name does not exist or if the second name already exists.

Updating the FileManager Program

This is the last time you will revisit the FileManager program. You will be adding a few new commands to make it more useful as a file browser. Specifically, you will add features to move, rename, copy, and delete files—all within DarkBASIC! You will find this updated version of the program on the CD in the folder for this chapter. The project is called FileManager3. Figure 15.7 shows what the new version of the program looks like.

The first few things that you need to add to this program are new global variables. These variables will keep track of which files need to be cut, copied, or pasted. Any file that is to be copied in this program will be marked first. Look for the following lines in the main portion of the source code.

```
DIM PageStartY(1)
DIM FileSpacing(1)
```

Now add the following lines after them.

```
DIM MarkedFileDir$(1)
DIM MarkedFile$(1)
```

Then look for the following lines in the main portion of the source code.

```
PageStartY(1) = 40
FileSpacing(1) = 16
```

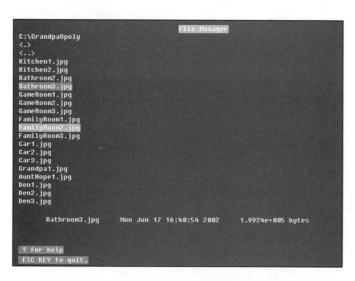

Figure 15.7

The new-and-improved FileManager3 program now has additional features.

Now add the following lines after them.

```
MarkedFileDir$(1) = ""
MarkedFile$(1) = ""
```

You only need to add one small part to the DisplayFiles function. This part will display the marked files in red. Look for the following lines in the DisplayFiles function.

```
    CENTER TEXT 320,380, TempString2$
ELSE
    INK White,Black
```

Then add the following lines of code after them.

```
CurrentDir$ = GET DIR$()
IF CurrentDir$ = MarkedFileDir$(1)
    IF TempString$ = MarkedFile$(1)
        INK White,Red
    ENDIF
ENDIF
```

You need to add a pretty hefty amount of code to the CheckKeyMovements function. You will be adding the keys for the MARK, CUT, COPY, and RENAME functions. Look for the following lines of code in the CheckKeyMovements function.

```
    IF UPPER$(INKEY$())="G"
        WHILE UPPER$(INKEY$()) = "G"
            SYNC
        ENDWHILE
        NewCommand(1) = 10
    ENDIF
```

Add the following lines after them.

```
    IF UPPER$(INKEY$())="M"
        WHILE UPPER$(INKEY$()) = "M"
            SYNC
        ENDWHILE
        NewCommand(1) = 11
    ENDIF
    IF UPPER$(INKEY$())="X"
        WHILE UPPER$(INKEY$()) = "X"
            SYNC
```

```
        ENDWHILE
        NewCommand(1) = 12
    ENDIF
    IF UPPER$(INKEY$())="C"
        WHILE UPPER$(INKEY$()) = "C"
            SYNC
        ENDWHILE
        NewCommand(1) = 13
    ENDIF
    IF UPPER$(INKEY$())="R"
        WHILE UPPER$(INKEY$()) = "R"
            SYNC
        ENDWHILE
        NewCommand(1) = 14
    ENDIF
```

Now you need to modify the ProcessCommands function. There are two things that
you need to do in this function. You need to replace one section of code and add
another. Look for the following section of code in CheckKeyMovements function.

```
` Delete a Directory
    IF CmdToProcess = 8
        ...
    ENDIF
```

Now just replace all the code in the "Delete a Directory." section with the following
lines of code.

```
` Delete a Directory or File
    IF CmdToProcess = 8
        DeleteDir$ = CurrentFile$(1)
        ` You do not want to delete . or the .. directory..
        ` Trust me on this
        IF CurrentFileType(1) = 1
            IF DeleteDir$ = "." THEN EXITFUNCTION
            IF DeleteDir$ = ".." THEN EXITFUNCTION
            tempstring$ = "Are you sure you want to delete " + DeleteDir$
            TEXT 10,400, tempstring$
            A$ = ASKYESNO$()
            IF A$ = "YES"
                DELETE DIRECTORY DeleteDir$
            ENDIF
```

```
    ELSE
        tempstring$ = "Are you sure you want to delete " + DeleteDir$
        TEXT 10,400, tempstring$
        A$ = ASKYESNO$()
        IF A$ = "YES"
            DELETE FILE DeleteDir$
        ENDIF
    ENDIF
    CLS
    DisplayInfo()
    DisplayFiles()
ENDIF
```

While you are still in the CheckKeyMovements function, look for the following section of code.

```
` Go to a new directory
    IF CmdToProcess = 10
        SET CURSOR 10,400
        INPUT "Type in the new location: ",newdir$
        IF PATH EXIST(newdir$) = 1
            CD newdir$
        ENDIF
        CLS
        DisplayInfo()
        DisplayFiles()
    ENDIF
```

Add the following lines below this code.

```
` Set Marked File
    IF CmdToProcess = 11
        MarkedFileDir$(1) = GET DIR$()
        MarkedFile$(1) = CurrentFile$(1)
        CLS
        DisplayInfo()
        DisplayFiles()
    ENDIF
` Move Marked File
    IF CmdToProcess = 12
        OldFile$ = MarkedFileDir$(1)+"\"+MarkedFile$(1)
```

```
            NewFile$ = GET DIR$()+"\"+MarkedFile$(1)
            MOVE FILE OldFile$, NewFile$
            MarkedFileDir$(1) = GET DIR$()
            CLS
            DisplayInfo()
            DisplayFiles()
        ENDIF
`  Copy Marked File
    IF CmdToProcess = 13
            OldFile$ = MarkedFileDir$(1)+"\"+MarkedFile$(1)
            NewFile$ = GET DIR$()+"\"+MarkedFile$(1)
            COPY FILE OldFile$, NewFile$
            MarkedFileDir$(1) = GET DIR$()
            CLS
            DisplayInfo()
            DisplayFiles()
    ENDIF
`  Rename File
    IF CmdToProcess = 14
            SET CURSOR 10,400
            INPUT "Type in the new name of the file: ",newname$
            IF newname$ <> ""
                RENAME FILE CurrentFile$(1),newname$
            ENDIF
            CLS
            DisplayInfo()
            DisplayFiles()
    ENDIF
```

The last thing you need to update in this version of the FileManager program is the help. Look for the following two lines in the DisplayHelp function.

```
PRINT "D          -- Change Drives"
PRINT "G          -- Goto a specified directory"
```

Add the following code below them.

```
PRINT "C          -- Mark File"
PRINT "X          -- Move Marked File"
PRINT "P          -- Copy Marked File"
PRINT "R          -- Rename File"
```

File Input/Output Commands

Up to this point, you have been exposed to the DarkBASIC commands to manipulate files and folders, but you have not actually used files to read or write information to disk. Therefore, I will spend the rest of this chapter showing you how to read and write files! There are many processes that benefit from storing data in files. For example, you might store the high scores for your game in a file. The most common use of file I/O is to create a data-driven game. By storing data outside your game, you can modify game data and items without recompiling the entire game. As games get more and more complex, the ability to edit the game-play without modifying the source code becomes a valuable timesaver. As an example, the game *Real War* uses a scripting language to handle many of the different aspects of the game, so it is possible to change the way the game plays without recompiling the source code.

Opening and Closing Files

After you know (or have created) the file you want to work with, you must open the file. There are two different methods for opening a file. You can open a file for reading or for writing. If you want to output data to a file, you must open it for writing. If you want to input data from a file, you need to open it for reading. After you have written or read all the data from the file, you must then close it. If you do not perform this step, you can write or read the wrong information later, resulting in corrupt data.

The OPEN TO READ Command

The OPEN TO READ command opens a file for reading. The command takes two parameters, the first of which is the file number. DarkBASIC supports up to 32 files open for reading or writing at the same time. The second parameter is the name of the file. The file must exist, or the command will fail.

Here is an example of the OPEN TO READ command:

```
OPEN TO READ 1,"NewFile.txt"
```

The OPEN TO WRITE Command

The OPEN TO WRITE command opens a file for writing. This command takes two parameters. The first is the file number, and the second is the name of the file. The file must exist, or the command will fail.

Here is an example of the OPEN TO WRITE command:

```
OPEN TO WRITE 1,"NewFile.txt"
```

The CLOSE FILE Command

The CLOSE FILE command closes a file number so that no more read or write operations can be performed on that file. This command takes one parameter—the number of the file that you want to close. The command will fail if the specified file is not already open.

> **TIP**
>
> Remember that DarkBASIC can only open 32 files at a time. If you need to open multiple files, make sure you close them with the CLOSE FILE command when you are finished.

Here is an example of the CLOSE FILE command:

```
CLOSE FILE 1
```

The FILE OPEN Command

The FILE OPEN command reports whether a file number is open or closed. This command takes one parameter—the file number. If a file has previously been opened, this command will return a 1; otherwise, it will return a 0.

Here is an example of the FILE OPEN command:

```
IsTheFileOpen = FILE OPEN(1)
```

The FILE END Command

The FILE END command lets you know when you have reached the end of an open file. It takes one parameter, which is the file number, and returns a 1 if the end of the file has been reached. Every time data is read, the end of the file should be checked. Data from a file will be invalid if it is read after the end of the file.

Here is an example of the FILE END command:

```
IsTheFileAtTheEnd = FILE END(1)
```

Integer File Commands

The integer READ and WRITE commands read or write an integer from a file, respectively. If you call enough of these commands, the FILE END command will equal 1.

The READ FILE Command

The READ FILE command reads one integer from a file and places it in a variable. The command takes two parameters. The first is the file number, and the second is the variable that you want to store the integer. An integer is four bytes in size.

The Read File program reads through any file and prints the integer values contained in that file. This program displays many numbers on the screen because it is displaying the integer values from that file. Figure 15.8 displays the output of this program on a 20-byte (5 integers) file.

```
----------------------------------
Beginner's Guide To Game Programming With DarkBASIC
Copyright (C)2002 Jonathan S. Harbour and Joshua R. Smith
Chapter 15 - File and Directory Operations: Managing the I/O
----------------------------------
REMEND

INPUT "What file would you like me to read? ", FileName$
IF FILE EXIST(FileName$) = 0
    PRINT "That file does not exist!"
    WAIT KEY
    END
ENDIF

OPEN TO READ 1,FileName$

Value = 0
WHILE FILE END(1) = 0
    READ FILE 1,Value
    PRINT STR$(Value)
ENDWHILE

CLOSE FILE 1
WAIT KEY
```

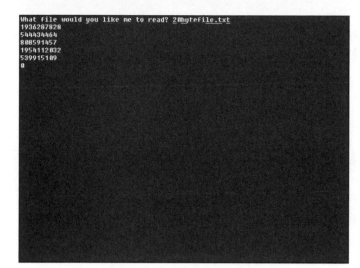

Figure 15.8 *The Read File program reads all the integers in the 20-byte file.*

The WRITE FILE Command

The WRITE FILE command writes one integer to a file. The command takes two parameters. The first is the file number, and the second is the value to write.

Byte File Commands

The byte READ and WRITE commands read or write one byte from or to a file, respectively. If you call enough of these commands, the FILE END command will equal 1 (which means true).

The READ BYTE Command

The READ BYTE command reads one byte from a file and places it in a variable. The command takes two parameters. The first is the file number, and the second is the variable that you want to store the byte.

The WRITE BYTE Command

The WRITE BYTE command writes one byte to a file. The command takes two parameters. The first is the file number, and the second is the byte to write. A byte ranges from 0 to 255.

Word (Two-Byte) File Commands

There are two commands for reading and writing word variables to a file. If you call enough of these commands, the FILE END command will equal 1. A word variable is equal to two bytes.

The READ WORD Command

The READ WORD command reads one word from a file and places it in a variable. The command takes two parameters. The first is the file number, and the second is the variable that you want to store the number.

The WRITE WORD Command

The WRITE WORD command writes one word number to a file. The command takes two parameters. The first is the file number, and the second is the variable to write. A word ranges from 0 to 65,535.

Long (Four-Byte) File Commands

The long number READ and WRITE commands read or write one long number to a file, respectively. These commands function similarly to the READ FILE and WRITE FILE commands. If you call enough of them, the FILE END command will equal 1. A long is equal to four bytes.

The READ LONG Command

The READ LONG command reads one long number from a file and places it in a variable. The command takes two parameters. The first is the file number, and the second is the variable that you want to store the number.

The WRITE LONG Command

The WRITE LONG command writes one word-sized number to a file. The command takes two parameters. The first is the file number, and the second is the word number to write. A byte ranges from 0 to 4,294,967,295.

Floating-Point Number File Commands

The floating-point number READ and WRITE commands read or write one number to a file, respectively. If you call enough of these commands, the FILE END command will equal 1. A float is 4 bytes.

The READ FLOAT Command

The READ FLOAT command reads one floating-point number from a file and places it in a variable. The command takes two parameters. The first is the file number, and the second is the variable that you want to store the number.

The WRITE FLOAT Command

The WRITE FLOAT command writes one floating-point number to a file. The command takes two parameters. The first is the file number, and the second is the number to write.

String File Commands

The string READ and WRITE commands read or write one sting from or to a file, respectively. If you call enough of these commands, the FILE END command will equal 1.

The READ STRING Command

The READ STRING command reads one string from a file and places it in a variable. The command takes two parameters. The first is the file number, and the second is the variable that you want to store the string. A newline (ASCII 13) character separates strings in a file.

The following program reads through any file and prints the strings contained in that file. Figure 15.9 displays the output of this program on the same 20-byte file as used in the Read File program. The difference is that this program displays the string that was stored in the file.

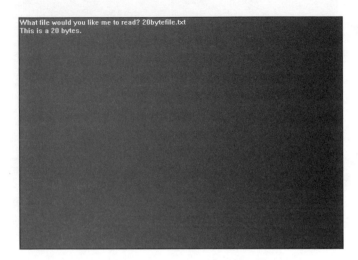

Figure 15.9

The program reads all the integers in the 20-byte file.

```
------------------------------------
Beginner's Guide To Game Programming With DarkBASIC
Copyright (C)2002 Jonathan S. Harbour and Joshua R. Smith
Chapter 15 - File and Directory Operations:  Managing the I/O
------------------------------------
REMEND

INPUT "What file would you like me to read? ", FileName$
IF FILE EXIST(FileName$) = 0
    PRINT "That file does not exist!"
    WAIT KEY
    END
ENDIF

OPEN TO READ 1,FileName$

Value$ = ""
WHILE FILE END(1) = 0
    READ STRING 1,Value$
    PRINT Value$
ENDWHILE

CLOSE FILE 1
WAIT KEY
```

The WRITE STRING Command

The WRITE STRING command writes a string to a file. The command takes two parameters. The first is the file number, and the second is the string to write.

Writing Your Own File

The Write File program creates a file and will write it in with whatever text you specify. Just like the SaveBitmap program in Chapter 10, this program will not work off of the CD-ROM. It must be copied to the hard drive because the CD-ROM is read-only (you can not write to it). Figure 15.10 displays the output this program.

```
This program demonstrates how to use the
DarkBASIC file read and write commands.

To Start off I need some information from you.
What is your name? Joshua
What is your favorite color? Blue
Why do you like DarkBasic? Because It is such a cool program.


OK. I am saving the file now.  Please wait.


Ok, I have written the file.
Now I am clearing the Variables

Variables are cleared!
Now reading the data from the file.
Your name is Joshua
Your favorite color is Blue
You like DarkBASIC because:
Because It is such a cool program.
```

Figure 15.10 *The Write File program shows you how to read and write to a file.*

```
REMSTART

----------------------------------

Beginner's Guide To Game Programming With DarkBASIC
Copyright (C)2002 Jonathan S. Harbour and Joshua R. Smith
Chapter 15 - Write File.

----------------------------------

REMEND

PRINT "This program demonstrates how to use the"
PRINT "DarkBASIC file read and write commands."
PRINT
PRINT "To Start off I need some information from you."
```

```
INPUT "What is your name? ", MyName$
INPUT "What is your favorite color? ", MyColor$
INPUT "Why do you like DarkBasic? ", WhyILike$
PRINT
PRINT
PRINT "OK, I am saving the file now.  Please wait."
PRINT
PRINT
IF FILE EXIST("MyTextFile.txt") = 1
    DELETE FILE "MyTextFile.txt"
ENDIF
OPEN TO WRITE 1,"MyTextFile.txt"
WRITE STRING 1,MyName$
WRITE STRING 1,MyColor$
WRITE STRING 1,WhyILike$
CLOSE FILE 1
PRINT "Ok, I have written the file."
PRINT "Now I am clearing the Variables"
MyName$ = ""
MyColor$ = ""
WhyILike$ = ""
PRINT
PRINT "Variables are cleared!"
PRINT "Now reading the data from the file."
OPEN TO READ 1,"MyTextFile.txt"
READ STRING 1,MyName$
READ STRING 1,MyColor$
READ STRING 1,WhyILike$
PRINT "Your name is "+MyName$
PRINT "Your favorite color is "+MyColor$
PRINT "You like DarkBASIC because:"
PRINT WhyILike$
WAIT KEY
```

Using the Clipboard

The Clipboard is memory that Windows has set aside to store and retrieve data. It is like a file, but you do not have to open or close it. Almost any program has access to this memory through its copy to Clipboard, cut to Clipboard, and paste from Clipboard commands. DarkBASIC gives you access to the Clipboard any time you want.

Reading from the Clipboard

If you want to read from the Clipboard, you can use the GET CLIPBOARD$ command, which is the DarkBASIC equivalent of pasting text in a word processor, e-mail software, or other program that supports copy and paste functions. The command takes no parameters, but it returns a string containing the contents of the Clipboard.

Saving to the Clipboard

Any time you need to save information to the Clipboard, you can use the WRITE TO CLIPBOARD command to store a string. This is the DarkBASIC equivalent of the copy feature in a copy-and-paste operation (such as in a word processor). The command takes one parameter—the string you want to save to the Clipboard.

Chapter Project: The GuessingGame Program

To fully appreciate the usefulness of file commands, you should write some sort of game that uses files to read or write data—hence, the GuessingGame program. In this game, the computer picks a random number and keeps track of how long it takes you to guess the number. The really interesting part is that the game stores the top five scores in a file.

GuessingGame is a simple program, but it is fun to play and it highlights the commands used in the second half of this chapter, involving file input and output. Figure 15.11 shows the output from the game.

TIP

There is a cheat in this game that helps to demonstrate the Clipboard commands. The game writes the random number that it has picked to the Clipboard. If you want to cheat, just look at the Clipboard to find the number. I will leave it up to you to figure out how to view the Clipboard while running the game.

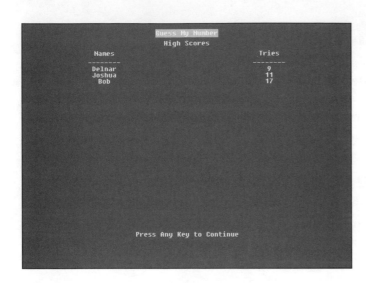

Figure 15.11
The GuessingGame program keeps track of high scores.

```
REMSTART
-----------------------------------
Beginner's Guide To Game Programming With DarkBASIC
Copyright (C)2002 Jonathan S. Harbour and Joshua R. Smith
Chapter 15 - File and Directory Operations:  Managing the I/O
-----------------------------------
REMEND

DIM HighName$(20)
DIM HighTries(20)
Playing = 1
SYNC RATE 30
SYNC ON
SET TEXT TRANSPARENT
WHILE Playing = 1
     DisplayTitle()
     PlayGame()
     Playing = PlayAgain()
ENDWHILE
END


` This function displays the title page for the game
```

```
FUNCTION DisplayTitle()
    Red = RGB(255,0,0)
    White = RGB(255,255,255)
    Black = RGB(0,0,0)
    INK White,Red
    CENTER TEXT 320,10, "Guess My Number"
    INK White,Black
    CENTER TEXT 320,400, "Press Any Key to Continue"
    SYNC
    DisplayHighScores()
    Counter = 1
    WHILE INKEY$() = ""
        Counter = Counter + 1
        SYNC
    ENDWHILE
    RANDOMIZE Counter
    WHILE INKEY$() <> ""
        SYNC
    ENDWHILE
ENDFUNCTION


` This plays the main game
FUNCTION PlayGame()
    MyNumber = RND(1000)
    YourNumber = -1
    Tries = 0
    TempString$ = ""
    WHILE YourNumber <> MyNumber
        Tries = Tries + 1
        CLS
        CENTER TEXT 320,10,"I have picked a number between 1 and 1000"
        CENTER TEXT 320,22,"You have to guess.  I will help you!"
        TEXT 10,420,TempString$
        SYNC
        SET CURSOR 10,400
        PRINT "What is your number? ";
        INPUT YourNumber
        SYNC
```

```
            IF YourNumber > MyNumber
                    TempString$ = "My Number is less then that number! (Lower)"
            ENDIF
            IF YourNumber < MyNumber
                    TempString$ = "My Number is greater then that number! (Higher)"
            ENDIF
            IF YourNumber = MyNumber
                    TempString$ = "You are correct.  Way to go"
            ENDIF
            IF Tries = 5 THEN WRITE TO CLIPBOARD STR$(MyNumber)
        ENDWHILE
        CLS
        CENTER TEXT 320,10,"I have picked a number between 1 and 1000"
        CENTER TEXT 320,22,"You have to guess.  I will help you!"
        TEXT 10,420, TempString$
        SYNC
        SYNC
        SLEEP 1000
        HighScore = CheckHighScore(Name$,Tries)
        IF HighScore
            CLS
            CENTER TEXT 320,10,"Congratulations, you have made it into the high scores"
            SET CURSOR 10,400
            SYNC
            INPUT "What is your name? ",Name$
            EnterHighScore(Name$,Tries)
        ENDIF
ENDFUNCTION

` This checks to see if the player
` want's to play again
FUNCTION PlayAgain()
    Flag = 0
    CLS
    CENTER TEXT 320,240,"Would you like to play again? Y/N"
    SYNC
    Answer$ = AskYesNo$()
    IF Answer$ = "YES" THEN Flag = 1
    ClS
    SYNC
```

```
ENDFUNCTION Flag

` This function displays the highscores
FUNCTION DisplayHighScores()
    CENTER TEXT 320,30,"High Scores"
    CENTER TEXT 160,50,"Names"
    CENTER TEXT 480,50,"Tries"
    CENTER TEXT 160,68,"-----"
    CENTER TEXT 480,68,"-----"

    IF FILE EXIST("HIGHSCORE.DAT") = 0 THEN EXITFUNCTION
    OPEN TO READ 1, "HIGHSCORE.DAT"
    ypos = 80
    FOR x = 1 TO 20
        READ STRING 1, Name$
        READ LONG 1, Tries
        IF Tries <> 0
            CENTER TEXT 160,ypos,Name$
            CENTER TEXT 480,ypos,STR$(Tries)
        ENDIF
        ypos = ypos + 12
    NEXT x
    CLOSE FILE 1
ENDFUNCTION

` This function records a new highscore
FUNCTION EnterHighScore(Name$,Tries)
    IF FILE EXIST("HIGHSCORE.DAT") = 0
        OPEN TO WRITE 1,"HIGHSCORE.DAT"
        WRITE STRING 1, LEFT$(Name$,20)
        WRITE LONG 1,Tries
        FOR X = 2 TO 20
            WRITE STRING 1," "
            WRITE LONG 1,0
        NEXT X
        CLOSE FILE 1
        EXITFUNCTION
    ENDIF
    OPEN TO READ 1,"HIGHSCORE.DAT"
```

```
        FOR X = 1 TO 20
            READ STRING 1,a$
            HighName$(X) = a$
            READ LONG 1, a
            HighTries(X) = a
        NEXT X
        CLOSE FILE 1
        strtoplace$ = Name$
        numtoplace = Tries
        FOR x = 1 TO 20
            IF HighTries(x) >= numtoplace OR HighTries(x) = 0
                tempstr$ = HighName$(x)
                tempnum = HighTries(x)
                HighName$(x) = strtoplace$
                HighTries(x) = numtoplace
                strtoplace$ = tempstr$
                numtoplace = tempnum
            ENDIF
        NEXT X
        DELETE FILE "HIGHSCORE.DAT"
        OPEN TO WRITE 1, "HIGHSCORE.DAT"
        FOR X = 1 TO 20
            WRITE STRING 1, HighName$(X)
            WRITE LONG 1, HighTries(X)
        NEXT X
        CLOSE FILE 1
ENDFUNCTION


` This function checks to see if a highscore
` qualifies.
FUNCTION CheckHighScore(Name$,Tries)
    IF FILE EXIST("HIGHSCORE.DAT") = 1
        EXITFUNCTION 1
    ENDIF
    OPEN TO READ 1,"HIGHSCORE.DAT"
    FOR X = 1 TO 20
        READ STRING 1,a$
        HighName$(X) = a$
        READ LONG 1, a
        HighTries(X) = a
```

```
      NEXT X
      CLOSE FILE 1
      Flag = 0
      FOR X = 1 TO 20
           IF HighTries(x) >= Tries OR HighTries(x) = 0
                 Flag = 1
           ENDIF
      NEXT X
ENDFUNCTION Flag


` This waits for a Y/N key
FUNCTION AskYesNo$
      ch$ = UPPER$(INKEY$())
      WHILE ch$ <> "Y" AND ch$ <> "N"
           ch$ = UPPER$(INKEY$())
           SYNC
      ENDWHILE
      IF ch$ = "Y" then Ret$ = "YES"
      IF ch$ = "N" then Ret$ = "NO"
      WHILE ch$ = "Y" OR ch$ = "N"
           ch$ = UPPER$(INKEY$())
           SYNC
      ENDWHILE
ENDFUNCTION Ret$
```

Summary

You have now covered the exhaustive concepts of file system management and file input and output programming in DarkBASIC. This chapter provided an introduction to the commands you will need to tackle these important subjects in your own game projects. In the end, you were shown a complete game that used file access to store the high scores for the game. You might want to recycle the functions in GuessingGame to add a high-score list to any games you write later. But why stop there? Enjoy your newfound power over files that you have discovered with DarkBASIC. When you have access to the file system, you can literally write any type of application or utility that you set your mind to . . . even if it isn't a game.

Chapter Quiz

The chapter quiz will help you retain the information that was covered in this chapter, as well as give you an idea of how well you're doing at understanding the subjects. The answers for this quiz can be found in Appendix A, "Answers to the Chapter Quizzes."

1. What information does the GET DIR$ command *not* contain?

   A. Drive

   B. Directory

   C. File size

   D. File name

2. The CD command in DarkBASIC stands for:

   A. Carry Duck

   B. Capture Data

   C. Cloak Darkness

   D. Change Directory

3. How many bits are in a byte?

   A. 16

   B. 12

   C. 8

   D. 32

4. What information does FILE SIZE return?

   A. A file size

   B. A file checksum

   C. A file name

   D. None of the above

5. Where does the data from the WRITE TO CLIPBOARD command go?

   A. The hard drive

   B. The screen

   C. The printer

   D. The Windows Clipboard

6. Which command opens HelloWorld.txt for reading as file #1?

    A. `FILE OPEN TO READ 1, "HelloWorld.txt"`

    B. `OPEN FILE FOR READ 1, "HelloWorld.txt"`

    C. `OPEN TO READ 1, "HelloWorld.txt"`

    D. `OPEN FOR READ 1, "HelloWorld.txt"`

7. Which command reads the number 1,000,000 in integer from file #1?

    A. `READ STRING 1, MILLION`

    B. `READ LONG 1, MILLION`

    C. `READ WORD 1, MILLION`

    D. `READ BYTE 1, MILLION`

8. Which command writes the string "Hello World" to file #1?

    A. `WRITE BYTE 1,"Hello World"`

    B. `WRITE FLOAT 1, "Hello World"`

    C. `WRITE STRING 1, "Hello World"`

    D. `WRITE LONG 1, "Hello World"`

9. Which command changes the file name "HelloWorld.txt" to "GoodBye.txt?"

    A. `DELETE FILE "Hello World.txt" "GoodBye.txt"`

    B. `COPY FILE "Hello World.txt" "GoodBye.txt"`

    C. `RENAME FILE "Hello World.txt" "GoodBye.txt"`

    D. `OPEN FILE "Hello World.txt" "GoodBye.txt"`

10. A bit can be 0, 1, or 2.

    A. True

    B. False

CHAPTER 16

PLAYING INTRO MOVIES AND CUT-SCENES

Animated movie sequences have become a standard feature of computer and video games, so much so that introductory movies and cut-scenes for games are often used as demo reels and trailers before the game is finished. If a high-end game is released without an introductory movie or narrative of some kind, it is possible that the game will make a poor first impression on reviewers and consumers alike. A two-minute game "teaser" trailer or introductory movie can take up to a year and cost upwards of a million dollars to produce, due to the excruciating detail put into the 3D animation sequences that are rendered for the movie. Game studios often hire 3D animators and concept artists to use programs such as Maya and LightWave for both game artwork and movies.

This chapter teaches you how to add intro movies and cut-scenes to your DarkBASIC programs. As you will learn, you can use DarkBASIC for the sole purpose of playing movie files, which can be embedded inside an executable. If you are an animator or a 3D modeler learning DarkBASIC to enhance your portfolio, you might use this feature to make your demos into self-running programs!

This chapter covers the following topics:

- Introduction to Movies
- Loading and Playing Movie Files
- Changing the Position and Size of a Movie
- Movie Trailers

Introduction to Movies

In the early days of video games, an intro movie was usually a paragraph of text on the screen with perhaps a single-channel soundtrack. As games became more complex and budgets were increased, intro movies and cut-scenes became more elaborate, moving from text to game engine cinematics. *Wing Commander II: Vengeance of the Kilrathi* was one of the first games to feature cut-scenes, and later games in the *Wing Commander* series followed suit to much acclaim, with custom movie-quality sets and popular actors reprising the roles of lead characters in the game.

Game Cinema

Wing Commander II was a trend-setting game featuring extraordinary movies that told the story within the game. Keep in mind that when this game came out, the average PC was a 486/33 with 8 MB of memory and an Adlib or Sound Blaster card. Windows 3.0 was not even around yet. That the game had movie sequences and voiceovers was extraordinary. Granted, the speech kit was an add-on for the game, sold separately. The game wasn't even distributed on a CD-ROM. Actually, CD-ROM technology had not hit the mainstream yet, so games were still being put on 5¼" or 3½" floppy diskettes (1.2 MB and 1.4 MB, respectively). The movie sequences in *Wing Commander II* were recorded on video and then digitized using a video capture card. In other words, the movies were not rendered in 3D as they are today.

Video capture movies were used in the follow-up *Wing Commander* games, but they dropped in popularity as the game industry became flooded with video-capture games in the great multimedia revolution. As a result, movies are almost always rendered in 3D today. If you are looking for ideas for how to create intro movies for your own games, consider recording a video of your game actually running (perhaps in demo mode), adding a catchy soundtrack, and using the demo trailer for your game as the intro movie.

What Is a Movie File?

Movie files store the video frames and audio streams that make up a movie sequence. The AVI (*Audio-Video Interleaved*) format was a standard for Windows multimedia PCs at the start of the multimedia revolution in the early 1990s, and it is still the most popular movie file format for Windows. However, there are many competing video formats, such as Apple's QuickTime (.mov), RealNetwork's RealMedia (.rm), and the somewhat more professional and platform-independent MPEG (.mpg) formats. Since that time, AVI has been expanded with multiple compressor-decompressor (*codec*) formats, making it extremely versatile at the expense of complexity. When encoding or decoding to or from an AVI, it can be confusing to figure out which codec to use. Despite the growing list, two formats are compatible with most AVI players—Indeo and Cinepak. If you have ever played around with a video capture card or video mastering software, you have likely come across these codecs.

Loading and Playing Movie Files

Despite the confusing plethora of audio-video formats and codecs, DarkBASIC makes loading and playing AVI files as simple as loading and displaying a bitmap image. Not only does DarkBASIC let you load and play a movie file with only a couple of lines of source code, you can also play several movies on the screen at the same time!

Basic Movie Playback Commands

There are quite a few commands to help you get the most out of your movie-going experience, but only a couple of those commands are absolutely necessary. This section will show you the commands that simply load and play a movie, along with some helper commands. First, I want to introduce you to the command to load a movie file.

The LOAD ANIMATION Command

You can use the LOAD ANIMATION command to load an AVI movie file into DarkBASIC. The syntax of the command is LOAD ANIMATION Filename, Animation Number.

The first parameter is the name of an AVI file, which is relative to the current folder in which the program was run. The second parameter is a number from 1 to 32, representing the position in which to store the movie in DarkBASIC. You can load up to 32 movies at a time and play any or all of them at any time. However, keep in mind that movie files can be large, and you might extinguish available memory by trying to load them all at once. It is usually better to load a movie, play it, and then delete it from memory (using the DELETE ANIMATION command, which I will cover later).

The ANIMATION EXIST Command

After you have loaded a movie file into DarkBASIC, there are several helper commands available to tell you about the movie. One such command is ANIMATION EXIST, which has the syntax Return Value = ANIMATION EXIST (Animation Number).

If the animation has been loaded, then the
ANIMATION EXIST command will return a 1; otherwise, it will return a 0. You can use this command
to determine whether a movie file loaded correctly. Another way to make sure the movie was
loaded correctly is to check its dimensions, as the
next two commands demonstrate.

> **NOTE**
>
> In DarkBASIC, the term
> *animation* is synonymous
> with the term *movie*.

The ANIMATION WIDTH Command

The ANIMATION WIDTH command returns the horizontal resolution of a movie after it
has been loaded by referencing the animation number parameter. The syntax for
the command is Return Value = ANIMATION WIDTH (*Animation Number*).

This command comes in handy when you want to resize or reposition the movie. As
I'll show you later in this chapter, you can scale the movie or center it on the screen.

The ANIMATION HEIGHT Command

The ANIMATION HEIGHT command returns the vertical resolution of a movie after it
has been loaded by referencing the animation number parameter. The syntax for
the command is Return Value = ANIMATION HEIGHT (*Animation Number*).

The PLAY ANIMATION Command

After you have loaded and verified a movie file, you can play it using the PLAY
ANIMATION command. The syntax for this command is PLAY ANIMATION *Animation
Number*, *Bitmap Number*, *Left*, *Top*, *Right*, *Bottom*.

The first parameter is required, but the others are optional. By specifying the
bitmap number, you can send playback to a specific bitmap. The last four parameters (*Left*, *Top*, *Right*, and *Bottom*) resize and reposition the movie on the screen.
This is demonstrated in the PlayAnim program, which I will cover shortly.

The ANIMATION PLAYING Command

Some movie files are short, and others can be very long. In fact, some games have
high-resolution intro movies that weigh in at several hundred megabytes. You can
use the ANIMATION PLAYING command to determine when a movie is done playing.
The syntax is Return Value = ANIMATION PLAYING (*Animation Number*).

The DELETE ANIMATION Command

After you have finished playing a particular movie that you might not need again, you should consider deleting it to free up memory and make room for other movies. You can delete a movie using the `DELETE ANIMATION` command. The syntax is `DELETE ANIMATION` *Animation Number.*

The PlayAnim Program

All right, how about a demonstration of loading and playing a movie file? Nothing beats a little source code to see how something works. I wrote the PlayAnim program just for that purpose. It is simple enough that you can see how easy it is to load and play a movie file. Take a look at Figure 16.1, which shows a movie file playing with the default resolution. Figure 16.2 shows a movie playing in full-screen mode, which is possible by simply changing the size parameters of the `PLAY ANIMATION` command.

Note that the PlayAnim program (and all other programs in this chapter) runs at 640×480 in 32-bit color mode. Although all of the sample programs run at this screen resolution, the color depth is not quite as important. Although 32-bit color is higher quality than 16-bit color, and special effects such as transparency are possible with 32-bit color mode, feel free to use either 32-bit or 16-bit color (using the third parameters of the `SET DISPLAY MODE` command). If your video card is unable to

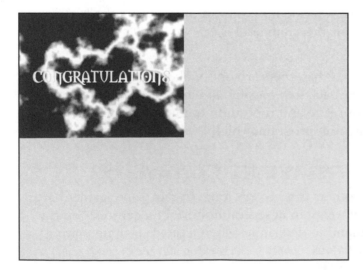

Figure 16.1 *The PlayAnim program loads and plays an AVI movie file using the default width and height of the movie.*

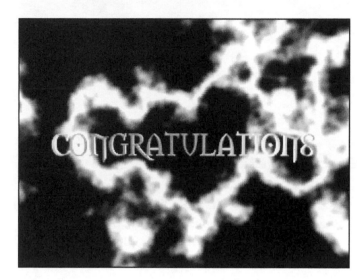

Figure 16.2 *The PlayAnim program can be set to run full screen by changing the* Right *and* Bottom *parameters to the resolution of the screen.*

run in 32-bit color mode (or if it runs slowly), change the display mode command so it uses 16-bit color instead. DarkBASIC Pro supports this command, but it is preferable to use the Project Manager to configure the video mode instead.

```
`-----------------------------------
`Beginner's Guide To DarkBASIC Game Programming
`Copyright (C)2002 Jonathan S. Harbour and Joshua R. Smith
`Chapter 16 - PlayAnim Program
`-----------------------------------

`initialize the program
SET DISPLAY MODE 640, 480, 32
HIDE MOUSE
CLS

`load background bitmap
LOAD BITMAP "background.bmp", 0

`load the animation file
LOAD ANIMATION "congrat2.avi", 1

`play the animation
PLAY ANIMATION 1, 0, 0, 320, 240
```

```
`wait for keypress
WAIT KEY

`remove the movie from memory
DELETE ANIMATION 1
END
```

Looping Movie Playback

One thing you probably noticed right away was how short the movie was in the PlayAnim program. It was only a few seconds long! That file, like many of the others in this chapter, is one of the movie files that comes with DarkBASIC. You can use those animated movies to enhance your game, such as by playing the Congratulations movie when the player wins or the Game Over movie when the game ends.

The LOOP ANIMATION Command

The animation in the PlayAnim program doesn't last long because that particular movie file simply is supposed to display the Congratulations message on the screen. But what if you want to repeat the movie after it has stopped? For example, you can use the LOOP ANIMATION command to loop the movie to play until the player presses a key or clicks a mouse button. The syntax for this command is LOOP ANIMATION *Animation Number*, *Bitmap Number*, *Left*, *Top*, *Right*, *Bottom*.

The last four parameters (*Left*, *Top*, *Right*, and *Bottom*) are optional, as is the *Bitmap Number* parameter. I will explain movie scaling shortly, but for now I'll focus on looping.

The ANIMATION LOOPED Command

When a movie is playing in loop mode, the ANIMATION LOOPED command returns a 1 for that movie; otherwise, it returns a 0. The syntax for the command is Return Value = ANIMATION LOOPED (*Animation Number*).

The STOP ANIMATION Command

Because a looping movie will continue to loop indefinitely, you need a way to stop the playback at some point (such as at the end of the program). You can stop playback of a movie using the STOP ANIMATION command. The syntax is STOP ANIMATION *Animation Number*.

The PAUSE ANIMATION Command

Now for some support commands, as promised. There are several handy commands you can use while a movie file is playing. For example, to pause playback at the current position, you can use the PAUSE ANIMATION command. The syntax is PAUSE ANIMATION *Animation Number*.

The ANIMATION PAUSED Command

When a movie has been paused, you can check the status of the paused property using the ANIMATION PAUSED command. The syntax is Return Value = ANIMATION PAUSED (*Animation Number*).

The RESUME ANIMATION Command

Another useful command is RESUME ANIMATION, which resumes playback after a movie has been paused. The syntax for this command is RESUME ANIMATION *Animation Number*.

Keep in mind that although these commands are all similar in syntax, you can use any animation number from 1 to 32 when calling them, which gives you the ability to manipulate multiple movies at the same time. I would think that playing just one movie on the screen would be enough to ask of DarkBASIC, but it goes a step further by allowing you to play several at a time!

The MultiAnim Program

The MultiAnim program plays four movies on the screen at the same time. By pressing the number keys 1 to 4, you can pause and resume playback of each of the four movies. The Esc key ends the program. Figure 16.3 shows the output of the MultiAnim program. This program is very demanding of your PC, so if it doesn't respond immediately to the number keys, just hold the key down for a second and you should see something happen.

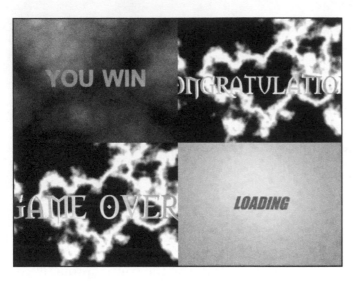

Figure 16.3 *The MultiAnim program plays four movie files at the same time and allows the user to pause and resume playback of each video stream.*

```
`----------------------------------
`Beginner's Guide To DarkBASIC Game Programming
`Copyright (C)2002 Jonathan S. Harbour and Joshua R. Smith
`Chapter 16 - MultiAnim Program
`----------------------------------

`initialize the program
SET DISPLAY MODE 640, 480, 16
HIDE MOUSE
DISABLE ESCAPEKEY
CLS

`load background bitmap
LOAD BITMAP "background.bmp", 0

`load and start each of the movies
LOAD ANIMATION "youwin1.avi", 1
LOOP ANIMATION 1
LOAD ANIMATION "congrat2.avi", 2
LOOP ANIMATION 2, 0, 320, 0, 640, 240
LOAD ANIMATION "gameover2.avi", 3
LOOP ANIMATION 3, 0, 0, 240, 320, 480
LOAD ANIMATION "loading3.avi", 4
LOOP ANIMATION 4, 0, 320, 240, 640, 480
```

```
`loop until ESC key pressed
REPEAT
    FOR N = 1 TO 4
        IF VAL(INKEY$()) = N
            IF ANIMATION PAUSED(N)
                RESUME ANIMATION N
            ELSE
                PAUSE ANIMATION N
            ENDIF
        ENDIF
    NEXT N

    `update the screen
    SYNC
UNTIL ESCAPEKEY()

`delete the movies
FOR N = 1 TO 4
    DELETE ANIMATION N
NEXT N
END
```

Changing the Position and Size of a Movie

Now that you've had a little experience playing and looping movie files, I'd like to explain some advanced playback features. This section will explain how to change the scale and position of a movie during playback, with some interesting results.

Changing the Position of a Movie

Although you can simply play a movie using the full resolution of the screen, it is far more likely that you will want to use DarkBASIC's fantastic movie-playing capabilities for many small animations in a game or program. To do this, you will need a way to reposition the playback to anyplace on the screen, and then return the position of the movie. Following are some commands that will help you to do just that.

The PLACE ANIMATION Command

PLACE ANIMATION is one of the most versatile movie playback commands in DarkBASIC. The syntax is PLACE ANIMATION *Animation Number, Left, Top, Right, Bottom.*

Using this command, you can reposition and scale a movie *during playback.* That is the significant phrase—*during playback.* You can set the scale and position using the PLAY ANIMATION command. However, after the movie has started, you must use PLACE ANIMATION to make changes during playback. The MoveAnim and ScaleAnim programs, which are featured later in this chapter, demonstrate how to use this command.

The ANIMATION POSITION X Command

When you are using the PLACE ANIMATION command, it is convenient to be able to return the position of the movie on the screen. There are two commands for determining the position of the movie. The first command, ANIMATION POSITION X, returns the X position of a movie. The syntax is Return Value = ANIMATION POSITION X (*Animation Number*).

The ANIMATION POSITION Y Command

The other command for determining the position of a movie is ANIMATION POSITION Y, which returns the Y position of a movie. The syntax is Return Value = ANIMATION POSITION Y (*Animation Number*).

The MoveAnim Program

I must admit, I just flew through those position commands! Here's a little something that will help explain the subject in more detail—a complete program called MoveAnim (see Figure 16.4). This program loops a movie while moving it around on the screen and bouncing it off the walls. If this program resembles a sprite demo, it's because the program has a game loop and it updates the movie's position and velocity, just like the sample programs in Chapter 11.

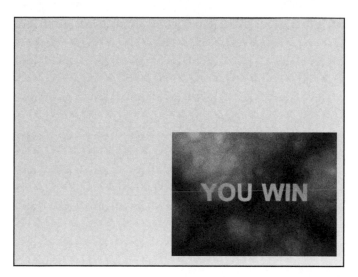

Figure 16.4 *The MoveAnim program moves the position of a movie on the screen while it is playing.*

```
`-----------------------------------
`Beginner's Guide To DarkBASIC Game Programming
`Copyright (C)2002 Jonathan S. Harbour and Joshua R. Smith
`Chapter 16 - MoveAnim Program
`-----------------------------------

`create some variables
X = 0
Y = 0
SPEEDX = 3
SPEEDY = 2

`initialize the program
SET DISPLAY MODE 640, 480, 32
HIDE MOUSE
DISABLE ESCAPEKEY
SYNC ON
CLS

`load background bitmap
LOAD BITMAP "background.bmp", 1
COPY BITMAP 1, 0

`load the animation file
LOAD ANIMATION "youwin1.avi", 1
```

```
`play the animation
LOOP ANIMATION 1

`loop until ESC key pressed
REPEAT
    `restore background under the movie
    COPY BITMAP 1, X, Y, X + 319, Y + 239, 0, X, Y, X + 319, Y + 239

    `update the X position
    X = X + SPEEDX
    IF X < 1 OR X > 315
        SPEEDX = SPEEDX * -1
    ENDIF

    `update the Y position
    Y = Y + SPEEDY
    IF Y < 1 OR Y > 235
        SPEEDY = SPEEDY * -1
    ENDIF

    `reposition the movie
    PLACE ANIMATION 1, X, Y, X + 320, Y + 240

    `update the screen
    SYNC
UNTIL ESCAPEKEY()
DELETE ANIMATION 1
END
```

Changing the Scale of a Movie

Moving the position of a movie is pretty impressive, but it is nothing compared to real-time scaling! *Scale* refers to not only the size of something, but also the ratio of width to height. Although you could scale the horizontal dimension of a 2D object to stretch it left to right, and you could likewise scale the vertical dimension to stretch it top to bottom, that is not true scaling (and it is not particularly useful). Scaling involves resizing both dimensions (horizontal and vertical) by the same amount. That is really the only way to get clean results with a movie.

To change the scale of a movie, you use the same command that you used earlier to reposition a movie—PLACE ANIMATION. For reference, the syntax for this command is PLACE ANIMATION *Animation Number, Left, Top, Right, Bottom*.

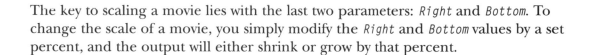

The key to scaling a movie lies with the last two parameters: *Right* and *Bottom*. To change the scale of a movie, you simply modify the *Right* and *Bottom* values by a set percent, and the output will either shrink or grow by that percent.

The ScaleAnim Program

To demonstrate movie scaling, I have written a program called ScaleAnim. Figure 16.5 shows a movie with a very small scale, and Figure 16.6 shows the same movie at 165% of its normal size, nearly filling the screen.

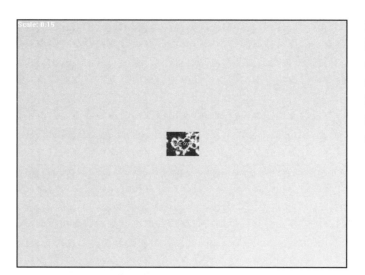

Figure 16.5 *The ScaleAnim program changes the scale of a movie during playback. Here, the movie is reduced to a very small size.*

Figure 16.6 *The ScaleAnim program loops the animation while changing the scale from 10% to 200%.*

```
`----------------------------------
`Beginner's Guide To DarkBASIC Game Programming
`Copyright (C)2002 Jonathan S. Harbour and Joshua R. Smith
`Chapter 16 - ScaleAnim Program
`----------------------------------

`create some variables
scale# = 1.0
change# = 0.05
SX = 0
SY = 0
X = 0
Y = 0

`initialize the program
SET DISPLAY MODE 640, 480, 32
HIDE MOUSE
DISABLE ESCAPEKEY
SYNC ON
CLS

`load background bitmap
LOAD BITMAP "background.bmp", 1
COPY BITMAP 1, 0
SET CURRENT BITMAP 0

`load the animation file
LOAD ANIMATION "gameover2.avi", 1

`play the animation
LOOP ANIMATION 1

`loop until ESC key pressed
REPEAT
    `redraw background
    COPY BITMAP 1, 0

    `change the scale
    scale# = scale# + change#
```

```
    IF scale# < 0.1 OR scale# > 2.0
        change# = change# * -1
    ENDIF


    `reposition the movie
    SX = INT(320 * scale#)
    SY =  INT(240 * scale#)
    X = 320 - SX / 2
    Y = 240 - SY / 2
    PLACE ANIMATION 1, X, Y, X + SX, Y + SY

    TEXT 0,0,"Scale: " + STR$(scale#)


    `update the screen
    SYNC
UNTIL ESCAPEKEY()
DELETE ANIMATION 1
END
```

Movie Trailers

So you can really get a feel for what an introductory movie is like, I recommend
that you download some movie or video game trailers from
http://www.apple.com/trailers or http://www.ifilm.com. However, some movie files
are not in a format supported by DarkBASIC. The three most popular movie formats are Windows Media, Apple QuickTime, and RealPlayer. To play a movie file, it
must be an AVI file in a standard format such as Indeo or Cinepak. As long as you
use a standard format when converting a movie file to AVI for use in DarkBASIC,
the movie will be playable. Many sample movies come with DarkBASIC, such as
those used in the sample programs in this chapter.

As for converting video files, there are numerous programs on the Internet that
you can download and try out or purchase. One such program that I recommend is
EO Video by McGray Ltd. You can learn more about EO Video and download a
trial version from http://www.eo-video.com. I like this program because it can convert from any movie format to another, and it can even combine multiple movie
files into a single output file using any codec (compressor-decompressor) format.

Feel free to modify the PlayMovie program to scale the movies to fill the whole screen. However, at higher than 320×240 (the most common resolution), some movies look grainy, so I prefer to watch them at their native resolution. The amazing thing about DarkBASIC is that you can compile the movies *into* the executable file by choosing Make Final from the File menu (or by pressing F7). Before you build the final executable, make sure that only the desired media files are in the current folder because DarkBASIC links all media files in the folder (in other words, DarkBASIC doesn't parse the source code for file names). DarkBASIC Pro, however, requires you to use the Media settings in the Project Manager. (Simply select the Media button at the bottom-right corner of the screen.)

The PlayMovie Program

The PlayMovie program is similar to the PlayAnim program with the added feature that it centers the movie on the screen. This program also shows how to check the horizontal and vertical resolution of the movie file so it can be centered properly. Previous programs in this chapter hard-coded the playback resolution.

```
`---------------------------------
`Beginner's Guide To DarkBASIC Game Programming
`Copyright (C)2002 Jonathan S. Harbour and Joshua R. Smith
`Chapter 16 - PlayMovie Program
`---------------------------------

`create some variables
Width = 0
Height = 0
X = 0
Y = 0

`initialize the program
SET DISPLAY MODE 640, 480, 32
HIDE MOUSE
DISABLE ESCAPEKEY
CLS

`modify the following line with the appropriate filename
LOAD ANIMATION "moviefile.avi", 1

`get resolution of the movie
```

```
Width = ANIMATION WIDTH(1)
Height = ANIMATION HEIGHT(1)
X = 320 - Width / 2
Y = 240 - Height / 2

`play the animation
PLAY ANIMATION 1, X, Y, X + Width, Y + Height

`wait for keypress
WAIT KEY

`remove the movie from memory
DELETE ANIMATION 1
END
```

Summary

This chapter explored the subject of playing movies for the introduction to a game and for cut-scenes within a game. DarkBASIC supports the AVI format most common on Windows PCs. It is capable of playing any Indeo, Cinepak, or similar codec in an AVI file. This chapter also showed you how to position a movie on the screen, how to move the movie during playback, and how to change the size of the movie by scaling the output rectangle. Finally, the chapter provided some exciting sneak peek trailers of popular games to use while testing the movie playback.

Chapter Quiz

The chapter quiz will help you retain the information that was covered in this chapter, as well as give you an idea about how well you're doing at understanding the subjects. The answers for this quiz can be found in Appendix A, "Answers to the Chapter Quizzes."

1. What does *codec* stand for?

    A. C source code
    B. Compressor-decompressor
    C. Compound decompression
    D. Condenser-defibrillator

2. Which movie file format does DarkBASIC support?

   A. MPG

   B. MOV

   C. WMV

   D. AVI

3. What are arguably the two most significant video codecs for the AVI format?

   A. QuickTime and RealMedia

   B. Indeo and Cinepak

   C. Video-1 and Video-CD

   D. DVD and MPEG-2

4. Which command plays a previously loaded movie file repeatedly?

   A. LOOP ANIMATION

   B. PLACE ANIMATION

   C. REPEAT ANIMATION

   D. PLAY ANIMATION

5. Which movie file format has an .mov extension?

   A. RealMedia

   B. Windows Media Player

   C. QuickTime

   D. MPEG

6. What is the maximum number of movies that can be played on the screen at once in a DarkBASIC program?

   A. 4

   B. 8

   C. 16

   D. 32

7. Which command changes the scale or size of a movie during playback?

   A. SCALE ANIMATION

   B. PLAY ANIMATION

   C. PLACE ANIMATION

   D. SET ANIMATION

8. Which command retrieves the current horizontal position of a movie?

    A. ANIMATION X

    B. ANIMATION POSITION X

    C. ANIMATION GET X

    D. GET ANIMATION X

9. Which command moves a movie to another position on the screen?

    A. MOVE ANIMATION

    B. PLACE ANIMATION

    C. SET ANIMATION

    D. POSITION ANIMATION

10. In what year was the game *Wing Commander II: Vengeance of the Kilrathi* released?

    A. 1989

    B. 1990

    C. 1991

    D. 1992

PART III

Advanced Topics: 3D Graphics and Multiplayer Programming

Welcome to Part III of *Beginner's Guide to DarkBASIC Game Programming*. Part III includes two chapters that cover the more advanced subjects of 3D graphics programming and multiplayer programming. These subjects are more suited to power users because they delve into topics that require a significant amount of prerequisite information and are not easy to explain in simple terms. The 3D chapter does a good job of explaining in detail the basics of 3D programming, from simple wire-frame triangles to complex textured scenes, replete with light sources and multiple cameras. Likewise, the multiplayer chapter explores the basic commands for connecting multiple PCs in a network-enabled game and then walks you through developing a complete game from scratch. This game, called Crazy CARnage, is a good resource to teach you how a complete game is written.

17 Fundamentals of 3D Graphics Programming

18 Multiplayer Programming: The Crazy CARnage Game

CHAPTER 17

FUNDAMENTALS OF 3D GRAPHICS PROGRAMMING

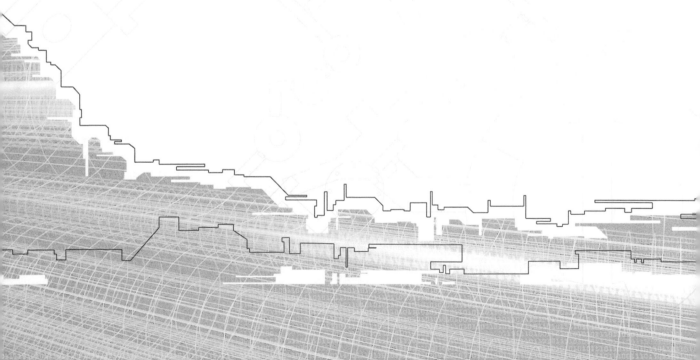

Today games are developed almost exclusively in 3D, and the era of the traditional 2D game is practically at an end. Although there are still many 2D games being developed for platforms such as Game Boy Advance, such games are in the minority and are highly proprietary. This chapter focuses on 3D graphics programming. You will learn the basics of how to create and draw 3D objects, such as triangles, rectangles, cubes, cones, and cylinders, as well as how to apply textures to such objects. This chapter provides you with what you might call a low-level view of 3D graphics, because you will have an opportunity to create 3D objects from scratch using source code, providing that extremely important foundation for more advanced techniques (such as meshes).

The one thing that this chapter does *not* do is bore you with 3D theory. Instead, I have designed this chapter to explain the specific DarkBASIC commands that you need to write 3D programs. There is value in understanding the underlying matrix mathematics involved in rendering a 3D scene, but the subject can become overwhelming quickly! Rather than spend time explaining the details, this chapter just shows you the steps for getting a 3D game up on the screen. After all, do you really care how a texture is wrapped around a mesh? If you do, then why are you reading a beginner book? Just kidding! But if you would like more depth, I recommend that you pick up a book dedicated to 3D programming, such as *Beginning Direct3D Game Programming* (Premier Press, 2001), which is listed in Appendix B, "Recommended Books and Web Sites."

This chapter is chock full of sample source code listings! If you struggle with any specific subject related to 3D graphics, you will surely be able to figure out what is going on by running the sample programs in this chapter. This chapter differs from the others in that the sample programs are for DarkBASIC Professional, rather than for standard DarkBASIC. If you are a regular DarkBASIC Pro user, then this will be welcome. However, if you have been using standard DarkBASIC throughout the book, you can load the projects (which are available for both versions) off the CD-ROM. You can also install DarkBASIC Pro to type in and run the programs in this chapter. (The DarkBASIC Pro demo is available on the CD-ROM.)

This chapter covers the following topics:

- Introduction to 3D Graphics
- Basic 3D Graphics Commands
- Lighting the Scene
- The 3D Camera

Introduction to 3D Graphics

The subject of 3D graphics truly consists of a monumental amount of information. Not only have entire books been written just about the basics of 3D graphics, but entire sets of volumes have been dedicated to the subject of advanced 3D rendering techniques. The 3D graphics business is a multi-billion dollar industry that encompasses video games and the motion picture industry, as well as commercial aviation and military applications. The astonishing thing about 3D graphics is how much they have improved over the years, both in theory and in application. There are techniques in use today, such as mip-mapping and multi-texturing, that are staggering in their realism. It is quite possible to mistake a real-time 3D demonstration for a pre-rendered video because the quality of rendered graphics today is so astonishing. Figure 17.1 shows a sample program called Light1, which comes with

Figure 17.1

The Light1 example program from DarkBASIC Professional, rendered with an ATI Mobility M4 (a laptop graphics chip)

DarkBASIC Professional. It shows just one example (among the many examples that come with the compiler) of the 3D capabilities built into DarkBASIC. In this example, only two light sources are used.

Although visual quality is really just a factor of your video card's features and capabilities, it does not take extraordinarily complex scenes to make a great game. Realism is definitely a good thing, but only if the majority of PCs in the world are able to run the game! The one thing you definitely do not want to do is limit the potential audience for your game by putting in so many high-quality scenes and models that it requires the very latest generation of video card to run the game. The latest generation Nvidia graphics accelerator is the GeForce4 Ti 4600 chip, which is capable of drawing 136 million vertices and 4.8 billion pixels per second. These numbers might not mean anything to you, but later in this chapter you will learn more about vertices and pixel fill rate. Take a look at Figure 17.2 for a photo of an MSI video card based on the Nvidia GeForce4 Ti 4200 chip.

You might have a similar video card in your PC, or something even more exotic! The point is that the video card does all the complicated work involved in rendering the 3D graphics in a game. In the old days before 3D accelerators came along (such as during the early '90s), the main CPU was tasked with doing all of the 3D calculations. Suffice it to say, CPUs in the early '90s were not particularly fast in the first place, let alone when required to render a 3D scene. Today, a single ATI Radeon 9700 chip is capable of more than a trillion calculations per second—many thousands of times faster than an original Intel Pentium chip.

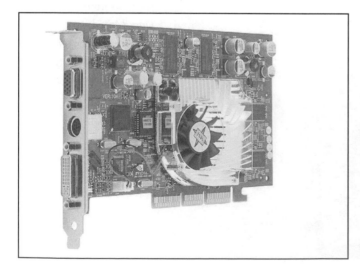

Figure 17.2

A GeForce4 Ti 4200 chip powers this video card. Notice the large heat sink and fan that keep the GPU chip from overheating.

Due to such advances in silicon technology, extraordinarily powerful graphics work-stations are available in the most common new PCs that you might peruse at a local computer store—usually for less than $2,000. Such a thing was unheard of just a few years ago! Figure 17.3 shows the same Light1 program running on a PC with a GeForce4, with all seven light sources enabled.

DarkBASIC does a great job of simplifying the complexity of programming 3D graphics with DirectX 8.1, with a large assortment of special effects and next-generation graphical features made possible by the latest video cards. One of the goals of this chapter is to demonstrate the difference that the video card can make in visual quality and performance because these factors are so important when it comes to 3D graphics programming. If you have an older video card, such as an ATI Rage 128, Nvidia TNT2, 3Dfx Voodoo3, or another video card that does not provide hardware transform and lighting (the increasingly hyped T&L feature), then you will likely not be able to use the advanced features available with the DirectX 8.1-based DarkBASIC Pro. However, the original DarkBASIC (often referred to as DBV1), which is based on DirectX 7.0a, will work fine with pre-T&L video cards. As a matter of fact, you can still use DarkBASIC Pro with an older video card, but some code won't run properly or at all. Therefore, in some cases I will show a sample program running on a low-end system, and then the same

Figure 17.3 *The Light1 example program rendered with a GeForce4 with all seven light sources enabled*

program running on a high-end system with the frame rate inhibitor turned off. That way, you will be able to compare raw performance to visual quality.

Introduction to Vertices

Now let's jump into the details and learn the basics of 3D graphics. Trust me, you will appreciate this information down the road when you start working with advanced 3D scenes and 3D objects. It's okay if you have never written a 3D program before, because this chapter will show you how to load and draw 3D objects on the screen. For now, let's start at the beginning.

What Is a Vertex?

The first question that you must ask before doing anything in 3D is: What is a vertex? It is the atom of the 3D realm, the lowest common denominator, the most basic entity of a 3D world. If you think of a 3D world as a pool of water, then a vertex is analogous to an H_2O molecule. A vertex is actually a point in geometric space. Do you have any experience with geometry? In high school, the class that unifies geometry and algebra is called trigonometry. Whether or not you are interested in the subject, I can't stress enough how a little background refresher in geometry will make you a more formidable 3D programmer. As the previous chapters in this book have testified, it takes a lot to explain the basics of something that is rather complicated—like programming a game.

Now, don't let me worry you. You won't need trigonometry to write a 3D game with DarkBASIC because it was designed to make game programming as simple as possible by handling all the math in the background, so to speak. In the 3D graphics world, trigonometry describes how 3D objects can be rotated, moved, and scaled on the screen. I will explain the different ways that DarkBASIC uses trigonometry to create 3D objects throughout this chapter.

TIP

The Math League is an awesome online resource for information related to trigonometry, geometry, and 3D math. It has a useful Web page that describes vertices and polygons at http://www.mathleague.com/help/geometry/polygons.htm.

A vertex can be described as a 3D geometric point. The 3D world is mapped around the Cartesian coordinate system. A 3D point has three components: X, Y, and Z. Three vertices

A *vertex* is a point in 3D space with **X**, **Y**, and **Z** coordinates.

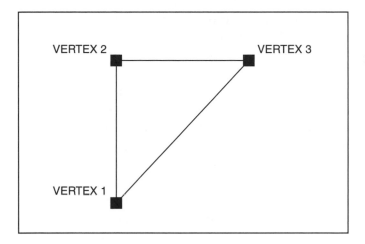

Figure 17.4 *Three vertices make up a polygon.*

make up a polygon, the basis for 3D graphics. Take a look at Figure 17.4 for an illustration of vertices.

Because 3D graphics are based on trigonometry, 3D formulas also use the Cartesian coordinate system for drawing, moving, rotating, and scaling vertices. The Cartesian coordinate system (shown in Figure 17.5) is the basis for all 3D graphics rendering.

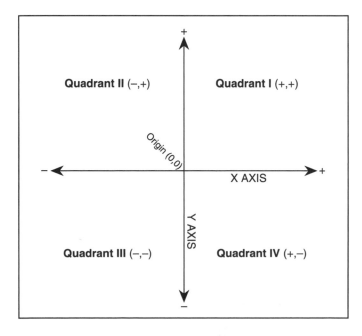

Figure 17.5 *3D math is based on the Cartesian coordinate system.*

However, in 3D space there are three dimensions on the coordinate system, requiring an additional axis called Z (see Figure 17.6). If you have a hard time visualizing the Z axis, just think of Z as moving away from you. Hold your hand in the air in front of your face and move it away from you, and then back toward you. That is the Z axis. The motion going away from you is the positive Z axis, and moving your hand back toward you is the negative Z axis. As for Figure 17.6, imagine the X and Y axes moving back and forth along the Z axis. That is exactly what happens when you are dealing with three dimensions. The lesser two dimensions are represented "on" the third dimension in what seems like many copies of those two dimensions. On the computer screen, when you are rendering an object in 3D space, the Z axis determines how far away the object is from the camera. Although there might be an absolute origin (0,0,0) in the 3D scene, you can think of the camera as the local origin. Every object in 3D space in relation to the game's camera can be represented by distance as a Z axis value.

Do this illustration and analogy help you to visualize the Z axis and the third dimension? If you understand this, then you also should be able to visualize the fourth dimension (or 4D), which is time. I don't want to sound like a guest speaker at a physics convention (or a science fiction convention, for that matter), but time is just as important in a 3D game as the other three dimensions. Unfortunately,

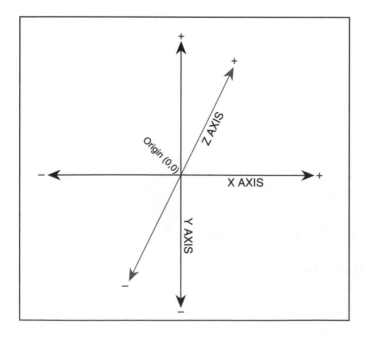

Figure 17.6

A 3D coordinate system with a Z axis

Table 17.1 Four-Dimensional Space and Time

Dimension	Axis	Description
First	X	Left and right
Second	Y	Up and down
Third	Z	In and out
Fourth	T	Forward and backward

there is no easy way to illustrate a 4D coordinate system on paper. Table 17.1 puts the four dimensions into words.

Let me take the illustration with your hand one step further to explain time. Hold up your hand again to represent an object in 3D space. If you move your hand left to right, it is moving on the X axis. Move your hand up and down, and that is the Y axis. As I explained before, move your hand away from you and then back, and that is the Z axis. Now what about the T axis, representing the fourth dimension of time? While still holding your hand out in front of you (and moving it any way you want), stand up and take a step forward. Now take a step back. You have just translated your imaginary hand coordinate system into the fourth dimension.

Interested in whacking your brain even further? It's really all just a matter of perspective. Imagine where you are located in relation to your surroundings. Your body is a coordinate system. You can move left to right, up and down, in and out, and forward and backward. But what if you are walking around doing this on a train or a commercial airplane? Your imaginary coordinate system stays with you, and yet that whole coordinate system is moving *in another coordinate system itself*! You have just imagined how a fifth dimension might work. Of course, that is not useful for anything other than a fascinating discussion.

Vertices Are the Point

A 3D scene is nothing more than a huge collection of points, which is all the computer really sees. The video card fills in the pixels between the points, and that's about all there is to 3D rendering. When you look at the stratospheric polygon counts announced with each new video card release, the figure is only relevant when you consider that a polygon can be made up of just three points. There is no rule that there *must* be something between the points, although common sense would dictate as much. Video card capabilities are published on tiny triangles, if not without pixels then perhaps with as few filled pixels as necessary to call it a polygon. What is the reasoning behind this? Why would anyone want to announce a polygon fill rate that is half the fill rate of a competitor's card? Realistically, fill rates are only as useful as the game that uses them, and that is the point at which true benchmarks should be measured. There might be a video card with published polygon fill rates of ten billion triangles that can only run *Jedi Knight II: Jedi Outcast* at 20 FPS at the highest resolution.

The quality of a rendered scene is far more important than raw fill rate. The latest video cards support not only hardware transform and lighting, but also full-screen anti-aliasing (or FSAA). This is a technique that smoothes the jagged edges of objects on the screen, making a game look more realistic and less pixelated. Transform and lighting (which is often referred to as T&L or TnL) is one of those unfortunate computing technologies, such as MMX, that everyone wants but that few understand. The first T&L chip was invented by Nvidia and called the GeForce GPU (*Graphics Processing Unit*). This new naming convention was nothing short of brilliant marketing on the part of Nvidia, and it made the GeForce chip clearly stand out as the next greatest thing in computer graphics.

The GeForce name comes from "geometry force," and sounds like the term "G-force," which is familiar to pilots and flight simulator fans. But to the core, this new chip *is* a geometry force—the first chip of its kind to offload the mathematics required to rotate, translate, and scale points in 3D, as well as apply lighting effects to a polygon. Thus the term *transform and lighting* was born. In fact, modern GPUs perform so many astounding special effects that T&L is hardly the latest thing any more. Now that a base standard for graphics has arisen from the competitive conflict between ATI and Nvidia—the two chief rivals of the PC graphics industry today—the technology has reached a plateau in which astounding quality in addition to breakneck performance is to be expected. New techniques such as bump-mapping are giving normally flat polygons a real-life texture that raises the quality bar a number of levels and brings cinema-quality graphics to computer games.

Introduction to Polygons

The ironic thing about all this new technology is that it all comes back to the vertices—the points that make up a polygon, which makes up an object, which creates a scene. Vertices are useless unless they are connected to form lines. Three connected lines make the simplest polygon—a triangle. Although it might seem like three lines would have six points, that is only relevant if the lines are disconnected. By adding each line to the end of another line, the three lines are connected with only three points. A polygon with three vertices is called a triangle. There are many types of polygons, as described in Table 17.2.

Table 17.2 Polygons and Vertex Count

Figure	Polygon Name	Number of Vertices
	Triangle	3
	Quadrilateral	4
	Pentagon	5
	Hexagon	6
	Heptagon	7
	Octagon	8
	Nonagon	9
	Decagon	10

Drawing a Wire-Frame Triangle

Ready for your first sample 3D program? Okay, this one is really short, but the educational value of this small program is significant when you read the paragraphs that follow the listing. For now, type this program into DarkBASIC Pro and then save it as Wireframe. Alternatively, you can load this project off the CD-ROM under the folder for this chapter. Recall that this listing and those that follow were written for DarkBASIC Pro and may require modification to run under standard DarkBASIC. You can simply load the projects off the CD-ROM for whichever version you prefer. Note that some features covered here are not available with standard DarkBASIC.

```
`----------------------------------
`Beginner's Guide To DarkBASIC Game Programming
`Copyright (C)2002 Jonathan S. Harbour and Joshua R. Smith
`Chapter 17 - Wireframe Program
`----------------------------------

`set up the screen
SYNC ON
SYNC RATE 30
COLOR BACKDROP RGB(0,0,0)
INK RGB(255,255,255),0

`create a triangle
MAKE OBJECT TRIANGLE 1,0,0,0,0,10,0,10,10,0

`center triangle at the origin
MOVE OBJECT LEFT 1, 5
MOVE OBJECT DOWN 1, 5

`draw the triangle as a wireframe
SET OBJECT WIREFRAME 1, 1

`drag camera back away from object
MOVE CAMERA -12

`wait for a keypress
```

```
REPEAT
    SYNC
UNTIL ESCAPEKEY() = 1

END
```

Now go ahead and run the program, and you should see a triangle like the one shown in Figure 17.7. If you look closely at the figure, it might seem a bit fuzzy at the edges. In fact, the lines are not quite distinct, particularly when you look at the output of the program in contrast to the printed figure.

Here, let me zoom in on the figure and show you a closer view of the triangle in Figure 17.8. Do you see how smooth the edges of the lines that make up this triangle look?

Now I will zoom in even closer, this time on the upper-right corner. Figure 17.9 has been scaled by a factor of eight so you can see up close what the lines of the triangle look like. Do you see how there is a somewhat brighter central line with several levels of darker shading around each pixel of the line? That dark-gray color was supposed to be white, because the Wireframe program was given a color of RGB (255,255,255), which is pure white. However, the GeForce4 automatically anti-aliased the scene, producing this altered representation of the white line. Although it is possible (and in some cases desirable) to turn off anti-aliasing in the Windows

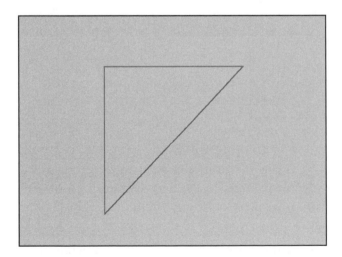

Figure 17.7 *The Wireframe program draws a wire-frame triangle on the screen.*

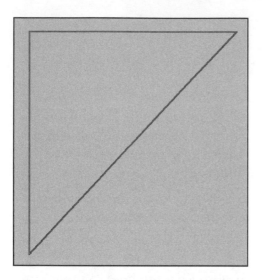

Figure 17.8 *The zoomed-in triangle produced by the Wireframe program*

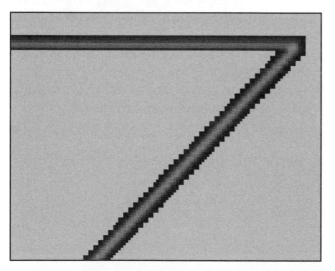

Figure 17.9 *A close-up view of one corner of the triangle produced by the Wireframe program shows anti-aliasing at work.*

Display Settings (via the Control Panel), a fully textured game world looks magnificent with this feature enabled. The only downside is that simple wire-frame polygons like this triangle will emphasize the imperfection that anti-aliasing inflicts on the geometry of a scene.

Some games look terrific with full-screen anti-aliasing (FSAA) turned on, while others run poorly, so it is up to you to decide whether to use FSAA (if your video card supports it, that is). There are also several different FSAA modes from which to choose. Consult your video card manufacturer as well as reviews to determine which FSAA method works best on your card. In the case of my GeForce4 Ti 4200, the card used to produce the triangle shown in the Wireframe program, I chose the Quincunx Antialiasing™ mode, as shown in the display settings in Figure 17.10.

One interesting thing you can do with the FSAA settings is select each mode in your display settings and then run a sample program in DarkBASIC Pro (such as the TexturedCube program later in this chapter) to see for yourself how each FSAA mode affects the quality and performance of the program. Better yet, run a complete game with each mode for a more effective demonstration!

Drawing a Wire-Frame Cube

Now you'll take the wire-frame concept a step further and draw a wire-frame cube. The only difference between a wired cube and a shaded cube is a command called SET OBJECT WIREFRAME, which must be set in order to view something in a wire-frame, but the results can be very interesting, not to mention educational. Figure 17.11 shows the WiredCube program with culling turned off. *Culling* is the process of removing non-visible polygons from an object in which a polygon is behind another polygon in the Z axis. Compare this to Figure 17.12, which shows the same cube with culling turned on (the default), hiding the invisible polygons.

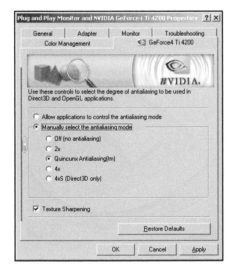

Figure 17.10

Anti-aliasing settings can drastically affect the quality and performance of your video card, so take care when choosing a high-quality mode that might produce a lower frame rate.

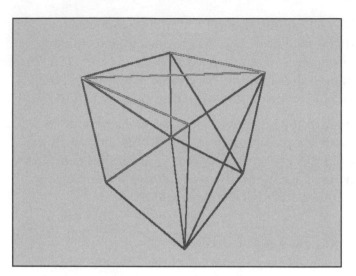

Figure 17.11 *The WiredCube program with culling turned off shows all of the triangles that make up the cube.*

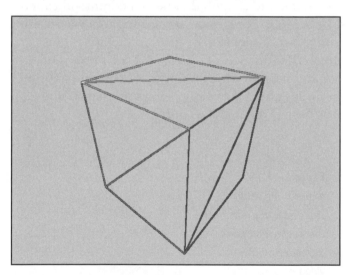

Figure 17.12 *The WiredCube program with culling turned on shows only those triangles in view of the camera.*

```
`-----------------------------------
`Beginner's Guide To DarkBASIC Game Programming
`Copyright (C)2002 Jonathan S. Harbour and Joshua R. Smith
`Chapter 17 - WiredCube Program
`-----------------------------------

`set up the screen
SYNC ON
```

```
SYNC RATE 30
COLOR BACKDROP RGB(0,0,0)
INK RGB(255,255,255),0

`create a triangle
MAKE OBJECT CUBE 1, 50

`draw the triangle as a wireframe
SET OBJECT WIREFRAME 1, 1

`uncomment to show away-facing polygons
`SET OBJECT CULL 1, 0

`move the camera out for a better view
POSITION CAMERA 50, 50, -60
POINT CAMERA 0, 0, 0

`wait for a keypress
REPEAT
    SYNC
UNTIL ESCAPEKEY() = 1

END
```

Drawing a Shaded Polygon

Wire-frame models make for an interesting discussion on 3D theory, but they are really not much to see. After all, who is writing wire-frame vector graphics games today? That sort of thing ended a couple decades ago! If you have a modern video card, it should be against the law to use your billion-operations-per-second GPU to draw wire-frame models. Therefore, I'm going to teach you how to add some color and shading to a polygon. Later, I will show you how to fully texture a polygon with a bitmap image, which is the goal of this discussion, and the way games are designed today.

A simple triangle without the SET OBJECT WIREFRAME command will result in a shaded white surface, which is rather dull. Instead of white, it is desirable to apply some other color to the surface when dealing with shaded polygons. To do so you can employ the SET OBJECT COLOR command, as the following Triangle program demonstrates. Figure 17.13 shows the output of the Triangle program, which draws and rotates a triangle on the screen. Figure 17.14 shows another random triangle

Figure 17.13
A triangle is made up of three vertices (and therefore three sides).

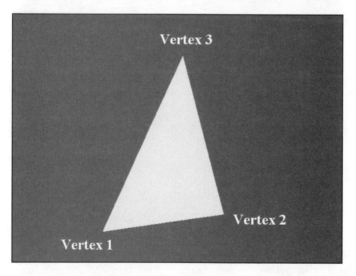

Figure 17.14 *The Triangle program demonstrates the simplest 3D object that can be rendered in DarkBASIC.*

on the screen, but I have added some labels to it so you can see the vertices that make up the polygon.

The Triangle program uses two new commands for working with polygons, XROTATE OBJECT and YROTATE OBJECT. These commands are passed the object number and a value by which the relevant axis should be rotated. To rotate an object in the same direction endlessly, you can use the OBJECT ANGLE X(), OBJECT ANGLE Y(), and OBJECT ANGLE Z() commands.

> ## NOTE
>
> At this late stage in the book, I have opted not to display the syntax for every command due to space considerations; there are hundreds of 3D commands in DarkBASIC Pro! Instead, I will simply teach by example, and you will get the hang of using these new commands simply by practice. If you would like detailed information about any command, refer to the **DarkBASIC Language Reference on the CD-ROM.**

```
`----------------------------------
`Beginner's Guide To DarkBASIC Game Programming
`Copyright (C)2002 Jonathan S. Harbour and Joshua R. Smith
`Chapter 17 - Triangle Program
`----------------------------------

`enable manual screen refresh
SYNC ON
SYNC RATE 100

`set some initial settings
HIDE MOUSE
COLOR BACKDROP RGB(0,40,40)
RANDOMIZE TIMER()

`create a colored triangle
MAKE OBJECT TRIANGLE 1,-10,-10,0,-10,10,0,10,10,0
COLOR OBJECT 1,RGB(RND(255),RND(255),RND(255))

`move camera back away from object
MOVE CAMERA -20

`main loop
REPEAT
    `rotate the X axis of the triangle
    XROTATE OBJECT 1, OBJECT ANGLE X(1) + 1
    `rotate the Y axis of the triangle
```

```
        YROTATE OBJECT 1, OBJECT ANGLE Y(1) + 1
        `update the screen
        SYNC
UNTIL ESCAPEKEY() = 1


`clean up
SHOW MOUSE
END
```

Drawing a Shaded Quadrilateral

A quadrilateral is a polygon with four vertices and four sides, which might not be
made up of right triangles. (In other words, it might not be a perfect rectangle.)
Most flat surfaces in a 3D scene are made up of triangles of varying sizes and
shapes, and that is what this sample program demonstrates. The Quadrilateral program creates a shape by combining two rectangles on the same plane. The result is
a two-tone quadrilateral surface, as shown in Figure 17.15.

Figure 17.16 shows the vertices that make up a polygon comprised of two triangles,
called a *triangle list*. Although this is the best way to visualize the process while
learning, there is actually an optimized way to render triangles that reduces the
number of vertices by having adjacent triangles simply share vertices. This is called
a *triangle strip*.

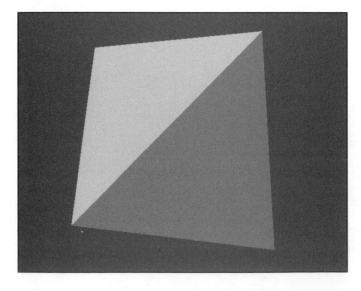

Figure 17.15
*A quadrilateral is
made up of two
joined triangles.*

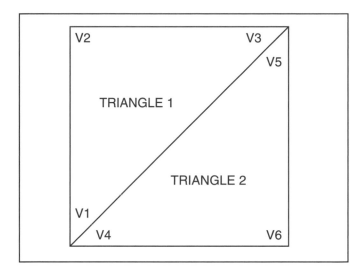

Figure 17.16
Polygons can be divided into interconnected triangles of varying levels of complexity.

Figure 17.17 shows another random quadrilateral, but I have inserted labels showing the position of each vertex and how the two triangles share two corners, similar to the diagram in Figure 17.16.

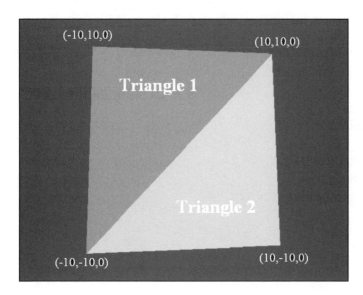

Figure 17.17
The output of the Quadrilateral program, with labels added to describe the vertices and triangles that make up the quadrilateral

```
`-----------------------------------
`Beginner's Guide To DarkBASIC Game Programming
`Copyright (C)2002 Jonathan S. Harbour and Joshua R. Smith
`Chapter 17 - Quadrilateral Program
`-----------------------------------

`enable manual screen refresh
SYNC ON
SYNC RATE 100

`set some initial settings
HIDE MOUSE
COLOR BACKDROP RGB(0,40,40)
RANDOMIZE TIMER()

`create a colored triangle
MAKE OBJECT TRIANGLE 1,-10,-10,0,-10,10,0,10,10,0
COLOR OBJECT 1,RGB(RND(255),RND(255),RND(255))
MAKE OBJECT TRIANGLE 2,-10,-10,0,10,10,0,10,-10,0
COLOR OBJECT 2,RGB(RND(255),RND(255),RND(255))

`move camera back away from object
MOVE CAMERA -20

`main loop
REPEAT
    `rotate the X axis of the triangle
    XROTATE OBJECT 1, OBJECT ANGLE X(1) + 1
    XROTATE OBJECT 2, OBJECT ANGLE X(2) + 1
    `rotate the Y axis of the triangle
    YROTATE OBJECT 1, OBJECT ANGLE Y(1) + 1
    YROTATE OBJECT 2, OBJECT ANGLE Y(2) + 1
    `update the screen
    SYNC
UNTIL ESCAPEKEY() = 1

`clean up
SHOW MOUSE
END
```

Drawing a Rectangle

DarkBASIC Pro has a `MAKE OBJECT PLAIN` command that creates a rectangle (a quadrilateral with 90-degree angles) without joining two triangles (as you did previously). Figure 17.18 shows the output of the Rectangle program, in which the rectangle is rotating in 3D space. I have also included a picture of the rectangle as a wire-frame by using the `SET OBJECT WIREFRAME` command, which you saw earlier. Figure 17.19 demonstrates how DarkBASIC Pro builds a stock "surface" out of triangles.

Figure 17.18

A simple plain object is made up of two right triangles and can be a root limb for a more complex object.

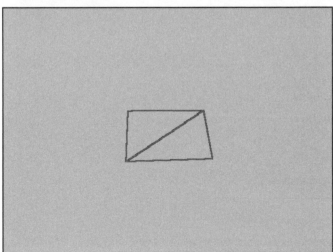

Figure 17.19

Setting the plain object to be drawn in wire-frame reveals that the object is actually made up of two triangles.

> **NOTE**
>
> In standard DarkBASIC, you use the SET OBJECT command to turn on wire-frame.

```
`---------------------------------
`Beginner's Guide To DarkBASIC Game Programming
`Copyright (C)2002 Jonathan S. Harbour and Joshua R. Smith
`Chapter 17 - Rectangle Program
`---------------------------------

`enable manual screen refresh
SYNC ON
SYNC RATE 100

`set some initial settings
HIDE MOUSE
COLOR BACKDROP RGB(0,40,40)
RANDOMIZE TIMER()

`create a colored triangle
MAKE OBJECT PLAIN 1, RND(10) + 1, RND(10) + 1
COLOR OBJECT 1,RGB(RND(255),RND(255),RND(255))

`uncomment to draw in wireframe
`SET OBJECT WIREFRAME 1, 1

`main loop
REPEAT
    `rotate the X axis of the triangle
    XROTATE OBJECT 1, OBJECT ANGLE X(1) - 0.75
    `rotate the Y axis of the triangle
    YROTATE OBJECT 1, OBJECT ANGLE Y(1) + 1
    `update the screen
    SYNC
UNTIL ESCAPEKEY() = 1

`clean up
SHOW MOUSE
END
```

Basic 3D Graphics Commands

That was quite a fast-paced first half of the chapter, wouldn't you agree? It has been fun, though, to learn all about wire-frame and solid objects and how DarkBASIC Pro creates objects and draws them. Now I would like to up the ante, so to speak, and give you more 3D graphics programming power by talking about some of the more powerful commands in DarkBASIC Pro.

> **NOTE**
>
> Although this chapter is geared for DarkBASIC Pro, I have not forgotten about DBVI users. The source code listings might be slightly different, but you can find DBVI versions of the sample programs in this chapter on the CD-ROM. I am focusing on DBPro to provide as much up-to-date information as possible.

Creating Stock Objects

You have already seen some of the stock objects in DarkBASIC Pro, such as the triangle, plain, and cube. Now I would like to cover all of the stock objects and then provide you with a demonstration program to show you how to use them.

The MAKE OBJECT TRIANGLE Command

I'll start with the easiest object, just for reference. This command is used to create a simple triangle in whatever shape you prefer. The syntax for this command is `MAKE OBJECT TRIANGLE Object Number, X1, Y1, Z1, X2, Y2, Z2, X3, Y3, Z3`.

There are so many parameters for this command because a triangle is the polygon by which all other 3D objects are constructed, and it requires the most flexibility. There are many different shapes and sizes possible with a triangle, not just the right-triangle variety with a 90-degree angle. With enough creativity, you can create any 3D object that you can imagine entirely out of triangles. This object is the building block of all others.

The MAKE OBJECT PLAIN Command

A plain is a quadrilateral (or rectangle) with two sets of equal sides and four right angles that equal 360 degrees in total. To create a rectangle, simply pass the width and height to the MAKE OBJECT PLAIN command. The syntax is MAKE OBJECT PLAIN *Object Number, Width, Height.*

The MAKE OBJECT CUBE Command

The MAKE OBJECT CUBE command constructs a cube that is comprised of six sides (and therefore 12 triangles). Due to the number of polygons involved, a cube has eight vertices—one for each corner. The important thing to remember is that this command constructs a cube of equal dimensions on all sides. (In contrast, the MAKE OBJECT BOX command builds an object with a different height, width, and depth.) The syntax for this command is MAKE OBJECT CUBE *Object Number, Size.*

The MAKE OBJECT BOX Command

The MAKE OBJECT BOX command creates a 3D object that is similar to a cube, but that might have different dimensions for the width, height, and depth. The result is akin to a 3D rectangle. (In contrast, the MAKE OBJECT CUBE command builds an object with the same height, width, and depth.) The format for this command is MAKE OBJECT BOX *Object Number, Width, Height, Depth.*

The MAKE OBJECT CYLINDER Command

To create a cylinder object, which you might use as a telephone pole or a drinking cup, use the MAKE OBJECT CYLINDER command. The syntax is MAKE OBJECT CYLINDER *Object Number, Size.*

The MAKE OBJECT CONE Command

The MAKE OBJECT CONE command creates a cone-shaped object that resembles an ice cream cone. The syntax is MAKE OBJECT CONE *Object Number, Size.*

The MAKE OBJECT SPHERE Command

A sphere is a complex 3D object consisting of many triangles in the proper orientation to give a spherical appearance (which you might use, for example, to render a planet in space). You can create a sphere using the MAKE OBJECT SPHERE command.

The syntax is MAKE OBJECT SPHERE *Object Number*, *Size*, *Rows*, *Columns*. You can use the *Rows* and *Columns* parameters for this command to provide DarkBASIC with more detail on the number of polygons in the sphere.

Transforming and Drawing 3D Objects

When you have created a stock 3D object using one of the commands covered earlier, you can then instruct DarkBASIC to manipulate and draw the object on the screen. Transforming is a process by which something changes orientation, position, or scale. The precise terms for this are rotation, translation, and scaling, respectively. *Rotation* refers to the angle by which an object is displayed on each of the three axes (X, Y, and Z). *Translation* is the process of moving an object in 3D space using the three axes. *Scaling* involves changing the size of an object.

Possibly the most important thing to consider when you are working in 3D is the viewpoint, or the position of the so-called "camera." Although there is no physical (or logical) camera in the 3D scene, it is a practical analogy to describe the process of setting the viewpoint (and viewport) of the scene. The camera can be moved and rotated independently of any 3D objects in the scene, which can be quite useful. Often the functioning of the camera will make or break a game, despite the amount of work that has gone into it. If the camera is unwieldy, moves too often, or prevents the player from seeing what is going on in the game (such as the infamous problem with the player walking "toward" the camera and thus being unable to see anything), it will simply ruin a game. You must take great care and pay attention to the code that positions the camera in a scene. Often the best policy is just to leave the camera at a bird's-eye view and let the game run normally below the camera. (This might be useful in a strategy war game, for example.)

Although scaling is also a transformation, I don't use it very often. Scaling might be useful if you wanted to use a common stock size for all enemies in a game, and you wanted to enlarge some models for boss characters. You might also have a stock size and want to reduce models; for instance, to render a flock of birds where the model size is rather large by default.

The MakeObjects Program

The MakeObjects program demonstrates how to create several stock 3D objects and then rotate and move those objects around in a circular formation. This program shows how to transform objects (remember: rotation, translation, and scaling) and position the camera. Figure 17.20 shows the output of the MakeObjects program running in normal mode, and Figure 17.21 shows the program running at the fastest possible speed (which is useful for benchmarking the game loop).

Figure 17.20
The MakeObjects program draws five stock 3D objects rotating in a circle on the screen.

Figure 17.21 *The MakeObjects program, running without a frame rate limit*

```
`-----------------------------------
`Beginner's Guide To DarkBASIC Game Programming
`Copyright (C)2002 Jonathan S. Harbour and Joshua R. Smith
`Chapter 17 - MakeObjects Program
`-----------------------------------

`create some arrays
DIM angle(5)
DIM posx(5)
DIM posz(5)

`initialize the program
SYNC ON
SYNC RATE 100
HIDE MOUSE
COLOR BACKDROP RGB(0,40,40)

`create a cube
MAKE OBJECT CUBE 1,50
COLOR OBJECT 1, rgb(255,0,0)

`create a cone
MAKE OBJECT CONE 2,50
COLOR OBJECT 2, RGB(0,255,0)

`create a sphere
MAKE OBJECT SPHERE 3,50
COLOR OBJECT 3, RGB(0,0,255)

`create a box
MAKE OBJECT BOX 4, 50, 25, 25
COLOR OBJECT 4, RGB(255,255,0)

`create a cylinder
MAKE OBJECT CYLINDER 5, 50
COLOR OBJECT 5, RGB(0,255,255)

`reposition the camera to get the whole view
PITCH CAMERA DOWN 25
MOVE CAMERA -200
```

```
`set initial angles for each object
angle(1) = 0
angle(2) = 72
angle(3) = 144
angle(4) = 216
angle(5) = 288
radius = 150


`start the loop
REPEAT
    `move the objects in a circle
    FOR n = 1 TO 5
        `calculate X position using cosine
        posx(n) = COS(angle(n)) * radius
        `calculate Y position using sine
        posz(n) = SIN(angle(n)) * radius
        `increment the angle
        angle(n) = angle(n) + 1
        `move and rotate the object
        POSITION OBJECT n, posx(n), 0, posz(n)
        XROTATE OBJECT n, OBJECT ANGLE X(n) + 1
        YROTATE OBJECT n, OBJECT ANGLE Y(n) + 0.5
    next n

    `display frame rate and update the screen
    TEXT SCREEN WIDTH()-80, SCREEN HEIGHT()-30, "FPS: " + STR$(SCREEN FPS())
    SYNC
UNTIL ESCAPEKEY() = 1

`clean up
SHOW MOUSE
END
```

Adding Textures to 3D Objects

For many years, video games used shaded polygons to build their 3D worlds; before that, they used wire-frame graphics. (Remember *Battlezone*?) What truly makes a game realistic, though, is the use of textures. Texturing is a process by which a bitmap image is pasted onto a polygon. That is the gist of it in simple terms. However, the process of mapping pixels to a polygon and even wrapping a texture around an entire 3D object is quite complicated. Add to this the real-world need for extreme speed in a texture mapper, and there can be some serious problems in a software-only solution. That is why all modern video cards paste textures to polygons in the hardware—the silicon 3D chip itself does the texture mapping. As you have probably noticed while playing a recent game, hardware 3D is impressive. Before hardware texture mapping was brought to the PC, software texture mapping code relied on a fast processor to work.

Half-Life featured a software texture mapper within its 3D engine that was quite sophisticated (which was no surprise, given that it was based on *Quake II*). However, the most impressive software-texturing algorithm in the world has no hope of competing with a hardware renderer. I remember the first time I saw a game running on a 3D-accelerated PC. It was the original *Quake*, running an OpenGL driver on a 3Dfx Voodoo card. The difference between software-rendered *Quake* and hardware-rendered *Quake* was astounding! Suffice it to say, it is a given today that all 3D games must be textured and hardware accelerated. Software-only solutions don't have a hope of competing (nor should anyone argue any longer against a game that is dependent on 3D hardware).

Loading a Texture

DarkBASIC makes texturing very easy. In fact, just slap yourself right now for not skipping to this part of the chapter. No wait, just kidding! There is true educational value to be had from going through the process. So many programmers today take the rendering pipeline for granted without considering exactly how much work is involved in drawing a complex textured 3D scene. I suppose after writing some 3D code in DarkBASIC, you will start to take it for granted too. Such is the nature of computers. Ah, well. Let me show you how to load a texture.

Basically, a texture is just a bitmap file. Why are they called textures then, rather than bitmaps? That's a funny question. Actually, doesn't "texture" have something to do with how things feel? When I think of the word texture, I am reminded of what the bark on a tree feels like, because that is a significant feeling. I also think of a brick wall as being very textured. Wait, that is bump-mapping. You know, computer science people are weird, okay? Please stop asking silly questions and just take my word for it that a texture is a bitmap.

You use the LOAD IMAGE command to load a texture. The format is LOAD IMAGE *Filename*, *Image Number*.

NOTE

Actually, a texture could be a JPG, PNG, BMP, TGA, DDS, or DIB file! Just thought I'd throw that little tidbit in here to confuse you a little more.

Applying a Texture to a Polygon

After you load a texture onto an image, you can apply that texture to a polygon using the TEXTURE OBJECT command. This command is quite easy to use, despite the complexity behind it. The format of the command is TEXTURE OBJECT *Object Number, Image Number*. Simply pass the object number and image number to the command, and the bitmap image stored in that image number will be textured onto the passed object (which can be a single polygon, a stock 3D object, or an object that you have constructed).

The TexturedCube Program

Texturing a 3D object is really easy to do, and I would like to provide you with a sample program to prove it. The TexturedCube program creates several stock objects, including a rotating cube in the center of the other objects with a texture applied to it. Figure 17.22 shows what the texture looks like. Hey, it's the DarkBASIC logo!

The TexturedCube program is similar to the MakeObjects program. I have removed two of the objects and placed the new cube in the center, rotating opposite of the motion of the other objects. Figure 17.23 shows the program running at normal speed, and Figure 17.24 shows the program running at top speed.

Figure 17.22
The DarkBASIC logo is used to texture a stock 3D object in the TexturedCube program.

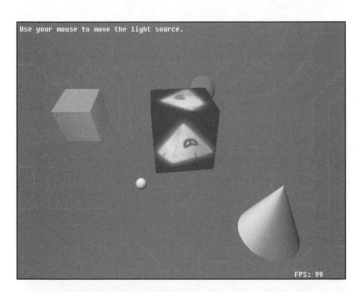

Figure 17.23
The TexturedCube program draws a textured cube with several colored objects rotating around it.

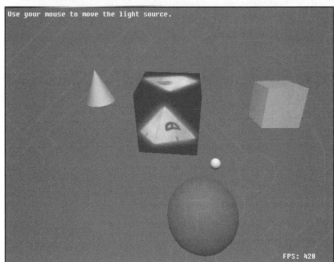

Figure 17.24
Running the TexturedCube program without a frame rate limiter results in a very high frame rate.

You can type this program into DarkBASIC Pro or load the project from the CD-ROM. If you are using DarkBASIC 1.0, there is a separate version of this program available.

```
`-----------------------------------
`Beginner's Guide To DarkBASIC Game Programming
`Copyright (C)2002 Jonathan S. Harbour and Joshua R. Smith
`Chapter 17 - TexturedCube Program
`-----------------------------------
```

```
`declare some arrays
DIM angle(4)
DIM posx(4)
DIM posz(4)

`initialize program
SYNC ON
SYNC RATE 100
HIDE MOUSE
COLOR BACKDROP RGB(0,60,60)

`create a light source
SET AMBIENT LIGHT 0
MAKE LIGHT 1
MAKE OBJECT SPHERE 9, 10
COLOR OBJECT 9, RGB(255,255,255)

`create the central textured cube
MAKE OBJECT CUBE 1, 75
LOAD IMAGE "pyramid.bmp",1
TEXTURE OBJECT 1, 1

`create a cone
MAKE OBJECT CONE 2, 50
COLOR OBJECT 2, RGB(0,255,0)

`create a sphere
MAKE OBJECT SPHERE 3, 50
COLOR OBJECT 3, RGB(0,0,255)

`create a cube
MAKE OBJECT CUBE 4, 50
COLOR OBJECT 4, RGB(255,0,0)

`position the camera
PITCH CAMERA DOWN 25
MOVE CAMERA -200

`set the starting position of each object
angle(2) = 0
```

```
    angle(3) = 135
    angle(4) = 270

    `set the radius of the rotation circle
    radius = 150

    `start the loop
    REPEAT
        `move the objects in a circle
        FOR n = 2 TO 4
            `set the X position with cosine
            posx(n) = COS(angle(n)) * radius
            `set the Y position wiht sine
            posz(n) = SIN(angle(n)) * radius
            `increment the angle
            angle(n) = angle(n) + 1
            `move the object
            POSITION OBJECT n,  posx(n), 0,  posz(n)
        NEXT n

        `rotate the objects individually
        YROTATE OBJECT 1, OBJECT ANGLE Y(1) + 0.5
        YROTATE OBJECT 2, OBJECT ANGLE Y(2) + 1
        XROTATE OBJECT 3, OBJECT ANGLE X(3) + 1
        XROTATE OBJECT 4, OBJECT ANGLE X(4) + 1

        `move the light source according to mouse position
        POSITION LIGHT 1, MOUSEX() - 320, 0, 240 - MOUSEY()
        POSITION OBJECT 9, MOUSEX() - 320, 0, 240 - MOUSEY()

        `display some text messages and refresh the screen
        TEXT 5, 5, "Use your mouse to move the light source."
        TEXT SCREEN WIDTH()-100,SCREEN HEIGHT()-30,"FPS: "+STR$(SCREEN FPS())
        SYNC
    UNTIL ESCAPEKEY() = 1

    `clean up
    SHOW MOUSE
    END
```

Lighting the Scene

The difference between a simple 3D game and a complex one is often the amount of varied lighting in the game. As one of the most complicated themes in 3D graphics programming, lighting is such a difficult task that many games feature pre-lit scenes to simulate the effects of light. For example, a streetlight might seem to emit a directional light on the ground when the texture of the ground below the light simply has been pre-rendered with the appearance of a light shining on it. This can result in a realistic scene that avoids the pitfalls involved in programming real-time lighting effects. Even when you are using a library that might include support for hardware lights supported in the video card, such as OpenGL or Direct3D, you must still design your game engine in such a way that textures and objects in the game are set up to support hardware lights. DarkBASIC Pro has support for many different types of real-time lights that affect the characters and surroundings in a game. The built-in lighting effects in DarkBASIC are so easy to set up and use that you will be surprised by the results.

Ambient Light

Ambient light is the uniform level of lighting throughout an entire scene. If you are standing in a room that is lighted by fluorescent light bulbs, such as in an office building, the level of light might be viewed as ambient, and there would be a certain ambient level in the room. If you stand outside on a bright sunny day, though, ambient light will be significantly different from the light level in an office building. The sun is a large bright-point light source. The sun emits so much light (and heat) that it might seem to be ambient, but it is not. For one thing, sunlight creates shadows on the ground under trees, buildings, people, or anything else. Ambient light by nature does not create shadows. You might think of ambient light as a filler—somewhat light fog that is not emitted from a specific source. Some people, myself included, have a hard time visualizing ambient light. It is easy to understand a directional light, a point light, or a spot light, but ambient light is an abstract concept. When 3D objects are rendered in a scene with ambient light, all faces are lit equally without shadow.

Setting the Ambient Light Level

You can set the level of ambient light using the SET AMBIENT LIGHT command. The format is SET AMBIENT LIGHT *Percentage Value*.

This command expects a single parameter, 0 to 100, indicating the value of ambient light to apply to the scene as a percentage. Setting ambient light to 100 results in no shadows, while a value of 0 is useful when you want to use directional lights in the scene (which I'll discuss further in the upcoming "Directional Lights" section).

Setting the Ambient Color

In addition to changing the level of ambient light, you also have the ability to change the color of the ambient light to any RGB color value using the COLOR AMBIENT LIGHT command. The syntax is COLOR AMBIENT LIGHT *Color Value*.

The AmbientLight Program

The best way to demonstrate how to use ambient light is by showing you a sample program. The AmbientLight program draws a textured cube in the center of the screen, rotates the cube, and oscillates the light level and the color of the ambient light. Figure 17.25 shows the AmbientLight program while near the peak of full ambient color, and Figure 17.26 shows the cube at a low ambient level. At the same time, varying degrees of RGB color are being changed while the program is running, producing some interesting texture colors.

Figure 17.25

The AmbientLight program demonstrates varying levels of ambient light in a scene.

Figure 17.26

A low ambient light setting in the AmbientLight program results in dark, shadowed textures.

```
`---------------------------------
`Beginner's Guide To DarkBASIC Game Programming
`Copyright (C)2002 Jonathan S. Harbour and Joshua R. Smith
`Chapter 17 - AmbientLight Program
`---------------------------------

`create some variables
Ambient = 0
Direction = 1
Red = 0
Green = 0
Blue = 0

`initialize program
SYNC ON
SYNC RATE 60
HIDE MOUSE
COLOR BACKDROP RGB(0,60,60)

`create a textured cube
MAKE OBJECT CUBE 1, 75
LOAD IMAGE "cube.bmp",1
TEXTURE OBJECT 1, 1
```

```
POSITION OBJECT 1, 0, -20, -120

`position the camera
PITCH CAMERA DOWN 25
MOVE CAMERA -30

`start the loop
REPEAT
    `rotate the objects individually
    YROTATE OBJECT 1, OBJECT ANGLE Y(1) + 1

    `update ambient variable
    Ambient = Ambient + Direction
    IF Ambient > 100
        Ambient = 100
        Direction = -1
    ENDIF
    IF Ambient < 0
        Ambient = 0
        Direction = 1
    ENDIF

    `set the ambient light
    SET AMBIENT LIGHT Ambient

    `update the ambient color variables
    IF Red > 254
        IF Green > 254
            IF Blue > 254
                Red = 0
                Green = 0
                Blue = 0
            ELSE
                Blue = Blue + 1
            ENDIF
        ELSE
            Green = Green + 1
        ENDIF
    ELSE
        Red = Red + 1
```

```
        ENDIF

        `set the ambient color
        COLOR AMBIENT LIGHT RGB(Red,Green,Blue)

        `display the ambient variable
        TEXT 10, 10, "Ambient level: " + STR$(Ambient)
        TEXT 10, 20, "Color: "+STR$(Red)+","+STR$(Green)+","+STR$(Blue)

        `update the screen
        SYNC
UNTIL ESCAPEKEY() = 1

`clean up
SHOW MOUSE
END
```

Ambient light will suffice for almost any game that you plan to write. Most of the time, you need nothing more than the default ambient light level. However, you might want to add some pizzazz to your games. In addition to ambient light, DarkBASIC Pro provides three special-case lights that you can use in your programs.

- Directional lights
- Point lights
- Spot lights

Directional Lights

Directional lights illuminate a scene in a conical shape that points to a specific location where the light source is located. A directional light is similar to a spotlight, but it does not have a changeable angle of effect. Probably the most obvious use for a directional light would be for a streetlamp or headlights on a car.

Creating a Directional Light

You can use the SET DIRECTIONAL LIGHT command to turn an existing light into a directional light. The syntax for this command is SET DIRECTIONAL LIGHT *Light Number*, *DirX*, *DirY*, *DirZ*. The *DirX*, *DirY*, and *DirZ* parameters define the direction that the light is pointing.

The DirectionalLight Program

I have written a program called DirectionalLight to demonstrate how to use directional lights. This program revolves a small sphere (representing the light source) in a circle around a larger sphere, constantly shining the directional light at the larger sphere. The result is a bright surface on the larger sphere that moves according to the position of the light source, as shown in Figure 17.27.

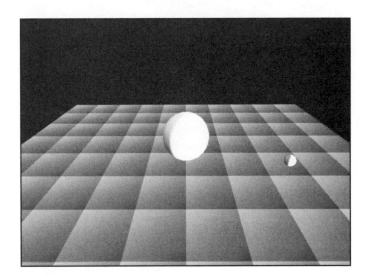

Figure 17.27
The DirectionalLight program demonstrates one of the many ways you can use directional lights.

```
`-----------------------------------

`Beginner's Guide To DarkBASIC Game Programming
`Copyright (C)2002 Jonathan S. Harbour and Joshua R. Smith
`Chapter 17 - DirectionalLight Program
`-----------------------------------

`create variables
posx = 0
posz = 0
angle = 0
radius = 200
```

```
`initialize program
SYNC ON
SYNC RATE 60
HIDE MOUSE
COLOR BACKDROP RGB(0,40,40)

`create the floor
MAKE MATRIX 1, 1000, 1000, 10, 10
LOAD IMAGE "floor.bmp", 2
POSITION MATRIX 1, -500, -100, -500
PREPARE MATRIX TEXTURE 1, 2, 1, 1
UPDATE MATRIX 1

`create the large sphere
MAKE OBJECT SPHERE 1, 100
COLOR OBJECT 1, RGB(245,200,0)

`create the small sphere
MAKE OBJECT SPHERE 2, 20
COLOR OBJECT 2, RGB(255,0,255)
POSITION OBJECT 2, 200, 0, 200

`create the directional light
MAKE LIGHT 1
SET DIRECTIONAL LIGHT 1, 0, 0, 0
`COLOR LIGHT 1, RGB(255,0,0)

`set up the camera
POSITION CAMERA 0, 200,  -400
POINT CAMERA 0, 0, 0

`start the loop
REPEAT
    `move the small sphere and light source
    posx = COS(angle) * radius
    posz = SIN(angle) * radius
    angle = angle + 1
```

```
        POSITION OBJECT 2, posx + 20, 0, posz + 20
        POSITION LIGHT 1, posx, 0, posz
        POINT LIGHT 1, 0, 0, 0

        `update the screen
        SYNC
UNTIL ESCAPEKEY() = 1

`clean up
SHOW MOUSE
END
```

Point Lights

Point lights are fascinating because they emit light in all directions and have a limited range, which allows for local lighting effects. One possible use for a point light is a projectile fired from a weapon, such as a plasma bolt fired from a gun in a futuristic tank battle or first-person shooter. Having a projectile that lights up objects that it passes is a particularly impressive special effect in a game. Keep in mind, however, that DarkBASIC has only a limited supply of lights available, and some video cards might not support hardware lights (which will slow down the program, because lighting effects are a serious drag on the processor).

Creating Point Lights

You can set an existing light to a point light by using the SET POINT LIGHT command. The format is SET POINT LIGHT *Light Number*, *PosX*, *PosY*, *PosZ*. The *PosX*, *PosY*, and *PosZ* parameters define the position of the light.

The PointLight Program

The PointLight program demonstrates how to use point lights. I was really happy with the way this program turned out because it surprised me the first time I ran it! The scene was supposed to be lit already, but I inadvertently set the ambient light level to a very low value. The result is that the point light circling the object in the center of the screen actually lights the surface of the object, which is a yellow sphere. The result is very interesting, as you can see in Figure 17.28.

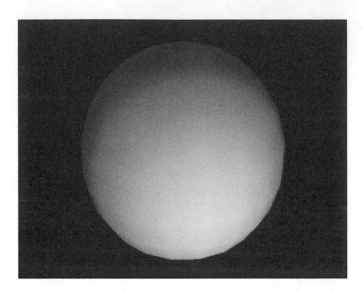

Figure 17.28

The PointLight program revolves a small point light around a sphere with low ambient light.

```
`-----------------------------------
`Beginner's Guide To DarkBASIC Game Programming
`Copyright (C)2002 Jonathan S. Harbour and Joshua R. Smith
`Chapter 17 - PointLight Program
`-----------------------------------

`create some variables
posx = 0
posz = 0
angle = 0
radius = 120

`initialize program
SYNC ON
SYNC RATE 60
HIDE MOUSE
COLOR BACKDROP RGB(0,0,0)

`set the ambient light
SET AMBIENT LIGHT 5

`create a point light
SET POINT LIGHT 0, 0, 0, 0
```

```
COLOR LIGHT 0, RGB(245,200,0)
SET LIGHT RANGE 0, 200

`create the central sphere
MAKE OBJECT SPHERE 1, 100
COLOR OBJECT 1, RGB(245,200,0)

`set up the camera
POSITION CAMERA 0, 50, -100
POINT CAMERA 0, 0, 0

`start the loop
REPEAT
    `orbit the point light around the sphere
    posx = COS(angle) * radius
    posz = SIN(angle) * radius
    angle = angle + 2
    POSITION LIGHT 0, posx, 0, posz

    `rotate the central sphere
    YROTATE OBJECT 1, OBJECT ANGLE Y(1) + 1

    `update the screen
    SYNC
UNTIL ESCAPEKEY() = 1

`clean up
SHOW MOUSE
END
```

Spot Lights

Spot lights are my favorite kind of light in DarkBASIC because color can be applied
to a spot light with attractive results. A spot light is similar to a directional light in
that there is a conical-shaped light source, but spot lights have the added benefit of
having internal and external light cone angles that you can set. The inner cone
determines how large the spot light will be when it strikes a surface, and the outer
cone determines how much residual light will pour out of the inner cone onto an
object in a faded manner.

Creating Spot Lights

You can set an existing light to a spot light by using the SET SPOT LIGHT command. The format is SET SPOT LIGHT *Light Number, Inner Angle, Outer Angle*.

The SpotLight Program

The SpotLight program is my favorite among the light source demos because it works so well and the result is fantastic (see Figure 17.29). By applying a different color to each of the two light sources in this program and shining them both at a textured cube, the result is very colorful and shows the great effects possible with spot lights. The only thing I might have done differently is to have the light sources move instead of the camera, but the result would have been attractive either way.

Figure 17.29
The SpotLight program demonstrates how to use spot lights.

```
`------------------------------------
`Beginner's Guide To DarkBASIC Game Programming
`Copyright (C)2002 Jonathan S. Harbour and Joshua R. Smith
`Chapter 17 - SpotLight Program
`------------------------------------

posx = 0
posz = 0
angle = 0
```

```
height = 150
radius = 400

`initialize program
SYNC ON
SYNC RATE 60
HIDE MOUSE
COLOR BACKDROP RGB(0,60,60)

`create a textured cube
MAKE OBJECT CUBE 1, 100
LOAD IMAGE "cube.bmp",1
TEXTURE OBJECT 1, 1

`create the "floor"
MAKE MATRIX 1, 1000, 1000, 10, 10
LOAD IMAGE "floor.bmp", 2
POSITION MATRIX 1, -500, -100, -500
PREPARE MATRIX TEXTURE 1, 2, 1, 1
UPDATE MATRIX 1

`marker object for green light
MAKE OBJECT SPHERE 10, 10
COLOR OBJECT 10, RGB(0,0,255)
POSITION OBJECT 10, 200, 0, 200

`create a green spot light
MAKE LIGHT 1
SET SPOT LIGHT 1, 30, 10
COLOR LIGHT 1, RGB(0,0,255)
POSITION LIGHT 1, 200, 0, 200
POINT LIGHT 1, 0, 0, 0

`marker object for red light
MAKE OBJECT SPHERE 11, 10
COLOR OBJECT 11, RGB(255,255,0)
POSITION OBJECT 11, -200, 0, -200

`create a red spot light
MAKE LIGHT 2
```

```
SET SPOT LIGHT 2, 30, 10
COLOR LIGHT 2, RGB(255,255,0)
POSITION LIGHT 2, -200, 0, -200
POINT LIGHT 2, 0, 0, 0

`start the loop
REPEAT
    `rotate the camera around the scene
    posx = COS(angle) * radius
    posz = SIN(angle) * radius
    angle = angle + 1
    POSITION CAMERA n,  posx, height,  posz
    POINT CAMERA 0, 0, 0

    `update the screen
    SYNC
UNTIL ESCAPEKEY() = 1

`clean up
SHOW MOUSE
END
```

The 3D Camera

Earlier in this chapter, you saw some possible uses for the camera, such as moving it around the perimeter of a scene instead of moving individual objects in the scene—a very useful technique, particularly when you just want to show off a 3D model that you have loaded. The camera is the most important aspect of the 3D engine, and DarkBASIC is no exception, although support for multiple cameras is a fascinating idea. The concept of a "camera" in 3D graphics is abstract. As far as DarkBASIC knows, there is a 3D world and there really is no computer screen or monitor. The 3D objects, lights, and cameras move around and do their thing regardless of whether or not someone is watching. In this sense, the word "watching" refers to not only the player—you, the programmer—but also to a camera. By default, DarkBASIC sets up camera 0 as the standard camera and displays the camera's view on the screen. However, you can just as easily create another camera elsewhere in the scene and set the screen to display what that camera is viewing! That is what I mean when I state that cameras are abstract views in 3D space. Often the impression is that a 3D scene is rendered on the screen using some sort of ray-tracing algorithm, and that impression somehow links the 3D objects to the screen as if they are glued in place. In fact, those objects are totally independent of the screen.

The 3D chip in your video card optimizes the mathematics involved in rendering these objects. The resulting impression of modern 3D graphics is that the scene can be rendered regardless of who is watching.

If there is no camera in place to display a scene on the screen, then the GPU will spend no time processing the scene. Although the CPU might continue to update the position of objects in the scene, rendering is by far the most intensive operation. This simply does not occur if there are no virtual cameras in place.

> **NOTE**
>
> All of the camera commands covered in this section are demonstrated in the CameraView program at the end of the chapter. Not all commands are represented here, only those that I deemed practical. For a complete reference to all of the camera commands, please refer to the DarkBASIC Language Reference on the CD.

Creating New Cameras

DarkBASIC provides a default camera (0) that is set slightly back (in the Z axis) and focused on 0,0,0. You will almost always need to move the default camera out a certain distance to see the objects in your scene, depending on their size. If you are writing a game such as a third-person shooter, you will probably want to set the camera just above and behind the main object in the game. You can use the default camera or create additional cameras using the MAKE CAMERA command. The syntax is MAKE CAMERA *Camera Number*.

After you create a new camera, you can position and point it to a new location in the scene, and then easily switch from one camera to another by simply calling the SET CURRENT CAMERA command, which immediately sets the view to that seen by the specified camera. The syntax of this command is SET CURRENT CAMERA *Camera Number*.

If you would rather display the feed of a particular camera right on the screen, you can do just that using the SET CAMERA VIEW command, which sets up a portion of the screen as an overlay video. The syntax is SET CAMERA VIEW *Camera Number, Left, Top, Right, Bottom*.

Getting and Setting the Camera's Position

It is your job to manage the camera's position. Although there is an AUTOCAM ON command, it simply focuses on the last 3D object that was created or loaded and does not follow the correct field of view. To set a camera's position in 3D space, you can use the POSITION CAMERA command in the syntax POSITION CAMERA *Camera Number*, *X*, *Y*, *Z*.

Any time you need to know the exact position of a camera or you need to move the camera based on its current position (for instance, to move the camera using absolute coordinates), you can use one of the following commands:

- CAMERA POSITION X(*Camera Number*)
- CAMERA POSITION Y(*Camera Number*)
- CAMERA POSITION Z(*Camera Number*)

Pointing the Camera

After positioning, the next most important factor to consider in camera management is the direction the camera is pointing. This determines what the camera is looking at and what is displayed on the screen (or in a window, as you will see later). To set a camera's direction, you can use the POINT CAMERA command, which is almost always necessary after moving the camera to a new location. The syntax is POINT CAMERA *Camera Number*, *X*, *Y*, *Z*.

Surprisingly, those are all the commands you need to effectively manage one or more cameras in a game. Again, if you would like to discover the more advanced camera-handling commands available, see the DarkBASIC Language Reference on the CD.

The CameraView Program

There are many more commands in DarkBASIC for manipulating and reading the status of the cameras in your programs, but I have covered only those commands that are immediately useful. To demonstrate how these commands work, I have written a program called CameraView. This program creates five cameras and positions them at various points in the scene, even moving the cameras in relation to objects. The top portion of the screen features five mini-overlays that show the view of each camera, in addition to the default camera (which fills the screen by default). See Figure 17.30 to get an idea what the output of the program looks like.

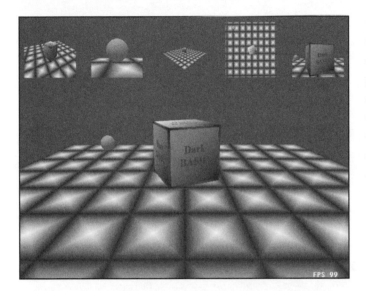

Figure 17.30 *The CameraView program demonstrates how to position and orient cameras in a scene and then display the output from each camera on the screen.*

NOTE

For a more in-depth overview of all the camera commands, please refer to the **DarkBASIC Language Reference on the CD.**

As has been the case throughout the book, I am taking liberty with the texture files that are referenced in this program and assuming that they exist. You can copy the texture files (floor.bmp and cube.bmp) to the program folder where you have saved the listing for CameraView, or you can create your own textures. The standard size for a texture is 512 pixels squared.

```
`---------------------------------
`Beginner's Guide To DarkBASIC Game Programming
`Copyright (C)2002 Jonathan S. Harbour and Joshua R. Smith
`Chapter 17 - CameraView Program
`---------------------------------

`create some variables
posx = 0
posz = 0
angle = 0
```

```
height = 150
radius = 300
screenw = SCREEN WIDTH()
screenh = SCREEN HEIGHT()

`initialize program
SYNC ON
SYNC RATE 100
HIDE MOUSE
COLOR BACKDROP RGB(0,60,60)

`create the "floor"
MAKE MATRIX 1, 1000, 1000, 10, 9
LOAD IMAGE "floor.bmp", 2
POSITION MATRIX 1, -500, -100, -500
PREPARE MATRIX TEXTURE 1, 2, 1, 1
UPDATE MATRIX 1

`create a textured cube
MAKE OBJECT CUBE 1, 100
LOAD IMAGE "cube.bmp",1
TEXTURE OBJECT 1, 1

`create the moving sphere
MAKE OBJECT SPHERE 2, 50
COLOR OBJECT 2, RGB(245, 0, 200)

`create and set up the cameras
MAKE CAMERA 1
SET CAMERA VIEW 1, 10, 10, 110, 110
MAKE CAMERA 2
SET CAMERA VIEW 2, screenw-110, 10, screenw-10, 110
MAKE CAMERA 3
SET CAMERA VIEW 3, 140, 10, 240, 110
MAKE CAMERA 4
POSITION CAMERA 4, 0, 600, 0
POINT CAMERA 4, 0, 0, 0
SET CAMERA VIEW 4, screenw-240, 10, screenw-140, 110
MAKE CAMERA 5
```

```
POSITION CAMERA 5, 900, 400, -900
POINT CAMERA 5, 0, 0, 0
SET CAMERA VIEW 5, screenw/2-50, 10, screenw/2+50, 110
POSITION CAMERA 0, 0, 100, -400
POINT CAMERA 0, 0, 0, 0

`start the loop
REPEAT
    `rotate the cube and point camera 2 at it
    YROTATE OBJECT 1, OBJECT ANGLE Y(1) + 1
    SET CAMERA TO FOLLOW 2, 0, 0, 0, 0, 200, 30, 1.0, 0

    `rotate a point around the scene
    posx = COS(angle) * radius
    posz = SIN(angle) * radius
    angle = angle + 1

    `move camera 1
    POSITION CAMERA 1,  posx, height,  posz
    POINT CAMERA 1, 0, 0, 0

    `move the sphere
    POSITION OBJECT 2, -1*posx, COS(angle)*posz/2, -1*posz+200

    `move camera 3
    X = OBJECT POSITION X(2)
    Y = OBJECT POSITION Y(2)
    Z = OBJECT POSITION Z(2)
    SET CAMERA TO FOLLOW 3, X, Y, Z, 0, 100, Y, 1.0, 0

    `display frame rate and update the screen
    TEXT screenw-70, screenh-20, "FPS " + STR$(SCREEN FPS())
    SYNC
UNTIL ESCAPEKEY() = 1

`clean up
SHOW MOUSE
END
```

Summary

Thus ends one of the longest and most complicated (but surely the most exciting!) chapters of the book thus far! I hope you have enjoyed this chapter, because 3D programming is where the action is, and this is what you should strive to master to write your own cutting-edge games. 2D games are fun and may always be around, but 3D is the place to be. To be honest, I personally find 3D programming just as easy as (if not easier than) 2D programming. It just seems that DarkBASIC handles all the details and makes it so much fun! It's wonderful to be able to write a 3D demo or even a complete game without having to learn matrix math or trigonometry. You can move or rotate any object, light source, or camera using only a single command. Now that's real programming power!

Chapter Quiz

The chapter quiz will help you retain the information that was covered in this chapter, as well as give you an idea about how well you're doing at understanding the subjects. You will find the answers for this quiz in Appendix A, "Answers to the Chapter Quizzes."

1. How many vertices (or angles) are required to make up a triangle?

   A. 2

   B. 3

   C. 4

   D. 5

2. Which coordinate system is used to calculate the position of points in a 3D program?

   A. Bilinear coordinate system

   B. Cartesian coordinate system

   C. Geometry coordinate system

   D. DirectX coordinate system

3. What is the name of the process that smoothes jagged edges in a 3D scene?

   A. Perspective-correct texture mapping

   B. Trilinear mip-mapping

   C. Real-time polygon count

   D. Full scene anti-aliasing

4. Which command creates a 360-degree quadrilateral?

   A. `MAKE OBJECT RECTANGLE`

   B. `MAKE OBJECT CUBE`

   C. `MAKE OBJECT TRIANGLE`

   D. `MAKE OBJECT SPHERE`

5. Which command sets the level of ambient light in the 3D scene to a uniform amount?

   A. `COLOR AMBIENT LIGHT`

   B. `AMBIENT LIGHT LEVEL`

   C. `SET AMBIENT LIGHT`

   D. `CHANGE AMBIENT LIGHT`

6. Which type of light source produces a colored light region in the shape of a sphere?

   A. Ambient light

   B. Point light

   C. Directional light

   D. Spot light

7. Which type of light source lets you set an inner and outer angle of effect?

   A. Ambient light

   B. Point light

   C. Directional light

   D. Spot light

8. How many sides do you need to make a cube?

   A. 4

   B. 6

   C. 8

   D. 10

9. Which command creates an overlay window on the screen for a camera?

   A. `SET CAMERA OVERLAY`

   B. `SET CAMERA OUTPUT`

   C. `SET CAMERA VIEW`

   D. `SET CAMERA WINDOW`

10. Which version of DirectX does DarkBASIC Professional directly support?

    A. DirectX 7.0
    B. DirectX 8.0
    C. DirectX 8.1
    D. DirectX 9.0

CHAPTER 18

MULTIPLAYER PROGRAMMING: THE CRAZY CARNAGE GAME

Y ou made it to the final chapter! Looking back, just think about all you have learned with DarkBASIC, from the basics of writing a program to 3D graphics. It has not always been easy! Now it is time to put all that you have learned to good use. In this chapter, I will show you how to write a complete game. Not just any game, but a 3D game. And that is not all—this game will support two players over a network! The network line can be a local area network (LAN) or it can be over the Internet with a phone line or cable/DSL. Regardless of the way you connect, you will be able to challenge a friend in the other room or across the globe to a game because DarkBASIC provides a consistent multiplayer programming interface. This multiplayer feature is based on DirectPlay—a component of DirectX 8.1.

This chapter will be the final one in your quest to learn about DarkBASIC, and I am confident that it will be a fun chapter for you! Specifically, I'll get into the multiplayer aspects of DarkBASIC and the use of memory blocks, and I'll add a few more 3D commands that build on the information from the last chapter. The final result is a multiplayer game called Crazy CARnage. I'm sure you have played vehicle combat games like *Twisted Metal: Black*, *Star Wars: Demolition*, and *Vigilante 8*. Crazy CARnage was based loosely on this game genre. Although I can't possibly begin to write a game as advanced and creative as *Twisted Metal: Black* in a single chapter, this game will at least show you how multiplayer games work and give you a good, solid overview of how to write a complete game.

This chapter will cover the following topics:

- Introduction to Multiplayer Games
- Packet Transport
- Establishing a Network Game
- Passing the Data
- Additional Multiplayer Commands
- Memory Blocks
- The Crazy CARnage Game!

Introduction to Multiplayer Games

Multiplayer games seem to be the wave of the future. Everyone from Microsoft to EA is making them now. Some of the most notable multiplayer games are *Quake III*, *Half-Life*, *Ultima Online*, *Real War: Rogue States*, and *Everquest*. Each of these games uses multiplayer capabilities in different ways to achieve the same goal: FUN.

Single-Player Versus Multiplayer

There is a question hanging around in the gaming world. Do consumers want multiplayer or single-player games? Multiplayer puts the world of human AI at your fingertips. There is no need to program the computer to simulate human behavior when you can just have humans do it for you. Single-player games, however, do have their place. Sometimes you just feel like playing a game without having to find someone else to play it with you. Single-player games are more story-driven, but that is changing as well.

Multiplayer Support in DarkBASIC

DarkBASIC uses the DirectPlay aspects of DirectX 8.1 to establish multiplayer games. DirectPlay is the network portion of DirectX. It supports all of the functions required to play a network game.

DarkBASIC has many different commands to provide multiplayer support. For example, with just a few commands, you can create a multiplayer connection. DarkBASIC supports two models of multiplayer connectivity—the client/server model and the peer-to-peer model. Each starts with a host (server) and a client; the difference is in how they pass around the packets. The default game settings use the peer-to-peer model.

> A *packet* is a collection of data to be processed that is sent from one computer to another.

The Client/Server Model

The client/server model designates one computer as the master controller and the rest of the computers as slaves. Each slave sends its packets to the master controller, which then dictates where the packets are sent. Imagine that there are three computers in a game—A, B, and C. If computer B is designated the master, computers A and C send their packets to B, which then sends the packets to the appropriate computer (A or C). Figure 18.1 shows the layout of the client/server model.

Anyone who has been in networking is very familiar with this model. This type of network connectivity is seen in systems such as Novell, UNIX, and Citrix, which generally include a server that hosts all the files and clients that connect to the server to retrieve files.

The Peer-to-Peer Model

The peer-to-peer model differs drastically from the client/server model. Although in DarkBASIC you start with the client/server for connection, that is where the similarities end. When all of the computers are connected to the game, there is no designated master controller. Every computer can send packets to any other computer. Imagine computers A, B, and C in this scenario. Computer A could send all of its

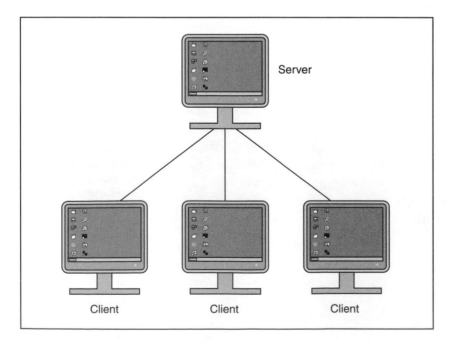

Figure 18.1
A client/server model

Server

Client   Client   Client

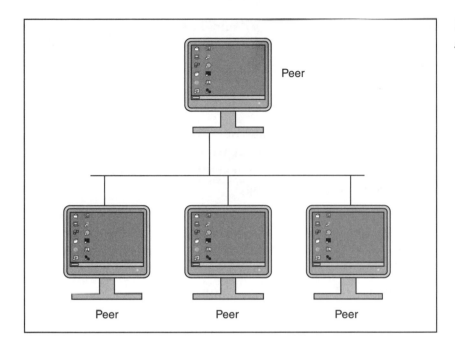

Figure 18.2
A peer-to-peer model

packets to both computers B and C. However, Computer A might have information only for Computer B, in which case it would send that data only to Computer B. The same applies to computers B and C. Figure 18.2 illustrates the peer-to-peer model.

You will find the peer-to-peer model mainly in Microsoft networking. In this model, one computer can talk to another computer without transferring any information through a central server. This is why, in a Microsoft network, you can connect from any computer to any other computer on the network without logging on to a master server. Higher functionalities of Microsoft networking merge both the client/server model and the peer-to-peer model.

Packet Transport

Once you are familiar with the network layout, you need to understand how the packets are transported around the network. There are many different types of transportation for packets. DarkBASIC supports four different types of network connections—serial (NULL modem), modem, IPX/SPX

> **Network connection is just a fancy term for the mode of transportation for network packets.**

(*Internet Packet Exchange/Sequenced Packet Exchange*), and TCP/IP (*Transmission Control Protocol/Internet Protocol*). In this book I will only cover one—TCP/IP, which is the most widely used protocol on networks today.

The TCP/IP Protocol

TCP/IP can be considered the taxicab of the Internet. Every time you view a Web page, TCP/IP transports the HTML packets to your Web browser. Every time you check your e-mail, TCP/IP transports the e-mail packets to your e-mail client. If you think about it, TCP/IP is really quite amazing.

TCP/IP transports your packets by using the IP address. Every computer that is connected to a network using TCP/IP has an IP address. Currently, this address consists of four numbers ranging from 1 to 255, each separated by a period. A typical IP address is 209.232.223.40. Figure 18.3 shows a typical TCP/IP network.

You're probably thinking, "If TCP/IP connects via numbered addresses, why do I type www.microsoft.com to get to Microsoft's Web site?" Well, there is a feature of the Internet known as DNS (*Domain Name System*) that converts IP addresses into numbers. Your computer keeps a repository that matches IP addresses to domain

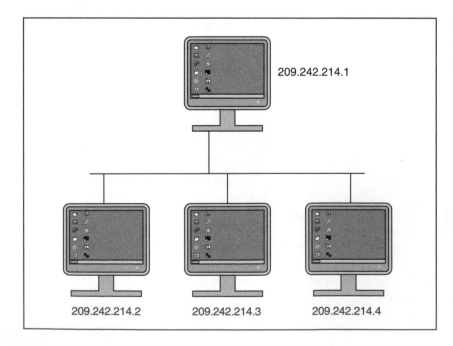

Figure 18.3

A typical TCP/IP network

names so you do not have to memorize all those numbers. If your computer doesn't know an IP address, it checks with another computer for the answer. Domain names are like nicknames. You only have one real name (such as Robert), but you can have many different nicknames (such as Bob, Pooh Bear, and Dogface). You only have one real IP address (such as 192.168.0.50), but you can have many different domain names (such as www.myaddress.com and www.bobshouse.com).

Selecting the Correct Transport

Now that you know about TCP/IP protocol, it's time to learn how to select it. This is a pretty easy task; you just need to know what number it is by using PERFORM CHECKLIST FOR NET CONNECTIONS. This command will fill the checklist with all the transports available. CHECKLIST STRING$ will contain the name of the protocol associated with that number. You will have to search for or specifically select TCP/IP.

Establishing a Network Game

After you select the connection, you must set up the game. A network game requires a minimum of two people. To that end, you need to call two different paths to create a network game—the client and server paths. There is only a difference of a single command between the two paths, but it's important to understand both of them.

Establishing the Server Path

In the client/server model, the server is the computer that is hosting the game. In the peer-to-peer model, the server is the starting point for the game, but everyone acts as a server after the game begins.

Before the game is established, you need to set the connection type that you got from PERFORM CHECKLIST FOR CONNECTIONS. Use the SET NET CONNECTION *Connection Number* command followed by a blank space in quotes: " ". You need the " " to establish that this computer is a host. The full command might look like this:

```
SET NET CONNECTION ConnectNumber, " "
```

The connection number variable, *ConnectNumber*, is the number you got from the PERFORM CHECKLIST FOR CONNECTIONS command.

After you set the game connection, you need to create a net game. To do so, you must use the CREATE NET GAME command, which looks like this:

`CREATE NET GAME GameName, PlayerName, NumberOfPlayers, Flag`

This command sets up DarkBASIC to accept other players into the game. *GameName* is the name of the game being hosted. *PlayerName* is your name in the game. *NumberOfPlayers* is the maximum number of players that you want to allow the game to include. You can have a maximum of 256 players including yourself in a game. *Flag* determines whether the game is connected in a peer-to-peer or client/server model. If *Flag* is a 1, the game is set to peer-to-peer. If *Flag* is a 2, the game is set to client/server. After the game is established, the server just waits for players.

Establishing the Client Path

Anyone that is not hosting a game is a client, and must connect to the host to play. Client computers first need to establish the connection by using the SET NET CONNECTION command, like this:

`SET NET CONNECTION ConnectionNumber, AddressData`

This is the same command used to establish the connection for the server, but you take a different approach in this instance. *AddressData* can either be blank ("") or it can have an address, such as 192.168.0.1 or www.mycomputer.com. *AddressData* is always a string and therefore its value must always be enclosed in quotes. If you leave *AddressData* blank, a dialog box will ask for any needed address data when the command is run. Figure 18.4 shows the Locate Session dialog box.

Finding the games on the host is almost as easy as finding the connections. After you have established the connection, use the PERFORM CHECKLIST FOR NET SESSIONS command. This will return a list of all the games running on the host computer. When you know what session to play, use the following command to establish a connection to the game.

`JOIN NET GAME SessionNumber, Playername`

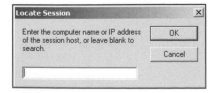

Figure 18.4 *The TCP/IP Locate Session dialog box*

SessionNumber is the number of the game you found using the PERFORM CHECKLIST FOR NET SESSIONS command. *Playername* is a string that contains your name.

Making the Connection

The following section of code will connect two computers using DarkBASIC. When you are running the program, you will have to specify whether the computer is the hosting machine or the client machine. If the computer is the client machine, the program will ask for the host's IP address. Figure 18.5 shows the output of a machine that is hosting a session. You will find this program on the CD in the Sources\Chapter18\NetworkConnect folder.

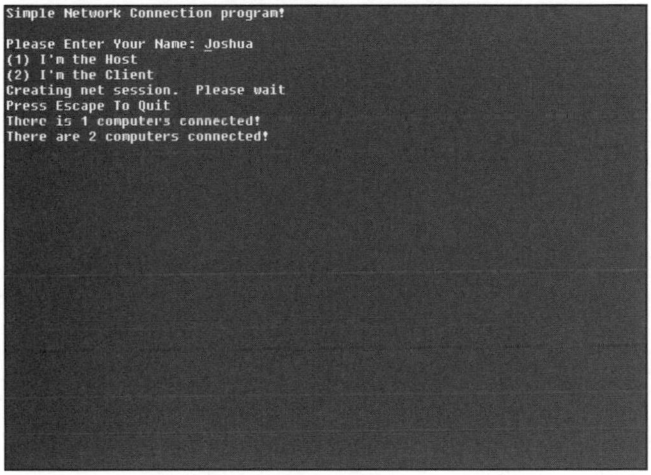

Figure 18.5
The NetworkConnect program demonstrates a host machine connected to a client machine.

```
REMSTART
----------------------------------
Beginner's Guide To DarkBASIC Game Programming
Copyright (C)2002 Jonathan S. Harbour and Joshua R. Smith
Chapter 8- NetworkConnect Program
----------------------------------
REMEND
SYNC ON
SYNC RATE 30
` Find the TCP/IP connection number
TcpIpNumber = FindTCPIPConnectionNumber()
PRINT "Simple Network Connection program!"
```

```
PRINT
SYNC
` Get their Name
INPUT "Please Enter Your Name: ", MyName$
SYNC
IF MyName$ = ""
    PRINT "You need to enter a name!"
    WAIT KEY
    END
ENDIF
` Find out who the host and clients are..
PRINT "(1) I'm the Host"
PRINT "(2) I'm the Client"
SYNC
A$ = ""
Answer = 0
` Get Host or Client
WHILE Answer = 0
    A$ = INKEY$()
    IF A$ = "1" THEN Answer = 1
    IF A$ = "2" THEN Answer = 2
ENDWHILE

` Do this if I'm the host..
IF Answer = 1
    PRINT "Creating net session.  Please wait"
    SYNC
    SLEEP 200
    SET NET CONNECTION TcpIpNumber, " "
    CREATE NET GAME "Sample Net session", MyName$, 16, 1
ENDIF

` Do this if I'm the client.
IF Answer = 2
    Input "Please enter the Hosts IP Address: ",AddressData$
    PRINT "Connecting to net session.  Please wait"
    SYNC
    SET NET CONNECTION TcpIpNumber, AddressData$
    PERFORM CHECKLIST FOR NET SESSIONS
    NumberOfGames =CHECKLIST QUANTITY()
```

```
        IF NumberOfGames = 0
            PRINT "No session found at that address"
            SYNC
            WAIT KEY
            END
        ENDIF
        JOIN NET GAME 1, MyName$
        PRINT "Connected to session!"
        SYNC
ENDIF
NumberOfPlayers = 0
LastNumberOfPlayers = 0
PRINT "Press Escape To Quit"
SYNC
`   Wait until the escape key it hit.
WHILE ESCAPEKEY()=0
    `  Look for more Net Players to display
    PERFORM CHECKLIST FOR NET PLAYERS
    NumberOfPlayers = CHECKLIST QUANTITY()
    `  If a player has entered or left.. display that.
    IF LastNumberOfPlayers <> NumberOfPlayers
        IF NumberOfPlayers = 1
            NewString$ = "There is "+STR$(NumberOfPlayers)
        ELSE
            NewString$ = "There are "+STR$(NumberOfPlayers)
        ENDIF
        NewString$ = NEWSTRING$ + " computers connected!"
        PRINT NewString$
        LastNumberOfPlayers = NumberOfPlayers
    ENDIF
    SYNC
ENDWHILE
END

`  Ths function will determine which NET CONNECTION number
`  is TCP/IP.
FUNCTION FindTCPIPConnectionNumber()
    Flag = 0
    CLS
    PERFORM CHECKLIST FOR NET CONNECTIONS
```

```
       FOR x = 1 TO CHECKLIST QUANTITY()
           Service$ = CHECKLIST STRING$(x)
           IF LEFT$(Service$,15)="Internet TCP/IP"
               Flag = x
           ENDIF
       NEXT x
ENDFUNCTION Flag
```

Passing the Data

After you have established the game, DarkBASIC provides you with many ways to pass data back and forth between the computers in the game. Passing data is a lot like passing notes in class. The data is written at your end, passed through the network, and read at the other end. If the other end has something to say to you, it performs the same series of events. The only difference between passing data and passing notes is that the teacher won't take your data and read it in front of the class.

Getting the Number and Names of Players

The very first piece of data you will probably want to obtain is the number of players and their names. You pass this data differently than the other data you send because it already resides on your computer. The PERFORM CHECKLIST FOR NET PLAYERS command will fill the checklist with the names and number of players in the game at the time the command is called. You can use this command to check to see whether someone else is in the game before you start it.

The checklist for PERFORM CHECKLIST FOR NET PLAYERS contains valuable information about the players. CHECKLIST STRING$(*PlayerNumber*) contains a string with that player's name. CHECKLIST VALUE A(*PlayerNumber*) contains a unique ID (or number) that was assigned to the player by the computer when he joined the game. This number will not change for the duration of the game; however, it is not the same on all computers in the game. CHECKLIST VALUE B(*PlayerNumber*) contains a special universal ID that is assigned to the player when he joins the game. This ID is the same for all of the computers on the network. CHECKLIST VALUE C(*PlayerNumber*) returns a 1 if you are the player. CHECKLIST VALUE D(*PlayerNumber*) returns a 1 if the player is the host of the game.

Sending Information

There are quite a few commands for sending different types of information over the network. Each command follows a basic form, as shown in the following line of code.

```
SEND NET MESSAGE TYPE PlayerNumber, Value
```

PlayerNumber is the number of the player to whom you want to send the data. If you want to send the information to everyone except yourself, *PlayerNumber* would be 0. Table 18.1 lists all the commands and what type of data they send.

Net message is DarkBASIC's terminology for a network packet. Any information sent over the network is considered a net message. You will see all packets from this point on referred to as net messages.

Table 18.1 Network Message Send Commands

Command	Data Type Sent
SEND NET MESSAGE INTEGER	Integer
SEND NET MESSAGE FLOAT	Float
SEND NET MESSAGE STRING	String
SEND NET MESSAGE MEMBLOCK	Memblock
SEND NET MESSAGE BITMAP	Bitmap
SEND NET MESSAGE IMAGE	Image
SEND NET MESSAGE SOUND	Sound
SEND NET MESSAGE MESH	3D mesh

Each of the commands sends a specific type of data. Some of the commands take longer to get to another computer than others. The SEND NET MESSAGE INTEGER command sends a small packet, whereas SEND NET MESSAGE IMAGE can send a very large packet containing all the data in the image. You'll notice that the last five commands have a flag parameter after them. This flag is there in case of network slowdown. If it is set to 1, it guarantees that the data will get to the other computer. DarkBASIC will drop any packets that don't have this flag if there is not enough time to send them.

Reading Information

There are many commands for reading the data that is available to the computer. Because you don't want to look for packets every turn, I will cover the NET MESSAGE EXISTS command first. This command returns a 1 if any messages are waiting to be processed. If no messages are waiting, there is no need to go through the process of reading them.

When you know that at least one message exists, you need to get that message. The GET NET MESSAGE command opens the packet so you can read it. For every message that comes to the computer, you must call a GET NET MESSAGE command. That is why when I am reading net messages; I simply do a loop while NET MESSAGE EXISTS is equal to 1.

After you have the message, and before you process it, you might want to know whom it is to and from. The NET MESSAGE PLAYER TO and NET MESSAGE PLAYER FROM commands return the player number to whom and from whom the message is sent, respectively. You should only use these commands if you need to know whom the message is from or to whom it is directed. In a client/server model, you will only get messages that are meant for you, so you can effectively ignore the NET MESSAGE PLAYER TO command. If your game requires you to keep track of whom the message is from (in the case of games with more than two players), the NET MESSAGE PLAYER FROM command will return the ID of the player who sent the message.

If the computer knows the message is for you and has dealt with whom it is from, you might want to know what type of message it is. If the wrong read message is called, the data will not be valid for what you read. NET MESSAGE TYPE returns an integer that dictates the type of net message that is waiting. Table 18.2 lists the return values and the types of data they represent.

The data type of the message waiting dictates what command you must call to retrieve the message. The commands will return the appropriate values for your game to process. NET MESSAGE INTEGER(), NET MESSAGE FLOAT(), and NET MESSAGE STRING$ all return values appropriate to the data type sent. The remaining five commands (NET MESSAGE MEMBLOCK, NET MESSAGE BITMAP, NET MESSAGE IMAGE, NET MESSAGE SOUND, and NET MESSAGE MESH) each have a parameter to indicate where to place the data (as referenced in Table 18.3).

Table 18.2 Network Message Return Values

Return Value	Data Type
1	Integer
2	Float
3	String
4	Memblock
5	Bitmap
6	Image
7	Sound
8	Mesh

Table 18.3 Network Message Types

Command	Data Type
NET MESSAGE INTEGER	Integer
NET MESSAGE FLOAT	Float
NET MESSAGE STRING$	String
NET MESSAGE MEMBLOCK	Memblock
NET MESSAGE BITMAP	Bitmap
NET MESSAGE IMAGE	Image
NET MESSAGE SOUND	Sound
NET MESSAGE MESH	Mesh

Let's Communicate

The ChatClient program demonstrates how to use the NET MESSAGE commands by creating a chat client. This program recycles some of the source code found in the NetworkConnect program because that code does not change. Figure 18.6 shows the host's point of view of the chat client with some sample chat. You will find this program on the CD in the Sources\Chapter18\ChatClient folder.

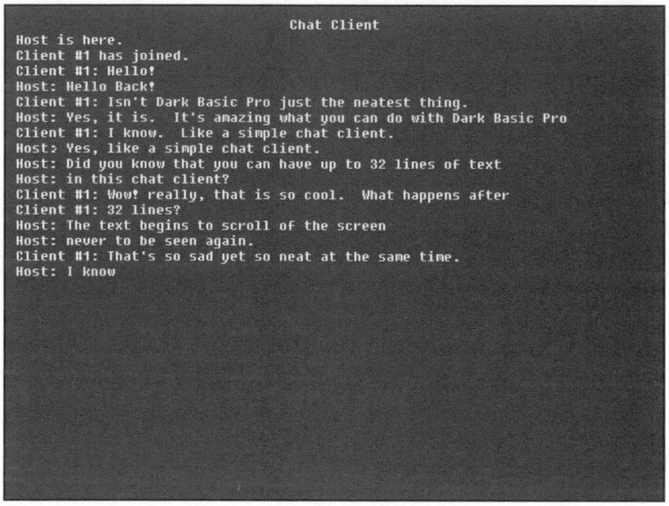

Figure 18.6 *The ChatClient program demonstrates using* NET MESSAGE *commands to create a chat client.*

```
REMSTART
----------------------------------
Beginner's Guide To DarkBASIC Game Programming
Copyright (C)2002 Jonathan S. Harbour and Joshua R. Smith
Chapter 18- ChatClient Program
----------------------------------
REMEND
SYNC ON
SYNC RATE 30

` Keep track of what was said and who said it.
DIM ChatText$(32)
DIM PlayersName$(1)
DIM NumberOfPlayers(1)
DIM LastNumberOfPlayers(1)
```

```
` Find the TCP/IP connection number
TcpIpNumber = FindTCPIPConnectionNumber()
PRINT "Simple network chat client!"
PRINT
SYNC
` Get their Name
INPUT "Please Enter Your Name: ", MyName$
PlayersName$(1) = MyName$
SYNC
SYNC
IF MyName$ = ""
    PRINT "You need to enter a name!"
    WAIT KEY
    END
ENDIF
` Find out who the host and clients are..
PRINT "(1) I'm the Host"
PRINT "(2) I'm the Client"
SYNC
SYNC
A$ = ""
Answer = 0
` Get Host or Client
WHILE Answer = 0
    A$ = INKEY$()
    IF A$ = "1" THEN Answer = 1
    IF A$ = "2" THEN Answer = 2
ENDWHILE
` Do this if I'm the host..
IF Answer = 1
    PRINT "Creating net session.  Please wait"
    SYNC
    SLEEP 200
    SET NET CONNECTION TcpIpNumber, " "
    CREATE NET GAME "Sample Net session", MyName$, 16, 1
ENDIF
` Do this if I'm the client.
IF Answer = 2
    Input "Please enter the Hosts IP Address: ",AddressData$
```

```
            PRINT "Connecting to net session.   Please wait"
            SYNC
            SET NET CONNECTION TcpIpNumber, AddressData$
            PERFORM CHECKLIST FOR NET SESSIONS
            NumberOfGames =CHECKLIST QUANTITY()
            IF NumberOfGames = 0
                 PRINT "No session found at that address"
                 SYNC
                 WAIT KEY
                 END
            ENDIF
            JOIN NET GAME 1, MyName$
            PRINT "Connected to session!"
            SYNC
    ENDIF
    ` Do the chat client
    ChatClient()
    END


    ` Ths function will determine which NET CONNECTION number
    ` is TCP/IP.
    FUNCTION FindTCPIPConnectionNumber()
        Flag = 0
        CLS
        PERFORM CHECKLIST FOR NET CONNECTIONS
        FOR x = 1 TO CHECKLIST QUANTITY()
            Service$ = CHECKLIST STRING$(x)
            IF LEFT$(Service$,15)="Internet TCP/IP"
                Flag = X
            ENDIF
        NEXT x
    ENDFUNCTION Flag


    ` This function does all the chat client functionality.
    FUNCTION ChatClient()
        ` Clears the chat text from the array..
        ClearChatText()
        `   Displays the initial players in the room.
        PERFORM CHECKLIST FOR NET PLAYERS
        NumberOfPlayers(1) = CHECKLIST QUANTITY()
```

```
    FOR x = 1 TO NumberOfPlayers(1)
        AddUserMessage(CHECKLIST STRING$(x))
    NEXT x

`   Send a comming in message
    C$ = PlayersName$(1)+" has joined."
    SEND NET MESSAGE STRING 0,C$
`    Displays the chat text..
    DisplayChatText()
`  Set the entry buffers.
    A$ = ""
    B$ = ""
    C$ = ""
    CLEAR ENTRY BUFFER
` Capture Text Input and process it accordingly
    WHILE ESCAPEKEY()=0
        CheckIncomingMessages()
        A$ = INKEY$()
        IF ASC(A$) = 8
            C$ = C$ + ENTRY$()
            C$ = LEFT$(C$,LEN(C$)-1)
            CLEAR ENTRY BUFFER
            CLS
            DisplayChatText()
        ENDIF
        B$ = C$ + ENTRY$()
        TEXT 10,460,B$
        IF RETURNKEY()=1 AND B$ <> ""
            SLEEP 250
`  Send Remote Message
            D$ = PlayersName$(1)+": "+B$
            SEND NET MESSAGE STRING 0,D$
`  Display Local Message
            AddStringToChat(D$)
            D$ = ""
            B$ = ""
            C$ = ""
            CLEAR ENTRY BUFFER
`  Display New Chat Window
            DisplayChatText()
```

```
            ENDIF
            SYNC
        ENDWHILE
ENDFUNCTION


` Scans the incoming messages for strings
` and displays them.
FUNCTION CheckIncomingMessages()
    GET NET MESSAGE
    IF NET MESSAGE EXISTS()=0 THEN EXITFUNCTION
    WHILE NET MESSAGE EXISTS()<>0
        MsgType = NET MESSAGE TYPE()
        IF MsgType = 3
            Msg$ = NET MESSAGE STRING$()
            AddStringToChat(Msg$)
            DisplayChatText()
        ENDIF
        GET NET MESSAGE
    ENDWHILE
ENDFUNCTION


` Message to display if a User has joined
FUNCTION AddUserMessage(Name$)
    NewString$ = Name$+" is here."
    AddStringToChat(NewString$)
ENDFUNCTION


` Adds a string to the ChatText$ array
FUNCTION AddStringToChat(a$)
    FOR x = 1 TO 32
        IF ChatText$(x) = ""
            ChatText$(x) = a$
            EXITFUNCTION
        ENDIF
    NEXT x
    FOR x = 32 TO 2
        y = x - 1
        ChatText$(y) = ChatText$(x)
    NEXT x
    ChatText$(32) = a$
ENDFUNCTION
```

```
`  Clears the ChatText$ Variables
FUNCTION ClearChatText()
    FOR x = 1 to 32
        ChatText$(x) = ""
    NEXT x
ENDFUNCTION


`  Displays the chat text on the screen
FUNCTION DisplayChatText()
    CLS
    SET CURRENT BITMAP 0
    CENTER TEXT 320,10,"Chat Client"
    FOR x = 1 TO 32
      TEXT 10,10+(x*15),ChatText$(x)
    NEXT x
ENDFUNCTION
```

Additional Multiplayer Commands

There are a few more multiplayer commands to cover. These commands give you a little extra data, as well as control over what is occurring. You don't need to use all of the commands to play a multiplayer game, but they do provide you with extra information.

The NET BUFFER SIZE() Command

The NET BUFFER SIZE() command returns how many messages are waiting to be received. This is the virtual pile of notes on your desk. If you don't want to process messages every time, you can use this command to determine how many are waiting before you process them. However, there is a limit to the number of packets that can be waiting. If you go over that limit, you will start losing them.

The FREE NET GAME Command

The FREE NET GAME command frees the current game so you can create a new one. Even though you can have multiple games from PERFORM CHECKLIST FOR NET SESSIONS, you can only have one game per application. Therefore, you need to free the game before starting a new one.

The NET GAME LOST() Command

The NET GAME LOST() command lets you know whether you have lost the current game. You should run this command to see whether the current net game has been freed. Once you know that it has, your program can quit the current game it is playing. There is no need to process or send any more net messages if no one is listening to them.

The CREATE NET PLAYER Command

The CREATE NET PLAYER command allows you to add your own players into the game. The command syntax is CREATE NET PLAYER *Playername$*, where *PlayerName$* is a string containing the name of the player you want to create. When you create or join a net game, a player is automatically created for you. This command allows you to add secondary or AI players or other local players to the same net game.

The FREE NET PLAYER Command

The FREE NET PLAYER command allows you to free a player from a net game. The command syntax is FREE NET PLAYER *PlayerNumber*, where *PlayerNumber* is the number of the player found in the PERFORM CHECKLIST FOR NET PLAYERS command. This is useful if you are dropping a local or AI player from the game because they have been destroyed or are no longer needed.

The NET PLAYER CREATED() Command

The NET PLAYER CREATED() command lets you know whether a net player was created by a CREATE NET PLAYER command. This command returns the number of the new net player that was created.

The NET PLAYER DESTROYED() Command

The NET PLAYER DESTROYED() command lets you know whether a net player was destroyed by a FREE NET PLAYER command. This command returns the number of the player that was destroyed.

Memory Blocks

One of the most power aspects of DarkBASIC
Professional is the ability to create and manipulate memory blocks (memblocks). A *memblock* can be any size and
can contain any data. Memblocks are powerful tools for
passing multiple bits of information over a single network packet. They are a defined size that can be broken
up into multiple bits of information. Figure 18.7 shows
one possible example of a memory block.

> **Memory blocks
> (memblocks) are chunks
> of memory allocated
> to store multiple types
> of information in one
> location. They have a
> specific size but do not
> conform to any specific
> data type. Memblocks
> can contain many
> different types of
> information in the
> same memory block.**

Creating Memory Blocks

Creating a memblock is similar to creating an image, bitmap, or sound. You simply
call the MAKE MEMBLOCK *Memblock Number, Size in Bytes* command. Make sure that
you set the size of the memblock large enough to fit all the data you will be storing
in it. The size is measured in bytes, so if you are placing four floats in the memory
block, you should allocate the size as 12 bytes (4×3).

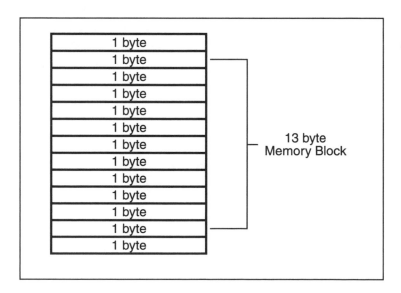

Figure 18.7

A sample memblock

Destroying Memory Blocks

Destroying a memblock is *very* important. If you do not destroy a memblock when you are finished using it, you can create a memory leak in your program. To destroy a memblock, just use the DELETE MEMBLOCK *Memblock Number* command. This command will destroy the memblock and free any memory associated with it.

Writing Data to Memory Blocks

Writing data into a memblock is pretty easy. DarkBASIC provides four different commands to write data into memblocks: WRITE MEMBLOCK BYTE, WRITE MEMBLOCK WORD, WRITE MEMBLOCK DWORD, and WRITE MEMBLOCK FLOAT. The syntax for each command looks like this:

```
WRITE MEMBLOCK BYTE MemblockNumber, Location, Value
WRITE MEMBLOCK WORD MemblockNumber, Location, Value
WRITE MEMBLOCK DWORD MemblockNumber, Location, Value
WRITE MEMBLOCK FLOAT MemblockNumber, Location, Value
```

Each of these commands has three parameters. The first parameter is the memblock number. This is the number you designated during the CREATE MEMBLOCK command. The second parameter is the location in the memblock to write the data. When you created the memory block you had to assign it a size that designated the maximum amount of data (in bytes) that can be placed into the memory block. Each value placed in a memblock takes up a specific amount of bytes. You do not want to overwrite any data that was previously written into a memblock by overwriting the bytes that contain that data. Table 18.4 contains the list of commands and the number of bytes of memory each uses.

Table 18.4 Memory Block WRITE Commands

Command	Data Size
WRITE MEMBLOCK BYTE	1
WRITE MEMBLOCK WORD	2
WRITE MEMBLOCK DWORD	4
WRITE MEMBLOCK FLOAT	4

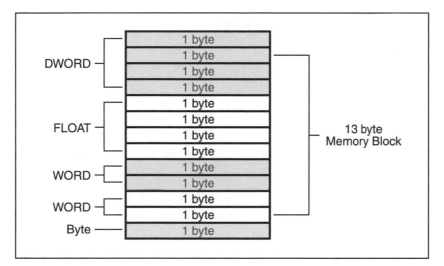

Figure 18.8 *A memblock with data and commands*

The third parameter of the WRITE MEMBLOCK commands is the value of the data itself. Figure 18.8 illustrates a memblock with data and the commands used to place that data into the memblock.

Reading Data from a Memory Block

Reading from a memory block is as easy as writing to one. There are four commands for reading from each memblock, and each command takes two parameters. The first parameter is the memblock number, and the second is the position in the memblock to start reading. Table 18.5 lists the commands for reading from a memblock. These commands return the values that you request from the memblock.

Table 18.5 Memblock Read Commands

Command	Data Size
MEMBLOCK BYTE	1
MEMBLOCK WORD	2
MEMBLOCK DWORD	4
MEMBLOCK FLOAT	4

Miscellaneous Memory Block Commands

There are a few other memblock commands that don't fall into the create/destroy or read/write categories. However, these commands are still useful for manipulating memblocks.

Copying Part of a Memory Block

The COPY MEMBLOCK *From, To, PosFrom, PosTo, Bytes* command copies the contents of one memory block to another. You can specify the locations in the memblock you are copying the data from and to, along with the size of the memory to copy.

Determining the Existence of a Memory Block

The MEMBLOCK EXISTS(*Memblock Number*) command indicates whether a memblock has been allocated. If the memblock has been allocated, this command returns a 0.

Retrieving the Size of a Memory Block

The GET MEMORYBLOCK SIZE(*Memblock Number*) command returns the size of the specified memblock.

Using Memblocks

Using memblocks is a tough concept to understand. The Memblock program shows you how to use them. This program asks for a few inputs, places the data into memblocks, and then returns the data stored in the memblock.

You can write this program using all variables, but the memblock is the most efficient way to collect data and send it as one net message. You will see the use of memblocks with net messages in the Crazy CARnage game. Figure 18.9 shows the output of the Memblock program. You can find the source for this program on the CD in the Sources\Chapter18\Memblock folder.

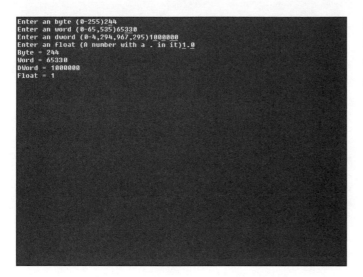

Figure 18.9 *The Memblock example demonstrates the use of memblocks.*

```
REMSTART
-----------------------------------
Beginner's Guide To DarkBASIC Game Programming
Copyright (C)2002 Jonathan S. Harbour and Joshua R. Smith
Chapter 18- Memblock Program
-----------------------------------
REMEND

CLS
` Create Memblock
MAKE MEMBLOCK 1,25
` Get the numbers
INPUT "Enter an byte (0-255)",MyByte
INPUT "Enter an word (0-65535)",MyWord
INPUT "Enter an dword (0-4294967295)",MyDWord
INPUT "Enter an float (A number with a . in it)",MyFloat#
` Make the Byte entered less than or equal to 255
WHILE MyByte > 255
    MyByte = MyByte - 255
ENDWHILE
```

```
` Make the Byte entered less than or equal to 65535
WHILE MyWord > 65535
    MyByte = MyByte - 65535
ENDWHILE
` Make the Byte entered less than or equal to 4294967295
WHILE MyDWord > 4294967295
    MyByte = MyByte - 4294967295
ENDWHILE
` Write the memory blocks
WRITE MEMBLOCK BYTE 1,0,MyByte
WRITE MEMBLOCK WORD 1,1,MyWord
WRITE MEMBLOCK DWORD 1,3,MyDWord
WRITE MEMBLOCK FLOAT 1,7,MyFloat#
` Clear the vars (to show memblocks are working)
MyByte = 0
MyWord = 0
MyDWord = 0
MyFloat# = 0.0
` Read the vars from the memblock
MyByte = MEMBLOCK BYTE(1,0)
MyWord = MEMBLOCK WORD(1,1)
MyDWord = MEMBLOCK DWORD(1,3)
MyFloat# = MEMBLOCK FLOAT(1,7)
` Display the vars gathered.
PRINT "Byte = "+STR$(MyByte)
PRINT "Word = "+STR$(MyWord)
PRINT "DWord = "+STR$(MyDWord)
PRINT "Float = "+STR$(MyFloat#)
`Delete Memory Block
DELETE MEMBLOCK 1
WAIT KEY
END
```

The Crazy CARnage Game!

"Gentlemen, start your engines!"

Are you ready to roll? It's time to work on the game! This will be the final project in the book. It's been a long road with many learning curves along the way, but I am confident that you will be able to understand this game without any problem. Crazy CARnage is a multiplayer car combat game. As I was writing this chapter, Crazy CARnage took many forms. One version had a level editor; another version was only single-player. Throughout the development of any game, you will make many revisions. It's the final product that counts, and it is up to you to decide on the final vision for a game.

Crazy CARnage uses two car models from the DarkMATTER collection. They are the Buggy models. It's so much fun to fight with buggies. Crazy CARnage also uses a skybox and ground texture from the DarkMATTER collection. This collection is an excellent source of material for those who are not necessarily artistically inclined. As you can tell, I'm not the world's best artist. I generated all of the other textures in the game.

TIP

If you have the full version of DarkBASIC, make sure you have the latest patch. You can find it at http://www.darkbasicpro.com. This game might not run correctly on the original version of DarkBASIC because it was developed with the 1.13 patch release.

You can find all the source for Crazy CARnage on the CD in the Chapter 18 source directory. All graphics, 3D models, sounds, and textures are located in this directory as well. The files are located in subfolders that are referenced through the game. If you copy the game to your hard drive to modify it, make sure you copy all the subfolders as well. After I walk you through the coding of this game, I will give you a list of add-ons and features I would love to see in the game. If you add any of them, feel free to e-mail the authors with a link to the game. We'd both love to see it.

The Menus

This game can be broken into two major sections. The first section is the menus. These menus help you decide which computer is the host and which is the client. Each player must decide his name and whether he will be a host or a client. Figure 18.10 displays the screen where you enter your name. This is all part of the menu section.

Figure 18.10
*The player name
entry screen*

The Game

After the games are connected from the host and client menus, you enter the second section—the actual gameplay. The up, down, left, and right arrows allow you to maneuver the car around the screen. The spacebar fires your weapon. You can display a radar by holding down the Shift key. The first player to lose all his health (shown in the red health bar) loses the game. There are boxes with power-ups scattered throughout the level; these power-ups include health, speed, weapon increase, and freeze. Figure 18.11 displays the game interface.

Figure 18.11
*The Crazy CARnage
game is all-out fun!*

When a player loses all of his health, the game is over, and the winner is declared. The winner of the game is the player who still has health remaining. After that, you return to the main menu. The game contains many TYPE and DIM commands. Good luck typing the program; if you get too frustrated, you can find the code listing on the CD in the Sources\Chapter18\CrazyCarnage folder.

```
SYNC RATE 30
SYNC ON
DISABLE ESCAPEKEY
AUTOCAM OFF


`  Special Type Defines
`  This Type Contains the Players Information
`  Their Name (NAME$)
`  And If they are that player (IAM)
DIM PlayerInfoName$(2)
DIM PlayerInfoIam(2)


`    This type references all the objects
`    Laid through the level
`    ObjectNumber is the DarkBASIC Object Number
`    ObjectType is the type of object
`    3 Health
`    4 Speed
`    5 Weapon
`    6 Freeze
DIM SpecialObjectsObjectNumber(256)
DIM SpecialObjectsObjectType(256)


`    This contains all the information about a
`    project (what the car files)
`    ObjectNumber is the DarkBASIC object number
`    ObjectSpeed is how fast the projectile is going.
`    ObjectTimer is the time the projectile has to live
`    ObjectOwner is who fired the projectile
`    ObjectDoneDamage indicates if the object has hit anything.
`    ObjectDamage is how much damage the object can/will do.
`    ObjectType is the type of projectile being shot.
DIM ProjectileObjectNumber(30)
DIM ProjectileObjectSpeed(30)
DIM ProjectileObjectTimer(30)
```

```
DIM ProjectileObjectLive(30)
DIM ProjectileObjectOwner(30)
DIM ProjectileObjectDoneDamage(30)
DIM ProjectileObjectDamage(30)
DIM ProjectileObjectType(30)

`   Type type contains all the variables about the car.
`   ObjectStartX is the starting X position of the car
`   ObjectStartZ is the starting Z position of the car.
`   There is no ObjectStartY because the car starts
`     on the ground.
`   CarWaponPower is how much Damage a shot from the
`     car does.
`   CarAngle is the Angle the car is facing.
`   CarSpeed is the speed the car is going.
`   CarMaxSpeed is how fast the car can go.
`   CarHealth is how much health the car has left.
`   ObjectNumber is the DarkBASIC object number
DIM CarInfoObjectStartX(2)
DIM CarInfoObjectStartZ(2)
DIM CarInfoCarWeaponPower(2)
DIM CarInfoCarAngle(2)
DIM CarInfoCarSpeed(2)
DIM CarInfoCarMaxSpeed(2)
DIM CarInfoCarHealth(2)
DIM CarInfoObjectNumber(2)

`  Global Dims
`  This Contains your name
DIM YourName$(1)
`  This contains what connection number
`  TCP/IP is
DIM ConnectType(1)
`  This contains if a network connection
`  was established.
DIM NoNetwork(1)
DIM MyPlayerNumber(1)
`   Contains what player number They am
`   either 1 or 2 and is the opposite of
`   MyPlayerNumber
DIM TheirPlayerNumber(1)
```

```
`  Fire Counter to delay firing
DIM FireCounter(1)
`  How many Special Objects are out there.
DIM SpecialObjCount(1)
`  Stores where the other player quit or not.
DIM HeQuit(1)
`  Determines if the radar needs to be displayed.
DIM ShowTheRadar(1)
`  Timer to freeze my car if need be.
DIM FreezeTimer(1)
`  I am the host this is 1
DIM IAmHost(1)

`  Initialize the global vars.
ShowTheRadar(1) = 0
FreezeTimer(1) = 0
SpecialObjCount(1) = 0
MyPlayerNumber(1)   = 1
TheirPlayerNumber(1)= 2
NoNetwork(1) = 1
IAmHost(1) - 1
`  Determing which connection is TCP/IP
CType = StandardNetworkStuff()
ConnectType(1) = CType
`  Process Menus and Play the game.
WHILE ProcessMenus()=1
    PlayGame()
ENDWHILE
END
```

The ProcessMenus() function displays all the initial menus for connecting the game. In the previous examples in this chapter, you used a simple text menu. However, most games don't use simple PRINT and INPUT menus. They have fancy graphics and menu selections. The ProcessMenus() function calls all the sub-functions for generating the look of the menu. You'll notice that this function returns a 1 or a 0 (based on the RetValue variable). This tells the main part of the program whether or not to play.

```
`  Processes all the game menus
FUNCTION ProcessMenus()
    Flag = 0
    RetValue = 1
```

```
` We need to loop until we have a game established..
` Once a game is establiched (or the player quits)
` Flag is set to 1.
` RetValue is used to determine if we need to play
` a game or not.
WHILE Flag=0
    ` Display the Main Menu.
    Command = MainMenu()
    ` If they quit the main menu..
    ` Don't play the game.
    IF Command = 3
        Flag = 1
        RetValue = 0
    ENDIF
    IF Command = 1
        NoNetwork(1) = 1
        Flag = 1
        RetValue = 1
    ENDIF
    `   Load up the Multiplayer menus
    IF Command = 2
        NoNetwork(1) = 0
        ` Get their name
        ReturnBack = GetNameScreen()
        IF ReturnBack <> -1
            MenuCommand = -1
            ` Find out whose hosting and whose a client..
            HostCommand = HostMenu()
            IF HostCommand = 1
                ` If we are hosting wait for the clients
                MenuCommand = WaitForHostMenu()
            ENDIF
            IF HostCommand = 2
                ` If we are a client, look for the host.
                MenuCommand = ConnectToHostMenu()
            ENDIF
            IF HostCommad = 3
                Flag = 1
                RetValue = 0
            ENDIF
            IF MenuCommand = -1
```

```
                    Flag = 0
                ELSE
                    Flag = 1
                ENDIF
            ELSE
                Flag = 0
            ENDIF
        ENDIF
    ENDWHILE
ENDFUNCTION RetValue
```

The PlayGame() function is the heart of Crazy CARnage. This function contains the main game loop and calls all the sub-functions required to play the game. All the images used in the interface (HUD—*Heads-Up Display*) are loaded in this function, which is executed after you've made your choices in the main menus. All the graphics for the HUD are located in the HUD subfolder. Also included in this function is the processing of the Shift key to display the radar.

```
REMSTART
 Play the main game...
REMEND
FUNCTION PlayGame()
    CarInfoCarWeaponPower(1) = 1
    CarInfoCarWeaponPower(2) = 1
    CarInfoCarMaxSpeed(1) = 1
    CarInfoCarMaxSpeed(2) = 1
`    Generates the Terrain for the Level
    GenerateLevel()
`   Loads all the images for the Heads up Display (HUD)
    LOAD IMAGE "Hud\Hud_All.bmp",20
    LOAD IMAGE "Hud\Radar.bmp",21
    LOAD BITMAP "Hud\GreenBar.bmp",2
    LOAD BITMAP "Hud\RedBar.bmp",3
    CREATE BITMAP 4,170,170

    SET CURRENT BITMAP 0

`   Initialized all the variables, models and sounds
    InitAllProjectiles()
    LoadSounds()
    LoadCarModels()
    InitialSpecialObjects()
```

```
SetCarLocation()
MyNumber = MyPlayerNumber(1)
TheirNumber = TheirPlayerNumber(1)
CarInfoCarAngle(MyNumber) = 0
CarInfoCarSpeed(MyNumber)=0
SendLocationPacket_Var = 0
FireCounter(1) = 0
Done = 0
HeQuit(1) = 0
MyObjectNumber = CarInfoObjectNumber(MyNumber)
TheirObjectNumber = CarInfoObjectNumber(TheirNumber)


` Main game loop... Exited when Done != 1
WHILE Done=0
    ` Check to see if radar should be displayed.
    IF SHIFTKEY()=1
        ShowTheRadar(1) = 1
    ELSE
        ShowTheRadar(1) = 0
    ENDIF
    ` Check to see if they quit.
    IF ESCAPEKEY()=1
        SendIQuitPacket()
        DONE = -1
    ENDIF
    ` If they quit, I should quit too..
    IF HeQuit(1) = 1
        DONE = -1
    ENDIF
    `   Process all the projectiles.
    ProcessProjectiles()
    `   Process all the network packets
    IF NoNetwork(1) = 0
        GET NET MESSAGE
        IF NET MESSAGE EXISTS()<>0
            ProcessNetMessages()
        ENDIF
        IF NET GAME LOST() = 1
          DONE = -1
        ENDIF
    ENDIF
```

```
``              `  Save the COORDs of my car.
                XLOC# = OBJECT POSITION X(MyObjectNumber)
                YLOC# = OBJECT POSITION Y(MyObjectNumber)
                ZLOC# = OBJECT POSITION Z(MyObjectNumber)
                YROT# = OBJECT ANGLE Y(MyObjectNumber)
                ` Set the camera to follow my car.
                SET CAMERA TO FOLLOW XLOC#, YLOC#,ZLOC#, YROT#, -12, 5, 1 ,1
                ` Reset my cars speed.
                CarInfoCarSpeed(MyNumber) = 0
                CarInfoCarSpeed(TheirNumber) = 0
                `  Check to see if I'm frozen
                IF FreezeTimer(1) > 0
                    SecondsLeft = FreezeTimer(1)-Timer()
                    SecondsLeft = SecondsLeft / 1000
                    IF SecondsLeft < 0 THEN SecondsLeft = 0
                    NewString$ = "Frozen: "+STR$(SecondsLeft)+" seconds."
                    TEXT 0,300,NewString$
                    IF TIMER() > FreezeTimer(1)
                        FreezeTimer(1) = 0
                    ENDIF
                    IF TIMER() < 10000
                        FreezeTimer(1) = 0
                    ENDIF
                ENDIF
                ` Check to see if my car is moving or turning.
                SendLocationPacket_Var = 0
                SendLocationPacket_Var = DriveCar(MyNumber)
                LookForSpaceBarFire(MyNumber)
                CarInfoCarAngle(MyNumber) = WRAPVALUE(CarInfoCarAngle(MyNumber))
                ` Move and turn my car based on the values determined above.
                YROTATE OBJECT MyObjectNumber,CarInfoCarAngle(MyNumber)
                MOVE OBJECT MyObjectNumber,CarInfoCarSpeed(MyNumber)
                ` IF my car is colliding, move it back.
                IF OBJECT COLLISION(MyObjectNumber,TheirObjectNumber) = 1
                    MOVE OBJECT MyObjectNumber, CarInfoCarSpeed(MyNumber)*-1
                ENDIF
                `  IF my car collides with the edge of the world.
                XLOC# = OBJECT POSITION X(MyObjectNumber)
                ZLOC# = OBJECT POSITION Z(MyObjectNumber)
                IF XLOC# <=0 OR XLOC# >=320
                    MOVE OBJECT MyObjectNumber, CarInfoCarSpeed(MyNumber)*-1
```

```
            ENDIF
            IF ZLOC# <=0 OR ZLOC# >=320
                MOVE OBJECT MyObjectNumber, CarInfoCarSpeed(MyNumber)*-1
            ENDIF
            `  Tell the other player I've moved..
            IF SendLocationPacket_Var =  1 THEN SendLocationPacket()

            `  Check for collisions to me...
            CheckForOtherCollisions(MyNumber)
            `  Check for collisions for them..
            CheckForOtherCollisions(TheirNumber)
            `  Display the HUD
            DisplayHud()
            `  Display the players names.
            DisplayPlayers()
            `  Determine the winnner
            `  Set's Done to the Player number
            `  if there is a winner.
            IF Done <> -1
                Done = GetWinner()
            ENDIF
            `Display What we've processed.
            SYNC
        ENDWHILE

        `  Send one final damage state so the other side knows who lost..
        SendDamageState()
        `  Clean up everything allocated..
        DELETE IMAGE 20
        DELETE IMAGE 21
        DELETE BITMAP 3
        DELETE BITMAP 2
        DELETE BITMAP 4
        DELETE SOUND 1
        DELETE SOUND 2
        DELETE SOUND 3
        KillSpecialObject()
        KillLevel()
        `  Reset the camera
        ResetCamera()
        `  If we have a winner display them.
```

```
        IF Done <> -1
            DisplayWinner(Done)
        ENDIF
        `  Free the net game so we can start anotherone.
        IF NET GAME EXISTS() = 1 THEN FREE NET GAME
        `   Delete the cars.
        DELETE OBJECT 2
        DELETE OBJECT 1
ENDFUNCTION
```

The next two functions, GenerateLevel() and KillLevel(), dcal with creating the world. GenerateLevel() loads the terrain, the terrain texture, and the background skybox. KillLevel() unloads the terrain, the terrain texture, and the background skybox. The terrain and terrain texture are located in the Terrain subfolder. The skybox is located in the Background subfolder.

```
`  Loads the Terrain, Terrain Texture, and
`  Skybox Texture.
FUNCTION GenerateLevel()
    `   Load the Terrain Texture
    LOAD IMAGE "Terrain\texture.bmp",10

    `   Make the Terrain
    MAKE MATRIX 1,320,320,10,10
    PREPARE MATRIX TEXTURE 1, 10, 1, 1

    `   Load the Skybox
    LOAD OBJECT "Background\sky01.x",3
    `   Turn off collision with the skybox as
    `   the car is inside the sky box and will
    `   always collide with it otherwise.
    SET OBJECT COLLISION OFF 3

    `   Set the Position, scale, and CULL of the
    `   Skybox.
    POSITION OBJECT 3,160,0,160
    SCALE OBJECT 3,5000,5000,5000
ENDFUNCTION

FUNCTION KillLevel()
    `   Free the Terrain
    DELETE MATRIX 1
```

```
`   Free the Skybox Object
DELETE OBJECT 3
`   Free the Terrain Texture
DELETE IMAGE 10
ENDFUNCTION
```

The next five functions—MainMenu(), HostMenu(), GetNameScreen(), ConnectToHostMenu(),
and WaitForHostMenu()—are the menus that are called by the ProcessMenu() function. The MainMenu() function has two options—to play the game and to quit. The
HostMenu() function has three options—to host the game, to join the game, or to
quit. The GetNameScreen() function gets the player's name and stores it in the
YourName$(1) variable. The ConnectToHostMenu() function establishes the client-side
connection to the game. The WaitForHostMenu() function establishes the host connection to the game. All the menus load their main graphics from the Menu subfolder. Each menu also loads the skybox (and rotates it) from the Background
subfolder.

```
`   Display the Main Menu
FUNCTION MainMenu()
    `   Sets the ambient Light
    SET AMBIENT LIGHT 100
    `   Loads Resources for this menu
    LOAD OBJECT "Background\sky01.x",3
    LOAD IMAGE "Menu\menu.bmp",1
    `   Set Variables
    Flag = 0
    BackgroundAngle = 0
    Black = RGB(0,0,0)
    Orange = RGB(255,102,0)
    SET CURSOR 10,10
    `   Loops until Flag <> 0
    WHILE Flag=0
        IF ESCAPEKEY()=1 THEN Flag = 3
        BackgroundAngle = BackgroundAngle + 1
        BackgroundAngle = WRAPVALUE(BackgroundAngle)
        YROTATE OBJECT 3,BackGroundAngle
        MX = MOUSEX()
        MY = MOUSEY()
        `   Check to see if Multiplayer was selected.
        IF MX >230 AND MX <500 AND MY >180 AND MY <225
            INK Orange,Black
            BOX 230,180,500,225
```

```
            IF MOUSECLICK() = 1 THEN Flag = 2
        ENDIF
        ` Check to see if Quit was selected.
        IF MX >230 AND MX <310 AND MY >390 AND MY <435
            INK Orange,Black
            BOX 230,390,310,435
            IF MOUSECLICK() = 1 THEN Flag = 3
        ENDIF
        ` Paste the main menu image on the screen.
        PASTE IMAGE 1,0,0,1
        SYNC
    ENDWHILE
    ` Free Resources used in this menu.
    DELETE IMAGE 1
    DELETE OBJECT 3
ENDFUNCTION Flag


`   Display the Host or Client Menu
FUNCTION HostMenu()
    ` Sets the ambient Light
    SET AMBIENT LIGHT 100
    ` Loads Resources for this menu         `
    LOAD OBJECT "Background\sky01.x",3
    LOAD IMAGE "Menu\Multiplayer.bmp",1
    ` Set Variables
    Flag = 0
    BackgroundAngle = 0
    Black = RGB(0,0,0)
    Orange = RGB(255,102,0)
    SET CURSOR 10,10


    ` This loop ask the player to Host or
    ` Join a game.
    ` Loops until FLAG <> 0
    WHILE Flag=0
        BackgroundAngle = BackgroundAngle + 1
        BackgroundAngle = WRAPVALUE(BackgroundAngle)
        YROTATE OBJECT 3,BackGroundAngle
        MX = MOUSEX()
        MY = MOUSEY()
        ` Check to see if host was selected.
```

```
            IF MX >230 AND MX <400 AND MY >110 AND MY <155
                INK Orange,Black
                BOX 230,110,400,155
                IF MOUSECLICK() = 1 THEN Flag = 1
            ENDIF
            ` Check to see if join was selected.
            IF MX >230 AND MX <500 AND MY >180 AND MY <225
                INK Orange,Black
                BOX 230,180,500,225
                IF MOUSECLICK() = 1 THEN Flag = 2
            ENDIF
            ` Check to see if quit was selected.
            IF MX >230 AND MX <310 AND MY >390 AND MY <435
                INK Orange,Black
                BOX 230,390,310,435
                IF MOUSECLICK() = 1 THEN Flag = 3
            ENDIF

            PASTE IMAGE 1,0,0,1
            SYNC
        ENDWHILE
        ` Free Resources used in this menu.
        DELETE IMAGE 1
        DELETE OBJECT 3
    ENDFUNCTION Flag

    FUNCTION GetNameScreen()
        ` Sets the ambient Light
        SET AMBIENT LIGHT 100
        ` Loads Resources for this menu
        LOAD OBJECT "Background\sky01.x",3
        LOAD IMAGE "Menu\NameOnly.bmp",1
        ` Set Variables
        Flag = 0
        BackgroundAngle = 0
        BLACK = RGB(0,0,0)
        WHITE = RGB(255,255,255)
        INK WHITE,BLACK
        SET CURSOR 10,10
        B$ = ""
        C$ = ""
```

```
        CLEAR ENTRY BUFFER
        ` This loop collects the players name.
        ` Loops until FLAG <> 0
        WHILE Flag=0
            IF ESCAPEKEY()=1 THEN Flag = -1
            BackgroundAngle = BackgroundAngle + 1
            BackgroundAngle = WRAPVALUE(BackgroundAngle)
            YROTATE OBJECT 3,BackGroundAngle
            IF RETURNKEY()=1 AND B$ <> ""
                WHILE RETURNKEY()=1
                ENDWHILE
                Flag = 1
            ENDIF
            CENTER TEXT 320,260,"Enter Your Name"
            A$ = INKEY$()
            IF ASC(A$) = 8
                C$ = C$ + ENTRY$()
                C$ = LEFT$(C$,LEN(C$)-1)
                CLEAR ENTRY BUFFER
            ENDIF

            B$ = C$ + ENTRY$()
            CENTER TEXT 320,280,B$

            PASTE IMAGE 1,0,0,1
            SYNC
        ENDWHILE
        ` Free Resources used in this menu.
        YourName$(1) = LEFT$(B$,LEN(B$)-1)

        DELETE IMAGE 1
        DELETE OBJECT 3
        CLEAR ENTRY BUFFER
ENDFUNCTION Flag

FUNCTION ConnectToHostMenu()
        ` Check for a valid network connection
        CType = ConnectType(1)
        IF CType = 0 THEN EXITFUNCTION 0
        IAmHost(1) = 0
        ` Sets the ambient Light
```

```
SET AMBIENT LIGHT 100
` Loads Resources for this menu
LOAD OBJECT "Background\sky01.x",3
LOAD IMAGE "Menu\NameOnly.bmp",1
` Set Variables
MyPlayerNumber(1) = 2
TheirPlayerNumber(1) = 1
MyNumber = MyPlayerNumber(1)
TheirNumber = TheirPlayerNumber(1)
MyName$ = YourName$(1)
Flag = 0
BackgroundAngle = 0
Black = RGB(0,0,0)
White = RGB(255,255,255)
INK White,Black
SET CURSOR 10,10
B$ = ""
C$ = ""
CLEAR ENTRY BUFFER
` This loop get's the IP address
` of the host you are connecting to.
` It loops until FLAG <> 0
WHILE Flag=0
    IF ESCAPEKEY()=1 THEN Flag = -1
    BackgroundAngle = BackgroundAngle + 1
    BackgroundAngle = WRAPVALUE(BackgroundAngle)
    YROTATE OBJECT 3,BackGroundAngle
    IF RETURNKEY()=1
        WHILE RETURNKEY()=1
        ENDWHILE
        Flag = 1
    ENDIF
    CENTER TEXT 320,260,"Enter Host Address"
    A$ = INKEY$()
    IF ASC(A$) = 8
        C$ = C$ + ENTRY$()
        C$ = LEFT$(C$,LEN(C$)-1)
        CLEAR ENTRY BUFFER
    ENDIF
    B$ = C$ + ENTRY$()
    CENTER TEXT 320,280,B$
```

```
            PASTE IMAGE 1,0,0,1
            SYNC
    ENDWHILE
    CLEAR ENTRY BUFFER
    ` Free Resources used in this menu.
    ` if ESCAPE was pressed.
    IF Flag = -1
            DELETE IMAGE 1
            DELETE OBJECT 3
            EXITFUNCTION Flag
    ENDIF
    SET NET CONNECTION CType,B$
    ` This loop waits until there are
    ` two players in the game.  This will
    ` rarely ever loop more than once.
    ` because you are the client (the
    ` second player to join).
    ` It loops until Flag <> 0
    Flag = 0
    WHILE Flag=0
        IF ESCAPEKEY()=1 THEN Flag = -1
        PERFORM CHECKLIST FOR NET SESSIONS
        IF CHECKLIST QUANTITY() = 1
            JOIN NET GAME 1,MyName$
            Flag = 1
        ENDIF
        BackgroundAngle = BackgroundAngle + 1
        BackgroundAngle = WRAPVALUE(BackgroundAngle)
        YROTATE OBJECT 3,BackGroundAngle
        CENTER TEXT 320,260,"Connecting to Client"
        PASTE IMAGE 1,0,0,1
        SYNC
    ENDWHILE
    ` Free Resources used in this menu.
    ` if ESCAPE was pressed.
    IF Flag = -1
        DELETE IMAGE 1
        DELETE OBJECT 3
        EXITFUNCTION Flag
    ENDIF
    GetPlayerNames()
```

```
        DELETE IMAGE 1
        DELETE OBJECT 3
ENDFUNCTION Flag


FUNCTION WaitForHostMenu()
        ` Check for a valid network connection
        CType = ConnectType(1)
        IF CType = 0 THEN EXITFUNCTION 0
        IAmHost(1) = 1
        SET NET CONNECTION CType," "
        MyName$ = YourName$(1)
        CREATE NET GAME "DualRacer", MyName$, 2
        ` Sets the ambient Light
        SET AMBIENT LIGHT 100
        ` Loads Resources for this menu
        LOAD OBJECT "Background\sky01.x",3
        LOAD IMAGE "Menu\NameOnly.bmp",1
        ` Set Variables
        MyPlayerNumber(1)=1
        TheirPlayerNumber(1)=2
        MyNumber = MyPlayerNumber(1)
        TheirNumber = TheirPlayerNumber(1)
        MyName$ = YourName$(1)
        Flag = 0
        BackgroundAngle = 0
        Black = RGB(0,0,0)
        White = RGB(255,255,255)
        INK White,Black
        SET CURSOR 10,10
        ` This look waits until two players are joined in the
        ` game created on this computer.
        ` It loops until Flag <> 0
        WHILE Flag=0
            IF ESCAPEKEY()=1 THEN Flag = -1
            BackgroundAngle = BackgroundAngle + 1
            BackgroundAngle = WRAPVALUE(BackgroundAngle)
            YROTATE OBJECT 3,BackGroundAngle
            PERFORM CHECKLIST FOR NET PLAYERS
            NumOfPlayers = CHECKLIST QUANTITY()
            IF CHECKLIST QUANTITY() = 2
                Flag = 1
```

```
                ENDIF
                IF RETURNKEY()=1
                    Flag = 3
                ENDIF
                CENTER TEXT 320,260,"Waiting for Client"
                NewString$ = "Players Waiting: "+STR$(NumOfPlayers)
                CENTER TEXT 320,280, NewString$
                PASTE IMAGE 1,0,0,1
                SYNC
        ENDWHILE

        `   Free the resources if ESC was pressed
        `   Includes freeing the game.
        IF Flag = -1
            FREE NET GAME
            DELETE IMAGE 1
            DELETE OBJECT 3
            EXITFUNCTION Flag
        ENDIF
        `   Loads the players names into the correct
        `   variables.
        GetPlayerNames()
        `   Free the resources if ESC was pressed
        DELETE IMAGE 1
        DELETE OBJECT 3
ENDFUNCTION Flag
```

The next four functions cover in-game displays. These functions deal with displaying player names, the HUD, and the radar. The GetPlayerNames() function stores the players' names in the PlayerInfo(...) structures. The DisplayPlayers() function displays the players' names on the screen. The DisplayHUD() function displays all the 2D graphics on the screen. The DisplayRadar() function displays the radar.

```
`   Records the players names into the
`   PlayerInfo... globals
FUNCTION GetPlayerNames
    PERFORM CHECKLIST FOR NET PLAYERS
    NUMOFPLAYERS = CHECKLIST QUANTITY()
    FOR x = 1 to NUMOFPLAYERS
        PlayerInfoName$(x) = CHECKLIST STRING$(x)
        IF PlayerInfoName$(x) = YourName$(1)
            PlayerInfoIam(x) = 1
```

```
        ELSE
            PlayerInfoIam(x) = 0
        ENDIF
    NEXT x
ENDFUNCTION


` Displays the players name on the screen
FUNCTION DisplayPlayers
    BLACK = RGB(0,0,0)
    WHITE = RGB(255,255,255)
    INK WHITE,BLACK
    FOR x = 1 to 2
        TEXT 10,(X*10)+20,PlayerInfoName$(x)
    NEXT x
ENDFUNCTION


` Displays the heads up display on the screen.
FUNCTION DisplayHud
    MyNumber = MyPlayerNumber(1)
    TheirNumber = TheirPlayerNumber(1)

    PASTE IMAGE 20,0,0,1

    COPY BITMAP 3,0,0,199,11,0,20,440,220,452
    COPY BITMAP 3,0,0,199,11,0,20,460,220,472

    ` Displays the health of both cars
    XSIZE = CarInfoCarHealth(MyNumber)*2
    IF XSIZE <> 0
        COPY BITMAP 2,0,0,XSIZE-1,11,0,20,440,20+XSIZE,452
    ENDIF
    XSIZE = CarInfoCarHealth(TheirNumber)*2
    IF XSIZE <> 0
        COPY BITMAP 2,0,0,XSIZE-1,11,0,20,460,20+XSIZE,472
    ENDIF

    If ShowTheRadar(1)=1 THEN DisplayRadar()

ENDFUNCTION

` Display the RADAR on the screen.
```

```
FUNCTION DisplayRadar()
    MyNumber = MyPlayerNumber(1)
    TheirNumber = TheirPlayerNumber(1)

    MyObjNumber = CarInfoObjectNumber(MyNumber)
    MyXPos = OBJECT POSITION X(MyObjNumber)
    MyYPos = OBJECT POSITION Z(MyObjNumber)

    TheirObjNumber = CarInfoObjectNumber(TheirNumber)
    TheirXPos = OBJECT POSITION X(TheirObjNumber)
    TheirYPos = OBJECT POSITION Z(TheirObjNumber)

    MyXPos = MyXPos / 2
    MyYPos = MyYPos / 2
    TheirXPos = TheirXPos / 2
    TheirYPos = TheirYPos / 2
    MyXPos = MyXPos+5
    MyYPos = MyYPos+5
    TheirXPos = TheirXPos+5
    TheirYPos = TheirYPos+5

    ` Dipslay the Players positions
    Grn = RGB(0,255,0)
    Red = RGB(255,0,0)
    Wht = RGB(255,255,255)
    SET CURRENT BITMAP 4
    PASTE IMAGE 21,0,0,0
    X1 = MyXPos-2
    X2 = MyXPos+2
    Y1 = MyYPos-2
    Y2 = MyYPos+2
    INK Green, Black
    BOX X1,Y1,X2,Y2
    X1 = TheirXPos-2
    X2 = TheirXPos+2
    Y1 = TheirYPos-2
    Y2 = TheirYPos+2
    INK Red, Black
    BOX X1,Y1,X2,Y2

    INK White, Black
```

```
` Display all projectiles being fired.
FOR x = 1 TO 30
    PObj = ProjectileObjectNumber(x)
    IF OBJECT EXIST(Pobj)
        ProX = OBJECT POSITION X(Pobj)
        ProY = OBJECT POSITION Z(Pobj)
        ProX = ProX/2
        ProY = ProY/2
        ProX = ProX+5
        ProY = ProY+5
        X1 = ProX-2
        X2 = ProX+2
        Y1 = ProY-2
        Y2 = ProY+2
        BOX X1,Y1,X2,Y2
    ENDIF
NEXT x
SET CURRENT BITMAP 0
COPY BITMAP 4,0,0,169,169,0,465,75,634,244
ENDFUNCTION
```

The next five functions deal with the bullets (projectiles) fired from the car. You'll see the number 30 show up a few times in these functions. That is because there are only 30 projectiles on the screen at any one time. Each player has 15 projectiles they can fire at any given time.

The InitAllProjectiles() function sets all the projectiles to their initial states. The ProcessProjectiles() function is the heart of what all the projectiles do. It processes their movements and checks to see whether they have dissipated. The DamagePlayer(PlayerNum, DamageDone) function applies damage to the specified player based on the damage done by the projectile. When this function is called, DamageDone is passed from the particle structures.

The ExplodeProjectile(ProjectileNum) function explodes a projectile when it is called. This function is called when a projectile has hit a player. The FireProjectTile(PlayerNum, ProjectileType) function sets up all the variables necessary to fire a projectile, creates the object, and sets it in motion.

```
` Sets all the projectiles to a base state
FUNCTION InitAllProjectiles
    FOR x = 1 to 30
        ProjectileObjectNumber(x) = 49+x
        ProjectileObjectSpeed(x) = 0
```

```
            ProjectileObjectLive(x) = 0
            ProjectileObjectTimer(x) = 0
            ProjectileObjectOwner(x) = 0
            ProjectileObjectDoneDamage(x) = 0
            ProjectileObjectDamage(x) = 0
            ProjectileObjectType(x) = 0
    NEXT x
ENDFUNCTION


`   Process all the projectiles.
FUNCTION ProcessProjectiles
    FOR x = 1 to 30
        ObjNumber = ProjectileObjectNumber(x)
        ObjSpeed = ProjectileObjectSpeed(x)
        ObjTimer = ProjectileObjectTimer(x)
        ` Make sure the object exists
        ` if it does not, that projectile
        ` has not been fired yet.
        IF OBJECT EXIST(ObjNumber)=1
            ` Move the projetile forward
            MOVE OBJECT ObjNumber, ObjSpeed
            ` Decrease the Projectiles timer.
            ProjectileObjectTimer(x) = ObjTimer - 1

            ` Check for the end of the projectile
            IF ProjectileObjectTimer(x) <= 10
                GHOST OBJECT ON ObjNumber
                FADE OBJECT ObjNumber,25
            ENDIF
            ` Free the projectile if it's at the end..
            IF ProjectileObjectTimer(x) <= 0
                ProjectileObjectLive(x) = 0
                ProjectileObjectOwner(x) = 0
                DELETE OBJECT ObjNumber
            ENDIF
        ENDIF
    NEXT x
ENDFUNCTION


` This function is called with a projectile
` collides with another player
```

```
FUNCTION DamagePlayer(PlayerNum , DamageDone)
    MyNumber = MyPlayerNumber(1)
    `  You can't get hit by your own projectile.
    IF PlayerNum <> MyNumber THEN EXITFUNCTION
    ` Reduce their health.
    CarInfoCarHealth(PlayerNum) = CarInfoCarHealth(PlayerNum) - DamageDone
    ` If the health is less then 0 make it equal to 0
    IF CarInfoCarHealth(PlayerNum) < 0
        CarInfoCarHealth(PlayerNum) = 0
    ENDIF
    `  Send the damage information to the other player.
    SendDamageState()
ENDFUNCTION


` This function is called when the projectile collides with a player.
FUNCTION ExplodeProjectile(ProjectileNum)
    ProjectileObjectTimer(ProjectileNum) = 10
    ProjectileObjectSpeed(ProjectileNum) = 0
    ProjectileObjectDoneDamage(ProjectileNum) = 1
ENDFUNCTION


`  The is called when a projectile needs to be fired.
FUNCTION FireProjectTile(PlayerNum, ProjectileType)
    Flag = 0
    ` This set of IF and for statements determine the
    ` next particle availible to you.
    IF PlayerNum = 1
        FOR x = 1 to 15
            IF ProjectileObjectLive(x) = 0
                Flag = x
                x = 30
            ENDIF
        NEXT x
    ELSE
        FOR x = 16 to 30
            IF ProjectileObjectLive(x) = 0
                Flag = x
                x = 30
            ENDIF
        NEXT x
    ENDIF
```

```
      ` If no particles are availible leave this function
      ` You don't want to fire blank particles.
      IF Flag = 0
           EXITFUNCTION Flag
      ENDIF
      `  Setup the Data for the Particle.
      ProjectileObjectOwner(Flag) = PlayerNum
      ProObjectNum = ProjectileObjectNumber(Flag)
      CarObjectNumber = CarInfoObjectNumber(PlayerNum)
      XPos# = OBJECT POSITION X(CarObjectNumber)
      YPos# = OBJECT POSITION Y(CarObjectNumber)
      ZPos# = OBJECT POSITION Z(CarObjectNumber)
      XRot# = OBJECT ANGLE X(CarObjectNumber)
      YRot# = OBJECT ANGLE Y(CarObjectNumber)
      ZRot# = OBJECT ANGLE Z(CarObjectNumber)
      ` Create the Particle VIA the MAKE OBJECT SPHERE
      ` command.
      MAKE OBJECT SPHERE ProObjectNum, 2
      ` SCALE POSITION and Size the particle.
      SCALE OBJECT ProObjectNum, 25,25,25
      POSITION OBJECT ProObjectNum,XPos#, YPos# + 1 , ZPOos#
      ROTATE OBJECT ProObjectNum, XRot#, YRot#, ZRot#
      MOVE OBJECT ProObjectNum, -2
      ` Turn on the collision for the particle.
      SET OBJECT COLLISION ON ProObjectNum
      SET OBJECT COLLISION TO BOXES ProObjectNum
      ` Set the remaining values for the Particle.
      CarMaxSpeed = CarInfoCarMaxSpeed(PlayerNum)*-1
      ProjectileObjectSpeed(Flag) = CarMaxSpeed-1
      ProjectileObjectTimer(Flag) = 100
      ProjectileObjectLive(Flag) = 1
      ProjectileObjectDamage(Flag) = CarInfoCarWeaponPower(PlayerNum)
      ProjectileObjectDoneDamage(Flag) = 0
      ProjectileObjectType(Flag) = ProjectileType
      ` Play the FIRE Sound.
      PLAY SOUND 1
ENDFUNCTION FLAG
```

If the PlayGame() function is the heart of this game, then the next six functions are the circulatory system. These are the veins and arteries of the program, passing the data around the network. The SendLocationPacket() function is called every time your car is moved. This command tells the other game to move the car on your behalf. The SendProjectilePacket(ObjectNum, ProjectileType) function is called every time a projectile is fired. This tells the other game to fire a projectile from the car on your behalf. The SendIQuitPacket() function is called when a player hits the Esc key. This lets the other game know that the player has quit. The SendDamageState() function is called whenever your projectiles hit your opponent. This lets the other game know that you have hit the other player.

The ProcessNetMessages() function is the brains of the operation. It takes all the messages sent from the other computer and processes them. It keeps track of the command that was sent through the memblock message and processes it accordingly. The StandardNetworkStuff() function finds the connection number for TCP/IP, which is needed to connect games via TCP/IP.

```
` Sends location packets..
FUNCTION SendLocationPacket()
    ` If there is no network.. don't send the packet.
    IF NoNetwork(1) = 1 THEN EXITFUNCTION
    MAKE MEMBLOCK 1,60
    ` Collectes the location information.
    MyNumber = MyPlayerNumber(1)
    MySpeed = CarInfoCarSpeed(MyNumber)
    MyObjectNumber = CarInfoObjectNumber(MyNumber)
    XPos# = OBJECT POSITION X(MyObjectNumber)
    YPos# = OBJECT POSITION Y(MyObjectNumber)
    ZPos# = OBJECT POSITION Z(MyObjectNumber)
    XRot# = OBJECT ANGLE X(MyObjectNumber)
    YRot# = OBJECT ANGLE Y(MyObjectNumber)
    ZRot# = OBJECT ANGLE Z(MyObjectNumber)

    MyHealth = CarInfoCarHealth(MyNumber)

    ` Writes all the location information into the memblcok.
    WRITE MEMBLOCK DWORD 1,1,1
    WRITE MEMBLOCK FLOAT 1,5,XPos#
    WRITE MEMBLOCK FLOAT 1,9,YPos#
    WRITE MEMBLOCK FLOAT 1,13,ZPos#
    WRITE MEMBLOCK FLOAT 1,17,XRot#
    WRITE MEMBLOCK FLOAT 1,21,YRot#
    WRITE MEMBLOCK FLOAT 1,25,ZRot#
    WRITE MEMBLOCK DWORD 1,29,MyHealth
    ` Sends the packet..
```

```
      SEND NET MESSAGE MEMBLOCK 0,1,1
      DELETE MEMBLOCK 1
   ENDFUNCTION


`  Sends projectile packets.
FUNCTION SendProjectilePacket(ObjectNum,ProjectileType)
      ` If there is no network.. don't send the packet.
      IF NoNetwork(1) = 1 THEN EXITFUNCTION
      MAKE MEMBLOCK 1,50
      ` Collects the Projectile information.
      MyNumber = MyPlayerNumber(1)
      NewNumber = ProjectileObjectNumber(ObjectNum)
      MyObjectNumber = CarInfoObjectNumber(MyNumber)
      XPos# = OBJECT POSITION X(MyObjectNumber)
      YPos# = OBJECT POSITION Y(MyObjectNumber)
      ZPos# = OBJECT POSITION Z(MyObjectNumber)
      XRot# = OBJECT ANGLE X(MyObjectNumber)
      YRot# = OBJECT ANGLE Y(MyObjectNumber)
      ZRot# = OBJECT ANGLE Z(MyObjectNumber)

      MyHealth = CarInfoCarHealth(MyNumber)

      ` Writes all the location
      ` and firing information
      ` into the memblcok.
      WRITE MEMBLOCK DWORD 1,1,2
      WRITE MEMBLOCK FLOAT 1,5,XPos#
      WRITE MEMBLOCK FLOAT 1,9,YPos#
      WRITE MEMBLOCK FLOAT 1,13,ZPos#
      WRITE MEMBLOCK FLOAT 1,17,XRot#
      WRITE MEMBLOCK FLOAT 1,21,YRot#
      WRITE MEMBLOCK FLOAT 1,25,ZRot#
      WRITE MEMBLOCK DWORD 1,29,ProjectileType
      WRITE MEMBLOCK DWORD 1,33,ObjectNum
      WRITE MEMBLOCK DWORD 1,37,MyHealth
      ` Sends the packet..
      SEND NET MESSAGE MEMBLOCK 0,1,1
      DELETE MEMBLOCK 1
ENDFUNCTION

` Sends the Quitting packet..
```

```
FUNCTION SendIQuitPacket()
    IF NoNetwork(1) = 1 THEN EXITFUNCTION
    MAKE MEMBLOCK 1,50
    WRITE MEMBLOCK DWORD 1,1,4
    ` Sends the packet..
    SEND NET MESSAGE MEMBLOCK 0,1,1
    DELETE MEMBLOCK 1
ENDFUNCTION


` Sends Damages State packets.
FUNCTION SendDamageState()
    ` If there is no network.. don't send the packet.
    IF NoNetwork(1) = 1 THEN EXITFUNCTION
    MAKE MEMBLOCK 1,50
    ` Collects damage information.
    MyNumber = MyPlayerNumber(1)
    MyHealth = CarInfoCarHealth(MyNumber)
    ` Writes the damage information to the MEMBLOCK.
    WRITE MEMBLOCK DWORD 1,1,5
    WRITE MEMBLOCK DWORD 1,5,MyHealth
    ` Sends the packet..
    SEND NET MESSAGE MEMBLOCK 0,1,1
    DELETE MEMBLOCK 1
ENDFUNCTION


` Processes all the network messages (Packets).
FUNCTION ProcessNetMessages()
    ` If there is no network.. don't process messages.
    IF NoNetwork(1) = 1 THEN EXITFUNCTION
    MAKE MEMBLOCK 2,50
    TheirNumber = TheirPlayerNumber(1)
    ` Loops while we still have some network messages to read..
    WHILE NET MESSAGE EXISTS()=1
        ` Get the message..
        NET MESSAGE MEMBLOCK 2

        ` The first DWORD in the message is the command
        CmdNumber = MEMBLOCK DWORD(2,1)
        ` This was a location packet..
        IF CmdNumber = 1
            TheirObjNum = CarInfoObjectNumber(TheirNumber)
```

```
            XPos# = MEMBLOCK FLOAT(2,5)
            YPos# = MEMBLOCK FLOAT(2,9)
            ZPos# = MEMBLOCK FLOAT(2,13)
            XRot# = MEMBLOCK FLOAT(2,17)
            YRot# = MEMBLOCK FLOAT(2,21)
            ZRot# = MEMBLOCK FLOAT(2,25)

            NewHealth = MEMBLOCK DWORD(2,29)
            CarInfoCarHealth(TheirNumber)  = NewHealth

            POSITION OBJECT TheirObjNum, XPos#, YPos#, ZPos#
            ROTATE OBJECT TheirObjNum, XRot#, YRot#, ZRot#
            CarInfoCarAngle(TheirNumber) = YRot
ENDIF
`   This was a Projectile Packet
IF CmdNumber = 2
    TheirObjNum = CarInfoObjectNumber(TheirNumber)
    XPos# = MEMBLOCK FLOAT(2,5)
    YPos# = MEMBLOCK FLOAT(2,9)
    ZPos# = MEMBLOCK FLOAT(2,13)
    XRot# = MEMBLOCK FLOAT(2,17)
    YRot# = MEMBLOCK FLOAT(2,21)
    ZRot# = MEMBLOCK FLOAT(2,25)

    NewHealth = MEMBLOCK DWORD(2,37)
    CarInfoCarHealth(TheirNumber)  = NewHealth

    POSITION OBJECT TheirObjNum, XPos#, YPos#, ZPos#
    ROTATE OBJECT TheirObjNum, XRot#, YRot#, ZRot#
    ProjectileType = MEMBLOCK DWORD(2,29)
    FireProjectTile(TheirNumber,ProjectileType)
ENDIF
`   This was a Quit Packet
IF CmdNumber = 4
    HeQuit(1) = 1
ENDIF
`   This was a damage packet.
IF CmdNumber = 5
    NewHealth = MEMBLOCK DWORD(2,5)
    CarInfoCarHealth(TheirNumber)  = NewHealth
ENDIF
```

```
            ` Get the next Message
            GET NET MESSAGE
        ENDWHILE
        DELETE MEMBLOCK 2
ENDFUNCTION
`   Determine what connection number
`   TCP/IP is.
FUNCTION StandardNetworkStuff()
    Flag = 0
    CLS
    PERFORM CHECKLIST FOR NET CONNECTIONS
    FOR x = 1 TO CHECKLIST QUANTITY()
        Service$ = CHECKLIST STRING$(x)
        IF LEFT$(Service$,15)="Internet TCP/IP"
            Flag = x
        ENDIF
    NEXT x
ENDFUNCTION Flag
```

The next three functions focus on the special objects. All the object textures are loaded from the Pieces subfolder. The `InitialSpecialObjects()` function initializes all the special objects and their placements using the `DATA` statements provided. To change the position of any special object in the world, just modify the `DATA` statements. The `ProcessSpecialObject(ObjectIndex,Player)` function affects a player based on the object with which they have collided. The `KillSpecialObject()` command frees all the special objects after a game is finished.

```
`   Data Format
`   Object Number, Xpos, Zpos, ObjectType

`   Health Powerups
DATA 55,250,3,31
DATA 25,150,3,31
DATA 178,192,3,31
DATA 299,170,3,31
DATA 49,21,3,31
DATA 62,130,3,31
DATA 71,49,3,31
DATA 99,112,3,31
DATA 57,38,3,31
DATA 22,245,3,31
```

```
` Speed Powerups
DATA 15,131,4,32
DATA 263,42,4,32
` Weapon Powerups
DATA 10,310,5,33
DATA 310,10,5,33
DATA 10,10,5,33
DATA 310,310,5,33
DATA 130,18,5,33
DATA 301,22,5,33
DATA 41,108,5,33
DATA 163,23,5,33
` Freeze Powerups
DATA 47,180,6,34
DATA 220,20,6,34
DATA 77,111,6,34
DATA 125,132,6,34


` Initializes all the special objects and their placements
FUNCTION InitialSpecialObjects()
    NewObjectNum = 500
    SpecialObjCount(1) = 0
    ObjCount = 1

    ` Load all the textures
    LOAD IMAGE "Pieces\Health.bmp",31
    LOAD IMAGE "Pieces\Speed.bmp",32
    LOAD IMAGE "Pieces\Weapon.bmp",33
    LOAD IMAGE "Pieces\Freeze.bmp",34

    FOR x = 1 TO 24
        READ Xloc
        READ Zloc
        READ ObjType
        READ TexNum
        MAKE OBJECT BOX NewObjectNum,2,2,2
        TEXTURE OBJECT NewObjectNum,TexNum
        POSITION OBJECT NewObjectNum, Xloc,1,Zloc
        SpecialObjectsObjectNumber(ObjCount) = NewObjectNum
        SpecialObjectsObjectType(ObjCount) = ObjType
```

```
            SET OBJECT COLLISION ON NewObjectNum
            ObjCount = ObjCount + 1
            NewObjectNum = NewObjectNum + 1
        NEXT x
        SpecialObjCount(1) = 24
ENDFUNCTION


`  Process the effects of special objects on the car.
FUNCTION ProcessSpecialObject(ObjectIndex,Player)
    TheirNumber = TheirPlayerNumber(1)
    MyNumber = MyPlayerNumber(1)
    PHealth = CarInfoCarHealth(Player)
    SpObjNum = SpecialObjectsObjectNumber(ObjectIndex)
    SELECT SpecialObjectsObjectType(ObjectIndex)
        `  Health Object
        CASE 3
            IF PHealth = 100 THEN EXITFUNCTION 0
            IF PHealth > 75
                CarInfoCarHealth(Player) = 100
            ELSE
                CarInfoCarHealth(Player) = PHealth + 25
            ENDIF
            IF OBJECT EXIST(SpObjNum)
                DELETE OBJECT SpObjNum
            ENDIF
        ENDCASE
        `  Speed Object
        CASE 4
            IF CarInfoCarMaxSpeed(Player) = 2 THEN EXITFUNCTION 0
            CarInfoCarMaxSpeed(Player) = CarInfoCarMaxSpeed(Player) + 1
            IF OBJECT EXIST(SpObjNum)
                DELETE OBJECT SpObjNum
            ENDIF
        ENDCASE
        `  Weapon Power UP
        CASE 5
            WepPow =CarInfoCarWeaponPower(Player)
            IF WepPow = 5 THEN EXITFUNCTION 0
            CarInfoCarWeaponPower(Player) = WepPow + 1
            IF OBJECT EXIST(SpObjNum)
                DELETE OBJECT SpObjNum
```

```
            ENDIF
        ENDCASE
        ` Speed Power UP.
        CASE 6
            IF Player = TheirNumber
                FreezeTimer(1) = TIMER()+10000
            ENDIF
            IF OBJECT EXIST(SpObjNum)
                DELETE OBJECT SpObjNum
            ENDIF
        ENDCASE
    ENDSELECT
ENDFUNCTION 1


`  Frees all unused special objects.
FUNCTION KillSpecialObject()
    SpecialCount = SpecialObjCount(1)
    FOR x = 1 TO SpecialObjCount(1)
        ObjNum = 499+x
        IF OBJECT EXIST(ObjNum)
            DELETE OBJECT ObjNum
        ENDIF
    NEXT x
    ` Frees the texturs as well.
    DELETE IMAGE 31
    DELETE IMAGE 32
    DELETE IMAGE 33
    DELETE IMAGE 34
ENDFUNCTION
```

The next six functions all deal with players' cars. The LoadCarModels() function loads all the cars into their respective objects. The car models are all located in the Models subfolder; each car model, in turn, is contained in a separate subfolder under that. The Beach Bug subfolder contains Player 1's car. The Beach Bug2 subfolder contains Player 2's car.

The LoadSounds() function loads all the sounds used in the game. The SetCarLocation() function places the two cars in the world. The DriveCar(CarNumber) function controls the movement of the car on the screen. Just like in the real world, you must be moving before you can turn. The LookForSpaceBarFire(CarNumber) function checks whether the spacebar has been pressed. If it has, the function fires a projectile.

The CheckForOtherCollisions(PlayerNumber) function drives the game. This function detects collisions between the players and the projectiles or special objects.

```
` Loads all the car models
FUNCTION LoadCarModels()
    ` Loads the models
    LOAD OBJECT "models\Beach Bug\H-Beach Bug-Move.x",1
    LOAD OBJECT "models\Beach Bug 2\H-Beach Bug 2-Move.x",2
    ` Set's their collision on
    SET OBJECT COLLISION TO BOXES 1
    SET OBJECT COLLISION TO BOXES 2
    SET OBJECT COLLISION ON 1
    SET OBJECT COLLISION ON 2
    ` Set their ObjectNumber
    CarInfoObjectNumber(1) = 1
    CarInfoObjectNumber(2) = 2
    ` Set their Health
    CarInfoCarHealth(1) = 100
    CarInfoCarHealth(2) = 100
ENDFUNCTION


`  Loads all the sounds used.
FUNCTION LoadSounds()
    LOAD SOUND "sounds\FIRE.WAV",1
    LOAD SOUND "sounds\HIT.WAV",2
    LOAD SOUND "sounds\PICKUP.WAV",3
ENDFUNCTION


`  Positions the car in the world.
FUNCTION SetCarLocation()
    XLoc# = 25
    ZLoc# = 25
    ObjNum = CarInfoObjectNumber(1)
    POSITION OBJECT ObjNum,XLoc#,0,ZLoc#
    XLoc# = 295
    ZLoc# = 295
    ObjNum = CarInfoObjectNumber(2)
    POSITION OBJECT ObjNum,XLoc#,0,ZLoc#
    ` Send an object packet so the other
    ` player knows where you are.
    SendLocationPacket()
```

```
    ENDFUNCTION

`   This function drives the car around
`   the world.
FUNCTION DriveCar(CarNumber)
`    If you are frozen, you can't drive.
     IF FreezeTimer(1) <> 0 THEN EXITFUNCTION 0
`     Set the variables.
     MyNumber = CarNumber
     SendLocationPacket_var = 0
     MaxCarSpeed = CarInfoCarMaxSpeed(MyNumber)
`     Check for Forward motion
     IF UPKEY()=1
         CarInfoCarSpeed(MyNumber)=MaxCarSpeed*-1
         SendLocationPacket_var = 1
     ENDIF
`     Check for backwards motion
     IF DOWNKEY()=1
         CarInfoCarSpeed(MyNumber)=MaxCarSpeed*1
         SendLocationPacket_var = 1
     ENDIF
     CurAngle = CarInfoCarAngle(MyNumber)
`     Check for Backwards motion and
`     Turning Left
     IF LEFTKEY()=1 AND CarInfoCarSpeed(MyNumber)>0
         CarInfoCarAngle(MyNumber) = CurAngle +5
         IF CarInfoCarAngle(MyNumber) > 360
             CarInfoCarAngle(MyNumber) = 5
         ENDIF
         SendLocationPacket_var = 1
     ENDIF
`     Check for Forwards motion and
`     Turning Left
     IF LEFTKEY()=1 AND CarInfoCarSpeed(MyNumber)<0
         CarInfoCarAngle(MyNumber) = CurAngle -5
         IF CarInfoCarAngle(MyNumber) < 0
             CarInfoCarAngle(MyNumber) = 355
         ENDIF
         SendLocationPacket_var = 1
     ENDIF
```

```
      `   Check for Backwards motion and
      `   Turning Right
      IF RIGHTKEY()=1 AND CarInfoCarSpeed(MyNumber)>0
          CarInfoCarAngle(MyNumber) = CurAngle -5
          IF CarInfoCarAngle(MyNumber) < 0
              CarInfoCarAngle(MyNumber) = 355
          ENDIF
          SendLocationPacket_var = 1
      ENDIF
      `   Check for Forwards motion and
      `   Turning Right
      IF RIGHTKEY()=1 AND CarInfoCarSpeed(MyNumber)<0
          CarInfoCarAngle(MyNumber) = CurAngle +5
          IF CarInfoCarAngle(MyNumber) > 360
              CarInfoCarAngle(MyNumber) = 5
          ENDIF
          SendLocationPacket_var = 1
      ENDIF
ENDFUNCTION SendLocationPacket_var


` Detects if the space bar was pressed
` and if it was, fires a projectile.
FUNCTION LookForSpaceBarFire(CarNumber)
    MyNumber = CarNumber
    ` Checks the fire counter to space out
    ` the projectiles.
    IF SPACEKEY()=1 AND FireCounter(1) = 0
        Flag = FireProjectTile(MyNumber,1)
        IF Flag <> 0
            SendProjectilePacket(FLAG,1)
        ENDIF
        FireCounter(1) = 5
    ENDIF
    IF FireCounter(1)>0
        FireCounter(1) = FireCounter(1) -1
    ENDIF
ENDFUNCTION

` Checks for collisions with other objects.
FUNCTION CheckForOtherCollisions(PlayerNumber)
```

```
TheirNumber = TheirPlayerNumber(1)
MyNumber = MyPlayerNumber(1)
CarObjNum = CarInfoObjectNumber(PlayerNumber)
` If the player isn't colliding, Quit..
ObjectNumColide = OBJECT COLLISION(CarObjNum,0)
IF ObjectNumColide = 0 THEN EXITFUNCTION
Flag = 0
` Check if the player is colliding with
` Projectiles
FOR x = 1 to 30
    PObjNum = ProjectileObjectNumber(x)
    PObjOwn = ProjectileObjectOwner(x)
    PObjDmg = ProjectileObjectDamage(x)
    IF ObjectNumColide = PObjNum and PObjOwn <> PlayerNumber
        SET OBJECT COLLISION OFF PObjNum
        DamagePlayer(PlayerNumber , PObjDmg)
        STOP SOUND 1
        PLAY SOUND 2
        ExplodeProjectile(x)
        Flag = 1
    ENDIF
NEXT x
` If they collided with a projectile quit..
` No need to process further.
IF Flag = 1 THEN EXITFUNCTION
` Check if the player is colliding with
` Special Objects
Flag = 0
FOR x = 1 TO 24
    IF ObjectNumColide = SpecialObjectsObjectNumber(x)
        Flag = x
        x = 25
    ENDIF
NEXT x

IF Flag <> 0
    NewFlag = ProcessSpecialObject(Flag,PlayerNumber)
ENDIF
ENDFUNCTION
```

The last three functions deal with winning and winning screens. The GetWinner() function determines whether there is a winner. If so, the function returns the winner's number. The DisplayWinner(WinnerNumber) function displays the winner on the winning screen. Both players can see who won the game. To leave this screen, the player simply presses the Esc key. The ResetCamera() function resets the camera for the winning screen.

```
` Determines the winner.
FUNCTION GetWinner()
    MyNumber = MyPlayerNumber(1)
    TheirNumber = TheirPlayerNumber(1)
    IF CarInfoCarHealth(MyNumber) <= 0
        EXITFUNCTION TheirNumber
    ENDIF
    IF CarInfoCarHealth(TheirNumber) <= 0
        EXITFUNCTION MyNumber
    ENDIF
ENDFUNCTION 0


` Displays the winning screen.
FUNCTION DisplayWinner(WinnerNumber)
    ` Sets the ambient light
    SET AMBIENT LIGHT 100
    `  Loads the skybox.
    LOAD OBJECT "Background\sky01.x",3
    Black = RGB(0,0,0)
    White = RGB(255,255,255)
    INK White,Black
    POSITION OBJECT CarInfoObjectNumber(WinnerNumber), 0,0,5
    MyNumber = MyPlayerNumber(1)
    TheirNumber = TheirPlayerNumber(1)
    IF WinnerNumber = MyNumber
        IF PlayerInfoIam(1) = 1
            WinnerText$ = PlayerInfoName$(1)
        ELSE
            WinnerText$ = PlayerInfoName$(2)
        ENDIF
    ENDIF
    IF WinnerNumber = TheirNumber
        IF PlayerInfoIam(1) = 0
```

```
            WinnerText$ = PlayerInfoName$(1)
        ELSE
            WinnerText$ = PlayerInfoName$(2)
        ENDIF
    ENDIF
    WinnerText$ = WinnerText$ +" is the winner"
    BackgroundAngle = 0
    WinObjNum = CarInfoObjectNumber(WinnerNumber)
    Flag = 0
    ` Waits until the ESCAPEKY is pressed.
    WHILE Flag=0
        BackgroundAngle = BackgroundAngle + 1
        BackgroundAngle = WRAPVALUE(BackgroundAngle)
        YROTATE OBJECT 3,BackGroundAngle
        YROTATE OBJECT WinObjNum ,BackGroundAngle
        CENTER TEXT 320,40,WinnerText$
        IF RETURNKEY()=1 THEN Flag = 1
        SYNC
    ENDWHILE
    ` Free the SkyBox
    DELETE OBJECT 3
ENDFUNCTION

` Resets the camera.
FUNCTION ResetCamera()
    POSITION CAMERA 0,0,0
    ROTATE CAMERA 0,0,0
ENDFUNCTION
```

The Extras

As I said before, I would like to see a few things added to this game. I had several great ideas that would not fit in the book. Here are a few ideas you can use to improve this game and make it that much better.

- **Different cars**. My favorite idea is to add more cars to the game. I love VWs, but there are more cars out there that you can use. Tanks, motorcycles, and police cars are just a few from the DarkMATTER collection. When you add the cars, just remember that when the multiplayer game is connected, the other computer needs to know what both cars are.

- **Car damage**. Another exciting aspect to add to the game would be car damage. It's not as hard as it sounds. You simply replace the car model with a more damaged model. Just remember that with health power-ups, your car could go back to a healthier state.

- **Different environments**. This game offers only one type of background and one type of texture for the terrain. It would be neat to have different worlds in which you can battle. The host could select the world before the game begins.

- **Multi-level terrain**. This problem is a little tougher to tackle, but you already have a small foothold on it by using the MAKE TERRAIN command. Check out the DarkBASIC Language Reference on the CD for a list of all the different terrain commands available.

- **More power-ups**. Weapons boost, speed boost, health, and freeze are nice power-ups, but not very creative. Try adding a few other power-ups, such as one that doubles the size of your car or one that makes the other player's controls go in reverse. The possibilities here are endless.

- **More weapons**. I'm using just a torpedo-type weapon, but more weapons would improve the game. I like weapons that people don't expect, such as hover jets or homing missiles.

- **Massively multiplayer capability**. A big undertaking for this game would be to make it massively multiplayer. Multiplayer can support two or more players, but what about a game of 32 or 64 cars? That would be massively multiplayer.

Summary

What an extensive chapter. Multiplayer and memblocks are the final components to make your games great. Feel free to modify the Crazy CARnage game to add more special effects and such. Use your imagination. If you come up with something really cool, let me know. I'd like to hear what you have done with the source code.

Chapter Quiz

The chapter quiz will help to reinforce the material you learned in this chapter, and will provide feedback on how well you have learned the subjects that were covered. For the answers to the quiz, refer to Appendix A, "Answers to the Chapter Quizzes."

1. Which component of DirectX does DarkBASIC utilize for multiplayer support?

   A. DirectNetwork
   B. DirectSound
   C. DirectPlay
   D. DirectConnect

2. A packet is . . .

   A. A series of commands sent to the hard drive
   B. A collection of data sent from one computer to another to be processed
   C. A jacket's cousin
   D. Slang for a packrat

3. Which of the following is *not* a domain name?

   A. www.yahoo.com
   B. slashdot.org
   C. 209.232.223.22
   D. www.cnn.com

4. What is considered the taxicab of the Internet?

   A. TCP/IP
   B. OC/UD
   C. MME/OB
   D. IPX/SPX

5. How many players can participate in a single net game?

   A. 4
   B. 256
   C. 16
   D. Unlimited

6. Which command returns the number of net messages waiting?

   A. MESSAGES WAITING
   B. MESSAGES EXIST
   C. GET NETMESSAGE
   D. NET BUFFER SIZE

7. What does the `Create Memblock` command do?

   A. Creates a memblock for reading and writing

   B. Deletes an existing memblock

   C. Prints a smiley face on the printer

   D. None of the above

8. How is the size of a memblock measured?

   A. In pixels

   B. In inches

   C. In dollars

   D. In bytes

9. What does the `WRITE MEMBLOCK WORD 1, 200, 4` command do?

   A. Writes 4 bytes to memblock 1, starting at byte 1

   B. Writes 200 bytes to memblock 1, starting at byte 4

   C. Writes 1 byte to memblock 4, starting at byte 200

   D. Writes 200 bytes to memblock 4, starting at byte 1

10. `GET MEMBLOCK SIZE(Memblock Number)` returns what information about a memblock?

   A. Its size in pixels

   B. Its size in inches

   C. Its size in dollars

   D. Its size in bytes

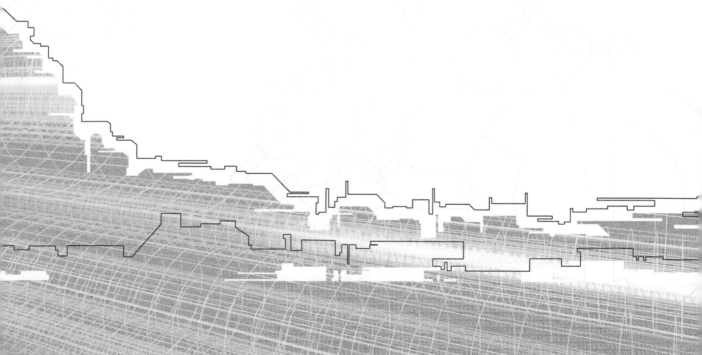

EPILOGUE

I feel as though we have just completed a long road trip together! Although I do not know you personally, I have gotten to know many readers and fans of my other books through online forums, so there is a certain feeling of coming full circle at this point. I hope you have found this book not just helpful, but invaluable as a reference and enjoyable to read. I have strived to leave no stone unturned and to cover everything you need to write cutting-edge games with DarkBASIC.

The goal of this book was first and foremost to teach the subject of computer programming, so there are many aspects of DarkBASIC that did not make it into the final book. This was inevitable because there are more than a thousand commands, and many subjects are just too difficult to incorporate into a beginner's book. DarkBASIC is now my favorite gaming language, and I find it a joy to use. My sincere hope is that you find DarkBASIC just as charming and pleasing to use, and that you keep this book by your side while you are writing your next game.

Contacting the Authors

Although every effort was made to ensure that the content and source code presented in this book are error-free, it is possible that errors in print or bugs in sample programs might have missed our scrutiny. Writing a book like this one is a tremendous effort, and with any large project, unintentional errors sometimes show up. Although many checks and review processes are followed before a book goes to print, some errors do occasionally slip by. If you have any problems with the source code, sample programs, or general theory in this book, please let us know. You can contact Jonathan at support@jharbour.com, and Joshua at joshua.smith@delnar.com. We will do our best to help you work though any problems. I also welcome your general comments about the book. I get several hundred e-mails a month from readers, and I respond to every one!

Finally, whether you are an absolute beginner or a seasoned professional, I invite you to join our discussion list on YahooGroups, where you will have an opportunity to share your games, ideas, and questions with other DarkBASIC fans! Membership is free and open to all. Just send an e-mail to the listserver at DarkBasic-Game-Programming-subscribe@yahoogroups.com, or visit the Web site at http://www.yahoogroups.com and search for the list by name. Of course, I also recommend that you visit the DarkBASIC home pages (http://www.darkbasic.com and http://www.darkbasicpro.com) regularly to keep up with the latest developments and any upgrades to the compiler. Also, be sure to check our Web sites for news and updates at http://www.jharbour.com and http://www.delnar.com. We look forward to hearing from you!

PART IV

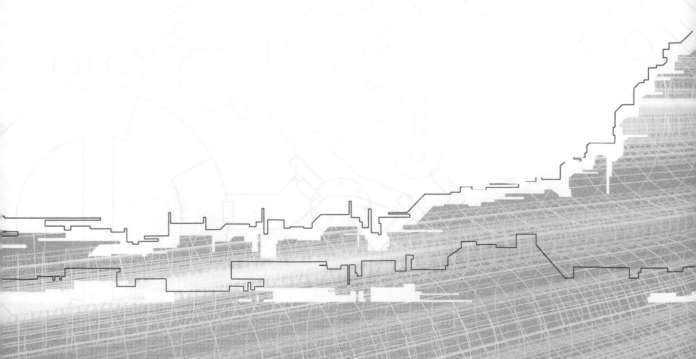

Welcome to Part IV, the appendixes for the book. This Part includes four appendixes of reference material, including answers to the chapter quizzes, a list of recommended game programming books and supporting Web sites, an ASCII chart, and a guide to the included CD-ROM.

A   Answers to the Chapter Quizzes

B   Recommended Books and Web Sites

C   ASCII Chart

D   Guide to the CD-ROM

APPENDIX A

Answers to the Chapter Quizzes

This appendix contains the answers to all the quiz questions from each chapter. I hope you got all the answers correct! If you miss more than four answers in any given quiz, I recommend that you go back and re-read the chapter in question and try again before proceeding, because each chapter builds upon the ones before it. Good Luck!

Chapter 1

1. B	6. D
2. C	7. A
3. D	8. C
4. A	9. D
5. A	10. B

Chapter 2

1. B	6. A
2. D	7. A
3. B	8. B
4. B	9. B
5. B	10. A

Chapter 3

1. C	6. A
2. B	7. C
3. C	8. D
4. A	9. B
5. A	10. B

Chapter 4

1. B	6. D
2. B	7. A
3. A	8. A
4. A	9. B
5. C	10. C

Chapter 5

1. C	6. D
2. B	7. B
3. D	8. B
4. B	9. C
5. A	10. A

Chapter 6

1. A	6. D
2. C	7. B
3. B	8. B
4. D	9. C
5. B	10. B

Chapter 7

1. D	6. B
2. A	7. B
3. D	8. D
4. B	9. C
5. A	10. C

Chapter 8

1. C	6. C
2. B	7. A
3. C	8. A
4. C	9. B
5. C	10. C

Chapter 9

1. B	6. A
2. A	7. C
3. B	8. D
4. A	9. C
5. B	10. B

Chapter 10

1. B	6. C
2. B	7. C
3. C	8. B
4. D	9. D
5. D	10. A

Chapter 11

1. A	6. B
2. C	7. C
3. A	8. C
4. D	9. A
5. B	10. D

Chapter 12

1. A	6. B
2. A	7. B
3. A	8. C
4. C	9. A
5. C	10. A

Chapter 13

1. A	6. C
2. C	7. B
3. D	8. A
4. B	9. B
5. B	10. C

Chapter 14

1. A	6. A
2. B	7. D
3. D	8. A
4. A	9. B
5. B	10. A

Chapter 15

1. C	6. C
2. D	7. B
3. C	8. C
4. A	9. C
5. D	10. B

Chapter 16

1. B	6. D
2. D	7. C
3. B	8. B
4. A	9. B
5. C	10. C

Chapter 17

1. B	6. B
2. B	7. D
3. D	8. C
4. A	9. C
5. C	10. C

Chapter 18

1. C	6. D
2. B	7. A
3. C	8. D
4. A	9. B
5. B	10. D

APPENDIX B

RECOMMENDED BOOKS AND WEB SITES

This appendix includes a list of books and Web sites that will help you master the subject of game programming with DarkBASIC (and other languages). This list includes books that I have written, as well as some of my favorites from Premier Press. Some titles might be out of print, or they might cover subjects that are long outdated but are still useful as references.

Recommended Books

Here is a list of good programming books that I highly recommend for beginners. If DarkBASIC is your first foray into computer programming, then you might want to stick with this book and peruse the list of Web sites until you feel ready to move on to another language. On the other hand, you might not be interested in learning anything other than DarkBASIC. I can certainly relate to that sentiment! You might be surprised by how much work it takes to write a complete game in a language other than DarkBASIC, so one or more of these books may be useful to you. Note that this list includes what I consider beginner books; I have intentionally left out advanced books. You can peruse the complete list of Premier Press books at http://www.premierpressbooks.com.

Beginning Direct3D Game Programming

Wolfgang F. Engel, et al. Premier Press. ISBN 0-7615-3191-2.

This book provides a good introduction to programming Direct3D, the 3D graphics component of DirectX, using the C language.

C Programming for the Absolute Beginner

Michael Vine. Premier Press. ISBN 1-931841-52-7.

This book teaches C programming using the free GCC compiler as its development platform. It sticks to the basics. You will learn the fundamentals of the C language without any distracting material or commentary, just the fundamentals of what you need to be a successful C programmer.

C++ Programming for the Absolute Beginner

Dirk Henkemans and Mark Lee. Premier Press. ISBN 1-931841-43-8.

If you are new to programming with C++ and you are looking for a solid introduction, this is the book for you. This book will teach you the skills you need for practical C++ programming applications, and how you can put these skills to use in real-world scenarios.

Game Design: The Art & Business of Creating Games

Bob Bates. Premier Press. ISBN 0-7615-3165-3.

This very readable and informative book is a great resource for learning how to design games—the high-level process of planning the game prior to starting work on the source code or artwork.

Game Programming All in One

Bruno Miguel Teixeira de Sousa. Premier Press. ISBN 1-931841-23-3.

This book provides everything you need to get started as a game developer using the C language. Divided into increasingly advanced sections, it covers the most important elements of game development. Beginners start with the basics of C programming early in the book. Later chapters move on to Windows programming and the main components of DirectX.

Microsoft C# Programming for the Absolute Beginner

Andy Harris. Premier Press. ISBN 1-931841-16-0.

Using game creation as a teaching tool, this book teaches not only C#, but also the fundamental programming concepts you need to learn any computer language. You will be able to take the skills you learn from this book and apply them to your own situations. *Microsoft C# Programming for the Absolute Beginner* is a unique book aimed at the novice programmer. Developed by computer science instructors, this series is the ideal tool for anyone with little to no programming experience.

Microsoft Visual Basic .NET Programming for the Absolute Beginner

Jonathan S. Harbour. Premier Press. ISBN 1-59200-002-9.

Whether you are new to programming with Visual Basic .NET or you are upgrading from Visual Basic 6.0 and you are looking for a solid introduction, this is the book for you. It teaches the basics of VB.NET by working through simple games that you will learn to create. You will acquire the skills you need for more practical Visual Basic .NET programming applications and learn how you can put these skills to use in real-world scenarios.

Multiplayer Game Programming

Todd Barron. Premier Press. ISBN 0-7615-3298-6.

This book is an intermediate-level programming guide for networked games. You will learn how to use the C and C++ languages to program the Windows Sockets API and DirectPlay. Two complete multiplayer games are included.

Pocket PC Game Programming: Using the Windows CE Game API

Jonathan S. Harbour. Premier Press. ISBN 0-7615-3057-6.

This book will teach you how to program a Pocket PC handheld computer using Visual Basic and Visual C++. It includes coverage of graphics, sound, stylus and button input, and even multiplayer capability. Numerous sample programs and games demonstrate the key topics you need to write complete Pocket PC games.

Programming Role-Playing Games with DirectX 8.0

Jim Adams. Premier Press. ISBN 1-931841-09-8.

This is a beginner book on programming role-playing games with C++. If you are a big RPG fan, you will enjoy this book! It includes a complete introduction to Windows programming, followed by detailed tutorials on DirectX, with coverage of RPG specifics such as inventory management, player statistics, and combat.

Swords & Circuitry: A Designer's Guide to Computer Role-Playing Games

Neal and Jana Hallford. Premier Press. ISBN 0-7615-3299-4.

This book is a fascinating overview of what it takes to develop a commercial-quality role-playing game, from design to programming to marketing.

Visual Basic Game Programming with DirectX

Jonathan S. Harbour. Premier Press. ISBN 1-931841-25-X.

This book is a comprehensive programmer's tutorial and a reference for everything related to programming games with Visual Basic. After a complete explanation of the Windows API graphics device interface meant to supercharge 2D sprite programming for normal applications, this book delves into DirectX 7.0 and 8.1 and covers every component of DirectX in detail, including Direct3D. Four complete games are included, demonstrating the code developed in the book.

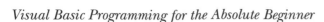

Visual Basic Programming for the Absolute Beginner

Michael Vine. Premier Press. ISBN: 0-7615-3553-5.

In addition to teaching Visual Basic, often the first language that aspiring programmers want to learn, this book teaches the fundamental programming concepts you need to grasp to learn any computer language. This is the perfect guide for anyone looking for an easy, non-intimidating introduction to Visual Basic and general programming concepts. Using game creation as a teaching tool, this book allows you to take the skills you learn and apply them to your own situations.

Recommended Web Sites

Following is a list of Web sites that you will find useful when you are learning DarkBASIC and as you start writing your own games.

Development Tools

The following Web sites focus on development tools, game libraries, compilers, and related resources, including sites specifically maintained by Microsoft.

DarkBASIC Home Page

http://www.darkbasic.com

This is the home page for DarkBASIC 1.0.

DarkBASIC Professional Home Page

http://www.darkbasicpro.com

This is the home page for DarkBASIC Professional.

Microsoft DirectX Home Page
http://www.microsoft.com/directx

This is Microsoft's main DirectX site, where you can download the latest version of DirectX.

Programming Sites

Following is a list of Web sites that focus on game programming, providing helpful information and source code for several languages and libraries.

Jonathan S. Harbour: Author's Home Page

http://www.jharbour.com

This is Jonathan's home page, with downloads, links, and resources for his books and interests.

Joshua R. Smith: Author's Home Page

http://www.delnar.com

This is Joshua's home page, with information on the commercial games that he has helped develop.

GameDev.net

http://www.gamedev.net

This is a well-respected online resource for all things related to game development.

Planet Source Code

http://www.planet-source-code.com

This is an archive of source code for many languages. If you ever need a particular algorithm or code example, this is a good source for that type of information.

APPENDIX C

ASCII Chart

This appendix contains a standard ASCII chart of character codes 0 to 255. To use an ASCII code, simply hold down the Alt key and type the appropriate value to insert the character. This method works in most text editors, including DarkBASIC. However, like some other text editors, DarkBASIC is not capable of displaying the special ASCII characters (such as codes 0 to 31).

Char	Value	Char	Value	Char	Value
null	000	→	026	4	052
☺	001	←	027	5	053
☻	002	∟	028	6	054
♥	003	↔	029	7	055
◆	004	▲	030	8	056
♣	005	▼	031	9	057
♠	006	space	032	:	058
•	007	!	033	;	059
◘	008	"	034	<	060
○	009	#	035	=	061
◙	010	$	036	>	062
♂	011	%	037	?	063
♀	012	&	038	@	064
♪	013	'	039	A	065
♫	014	(	040	B	066
☼	015	)	041	C	067
►	016	*	042	D	068
◄	017	+	043	E	069
↕	018	,	044	F	070
‼	019	-	045	G	071
¶	020	.	046	H	072
§	021	/	047	I	073
▬	022	0	048	J	074
↨	023	1	049	K	075
↑	024	2	050	L	076
↓	025	3	051	M	077

Char	Value	Char	Value	Char	Value
N	078	n	110	Ä	142
O	079	o	111	Å	143
P	080	p	112	É	144
Q	081	q	113	æ	145
R	082	r	114	Æ	146
S	083	s	115	ô	147
T	084	t	116	ö	148
U	085	u	117	ò	149
V	086	v	118	û	150
W	087	w	119	ù	151
X	088	x	120	ÿ	152
Y	089	y	121	Ö	153
Z	090	z	122	Ü	154
[	091	{	123	¢	155
\	092	|	124	£	156
]	093	}	125	¥	157
^	094	~	126	₧	158
_	095	Δ	127	ƒ	159
`	096	Ç	128	á	160
a	097	ü	129	í	161
b	098	é	130	ó	162
c	099	â	131	ú	163
d	100	ä	132	ñ	164
e	101	à	133	Ñ	165
f	102	å	134	ª	166
g	103	ç	135	º	167
h	104	ê	136	¿	168
i	105	ë	137	⌐	169
j	106	è	138	¬	170
k	107	ï	139	½	171
l	108	î	140	¼	172
m	109	ì	141	¡	173

Char	Value	Char	Value	Char	Value
«	174	╩	202	µ	230
»	175	╦	203	γ	231
▒	176	╠	204	Φ	232
▓	177	═	205	Θ	233
█	178	╬	206	Ω	234
│	179	╧	207	δ	235
┤	180	╨	208	∞	236
╡	181	╤	209	Ø	237
╢	182	╥	210	∈	238
╖	183	╙	211	∩	239
╕	184	╘	212	≡	240
╣	185	╒	213	±	241
║	186	╓	214	≥	242
╗	187	╫	215	≤	243
╝	188	╪	216	⌠	244
╜	189	┘	217	⌡	245
╛	190	┌	218	÷	246
┐	191	█	219	≈	247
└	192	▄	220	°	248
┴	193	▌	221	•	249
┬	194	▐	222	·	250
├	195	▀	223	√	251
─	196	α	224	ⁿ	252
┼	197	ß	225	²	253
╞	198	Γ	226	■	254
╟	199	π	227	_(blank character)	255
╚	200	Σ	228		
╔	201	σ	229σ		

APPENDIX D

GUIDE TO THE CD-ROM

The CD-ROM that comes with this book contains some important files that you will want to use when working through the sample programs in the book. The CD comes with an Autorun menu for installing the various demos and source code files to your hard drive. The CD menu will also include any extras that we can pack onto the CD at the last minute, so be sure to look through all the options on the menu.

Source Code Files

The most important files on the CD are the source code files for the sample projects in the book. The projects are stored in folders that are organized by chapter in the root \Sources folder. Inside \Sources, you will find two subfolders: Sources\DarkBASIC and Sources\DBPro. These subfolders contain the source code for the sample programs in the book, modified to work with DarkBASIC 1.0 and DarkBASIC Professional, respectively. For instance, you can find the projects for Chapter 10 in two places: Sources\DarkBASIC\CH10 (for DarkBASIC 1.0) and Sources\DBPro\CH10 (for DBPro).

DarkBASIC Premier Trial Edition

This book is about writing programs with DarkBASIC, so I have included a trial version of the DarkBASIC compiler that you can install and use while reading the book. It is located in \Software\DarkBASIC, and there is a CD menu item that will run the installer. The friendly folks at Dark Basic Software Ltd have created a custom version of the compiler just for this book, called "DarkBASIC Premier Trial Edition." The compiler is limited to 30 days of use, and you will be able to run the programs in the book during that time. After the 30 days, you can purchase the retail version of DarkBASIC to continue using this product.

DarkBASIC Professional Demo Version

In addition to the Premier Trial Edition of DarkBASIC 1.0, we have also included the demo version of DarkBASIC Professional. Many of the programs in the book will run in DarkBASIC Professional, so you will want to try out this awesome new version of DarkBASIC! You can use either version to run the programs in the book; just refer to the appropriate folder under \Sources. I highly recommend that you start with DarkBASIC 1.0 until you have mastered the language because it is easier to use than DarkBASIC Professional. However, in case you still want to try out DBPro, it is located in \Software\DBPro, and there is a CD menu item that will run the installer.

DirectX 8.1 Runtime

DarkBASIC requires that you install DirectX 8.1 or later. The DirectX runtime is located on the CD in a folder called \DirectX. Simply run the dxsetup.exe program to install DirectX—that is all you need to do before running the sample programs for the book! Note that installing DirectX usually requires a reboot of your PC.

Demo Versions of Games

DarkBASIC has a huge fan base of programmers who have written some compelling games and demos, and we have included some of those programs on the CD. Take a look at the \Games folder to see the list of games and demos that we have included. In each case, you will need to either install the program or simply run it right from the CD. Some of these programs might be really big because DarkBASIC can attach the media files to an executable program, so you may want to check the size of the \Games folder before copying the whole thing to your hard drive, if you are so inclined.

Trial Versions of Software

In addition to the game demos, there are also trial versions of several very useful development tools, including Cool Edit 2000 (a sound effects editor), Paint Shop Pro 7 (a graphics editor), and Anim8or (a fantastic free 3D modeling program that is compatible with 3D Studio Max). The CD menu will help you install these programs on your PC.

Index